ELFQUEST:
THE GRAND
QUEST
VOLUME TEN

WENDY &
RICHARD PINI

ELFQUEST:
THE **GRAND**
QUEST
VOLUME TEN

WRITTEN BY
WENDY & RICHARD PINI

ART BY
WENDY PINI

LETTERING BY
RICHARD PINI

ELFQUEST: THE GRAND QUEST VOLUME TEN
Published by DC Comics. Cover, timeline, character
bios, and compilation copyright © 2005 Warp
Graphics, Inc. All Rights Reserved.

Originally published in single magazine form in
ELFQUEST: KINGS OF THE BROKEN WHEEL 1-3.
Copyright © 1990 Warp Graphics, Inc. All Rights
Reserved. All characters, their distinctive
likenesses and related elements featured in this
publication are trademarks of Warp Graphics, Inc.
The stories, characters and incidents featured in
this publication are entirely fictional. DC Comics
does not read or accept unsolicited submissions
of ideas, stories or artwork.

DC Comics, 1700 Broadway, New York, NY 10019
A Warner Bros. Entertainment Company
Printed in Canada. First Printing.
ISBN: 1-4012-0506-2

The ElfQuest Saga is an ever-unfolding story spanning countless millennia that follows the adventures of humans, trolls and various elfin tribes. Some of the events that occur prior to the time of this volume are outlined below using the very first published ElfQuest story as a benchmark.

OUR STORY BEGINS HERE...
7 YEARS LATER

Recognition gives Cutter and Leetah twin children, *Ember* and *Suntop*. The Wolfriders set out to find and unite other elfin tribes. They discover fabled Blue Mountain where they meet bizarre, winged *Tyldak* and the beautiful, enigmatic *Winnowill*, who jealously protects her control over the mountain's secrets.

On the way to the frozen northlands, brutal mountain trolls attack and the Wolfriders are barely saved by the *Go-Back* elves. Their leader, *Kahvi*, allies the Go-Backs with the Wolfriders and forest trolls to win the Palace.

The Wolfriders' lives are peaceful again – until Glider *Aroree* kidnaps *Windkin* to give to Winnowill. The betrayal propels Cutter and his tribe into another conflict. Meanwhile, Rayek seeks out Winnowill, whom he naively regards as an equal. The Black Snake seduces him into serving her cause – to turn Blue Mountain into a spaceship to return all pure-blooded elves to their starhome.

In the final battle between Cutter and Winnowill, Blue Mountain itself is destroyed along with most of the Glider elves, and Winnowill is banished forever to a deserted island in the middle of the ocean. The elves are left to pick up the tattered threads of their lives...

2,000 - 3,000 YEARS BEFORE

Goodtree, eighth chief of the Wolfriders, founds a new Holt deep in the woods and creates the Father Tree where the Wolfriders can all live. Her son, *Mantricker*, reopens the struggle with nomadic humans. Mantricker's son, *Bearclaw*, discovers Greymung's trolls living in the tunnels beneath the Holt. Bearclaw becomes the Wolfriders' tenth chief.

In the distant Forbidden Grove near Blue Mountain, *Petalwing* and the preservers tirelessly protect their mysterious wrapstuff bundles.

9,000 YEARS BEFORE

Wolfrider chief Timmorn feels the conflict between his elf and wolf sides, and leaves the tribe to find his own destiny. *Rahnee the She-Wolf* takes over as leader, followed by her son *Prey-Pacer*.

10,000 YEARS BEFORE

Over time, the High Ones become too many for their faraway planet to support. *Timmain's* group discovers the World of Two Moons, but as their crystalline ship approaches, the High Ones crash-land far in the new world's past. Primitive humans greet them with brutality. The elfin High Ones and their troll attendants scatter into the surrounding forest. To survive, Timmain magically takes on a wolf's form and hunts for the other elves. *Timmorn*, first chief of the Wolfriders, is born.

0	
1,000	
2,000	
3,000	
4,000	
5,000	
6,000	
7,000	
8,000	
9,000	
10,000	

TIMELINE

0	

FIRE & FLIGHT

The peace is an illusion, and humans burn the Wolfriders from their forest home. Cutter and his band are driven into a vast desert where they discover new elves, the Sun Folk. Cutter Recognizes the Sun Folk's healer Leetah, and the two groups unite.

475

600

1,000

2,000

6 YEARS BEFORE

The feud between elves and humans ends – seemingly – with the death of Bearclaw. Cutter takes the chief's lock and assumes leadership of the tribe.

25 YEARS BEFORE

Joyleaf gives birth to a son, *Cutter*, who forms a fast friendship with *Skywise*. The two become brothers "in all but blood."

3,000

475 YEARS BEFORE

Bearclaw begins a long feud with a tribe of humans who have claimed the land near the Holt. Although both sides suffer over the years, neither can prevail, neither gives in.

4,000

600 YEARS BEFORE

In an oasis called the Sun Village deep in the desert to the south of the Holt, *Rayek* is born. *Leetah* is born twelve years later.

5,000

4,000 YEARS BEFORE

Freefoot leads the Wolfriders during a prosperous, quiet time. Freefoot's son, Oakroot, subsequently becomes chief and later takes the name *Tanner*.

7,000 YEARS BEFORE

Swift-Spear, fourth chief, goes to war for the first time against humans of a nearby village. The humans leave, and he takes the name *Two-Spear*. When his sister *Huntress Skyfire* challenges his chieftainship, the tribe splits. Two-Spear leaves, and Skyfire becomes chief.

6,000

7,000

8,000

10,000 - 8,000 YEARS BEFORE

Descendants of the High Ones wander the world. *Savah* and her family settle the Sun Village in the desert. *Lord Voll* and the Gliders move into Blue Mountain and shut themselves away from the world.

Guttlekraw becomes king of the trolls. Over time, they tunnel under the future Holt of the Wolfriders.

Greymung rebels against Guttlekraw, who flees north. *Winnowill* gives birth to Two-Edge.

9,000

10,000

The ElfQuest saga spans thousands of years and to date has introduced readers to hundreds of characters. At the time of the stories in this volume, these are the major characters you will meet and get to know.

THE WOLFRIDERS

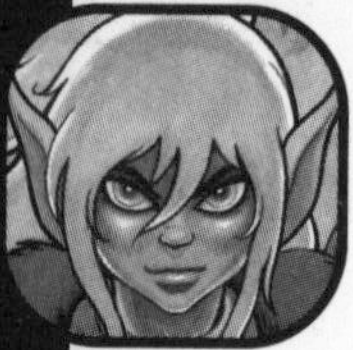

CUTTER

While his name denotes his skill with a sword, Cutter is not a cold and merciless death-dealer. Strong in his beliefs, he will nevertheless bend even the most fundamental of them if the well-being of his tribe is at stake. Skywise believes that what sets Cutter apart from all past Wolfrider chieftains is his imagination and ability to not only accept change, but take advantage of it.

LEETAH

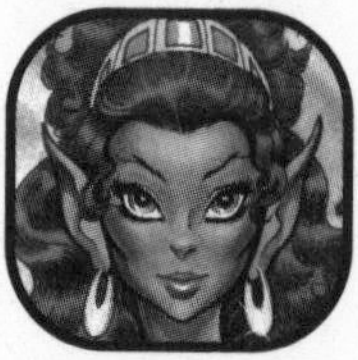

Her name means "healing light" and – as the Sun Folk's healer – she is the village's most precious resource. For over 600 years she has lived a sheltered life, surrounded by love and admiration, knowing little of the world beyond her desert oasis. Though delicate-seeming, beneath her beauty lies a wellspring of strength that has yet to be tested. She dislikes the death she has caused but understands it is The Way.

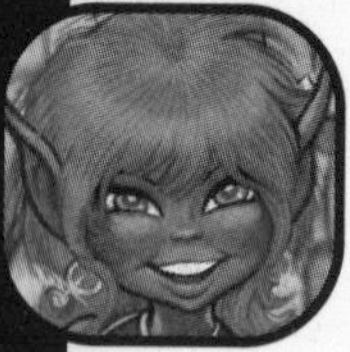

EMBER

Named for her fire-red hair, Ember is destined to be the next chief of the Wolfriders. As such, she constantly watches and learns from her father's actions; she also learns gentler skills from Leetah. As Cutter was a unique blend of his own parents' qualities, so too is Ember. She has recently begun experiencing what it will mean to lead.

SUNTOP

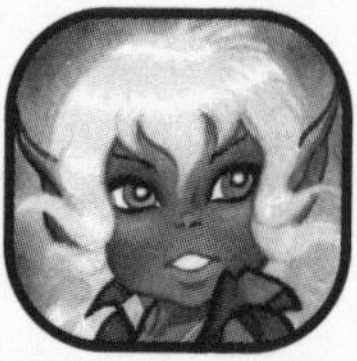

Suntop is the gentle, enigmatic son of Cutter and Leetah. Although a true Wolfrider, Suntop was born in the Sun Village and considers it home. Content that Ember will become chief of the Wolfriders, he says of himself, "I'll be what I'll be." Suntop has powerful mental abilities; his "magic feeling," as he calls it, alerts him when magic is being used by other elves.

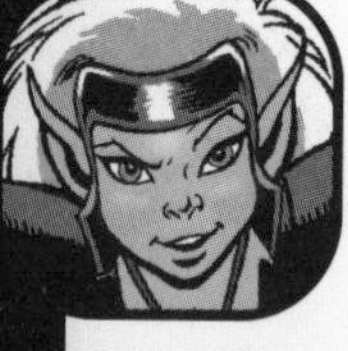

SKYWISE

Orphaned at birth, Skywise is the resident stargazer of the Wolfriders, and only his interest in elf maidens rivals his passion for understanding the mysteries of the universe. Skywise is Cutter's counselor, confidant, and closest friend. While he is capable of deep seriousness, nothing can diminish Skywise's jovial and rakish manner.

STRONGBOW

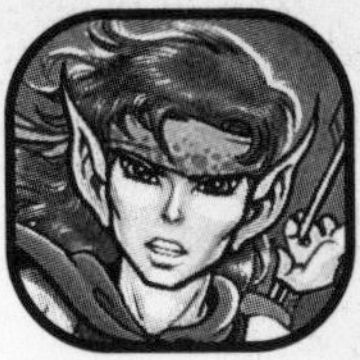

Strongbow is the reserved, silent master archer of the Wolfriders. Ever the devil's advocate, he is often proved right but finds no value in saying "I told you so." Strongbow is extremely serious, rarely smiles, and prefers sending to audible speech. He is completely devoted to his lifemate, Moonshade, and intensely proud of their son Dart. Having taken an elf's life in the battle of Blue Mountain, however, his soul is now shaken.

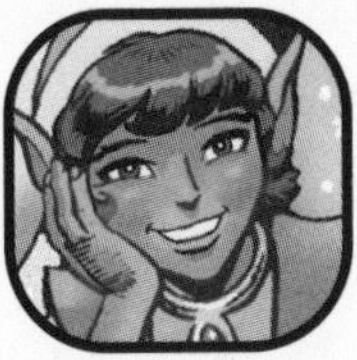

SCOUTER

Scouter has the sharpest eyes of all the Wolfriders. He is steadfast, loyal, and often overprotective. He is also extremely intolerant of anyone, tribemates included, whom he perceives as putting his loved ones in jeopardy. Dewshine and Scouter have been lovemates for most of their lives, yet are not Recognized.

DEWSHINE

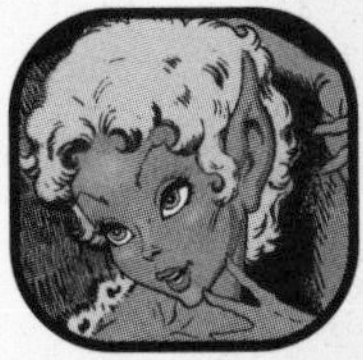

Swift and graceful as a deer, Dewshine is the most agile and free-spirited of the Wolfriders — and that takes some doing! She has a beautiful voice, full of melody and laughter. Song and dance are passions with her, and she has a talent for mimicking birdsong. Dewshine came to Recognition early and unexpectedly, with the shapechanged Glider Tyldak and together they had a son, Windkin.

CLEARBROOK

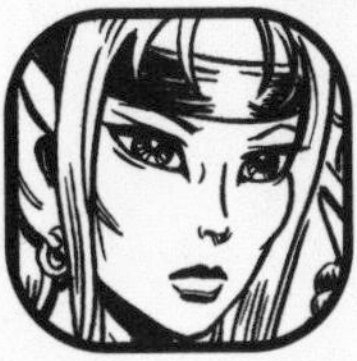

Calm, dignified and thoughtful, choosing her words carefully, Clearbrook is the eldest female Wolfrider. Her quiet advice is always welcomed. When she lost her lifemate, One-Eye, in the quest for the Palace, Clearbrook turned into a fierce and vengeful angel of death. Both mother figure and warrior, Clearbrook is now an advocate of forgiveness and letting go of the past – but her path to that understanding has been harrowing.

KAHVI

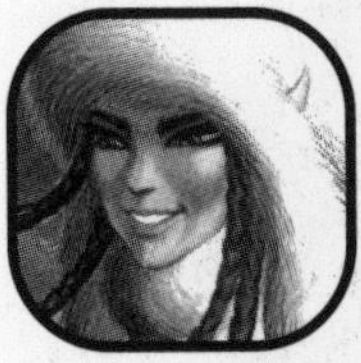

Kahvi is the devil-may-care leader of the northern elf tribe called the Go-Backs (so named because they hope someday to "go back" to the Palace of the High Ones). She is a superb fighter, even to the point of recklessness, who believes that life is to be lived to the fullest every day. She endured the loss of her daughter Vaya and is now forging a new life for her people. Recently, she gave birth to Rayek's daughter, but kept the knowledge from the father.

RAYEK

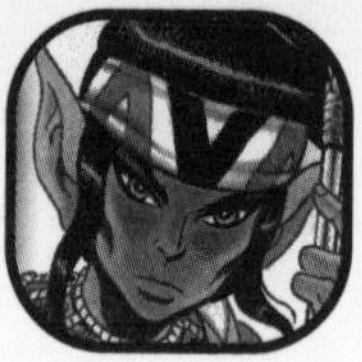

Vain and prideful, Rayek is chief hunter for the Sun Village and never tires of boasting of his superior skills. The same age as Leetah, he has spent nearly all those years as the healer's friend — always hoping that she will see him as more than simply that. He is a superb athlete, and skilled in both magic and weaponry. Thought lost, he returned with the Go-Backs and helped save Cutter's life. He now resides within the Palace.

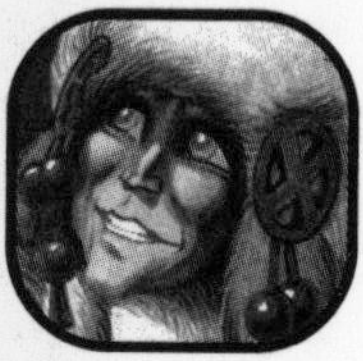

EKUAR

Ekuar is one of the most ancient elves on the World of Two Moons. He is a rock-shaper, who long ago was abducted by trolls who forced him to use his powers to search for precious metals and gems. To keep him in line, the trolls tortured and maimed the gentle elf, but rather than becoming bitter, Ekuar has turned his misfortune into an outlook that is amazingly life-affirming!

FRIENDS

PETALWING

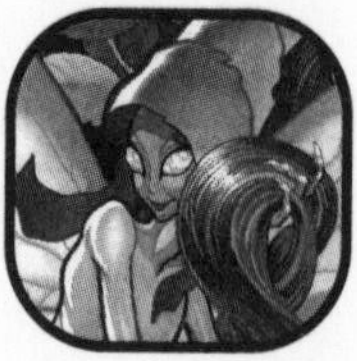

Petalwing is a Preserver — a carefree, fairylike creature that arrived on the World of Two Moons with the original High Ones. Petalwing lives under the grand illusion that "highthings" (elves) cannot live without it, and must be watched over and protected. Petalwing is the closest thing that the Preservers have to a leader. Cutter considers Petalwing to be a major annoyance; the sprite is unperturbed by this.

THE TROLLS

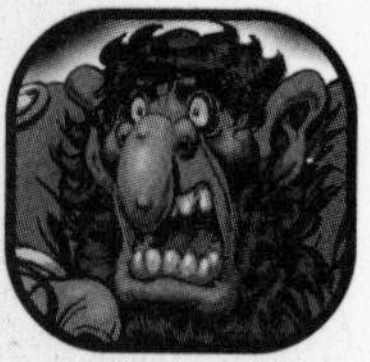

PICKNOSE

His name was inspired by his most prominent facial feature, which resembles the curved business end of a pick. The success of Picknose's interactions with the Wolfriders has been mixed at best, for while he does possess a sort of honor, he is also an opportunist of the first water. Currently King of the mountain trolls, Picknose is ever seeking opportunity.

OLD MAGGOTY

Old Maggoty was caught by Bearclaw one night stealing dreamberries near the Wolfriders' Holt. The two then became liaisons for their respective peoples in matters of trade. Old Maggoty is a master of herb lore and is renowned for brewing dreamberry wine, a potent lavender distillation that can set even the strongest-stomached elf on his pointed ear.

ODDBIT

Oddbit embodies all the troll maidenly virtues: she's greedy, deceptive, manipulative, coy, vain and fickle. She is the ultimate material girl, adorning the footstools of both King Guttlekraw and, later, King Greymung. After Picknose rescued her, Oddbit kept the lovesick troll dangling for years.

IN THE PREVIOUS VOLUME

Dart leads a band from the Sun Village to help the Wolfriders, who are engaged in a battle for power with Winnowill. As Cutter and his cohort approach Blue Mountain, Winnowill sees to it that her human protectors, the Hoan G'Tay Sho, will not stop defending Blue Mountain until every elf is dead.

What is unexpected, however, is Rayek's arrival in the mountain and his meeting with the dark sorceress. Winnowill senses what Rayek desires and she begins a dance of seduction that he is only too willing to join.

Outside, the conflict between human and Wolfrider is evenly matched until the humans threaten the new Holt with fire. Dart's timely arrival turns the tide and eliminates the Hoan G'Tay Sho's threat.

Winnowill's grand project – to turn the entire interior of Blue Mountain into an even greater Egg – is completed and it rises into the sky, casting off the shell of the mountain. Before it can fly off, Cutter arrives to stop her. Leetah attempts to heal Winnowill's black soul, learning of her past in the process. Subdued, Winnowill watches as her plans literally begin to fall apart – the mountain continues to crumble and the great Egg falls from the sky, destroyed. The elves within barely escape with their lives.

Clear of the debris, the freed humans warily watch the various elfin groups joyfully reunite. The moment is shattered, though, when Kureel, astride his great bird, attacks the assemblage. The rampage is ended only by Strongbow's arrow – the first time an elf has killed an elf.

With Winnowill stranded on a deserted island by Tyldak, the various elf tribes seek respite. Nonna and Adar bid their friends farewell and the elves are left, with Cutter, to ponder their future.

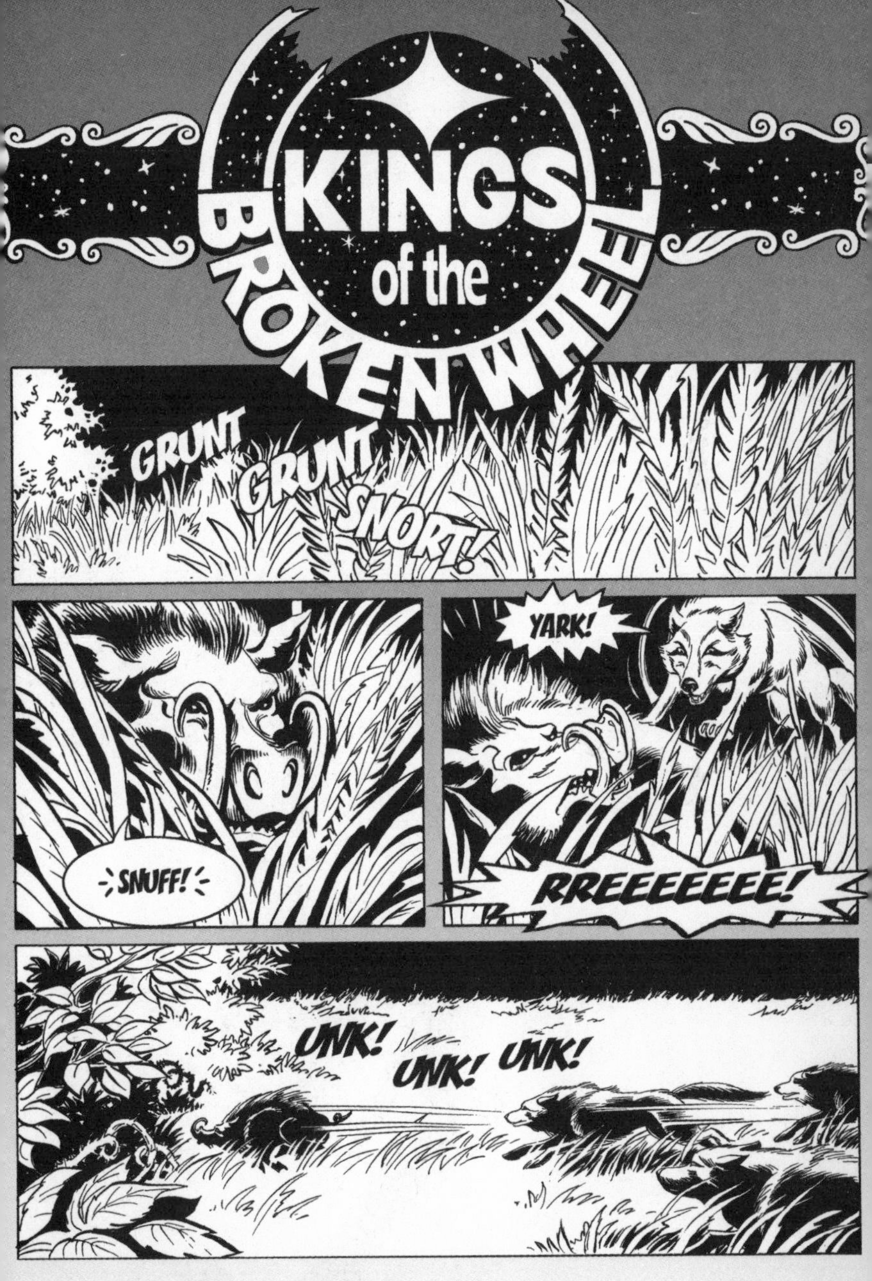
KINGS of the BROKEN WHEEL
GRUNT
GRUNT
SNORT!
SNUFF!
YARK!
RREEEEEEEE!
UNK!
UNK!
UNK!

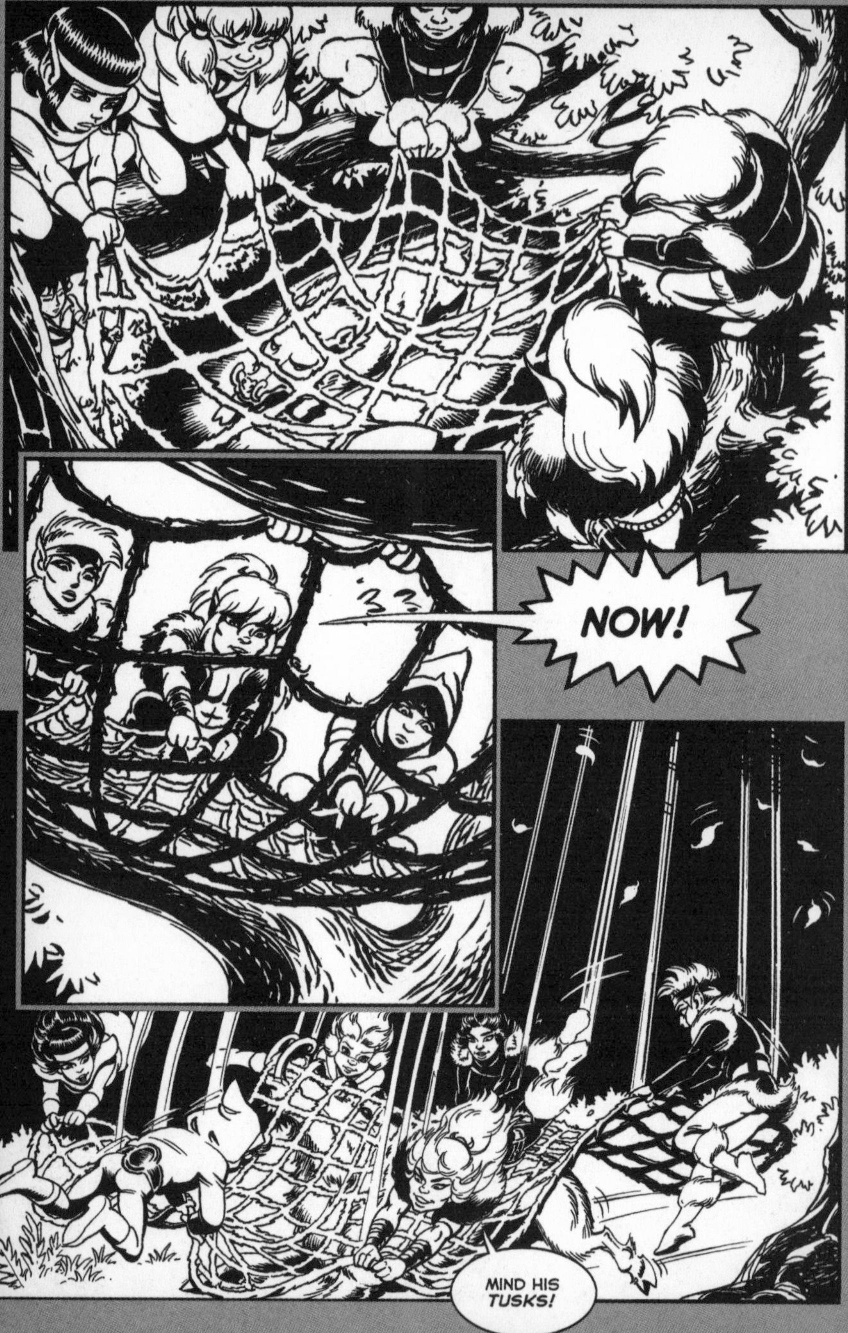
NOW!
MIND HIS TUSKS!

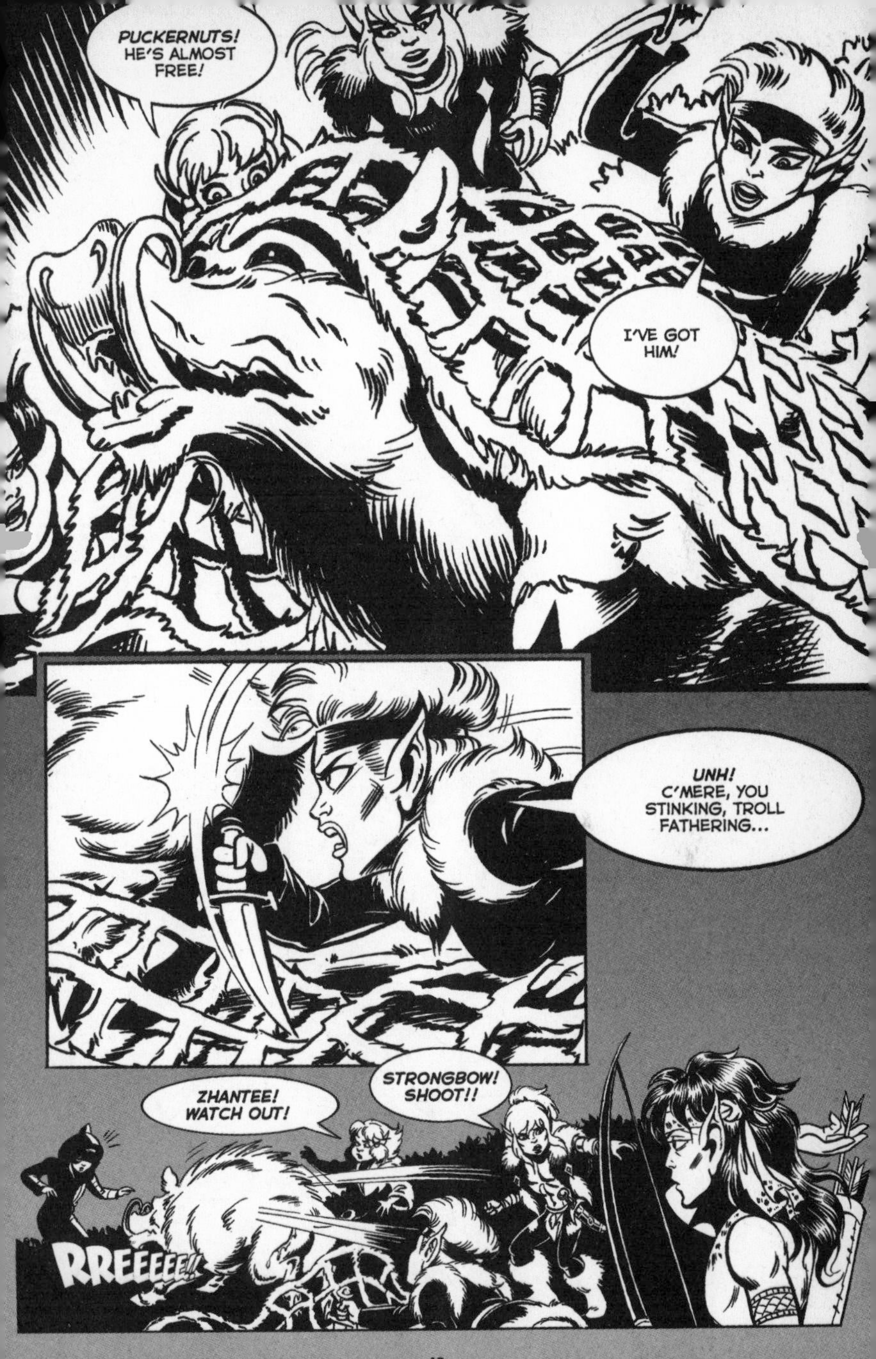
PUCKERNUTS! HE'S ALMOST FREE!
I'VE GOT HIM!
UNH! C'MERE, YOU STINKING, TROLL FATHERING...
ZHANTEE! WATCH OUT!
STRONGBOW! SHOOT!!
RREEEEEE!!

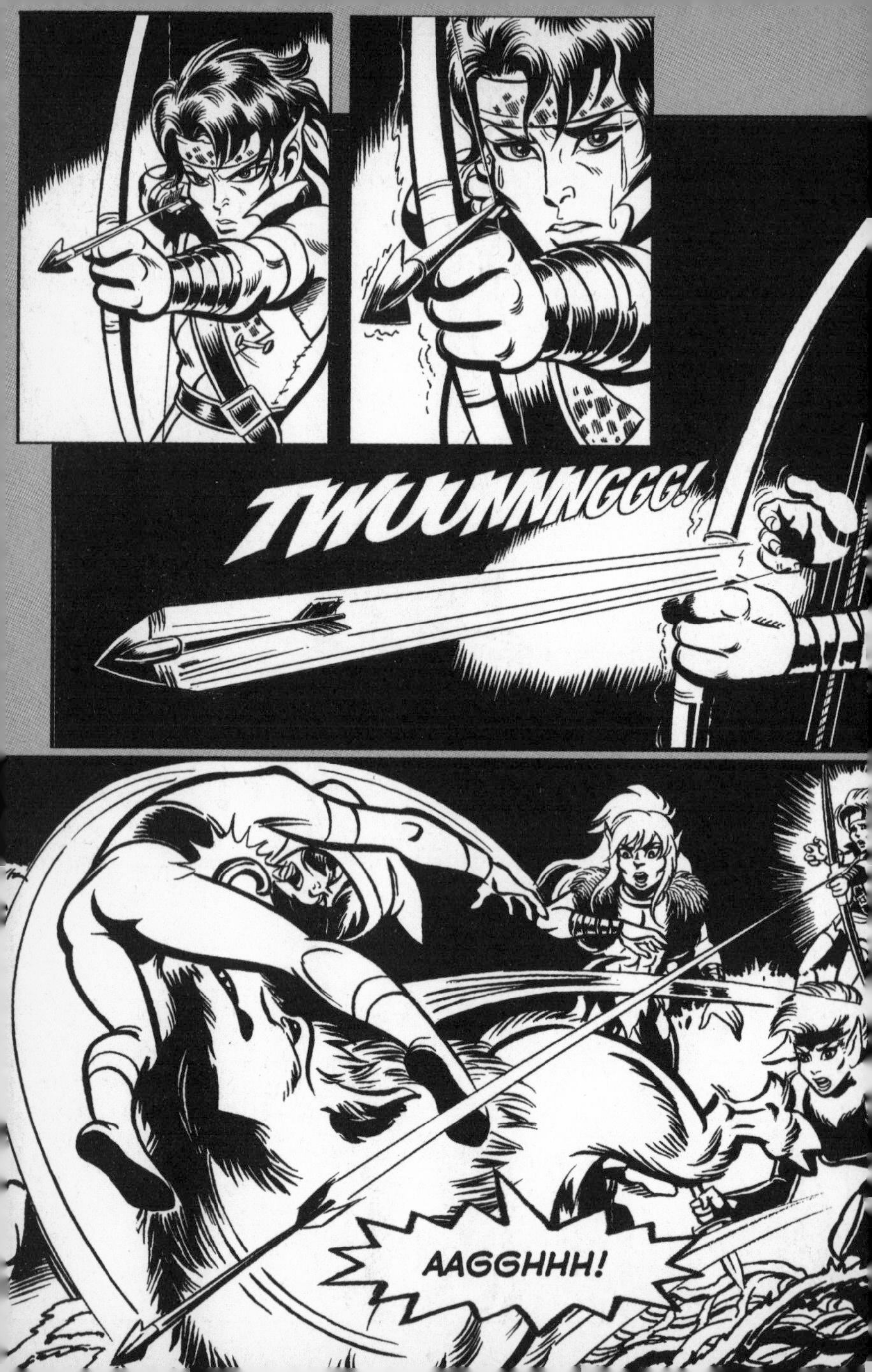
TWUUNNNGGG!
AAGGHHH!

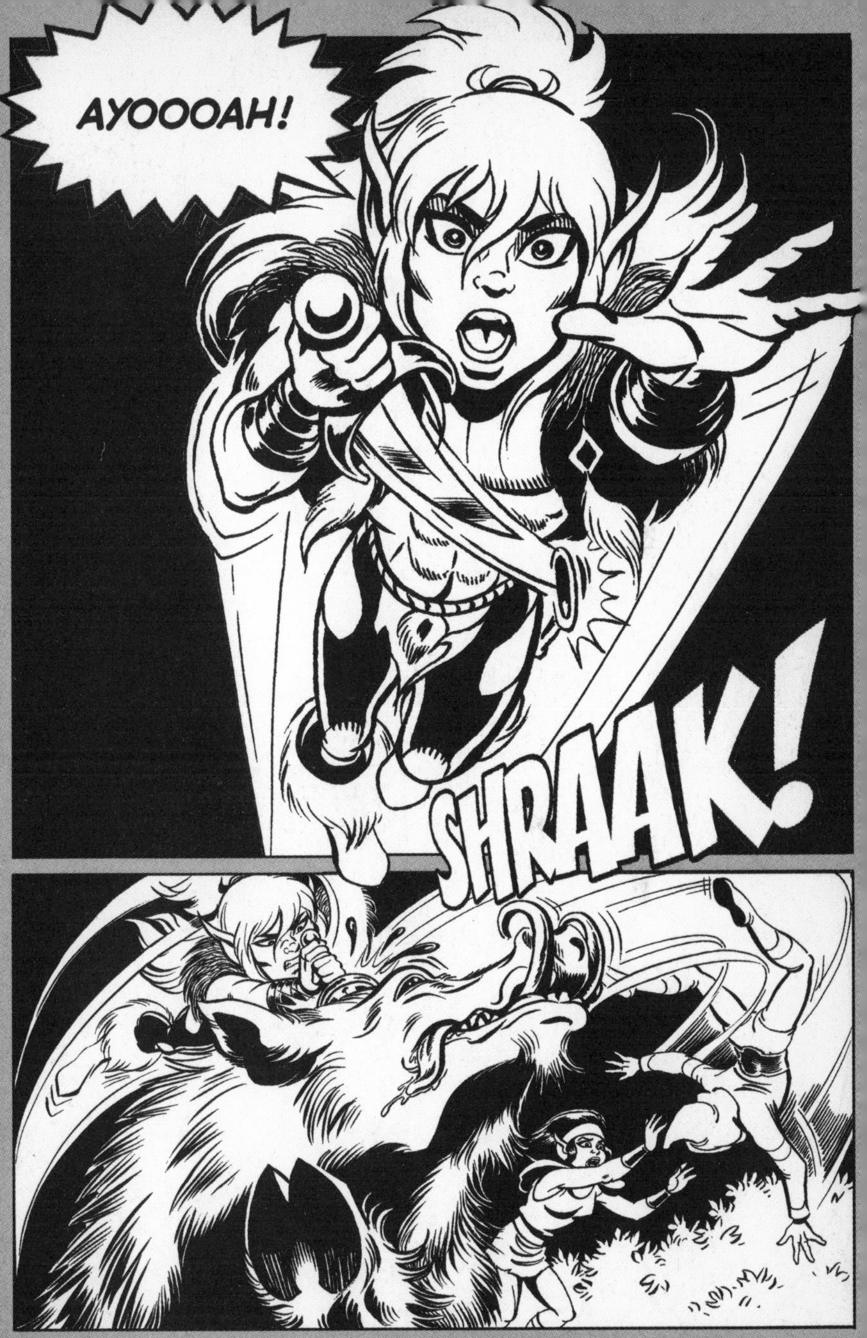
AYOOOAH!
SHRAAK!

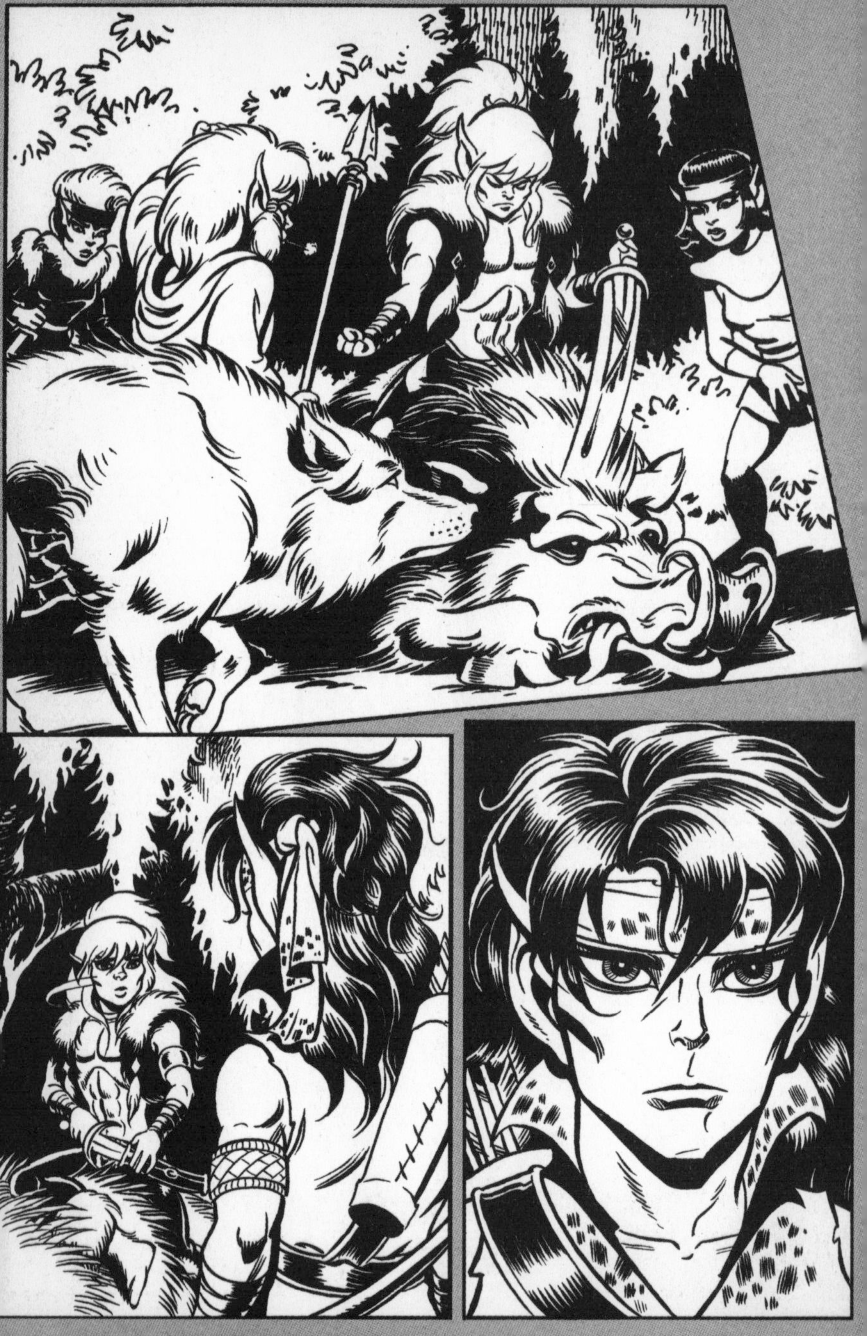

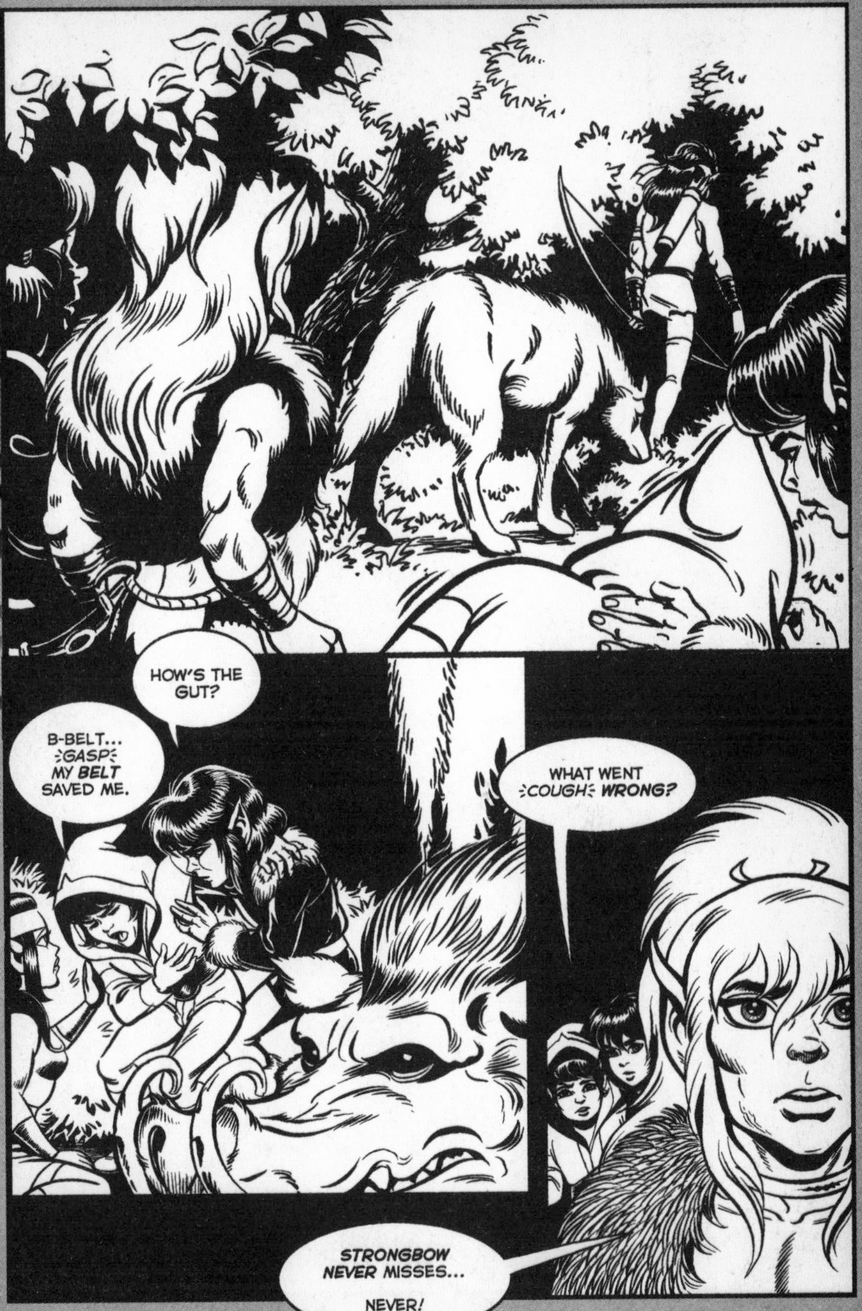
HOW'S THE GUT?
B-BELT... GASP MY BELT SAVED ME.
WHAT WENT COUGH WRONG?
STRONGBOW NEVER MISSES... NEVER!

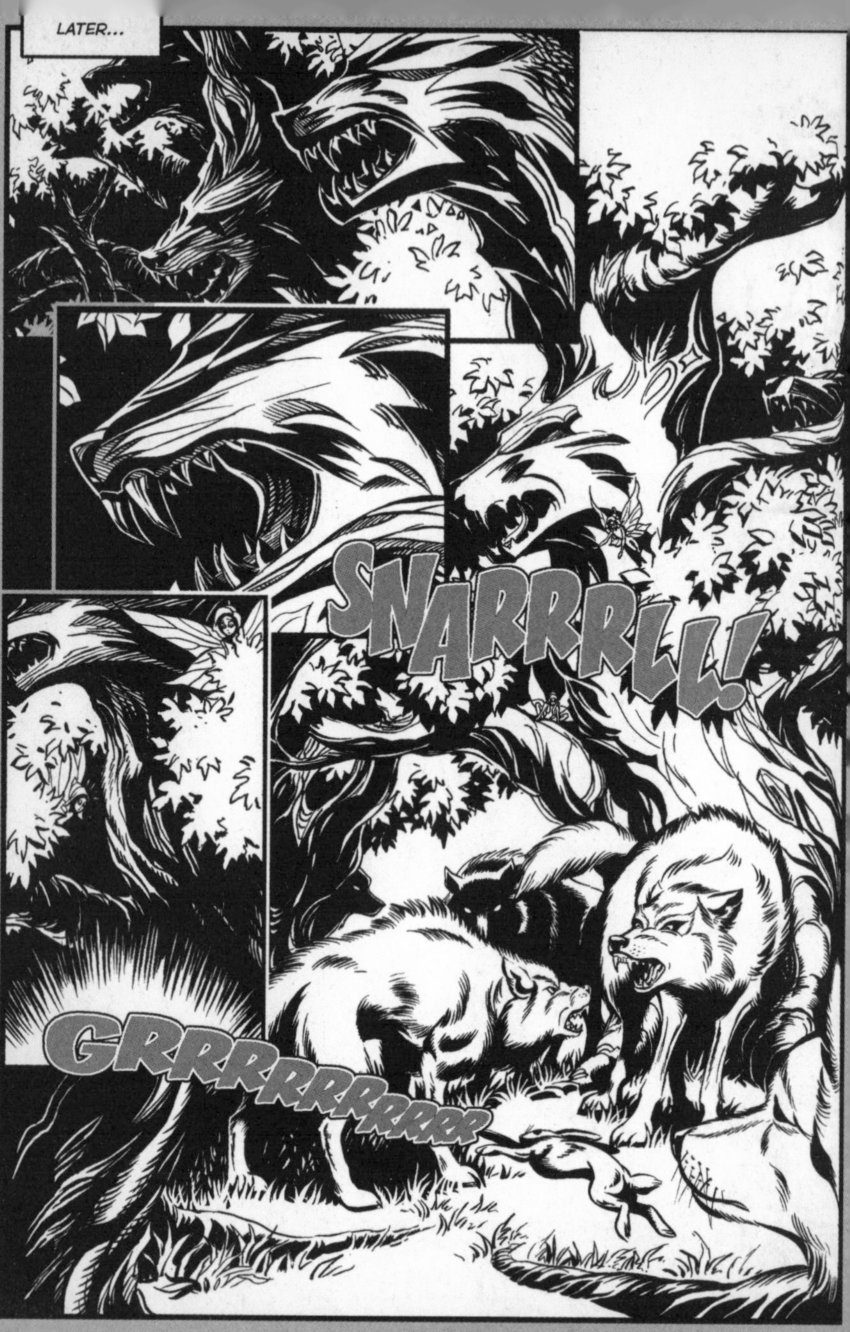
LATER...
SNARRRLL!
GRRRRRRRRRRR

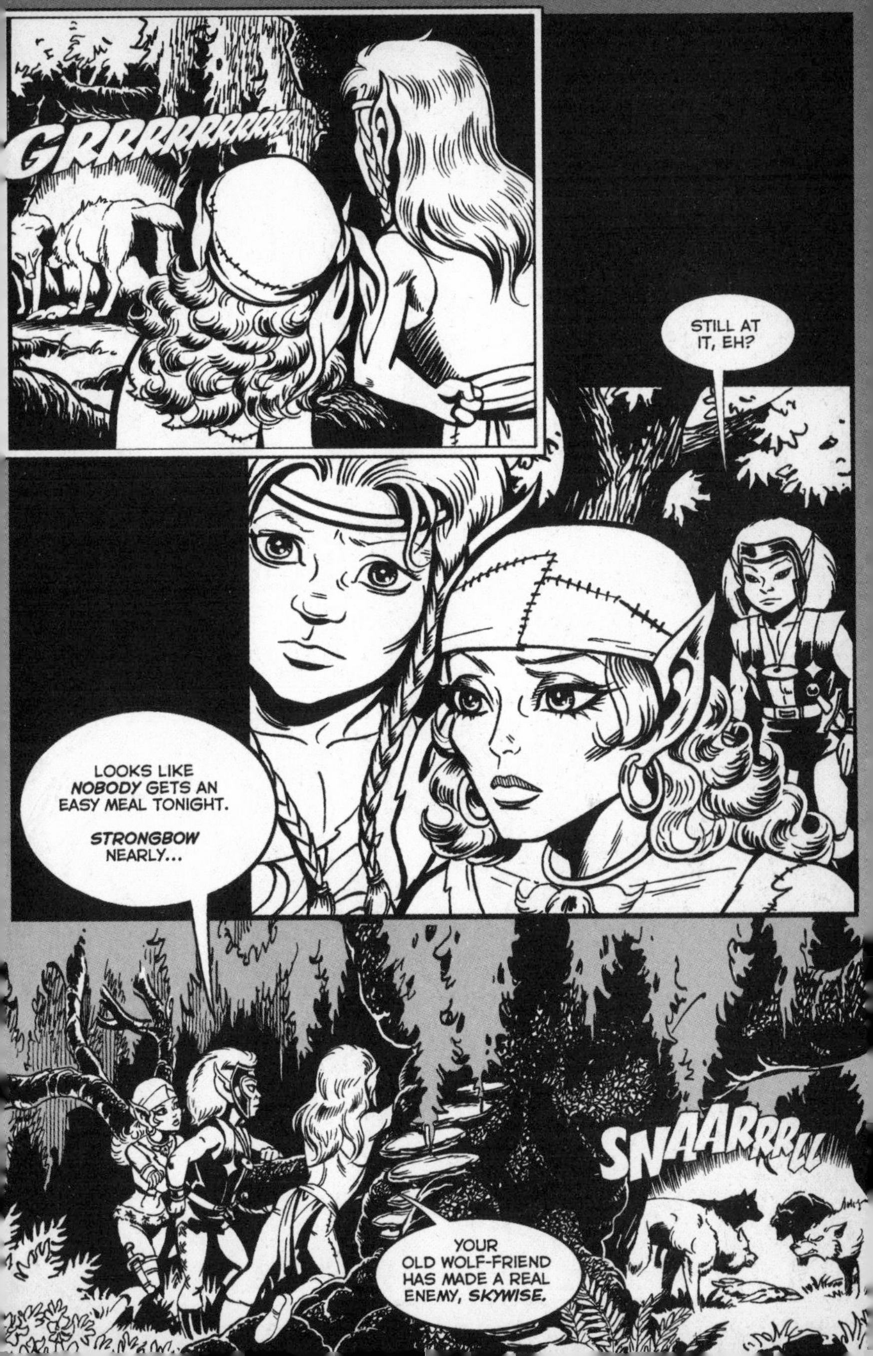
GRRRRRRRRRR
STILL AT IT, EH?
LOOKS LIKE *NOBODY* GETS AN EASY MEAL TONIGHT.
STRONGBOW NEARLY...
SNAARRRLL
YOUR OLD WOLF-FRIEND HAS MADE A REAL ENEMY, *SKYWISE.*

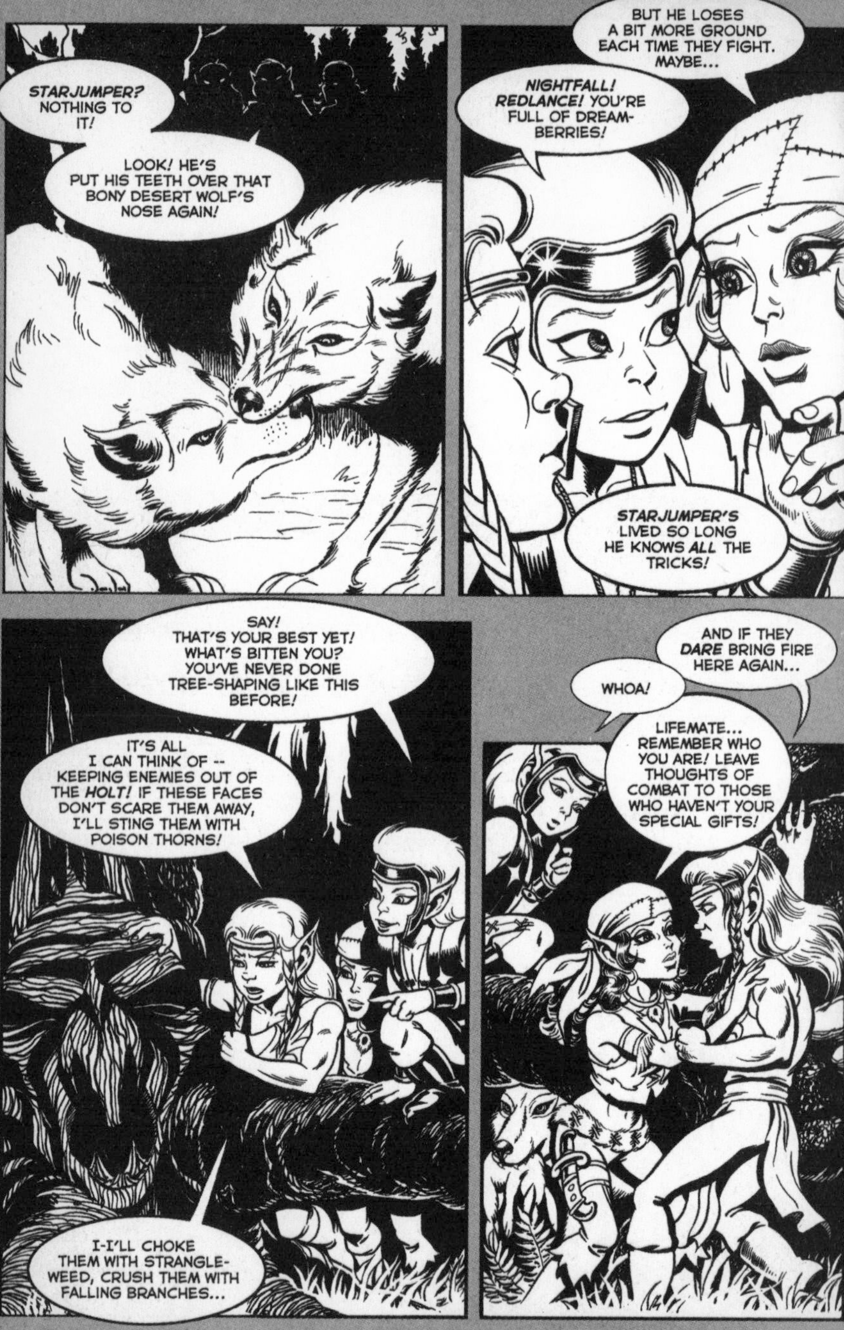
STARJUMPER? NOTHING TO IT!
LOOK! HE'S PUT HIS TEETH OVER THAT BONY DESERT WOLF'S NOSE AGAIN!
BUT HE LOSES A BIT MORE GROUND EACH TIME THEY FIGHT. MAYBE...
NIGHTFALL! REDLANCE! YOU'RE FULL OF DREAM-BERRIES!
STARJUMPER'S LIVED SO LONG HE KNOWS ALL THE TRICKS!
SAY! THAT'S YOUR BEST YET! WHAT'S BITTEN YOU? YOU'VE NEVER DONE TREE-SHAPING LIKE THIS BEFORE!
IT'S ALL I CAN THINK OF -- KEEPING ENEMIES OUT OF THE HOLT! IF THESE FACES DON'T SCARE THEM AWAY, I'LL STING THEM WITH POISON THORNS!
I-I'LL CHOKE THEM WITH STRANGLE-WEED, CRUSH THEM WITH FALLING BRANCHES...
AND IF THEY DARE BRING FIRE HERE AGAIN...
WHOA!
LIFEMATE... REMEMBER WHO YOU ARE! LEAVE THOUGHTS OF COMBAT TO THOSE WHO HAVEN'T YOUR SPECIAL GIFTS!

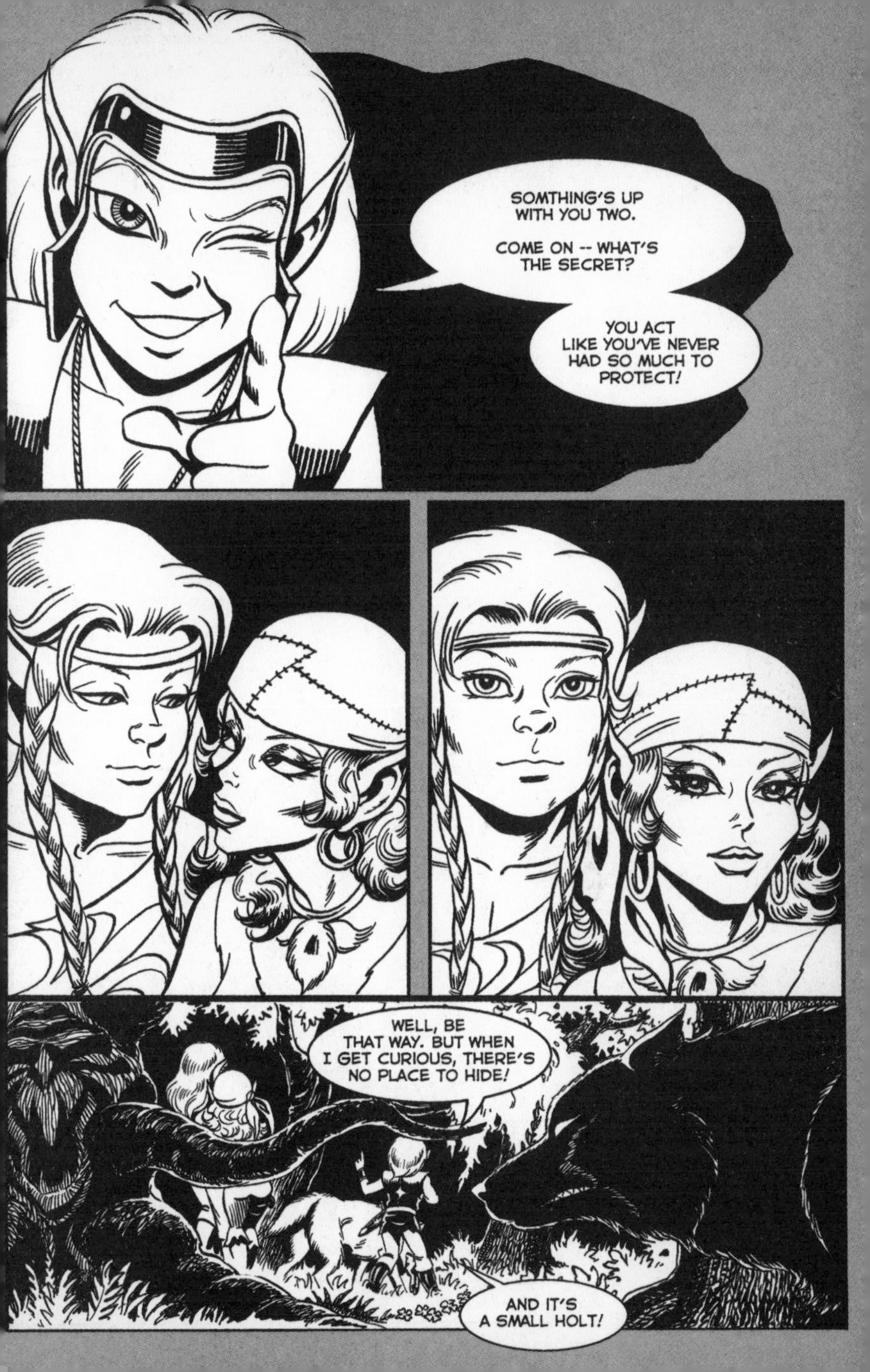
SOMTHING'S UP WITH YOU TWO.
COME ON -- WHAT'S THE SECRET?
YOU ACT LIKE YOU'VE NEVER HAD SO MUCH TO PROTECT!
WELL, BE THAT WAY. BUT WHEN I GET CURIOUS, THERE'S NO PLACE TO HIDE!
AND IT'S A SMALL HOLT!

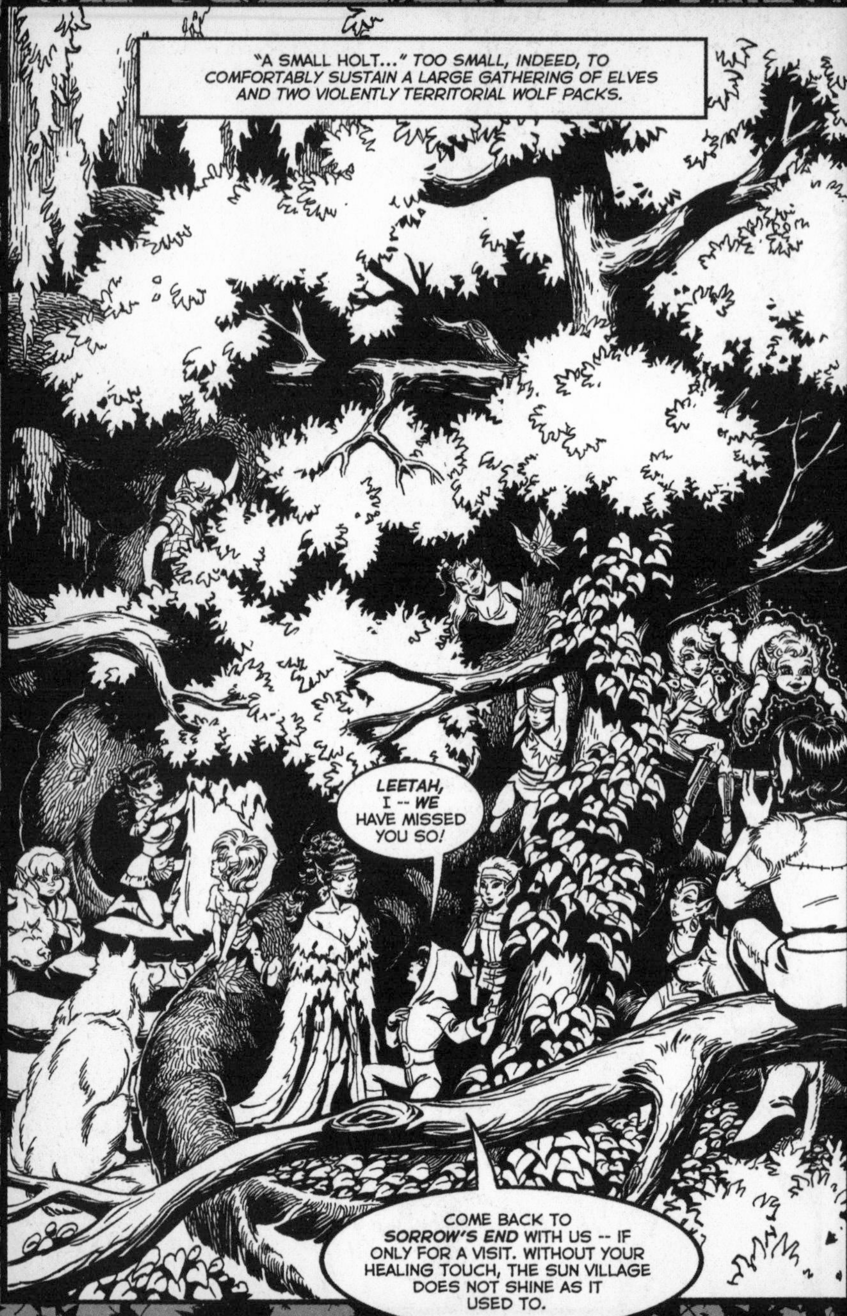
"A SMALL HOLT..." TOO SMALL, INDEED, TO COMFORTABLY SUSTAIN A LARGE GATHERING OF ELVES AND TWO VIOLENTLY TERRITORIAL WOLF PACKS.
LEETAH, I -- WE HAVE MISSED YOU SO!
COME BACK TO SORROW'S END WITH US -- IF ONLY FOR A VISIT. WITHOUT YOUR HEALING TOUCH, THE SUN VILLAGE DOES NOT SHINE AS IT USED TO.

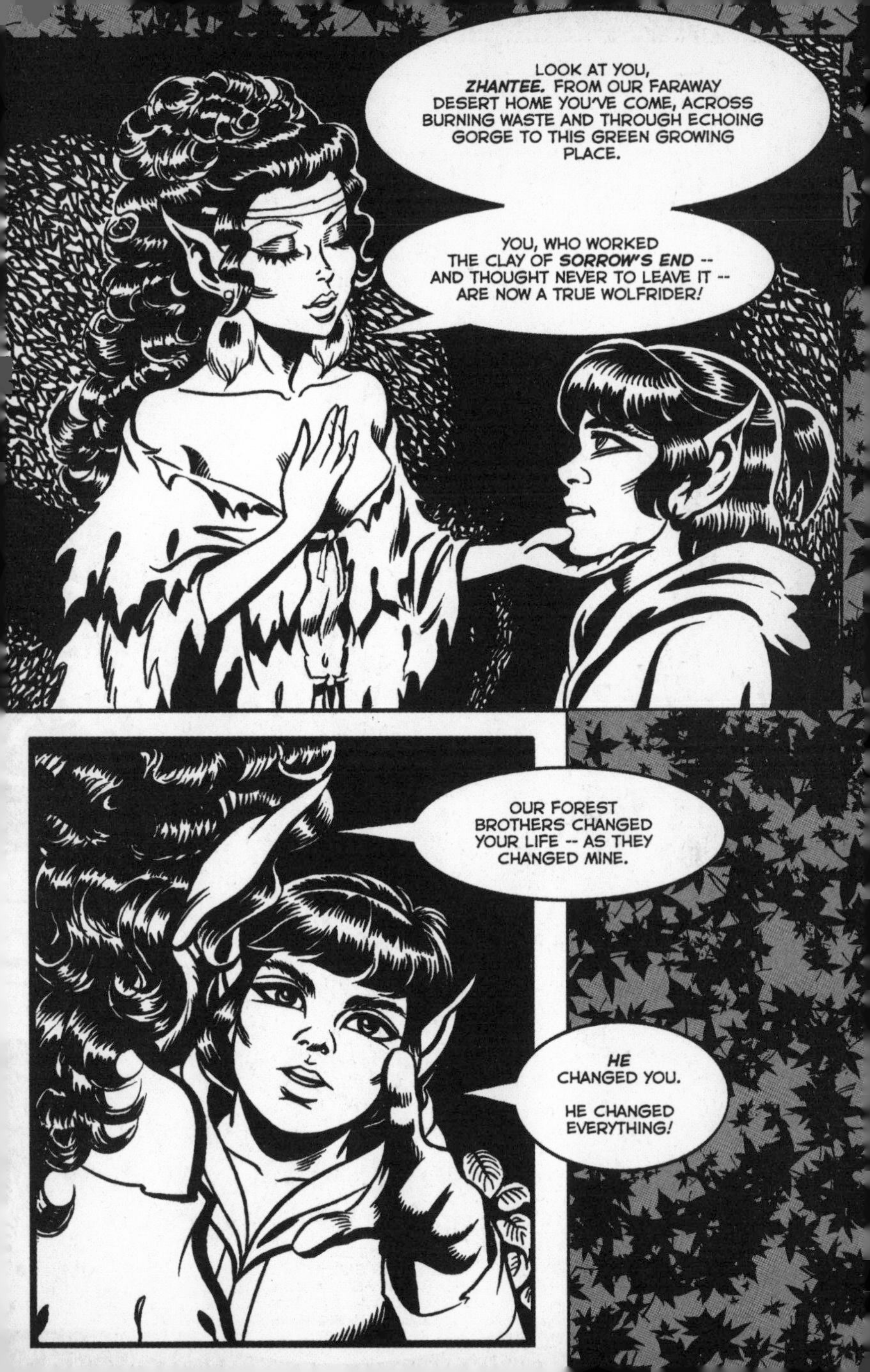
LOOK AT YOU, ZHANTEE. FROM OUR FARAWAY DESERT HOME YOU'VE COME, ACROSS BURNING WASTE AND THROUGH ECHOING GORGE TO THIS GREEN GROWING PLACE.
YOU, WHO WORKED THE CLAY OF SORROW'S END -- AND THOUGHT NEVER TO LEAVE IT -- ARE NOW A TRUE WOLFRIDER!
OUR FOREST BROTHERS CHANGED YOUR LIFE -- AS THEY CHANGED MINE.
HE CHANGED YOU.
HE CHANGED EVERYTHING!

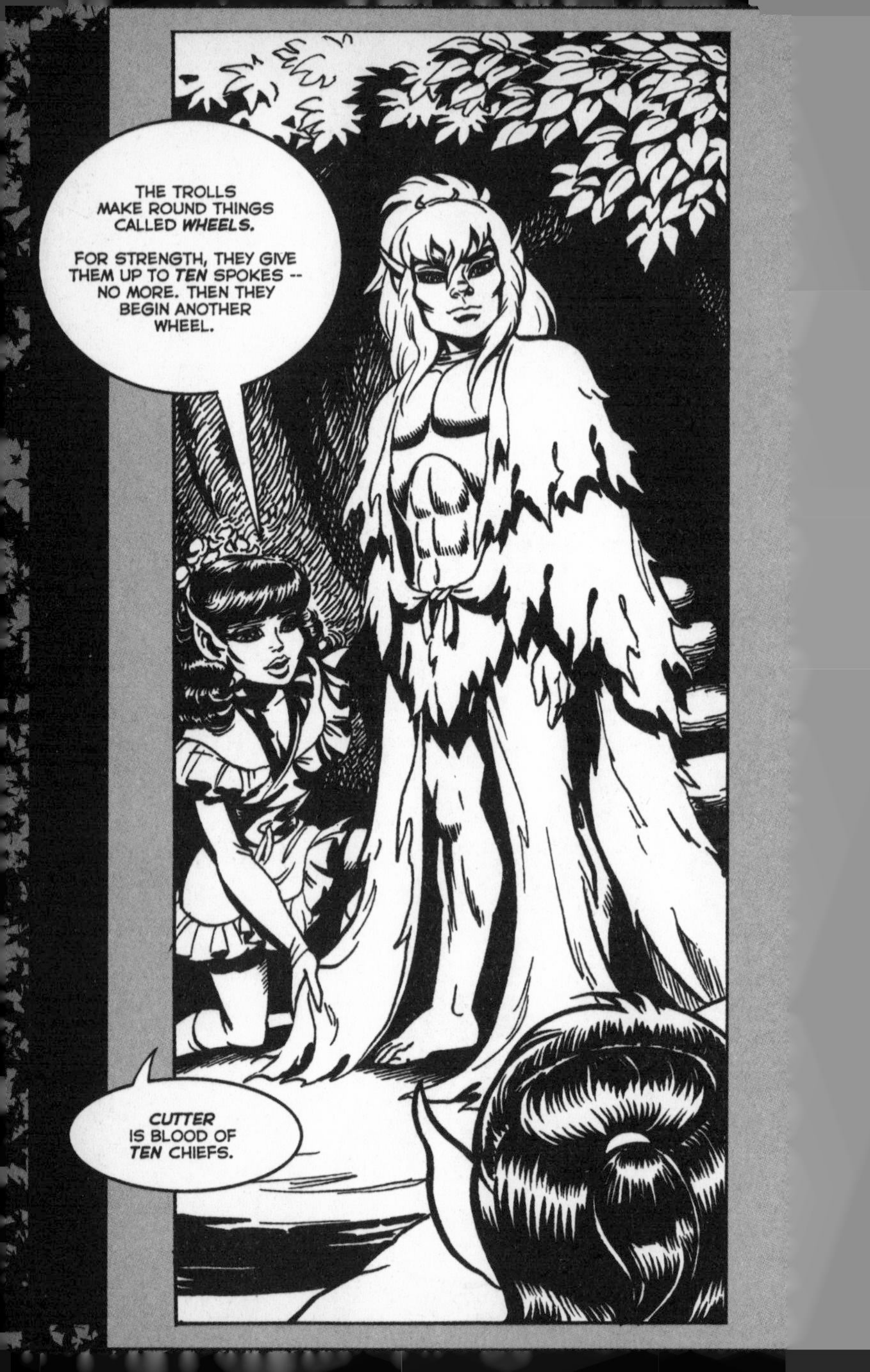
THE TROLLS MAKE ROUND THINGS CALLED *WHEELS.*
FOR STRENGTH, THEY GIVE THEM UP TO *TEN* SPOKES -- NO MORE. THEN THEY BEGIN ANOTHER WHEEL.
CUTTER IS BLOOD OF *TEN* CHIEFS.

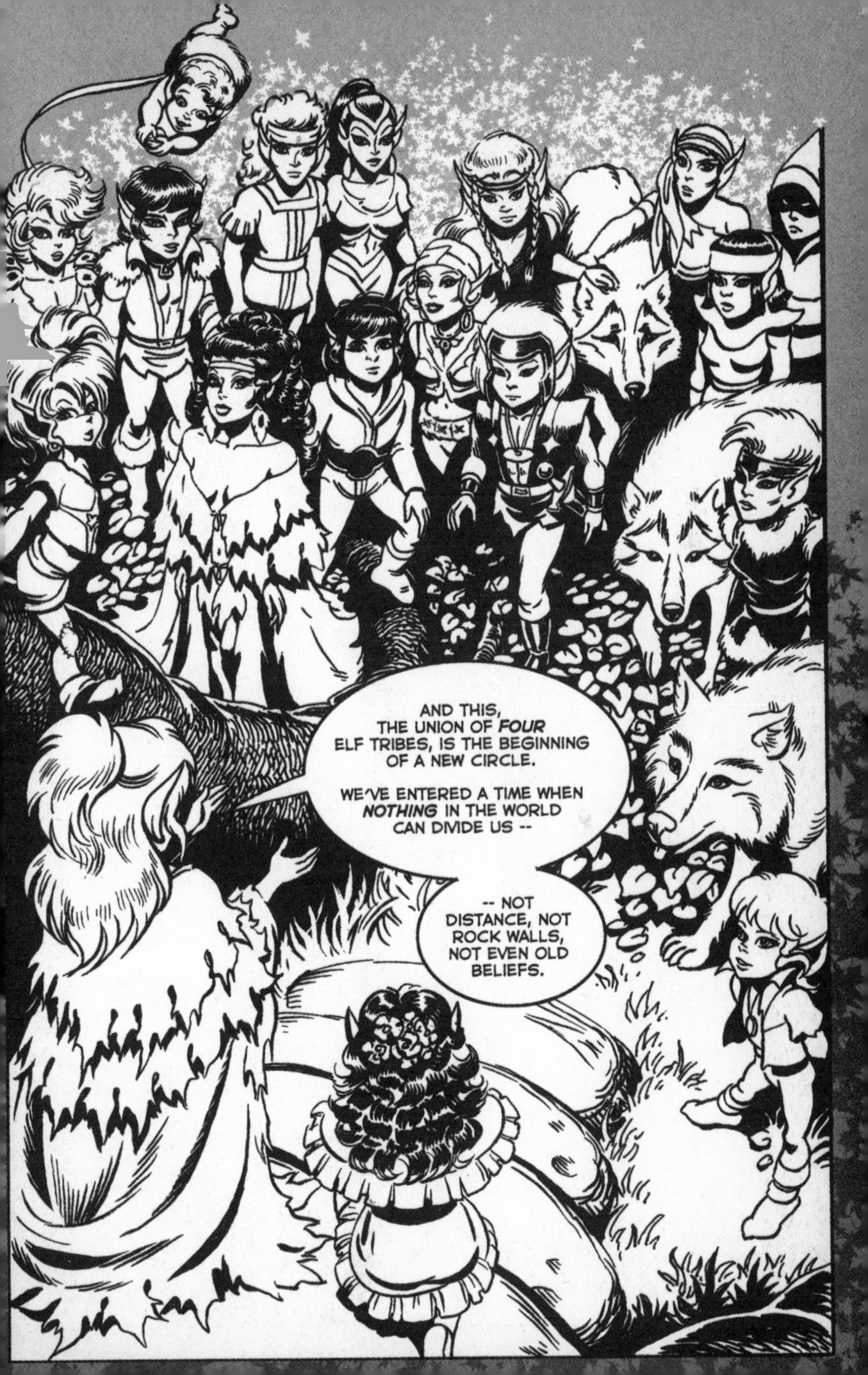
AND THIS, THE UNION OF *FOUR* ELF TRIBES, IS THE BEGINNING OF A NEW CIRCLE.
WE'VE ENTERED A TIME WHEN *NOTHING* IN THE WORLD CAN DIVIDE US --
-- NOT DISTANCE, NOT ROCK WALLS, NOT EVEN OLD BELIEFS.

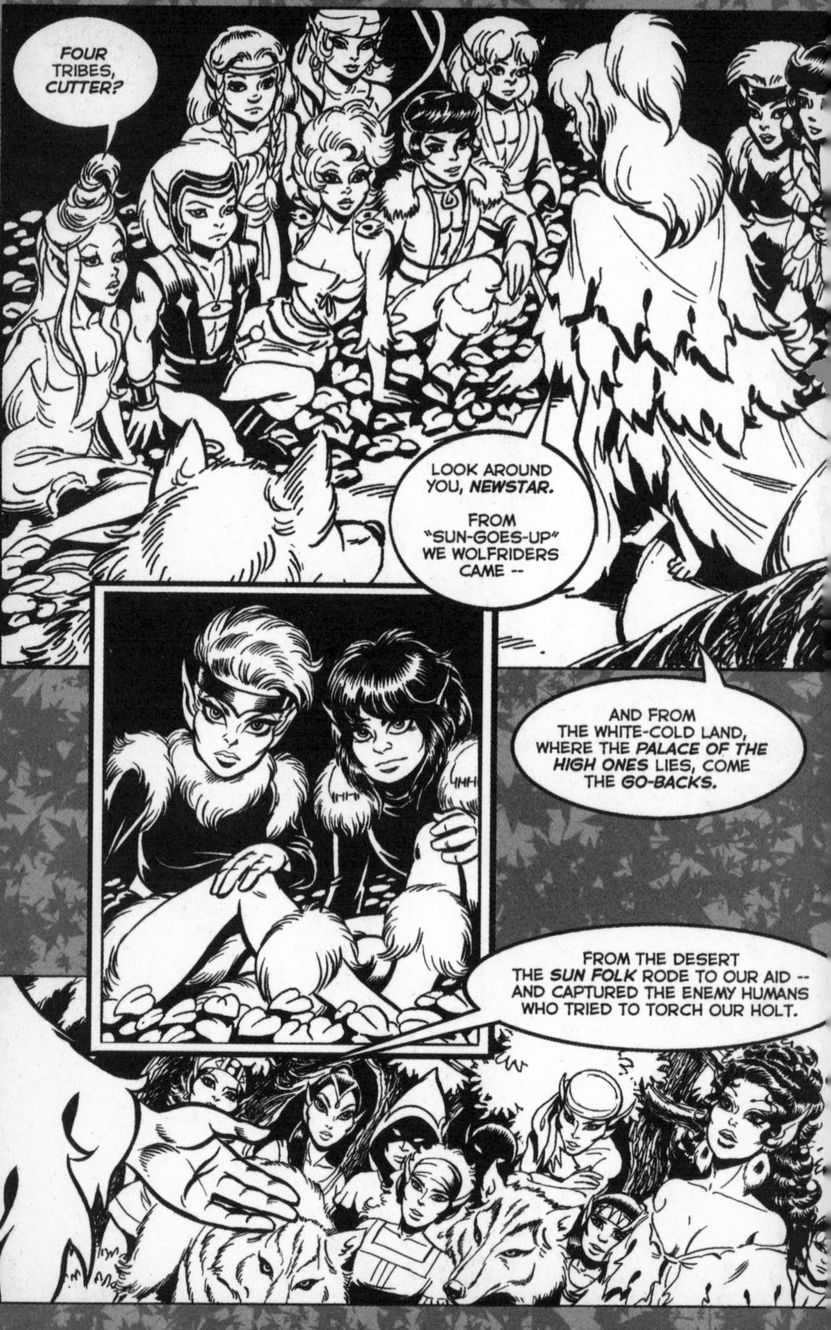
FOUR TRIBES, CUTTER?
LOOK AROUND YOU, NEWSTAR.
FROM "SUN-GOES-UP" WE WOLFRIDERS CAME --
AND FROM THE WHITE-COLD LAND, WHERE THE PALACE OF THE HIGH ONES LIES, COME THE GO-BACKS.
FROM THE DESERT THE SUN FOLK RODE TO OUR AID -- AND CAPTURED THE ENEMY HUMANS WHO TRIED TO TORCH OUR HOLT.

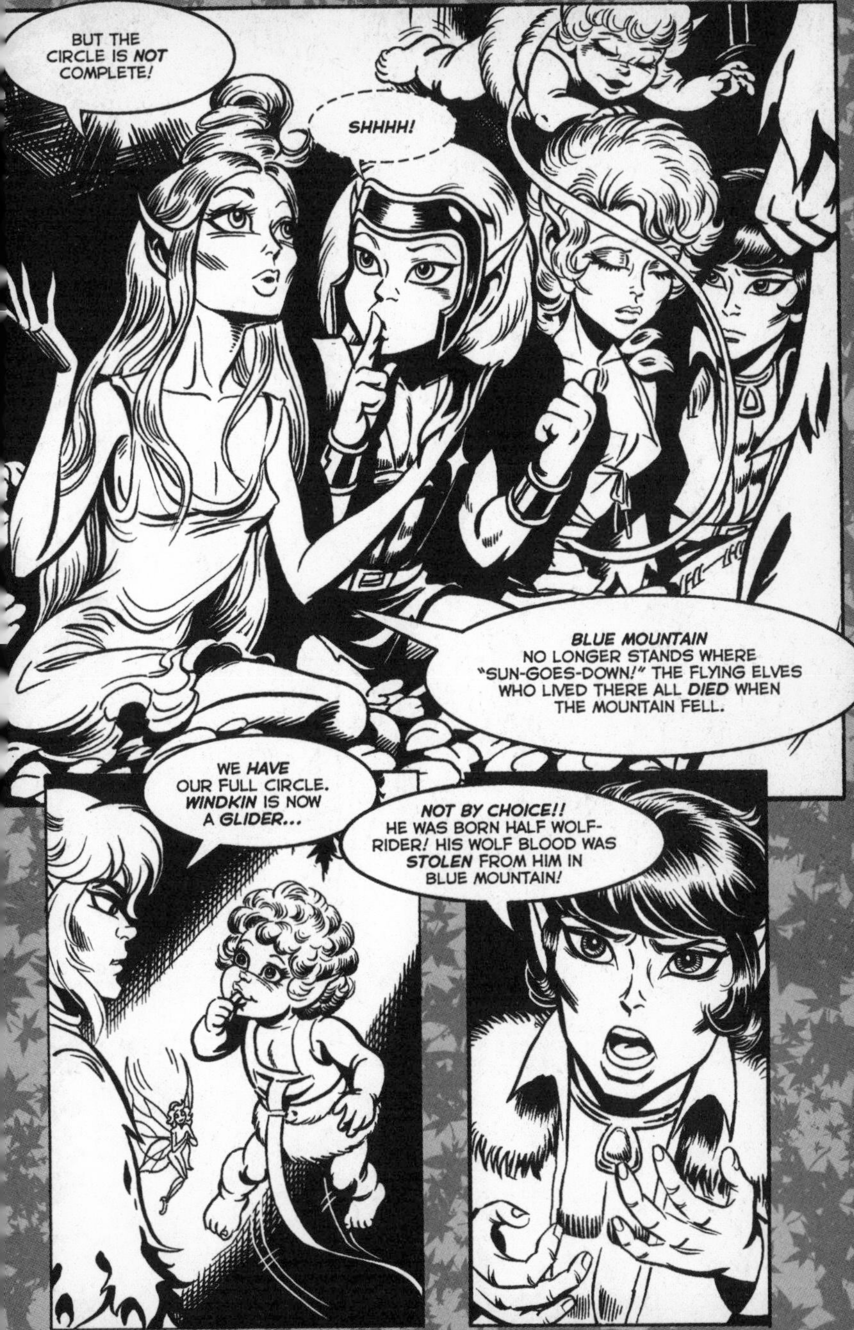

BUT THE CIRCLE IS *NOT* COMPLETE!
SHHHH!
BLUE MOUNTAIN NO LONGER STANDS WHERE "SUN-GOES-DOWN!" THE FLYING ELVES WHO LIVED THERE ALL *DIED* WHEN THE MOUNTAIN FELL.
WE *HAVE* OUR FULL CIRCLE. *WINDKIN* IS NOW A *GLIDER*...
NOT BY CHOICE!! HE WAS BORN HALF WOLF-RIDER! HIS WOLF BLOOD WAS *STOLEN* FROM HIM IN BLUE MOUNTAIN!

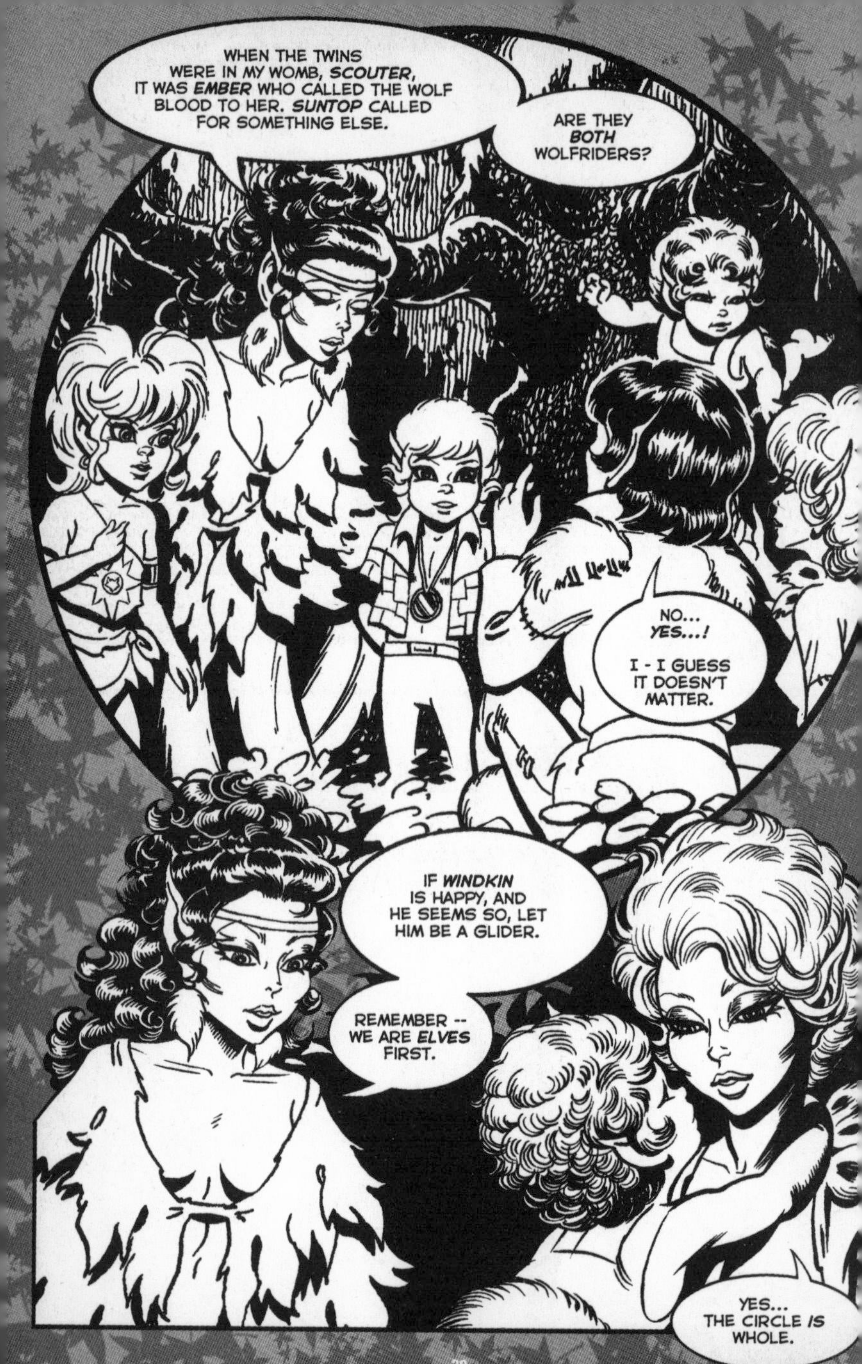

WHEN THE TWINS WERE IN MY WOMB, *SCOUTER*, IT WAS *EMBER* WHO CALLED THE WOLF BLOOD TO HER. *SUNTOP* CALLED FOR SOMETHING ELSE.
ARE THEY *BOTH* WOLFRIDERS?
NO... *YES...!* I - I GUESS IT DOESN'T MATTER.
IF *WINDKIN* IS HAPPY, AND HE SEEMS SO, LET HIM BE A GLIDER.
REMEMBER -- WE ARE *ELVES* FIRST.
YES... THE CIRCLE *IS* WHOLE.

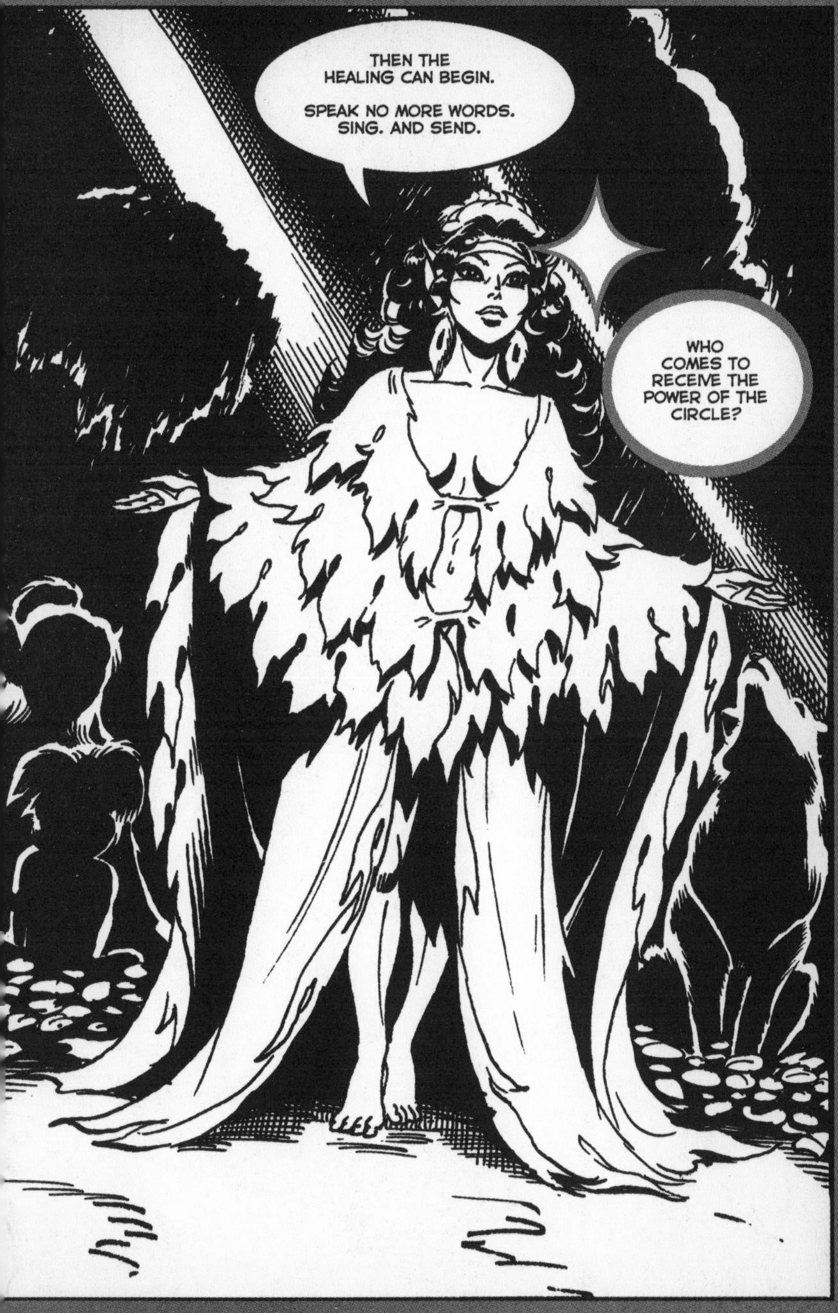
THEN THE HEALING CAN BEGIN.
SPEAK NO MORE WORDS. SING. AND SEND.
WHO COMES TO RECEIVE THE POWER OF THE CIRCLE?

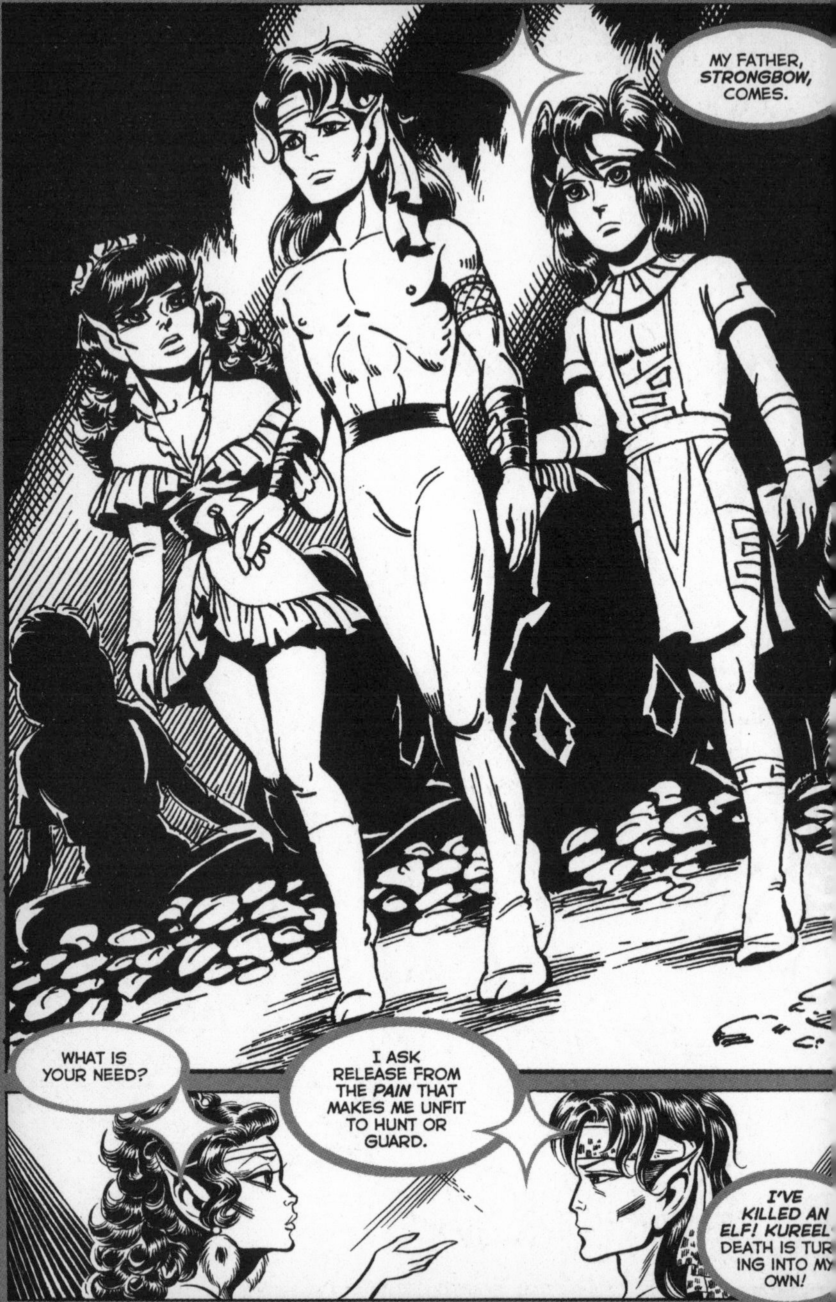
MY FATHER, STRONGBOW, COMES.
WHAT IS YOUR NEED?
I ASK RELEASE FROM THE PAIN THAT MAKES ME UNFIT TO HUNT OR GUARD.
I'VE KILLED AN ELF! KUREEL DEATH IS TUR ING INTO MY OWN!

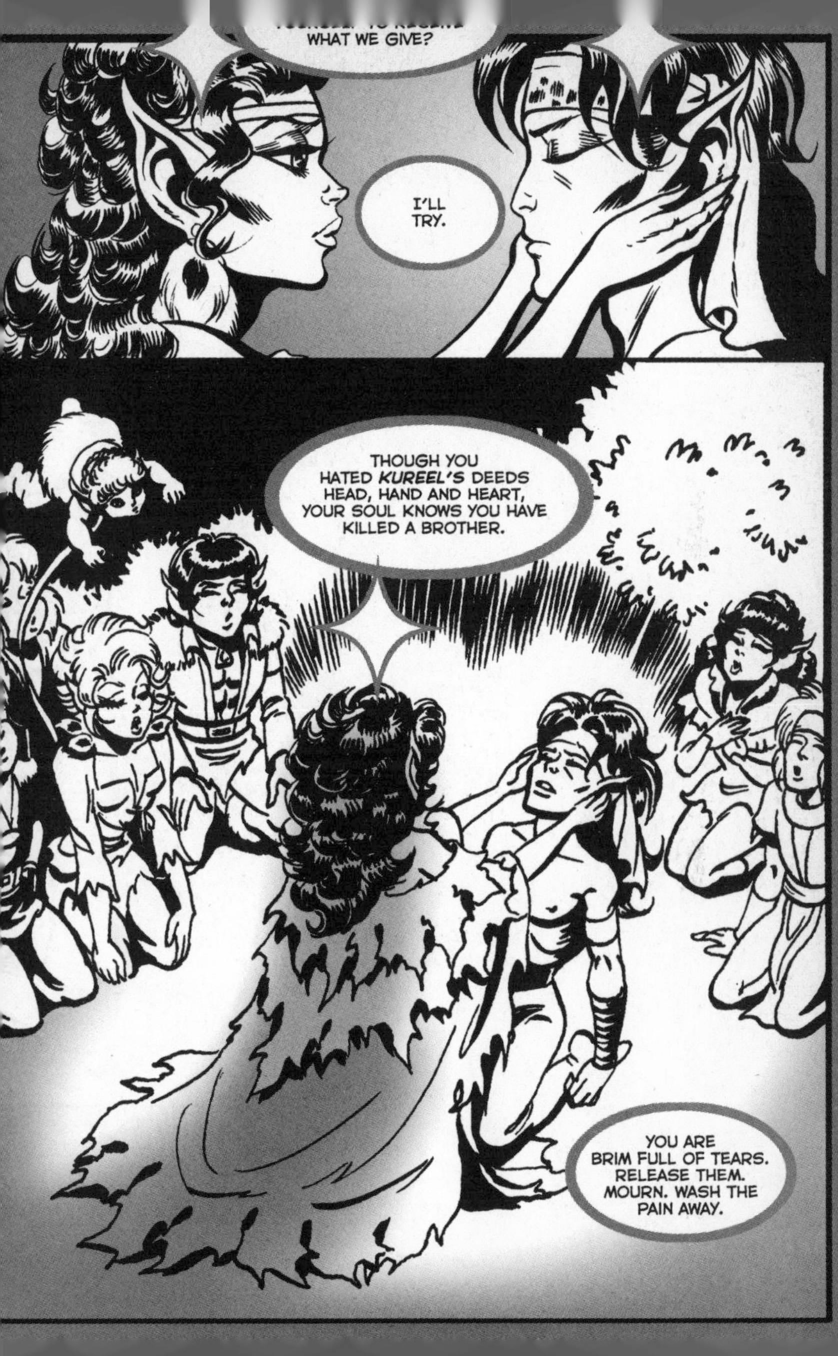
WHAT WE GIVE?
I'LL TRY.
THOUGH YOU HATED KUREEL'S DEEDS HEAD, HAND AND HEART, YOUR SOUL KNOWS YOU HAVE KILLED A BROTHER.
YOU ARE BRIM FULL OF TEARS. RELEASE THEM. MOURN. WASH THE PAIN AWAY.

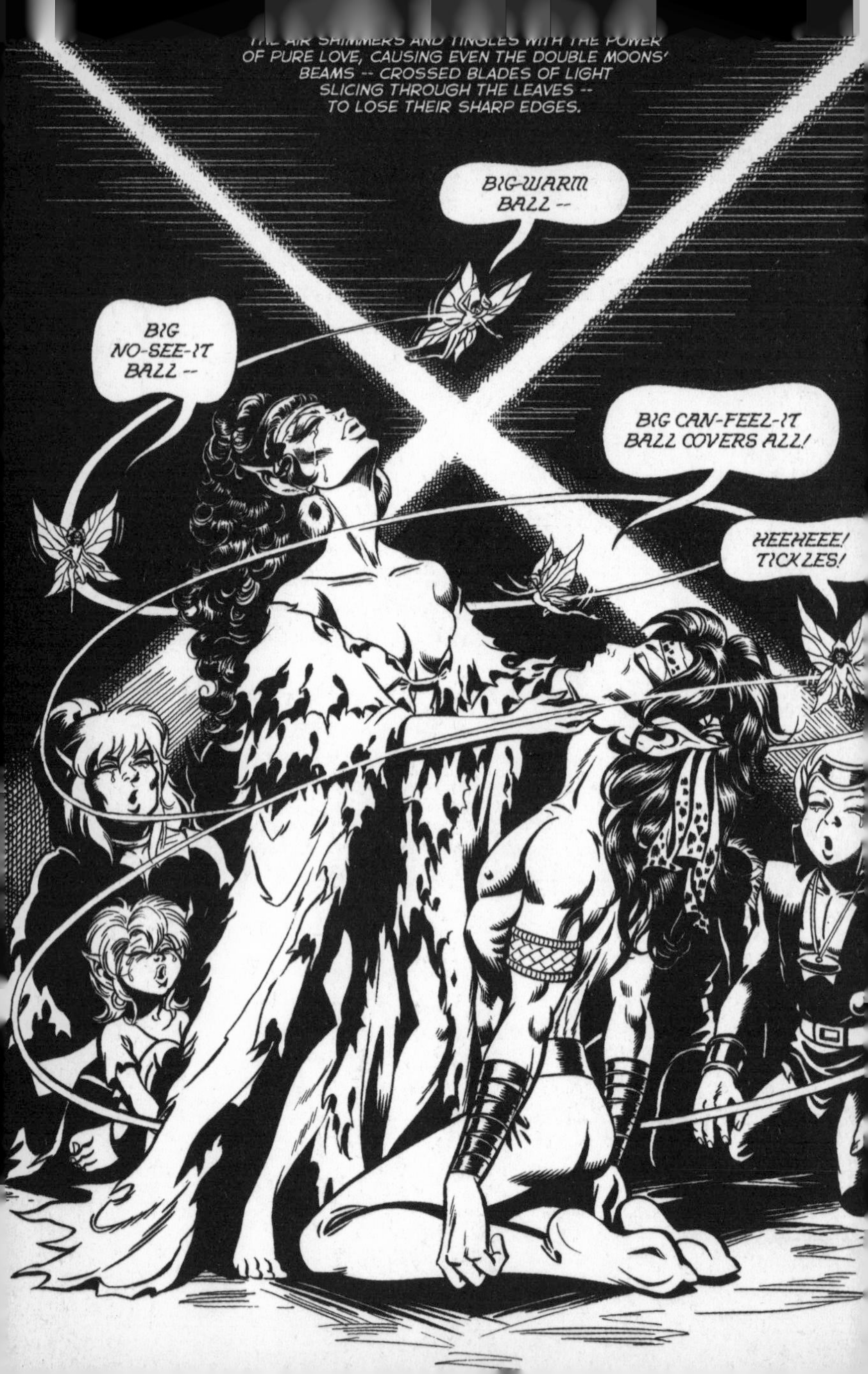
THE AIR SHIMMERS AND TINGLES WITH THE POWER
OF PURE LOVE, CAUSING EVEN THE DOUBLE MOONS'
BEAMS -- CROSSED BLADES OF LIGHT
SLICING THROUGH THE LEAVES --
TO LOSE THEIR SHARP EDGES.
BIG-WARM BALL --
BIG NO-SEE-IT BALL --
BIG CAN-FEEL-IT BALL COVERS ALL!
HEEHEEE! TICKLES!

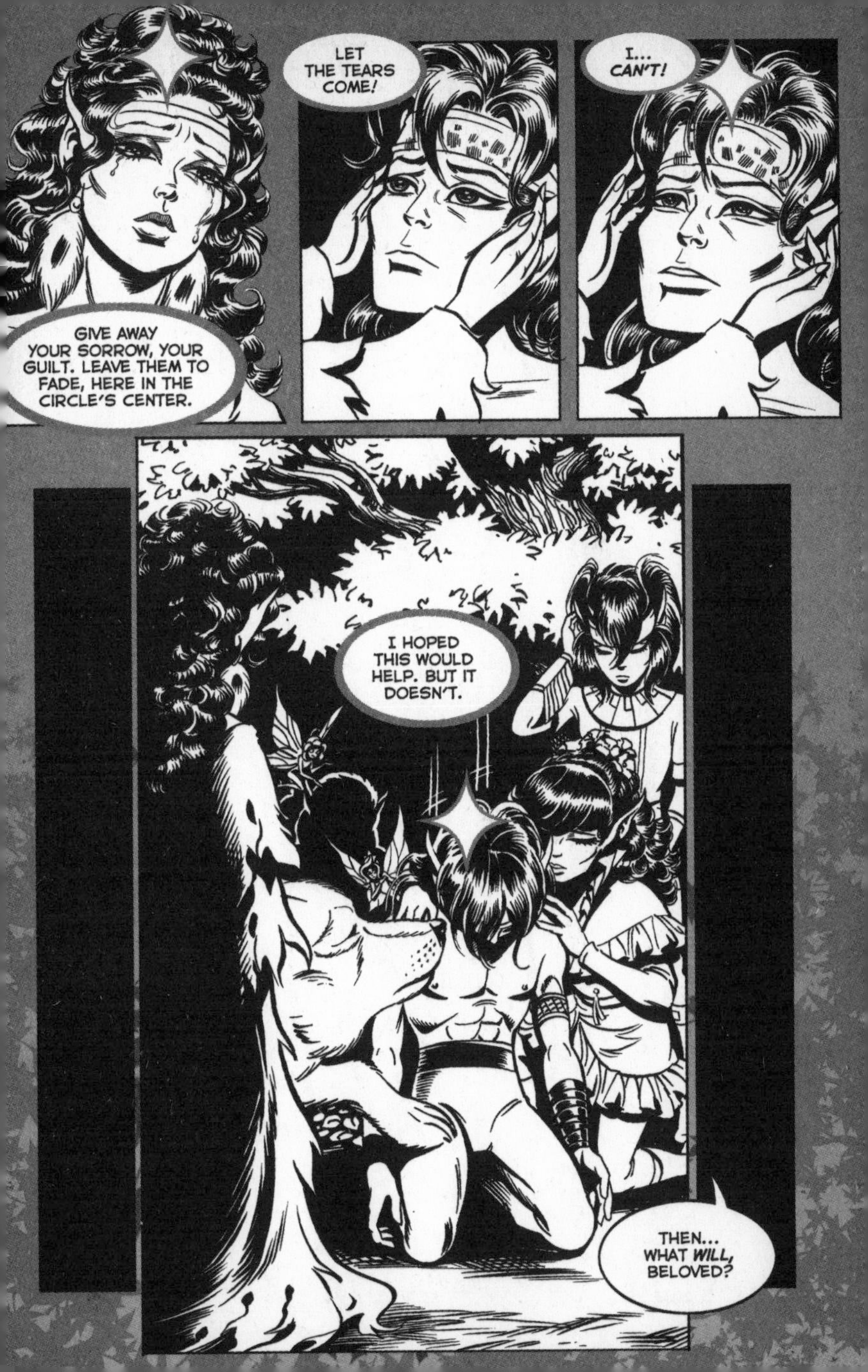
GIVE AWAY YOUR SORROW, YOUR GUILT. LEAVE THEM TO FADE, HERE IN THE CIRCLE'S CENTER.
LET THE TEARS COME!
I... *CAN'T!*
I HOPED THIS WOULD HELP. BUT IT DOESN'T.
THEN... WHAT *WILL*, BELOVED?

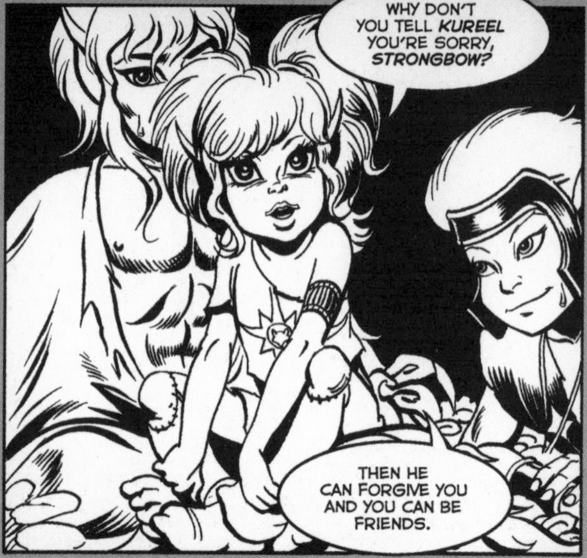
WHY DON'T YOU TELL KUREEL YOU'RE SORRY, STRONGBOW?
THEN HE CAN FORGIVE YOU AND YOU CAN BE FRIENDS.

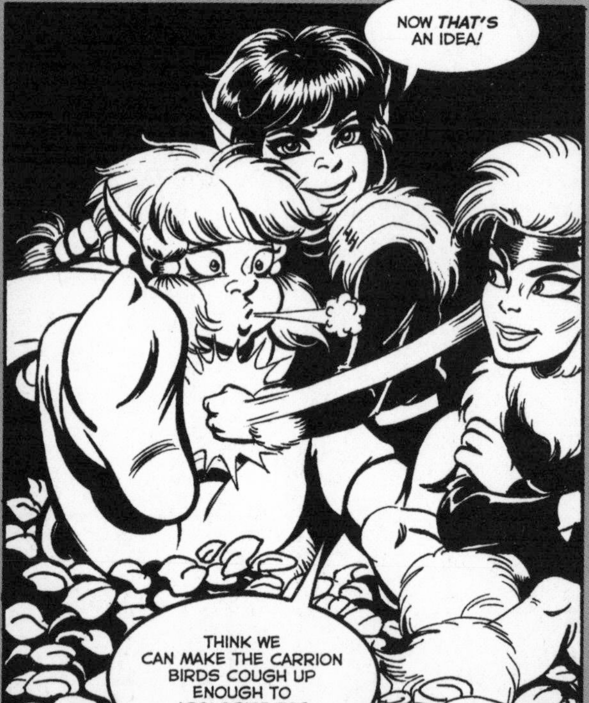
NOW THAT'S AN IDEA!
THINK WE CAN MAKE THE CARRION BIRDS COUGH UP ENOUGH TO APOLOGIZE TO?

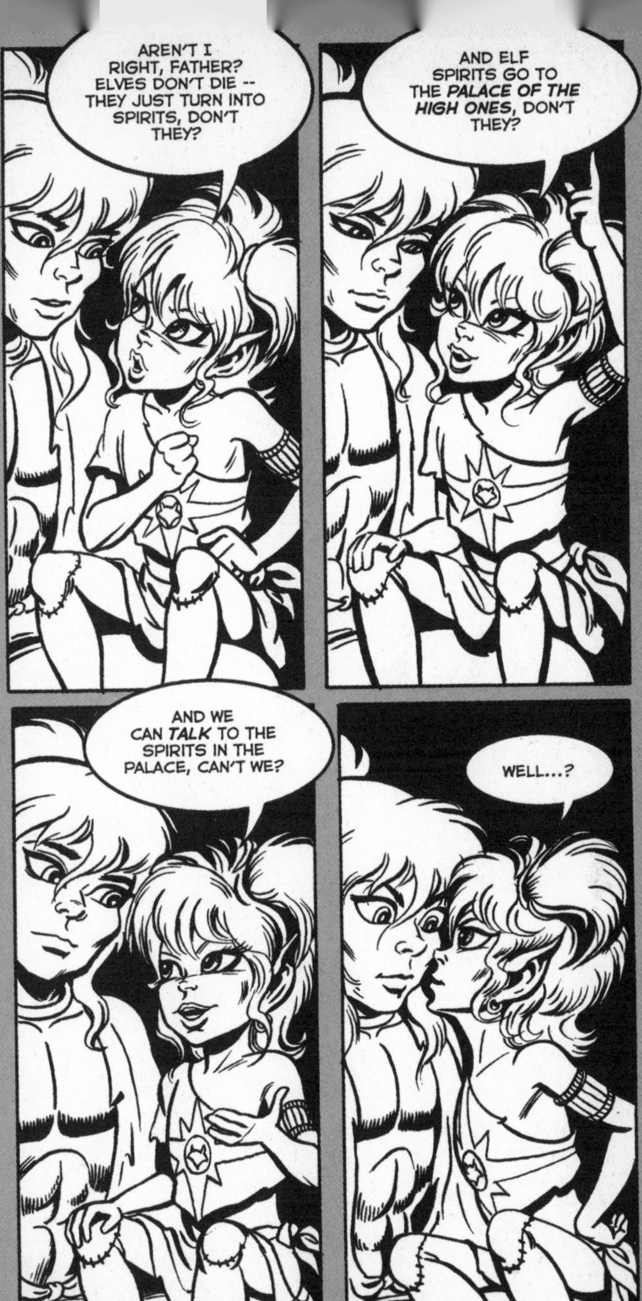
AREN'T I RIGHT, FATHER? ELVES DON'T DIE -- THEY JUST TURN INTO SPIRITS, DON'T THEY?
AND ELF SPIRITS GO TO THE *PALACE OF THE HIGH ONES*, DON'T THEY?
AND WE CAN *TALK* TO THE SPIRITS IN THE PALACE, CAN'T WE?
WELL...?

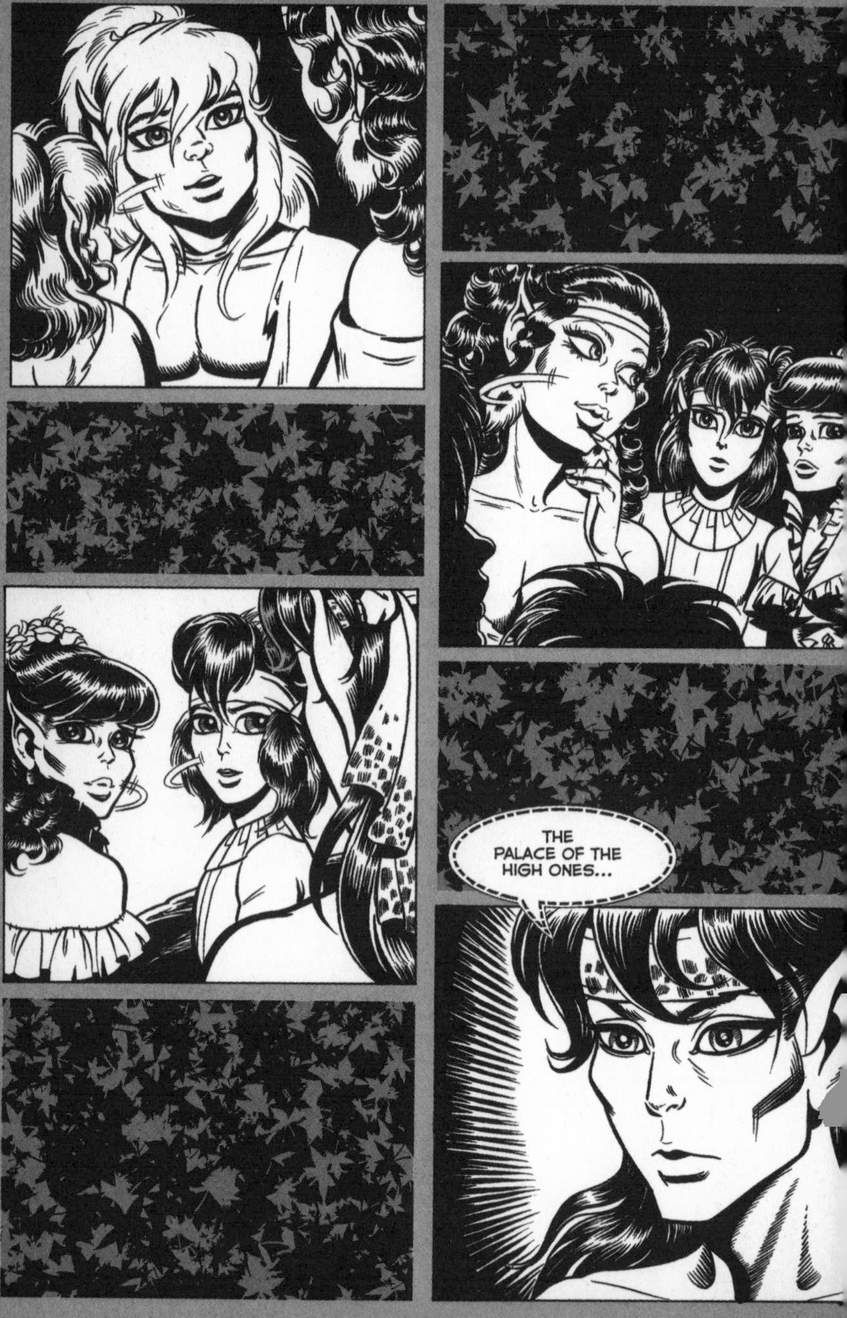
THE PALACE OF THE HIGH ONES...

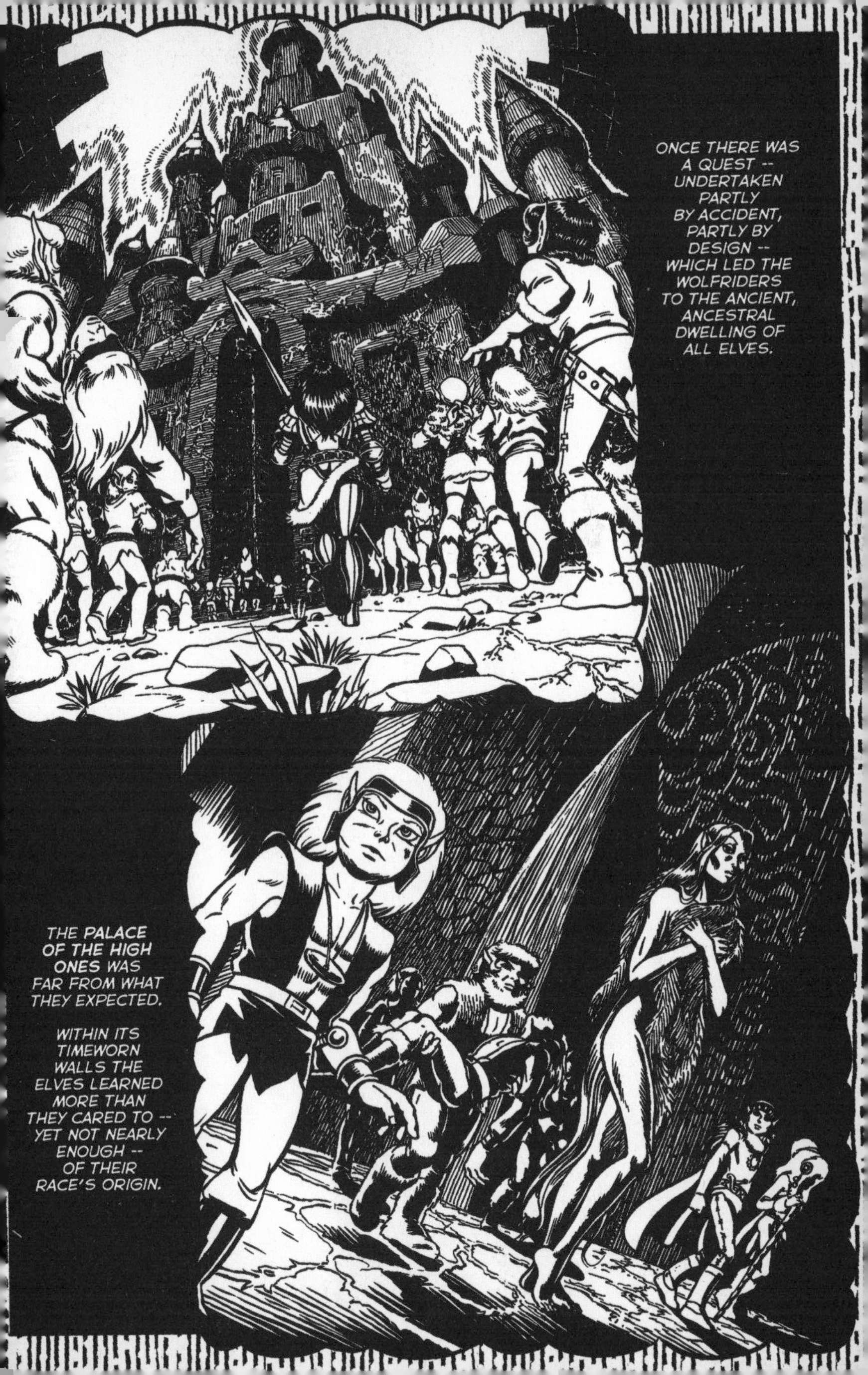
ONCE THERE WAS A QUEST -- UNDERTAKEN PARTLY BY ACCIDENT, PARTLY BY DESIGN -- WHICH LED THE WOLFRIDERS TO THE ANCIENT, ANCESTRAL DWELLING OF ALL ELVES.
THE PALACE OF THE HIGH ONES WAS FAR FROM WHAT THEY EXPECTED.
WITHIN ITS TIMEWORN WALLS THE ELVES LEARNED MORE THAN THEY CARED TO -- YET NOT NEARLY ENOUGH -- OF THEIR RACE'S ORIGIN.

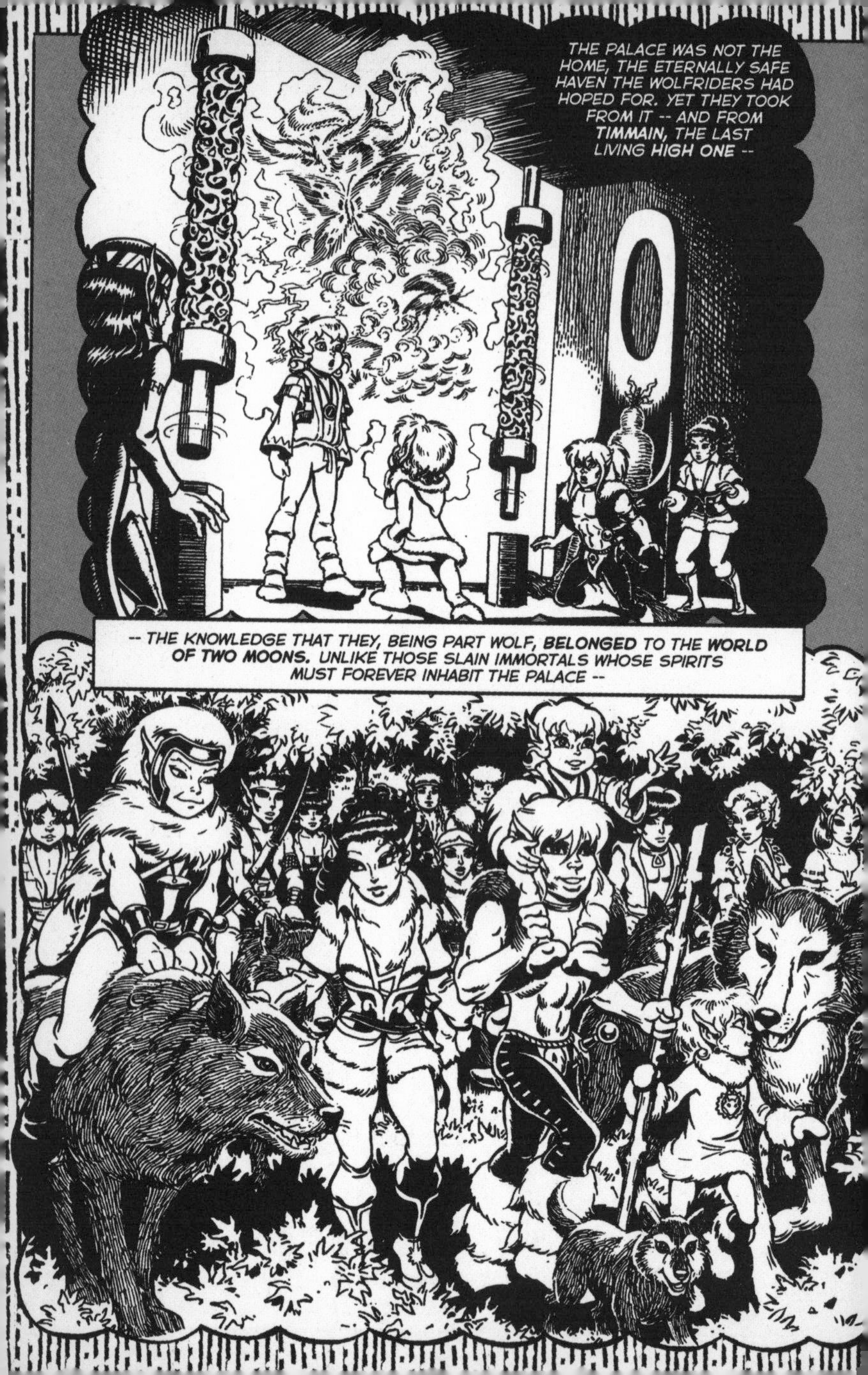
THE PALACE WAS NOT THE HOME, THE ETERNALLY SAFE HAVEN THE WOLFRIDERS HAD HOPED FOR. YET THEY TOOK FROM IT -- AND FROM TIMMAIN, THE LAST LIVING HIGH ONE --
-- THE KNOWLEDGE THAT THEY, BEING PART WOLF, BELONGED TO THE WORLD OF TWO MOONS. UNLIKE THOSE SLAIN IMMORTALS WHOSE SPIRITS MUST FOREVER INHABIT THE PALACE --

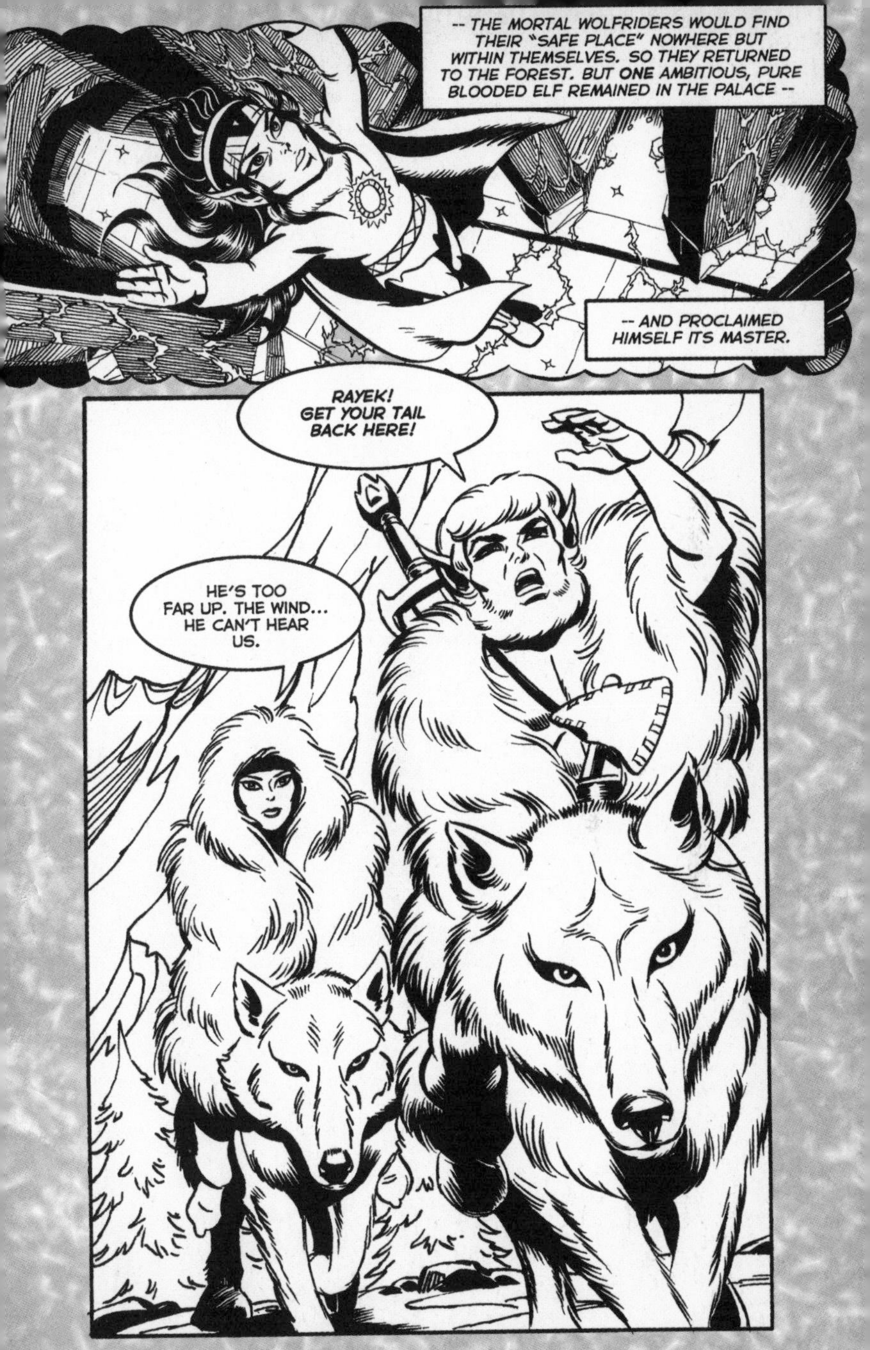
-- THE MORTAL WOLFRIDERS WOULD FIND THEIR "SAFE PLACE" NOWHERE BUT WITHIN THEMSELVES. SO THEY RETURNED TO THE FOREST. BUT ONE AMBITIOUS, PURE BLOODED ELF REMAINED IN THE PALACE --
-- AND PROCLAIMED HIMSELF ITS MASTER.
RAYEK! GET YOUR TAIL BACK HERE!
HE'S TOO FAR UP. THE WIND... HE CAN'T HEAR US.

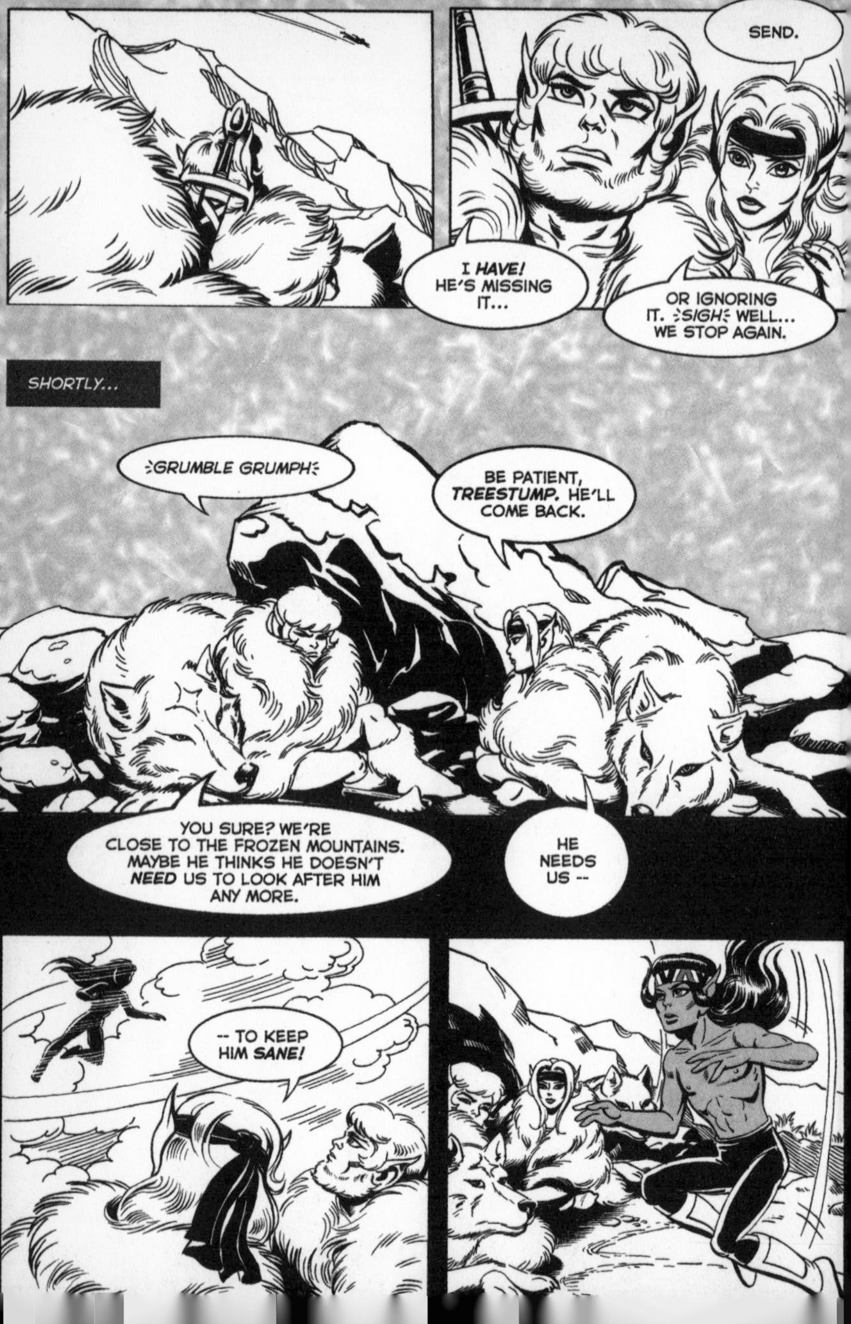
SEND.
I HAVE! HE'S MISSING IT...
OR IGNORING IT. ⁝SIGH⁝ WELL... WE STOP AGAIN.
SHORTLY...
⁝GRUMBLE GRUMPH⁝
BE PATIENT, TREESTUMP. HE'LL COME BACK.
YOU SURE? WE'RE CLOSE TO THE FROZEN MOUNTAINS. MAYBE HE THINKS HE DOESN'T NEED US TO LOOK AFTER HIM ANY MORE.
HE NEEDS US --
-- TO KEEP HIM SANE!

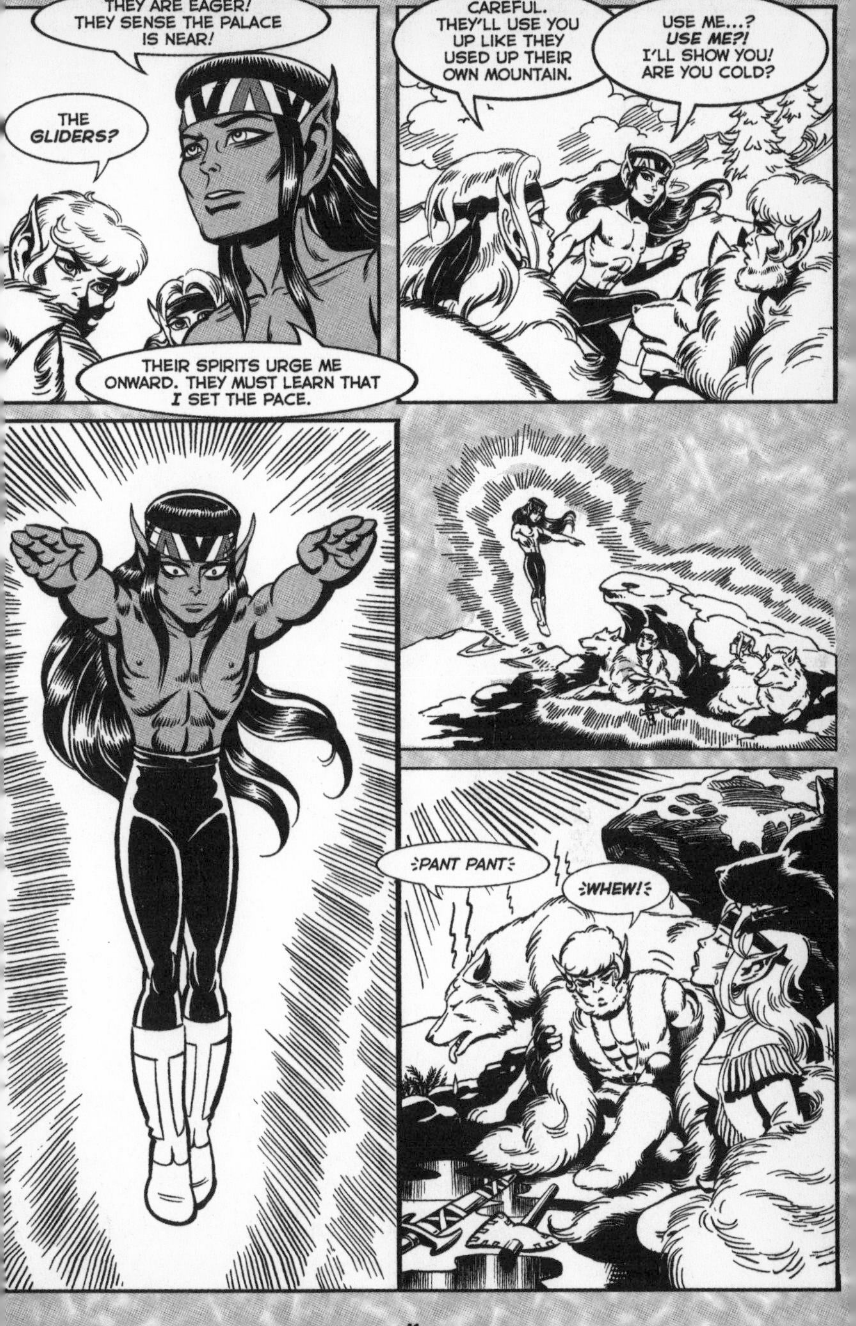
THEY ARE EAGER! THEY SENSE THE PALACE IS NEAR!
THE GLIDERS?
THEIR SPIRITS URGE ME ONWARD. THEY MUST LEARN THAT I SET THE PACE.
CAREFUL. THEY'LL USE YOU UP LIKE THEY USED UP THEIR OWN MOUNTAIN.
USE ME...? USE ME?! I'LL SHOW YOU! ARE YOU COLD?
PANT PANT
WHEW!

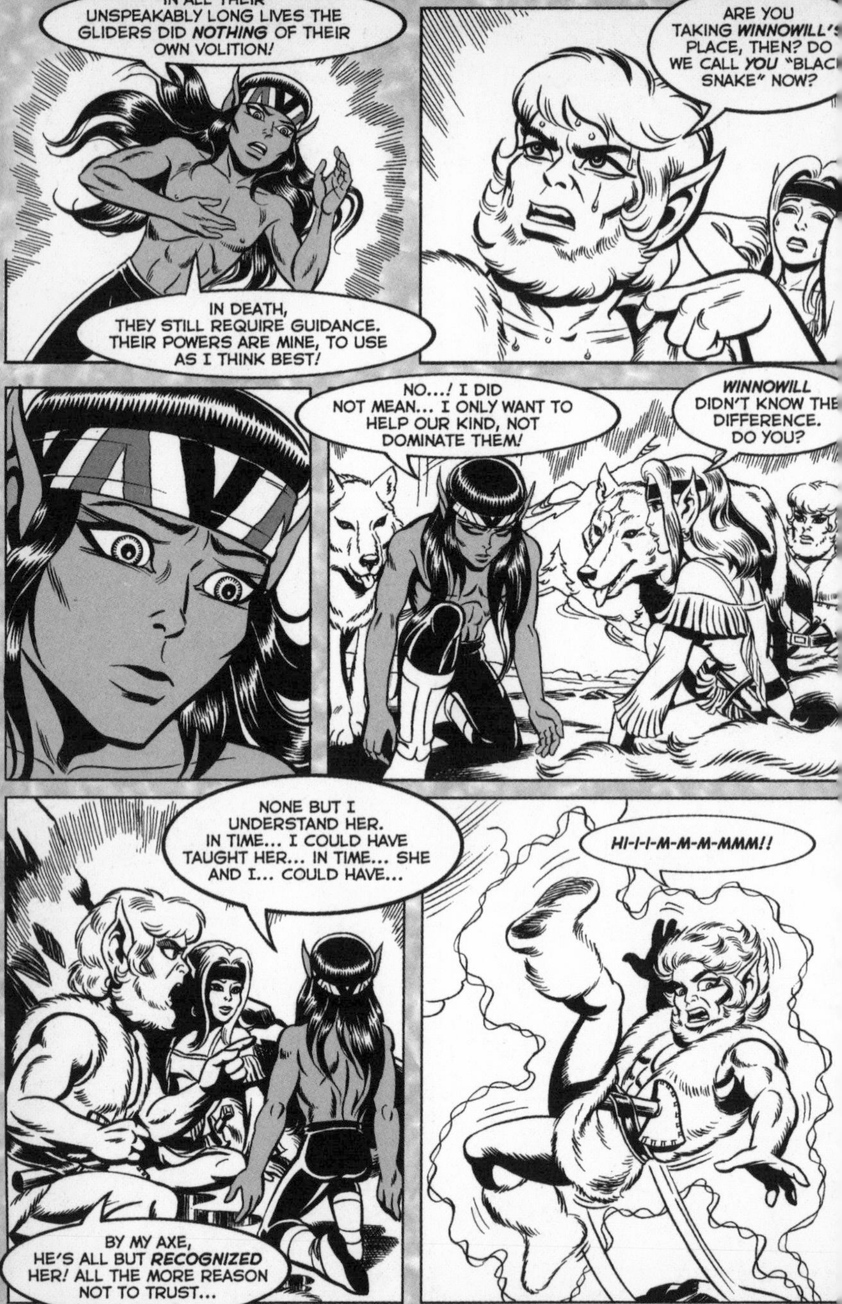
IN ALL THEIR UNSPEAKABLY LONG LIVES THE GLIDERS DID *NOTHING* OF THEIR OWN VOLITION!
IN DEATH, THEY STILL REQUIRE GUIDANCE. THEIR POWERS ARE MINE, TO USE AS I THINK BEST!
ARE YOU TAKING *WINNOWILL'S* PLACE, THEN? DO WE CALL *YOU* "BLACK SNAKE" NOW?
NO...! I DID NOT MEAN... I ONLY WANT TO HELP OUR KIND, NOT DOMINATE THEM!
WINNOWILL DIDN'T KNOW THE DIFFERENCE. DO YOU?
NONE BUT I UNDERSTAND HER. IN TIME... I COULD HAVE TAUGHT HER... IN TIME... SHE AND I... COULD HAVE...
BY MY AXE, HE'S ALL BUT *RECOGNIZED* HER! ALL THE MORE REASON NOT TO TRUST...
HI-I-I-M-M-M-MMM!!

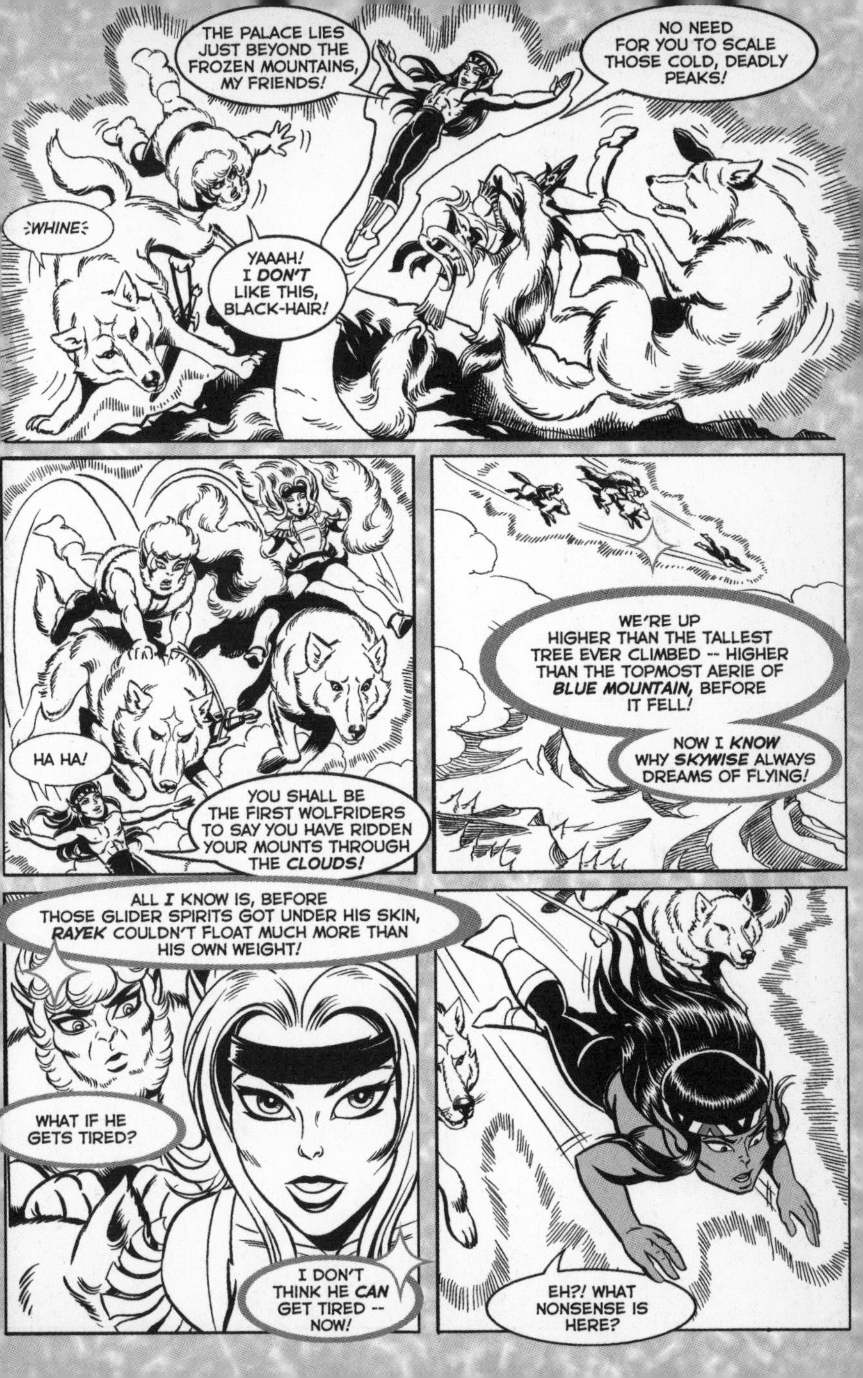

THE PALACE LIES JUST BEYOND THE FROZEN MOUNTAINS, MY FRIENDS!
NO NEED FOR YOU TO SCALE THOSE COLD, DEADLY PEAKS!
WHINE
YAAAH! I DON'T LIKE THIS, BLACK-HAIR!
HA HA!
YOU SHALL BE THE FIRST WOLFRIDERS TO SAY YOU HAVE RIDDEN YOUR MOUNTS THROUGH THE CLOUDS!
WE'RE UP HIGHER THAN THE TALLEST TREE EVER CLIMBED -- HIGHER THAN THE TOPMOST AERIE OF BLUE MOUNTAIN, BEFORE IT FELL!
NOW I KNOW WHY SKYWISE ALWAYS DREAMS OF FLYING!
ALL I KNOW IS, BEFORE THOSE GLIDER SPIRITS GOT UNDER HIS SKIN, RAYEK COULDN'T FLOAT MUCH MORE THAN HIS OWN WEIGHT!
WHAT IF HE GETS TIRED?
I DON'T THINK HE CAN GET TIRED -- NOW!
EH?! WHAT NONSENSE IS HERE?

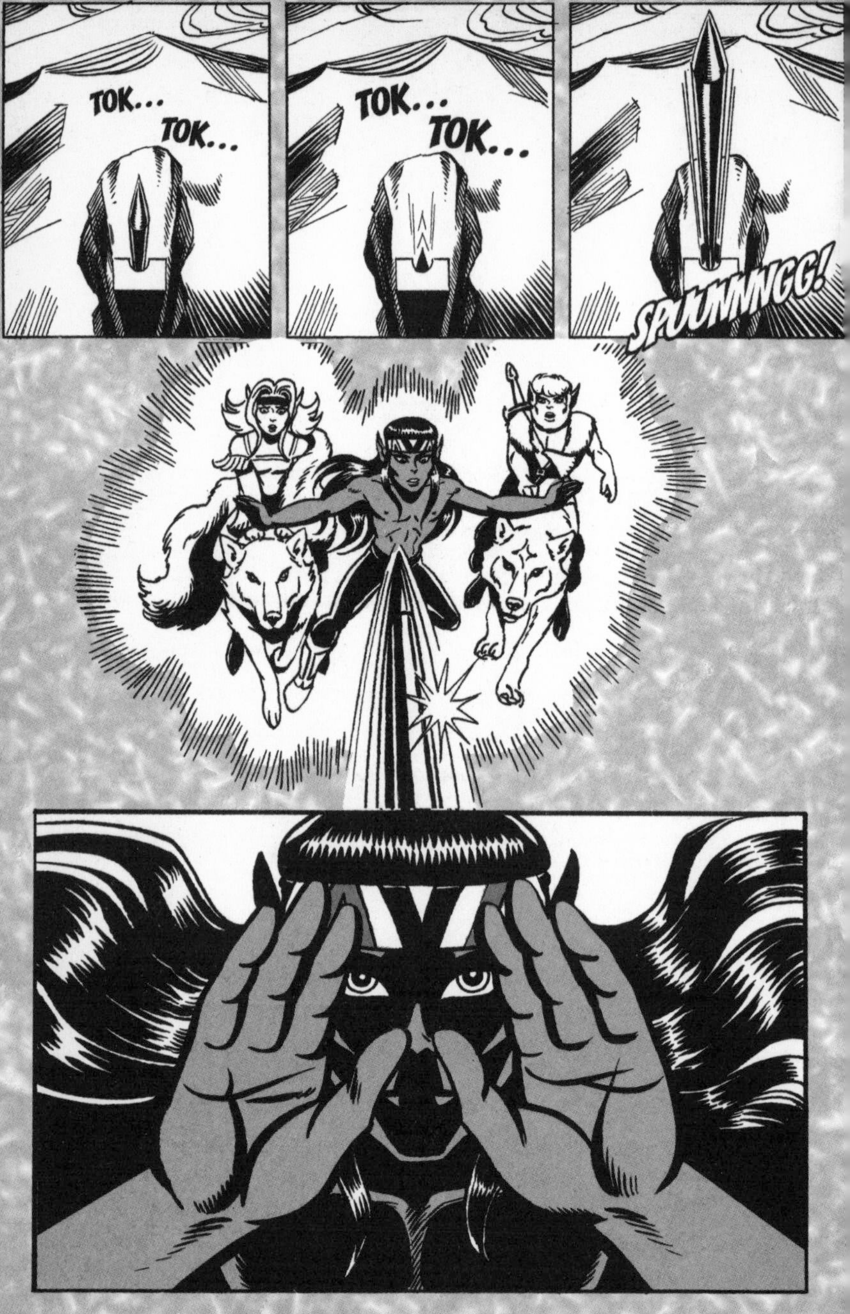
TOK...
TOK...
TOK...
TOK...
SPUUNNNGG!

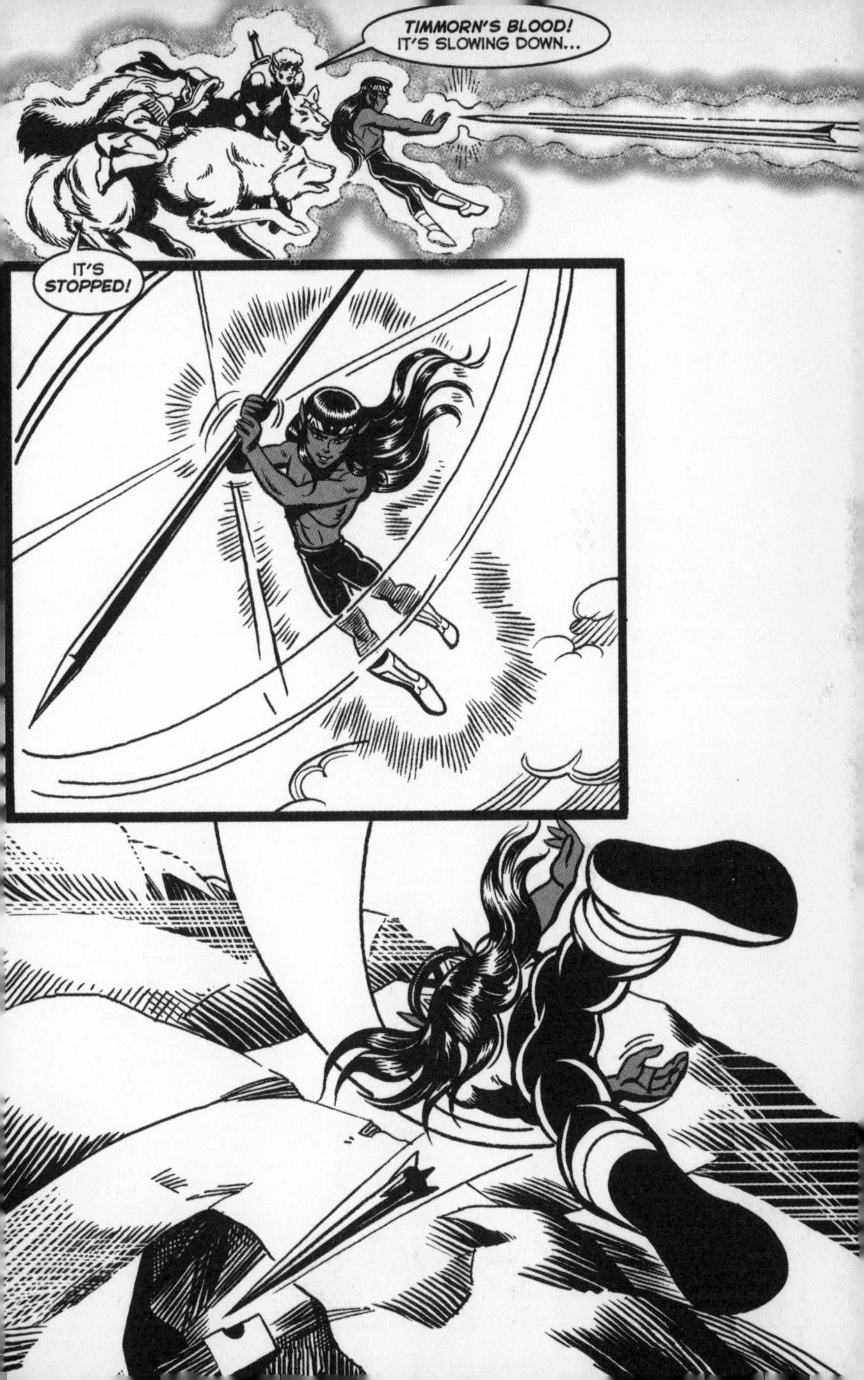
TIMMORN'S BLOOD! IT'S SLOWING DOWN...
IT'S STOPPED!

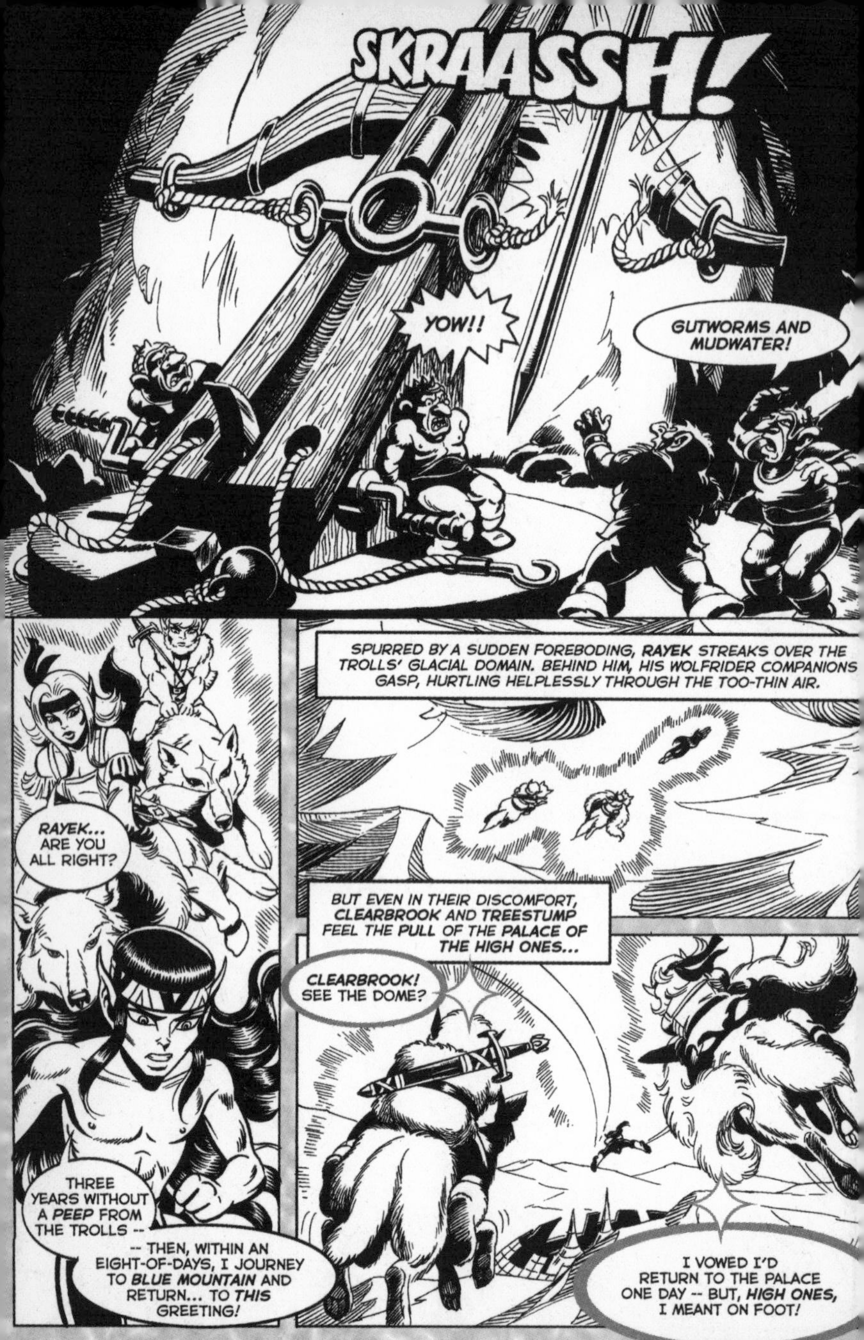
SKRAASSH!
YOW!!
GUTWORMS AND MUDWATER!
RAYEK... ARE YOU ALL RIGHT?
THREE YEARS WITHOUT A PEEP FROM THE TROLLS --
-- THEN, WITHIN AN EIGHT-OF-DAYS, I JOURNEY TO BLUE MOUNTAIN AND RETURN... TO THIS GREETING!
SPURRED BY A SUDDEN FOREBODING, RAYEK STREAKS OVER THE TROLLS' GLACIAL DOMAIN. BEHIND HIM, HIS WOLFRIDER COMPANIONS GASP, HURTLING HELPLESSLY THROUGH THE TOO-THIN AIR.
BUT EVEN IN THEIR DISCOMFORT, CLEARBROOK AND TREESTUMP FEEL THE PULL OF THE PALACE OF THE HIGH ONES...
CLEARBROOK! SEE THE DOME?
I VOWED I'D RETURN TO THE PALACE ONE DAY -- BUT, HIGH ONES, I MEANT ON FOOT!

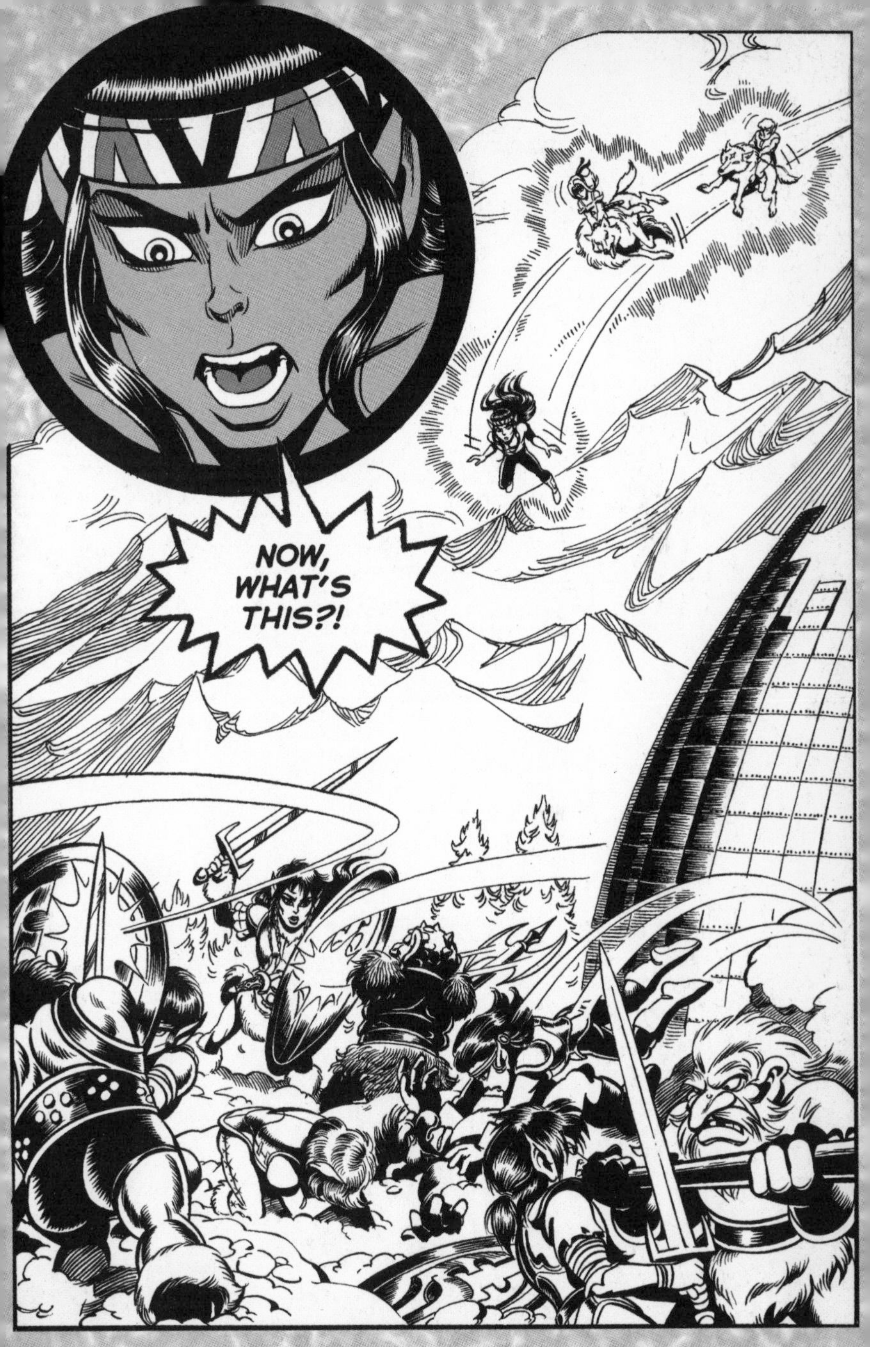
NOW, WHAT'S THIS?!

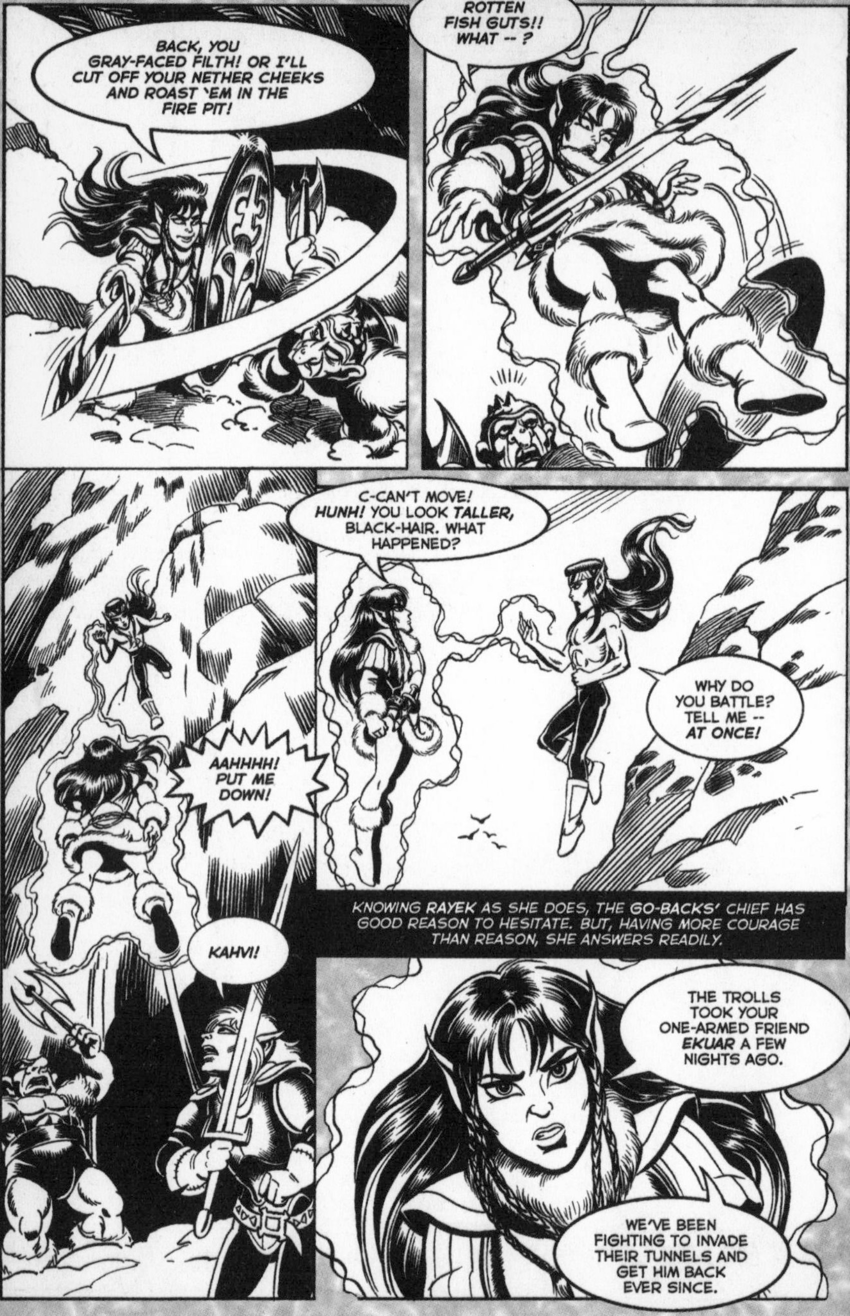
BACK, YOU GRAY-FACED FILTH! OR I'LL CUT OFF YOUR NETHER CHEEKS AND ROAST 'EM IN THE FIRE PIT!
ROTTEN FISH GUTS!! WHAT -- ?
C-CAN'T MOVE! HUNH! YOU LOOK TALLER, BLACK-HAIR. WHAT HAPPENED?
AAHHHH! PUT ME DOWN!
WHY DO YOU BATTLE? TELL ME -- AT ONCE!
KNOWING RAYEK AS SHE DOES, THE GO-BACKS' CHIEF HAS GOOD REASON TO HESITATE. BUT, HAVING MORE COURAGE THAN REASON, SHE ANSWERS READILY.
KAHVI!
THE TROLLS TOOK YOUR ONE-ARMED FRIEND EKUAR A FEW NIGHTS AGO.
WE'VE BEEN FIGHTING TO INVADE THEIR TUNNELS AND GET HIM BACK EVER SINCE.

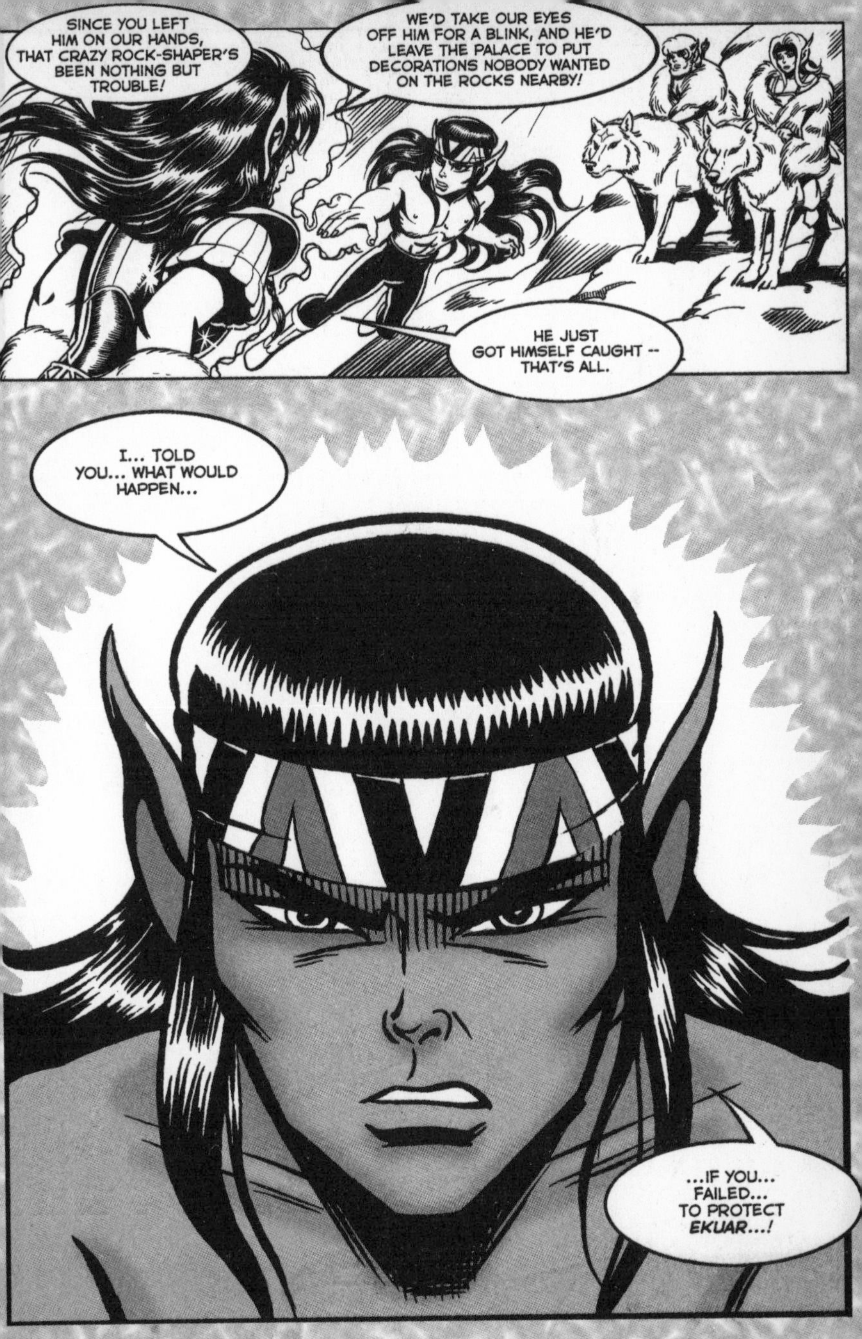
SINCE YOU LEFT HIM ON OUR HANDS, THAT CRAZY ROCK-SHAPER'S BEEN NOTHING BUT TROUBLE!
WE'D TAKE OUR EYES OFF HIM FOR A BLINK, AND HE'D LEAVE THE PALACE TO PUT DECORATIONS NOBODY WANTED ON THE ROCKS NEARBY!
HE JUST GOT HIMSELF CAUGHT -- THAT'S ALL.
I... TOLD YOU... WHAT WOULD HAPPEN...
...IF YOU... FAILED... TO PROTECT *EKUAR*...!

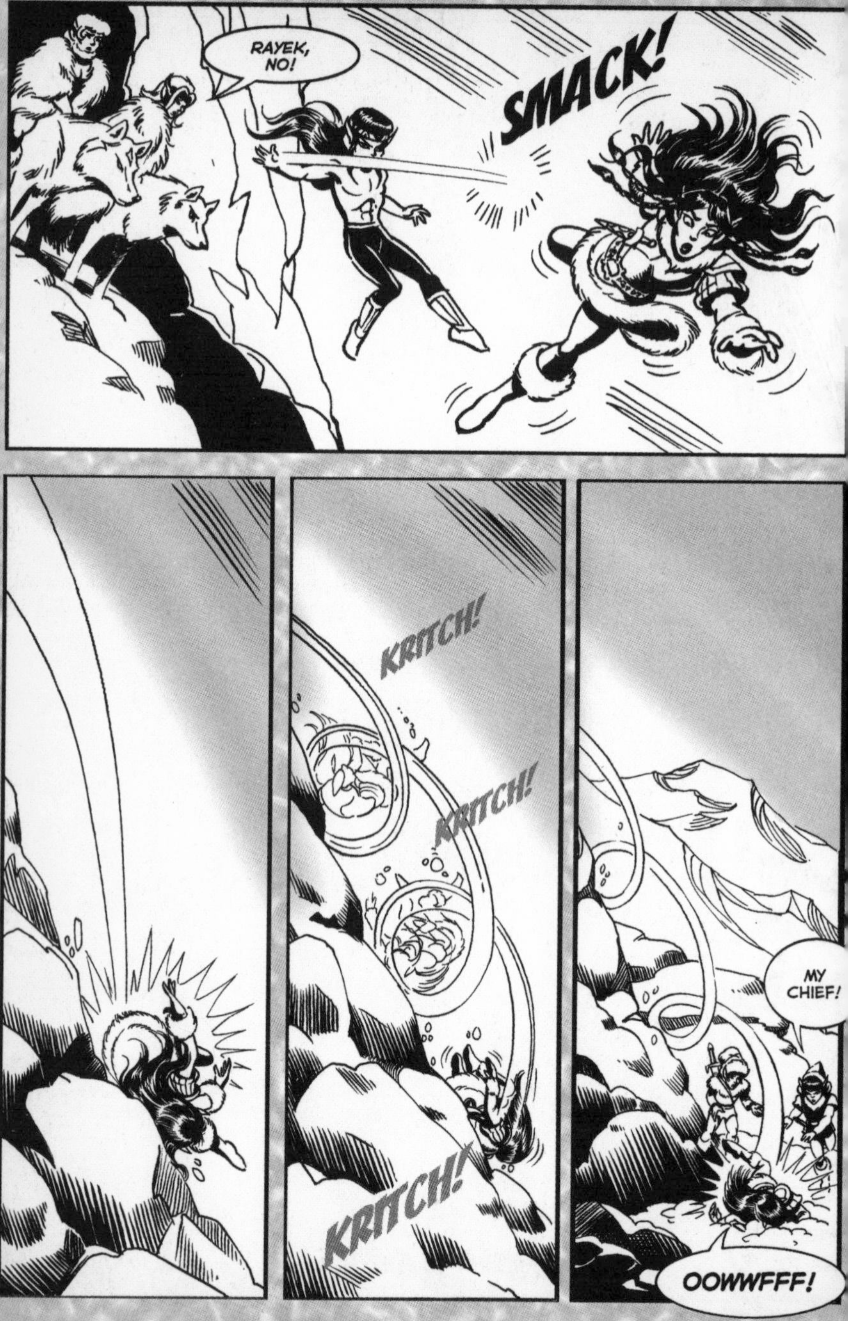
RAYEK, NO!
SMACK!
KRITCH!
KRITCH!
KRITCH!
MY CHIEF!
OOWWFFF!

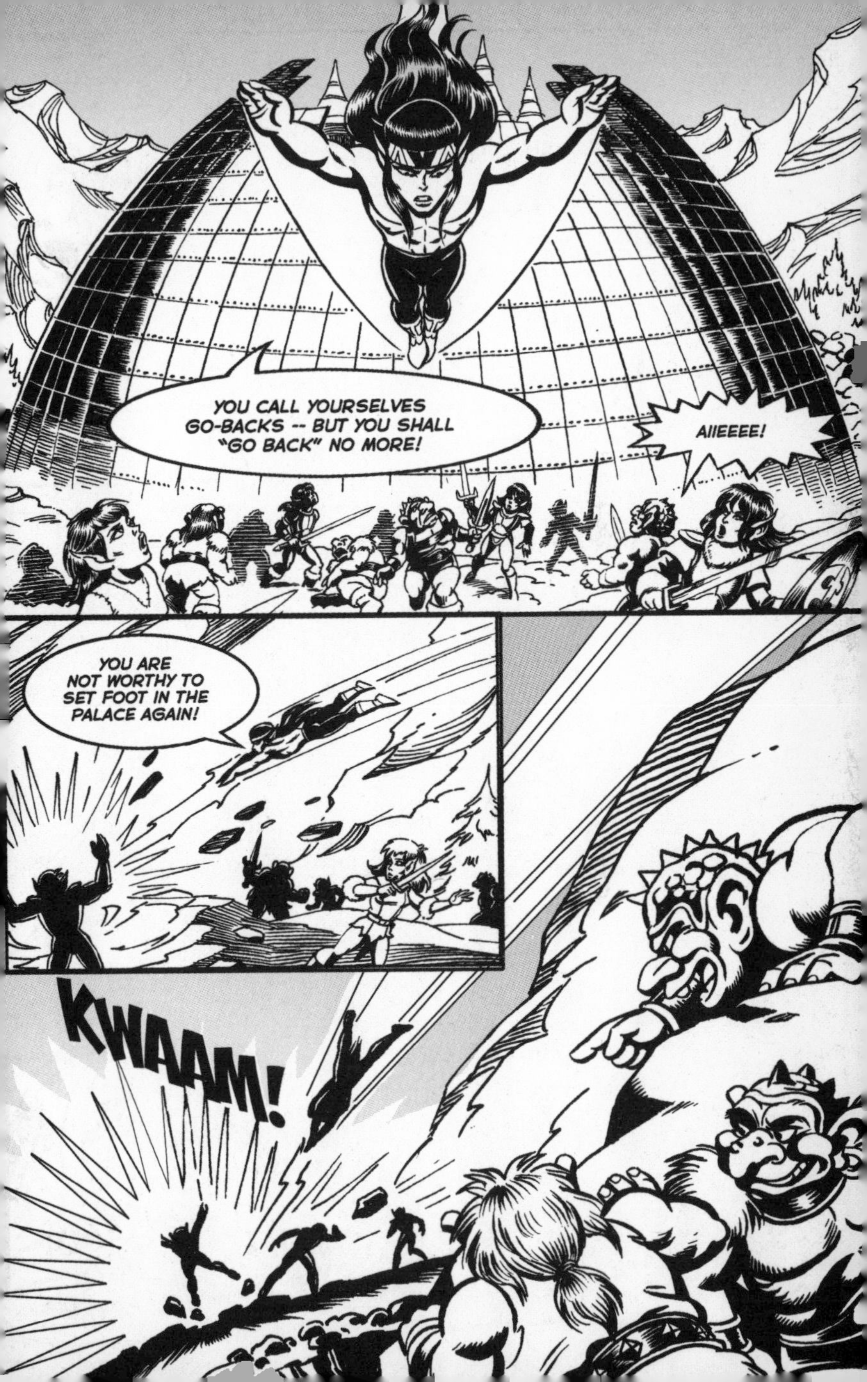
YOU CALL YOURSELVES GO-BACKS -- BUT YOU SHALL "GO BACK" NO MORE!
AIIEEEE!
YOU ARE NOT WORTHY TO SET FOOT IN THE PALACE AGAIN!
KWAAM!

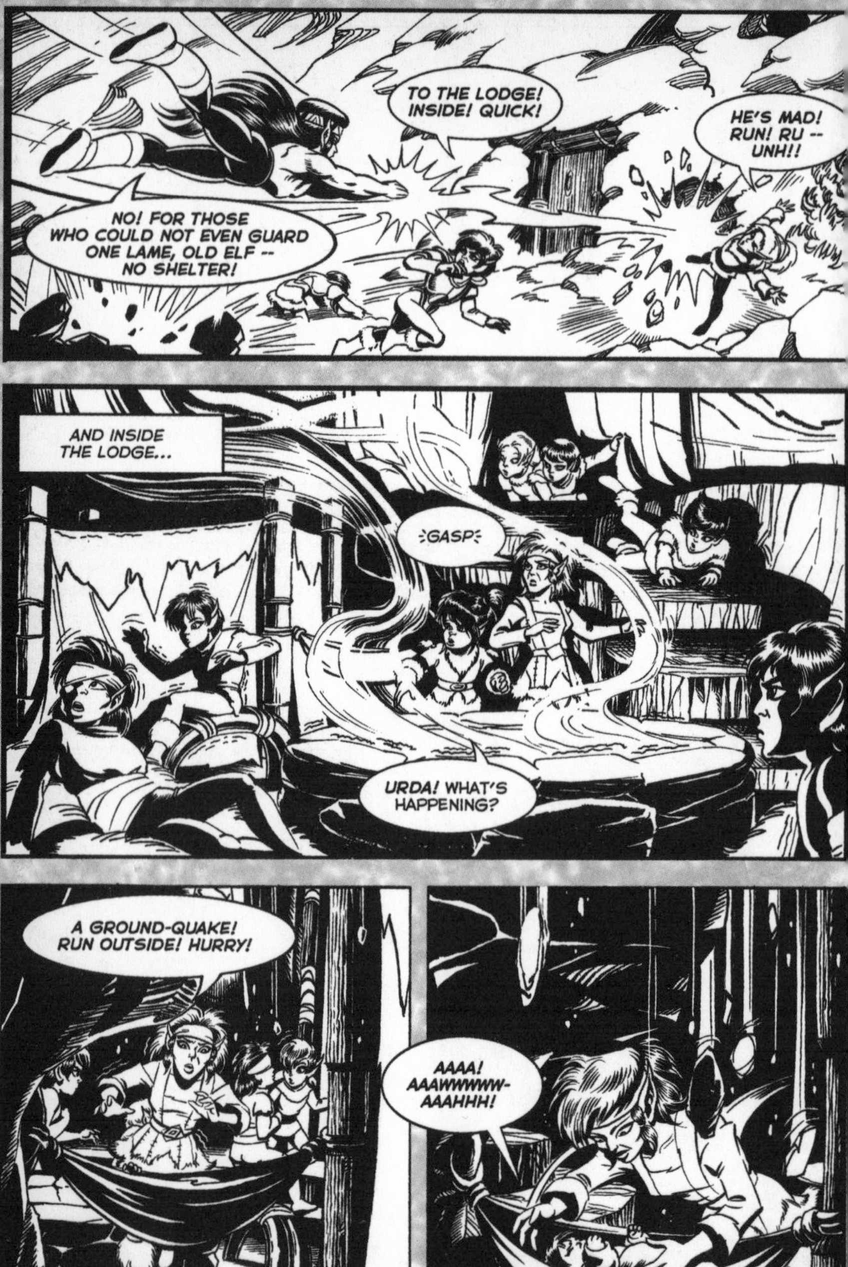
TO THE LODGE! INSIDE! QUICK!
NO! FOR THOSE WHO COULD NOT EVEN GUARD ONE LAME, OLD ELF -- NO SHELTER!
HE'S MAD! RUN! RU -- UNH!!
AND INSIDE THE LODGE...
GASP
URDA! WHAT'S HAPPENING?
A GROUND-QUAKE! RUN OUTSIDE! HURRY!
AAAA! AAAWWWWW-AAAHHH!

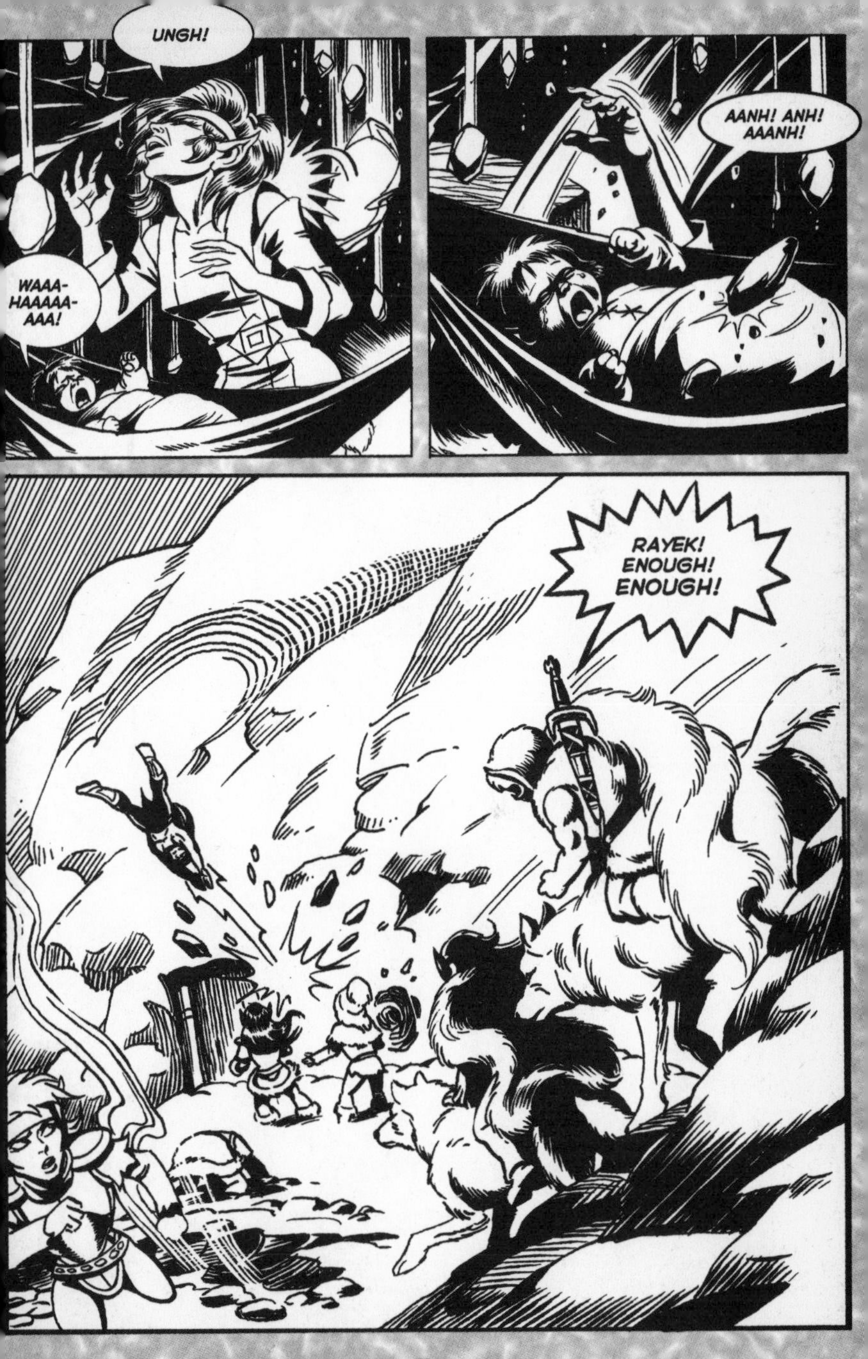
UNGH!
WAAA-HAAAAA-AAA!
AANH! ANH! AAANH!
RAYEK! ENOUGH! ENOUGH!

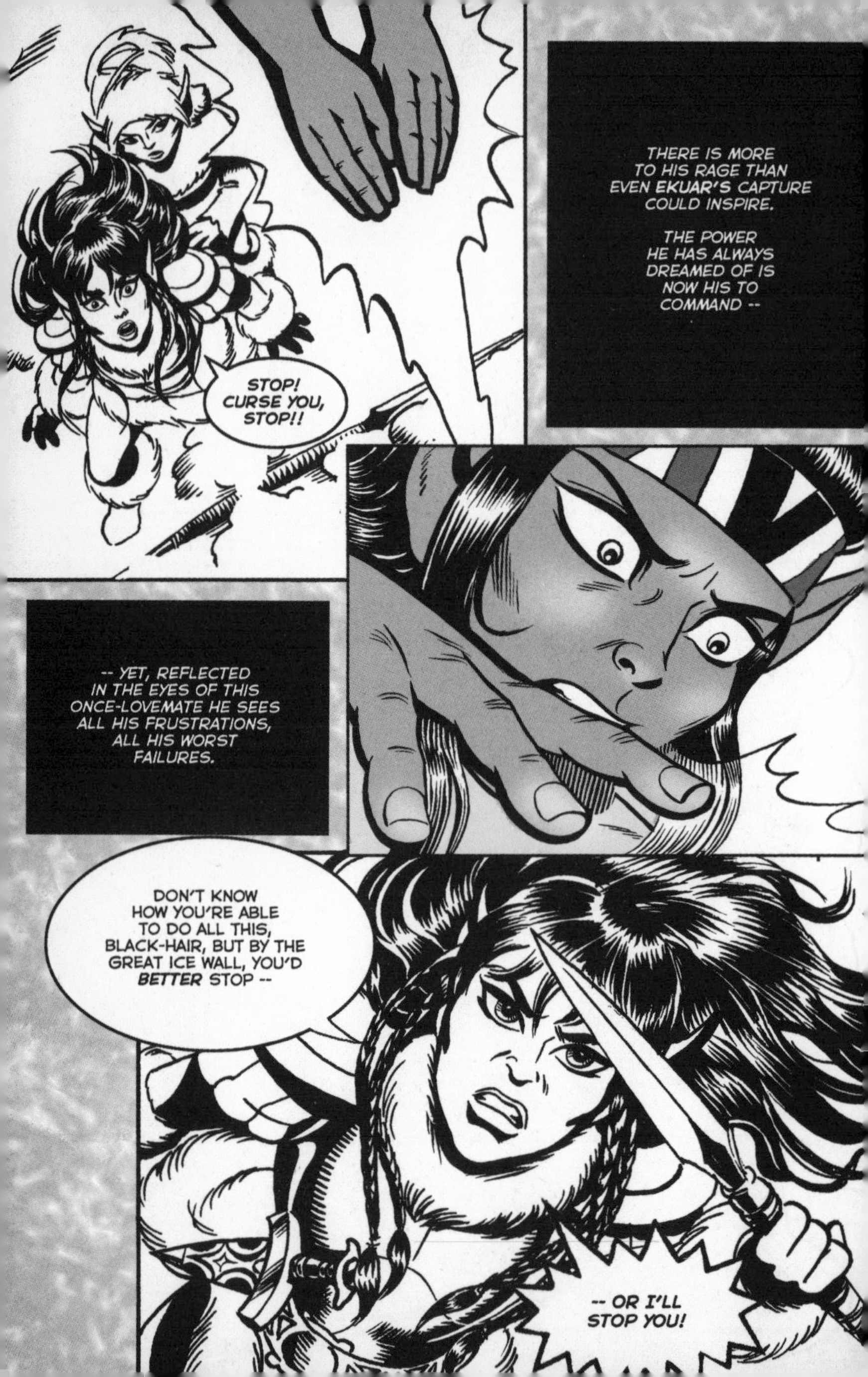
THERE IS MORE TO HIS RAGE THAN EVEN EKUAR'S CAPTURE COULD INSPIRE.
THE POWER HE HAS ALWAYS DREAMED OF IS NOW HIS TO COMMAND --
STOP! CURSE YOU, STOP!!
-- YET, REFLECTED IN THE EYES OF THIS ONCE-LOVEMATE HE SEES ALL HIS FRUSTRATIONS, ALL HIS WORST FAILURES.
DON'T KNOW HOW YOU'RE ABLE TO DO ALL THIS, BLACK-HAIR, BUT BY THE GREAT ICE WALL, YOU'D BETTER STOP --
-- OR I'LL STOP YOU!

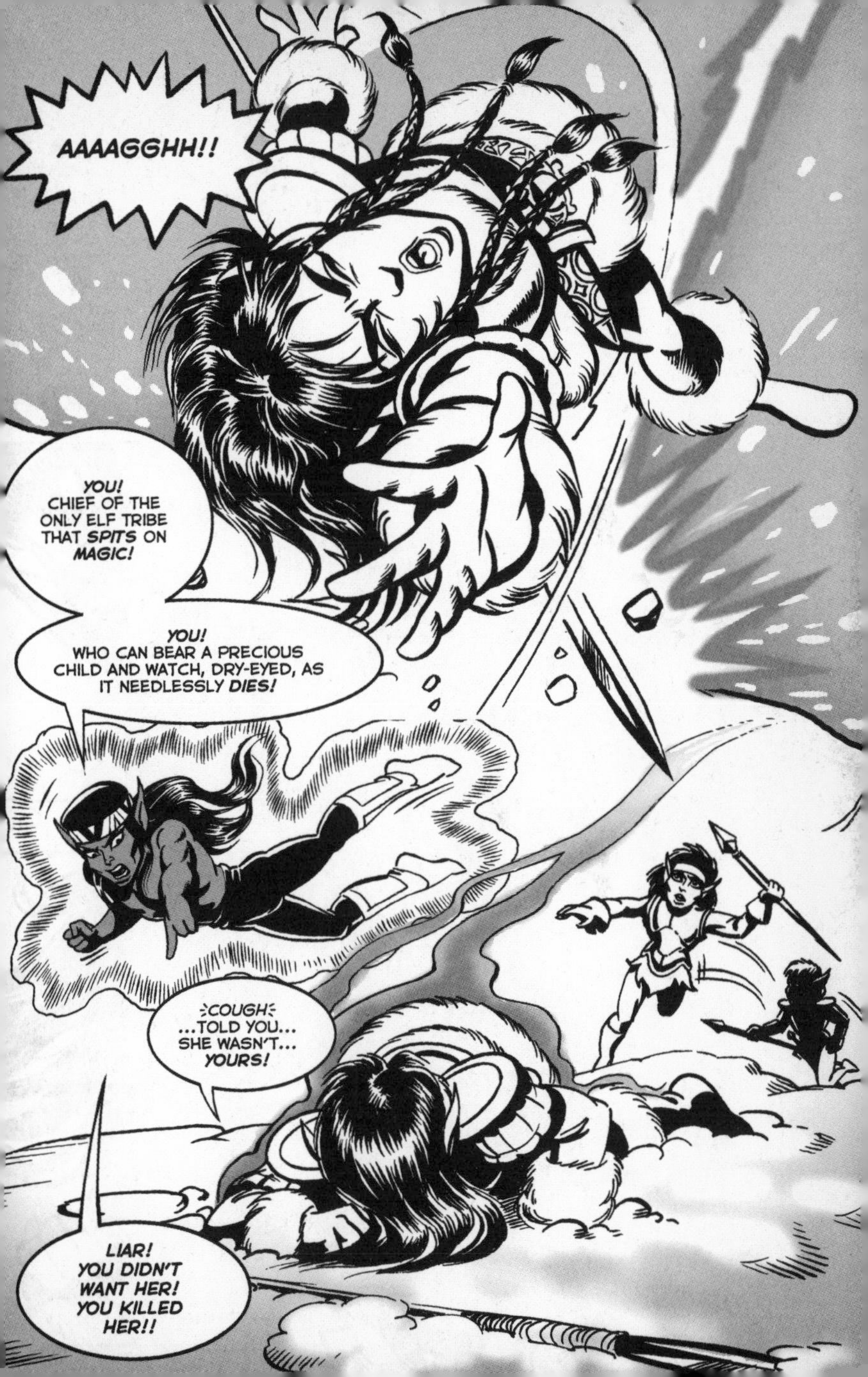
AAAAGGHH!!
YOU! CHIEF OF THE ONLY ELF TRIBE THAT SPITS ON MAGIC!
YOU! WHO CAN BEAR A PRECIOUS CHILD AND WATCH, DRY-EYED, AS IT NEEDLESSLY DIES!
COUGH ...TOLD YOU... SHE WASN'T... YOURS!
LIAR! YOU DIDN'T WANT HER! YOU KILLED HER!!

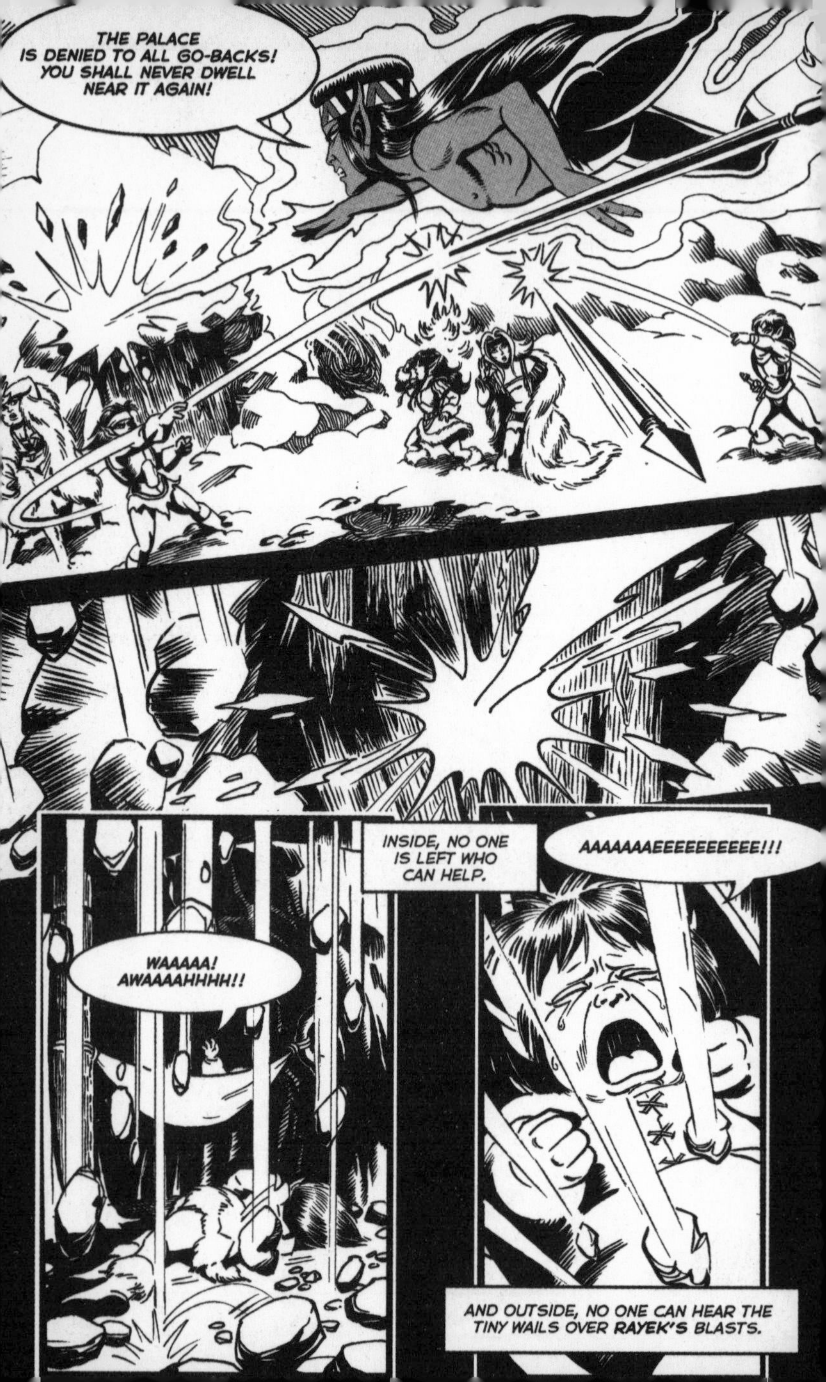
THE PALACE IS DENIED TO ALL GO-BACKS! YOU SHALL NEVER DWELL NEAR IT AGAIN!
INSIDE, NO ONE IS LEFT WHO CAN HELP.
AAAAAAAEEEEEEEEEE!!!
WAAAAA! AWAAAAHHHH!!
AND OUTSIDE, NO ONE CAN HEAR THE TINY WAILS OVER RAYEK'S BLASTS.

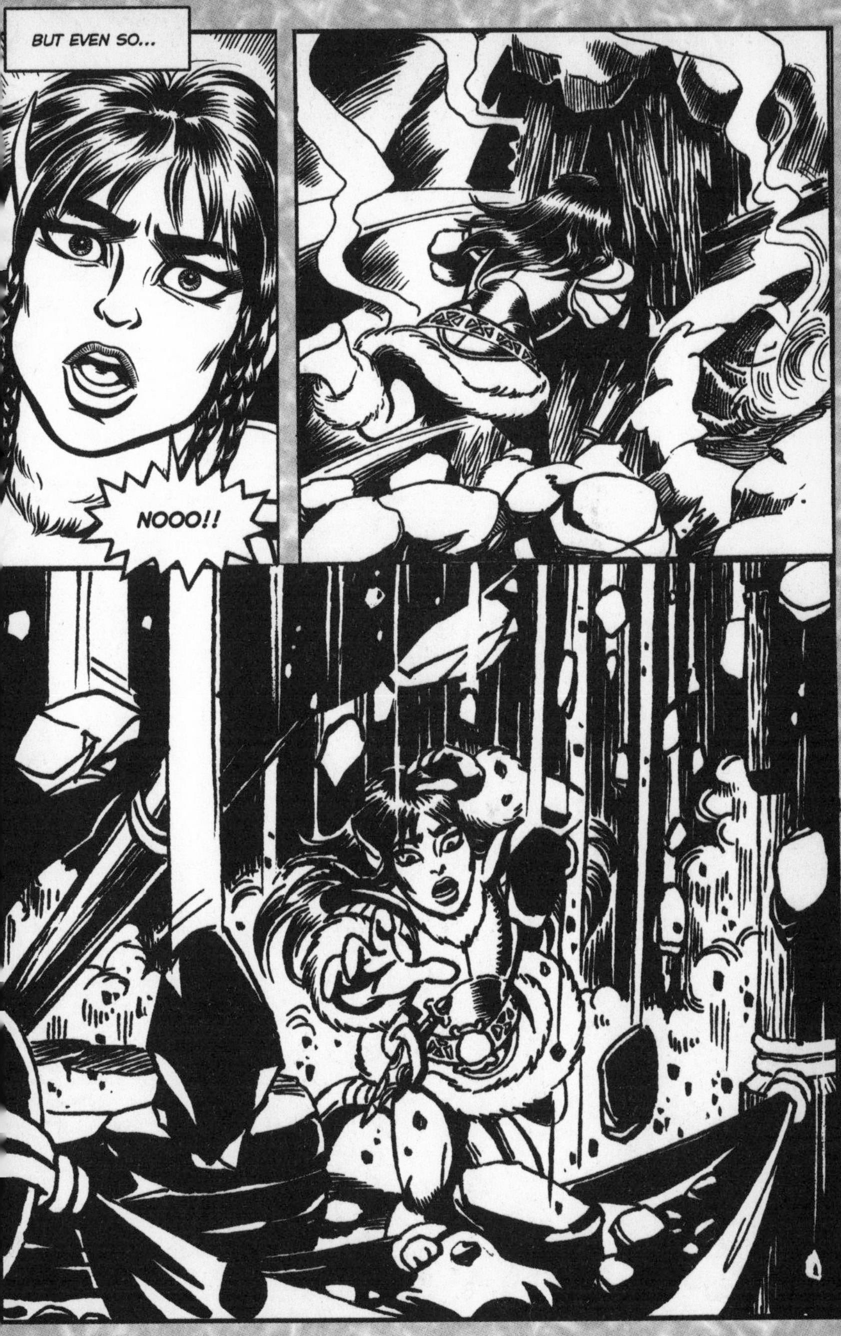
BUT EVEN SO...
NOOO!!

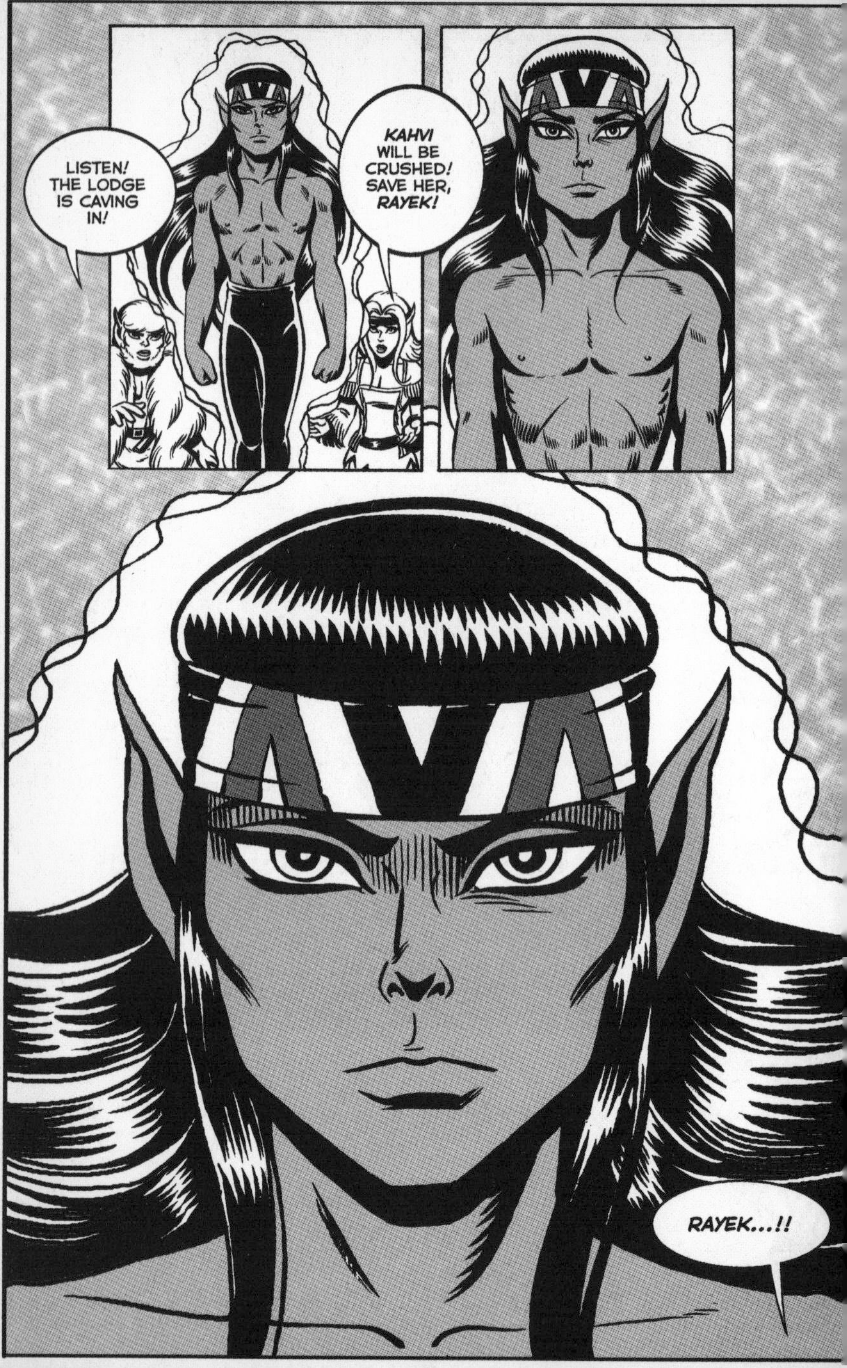
LISTEN! THE LODGE IS CAVING IN!
KAHVI WILL BE CRUSHED! SAVE HER, RAYEK!
RAYEK...!!

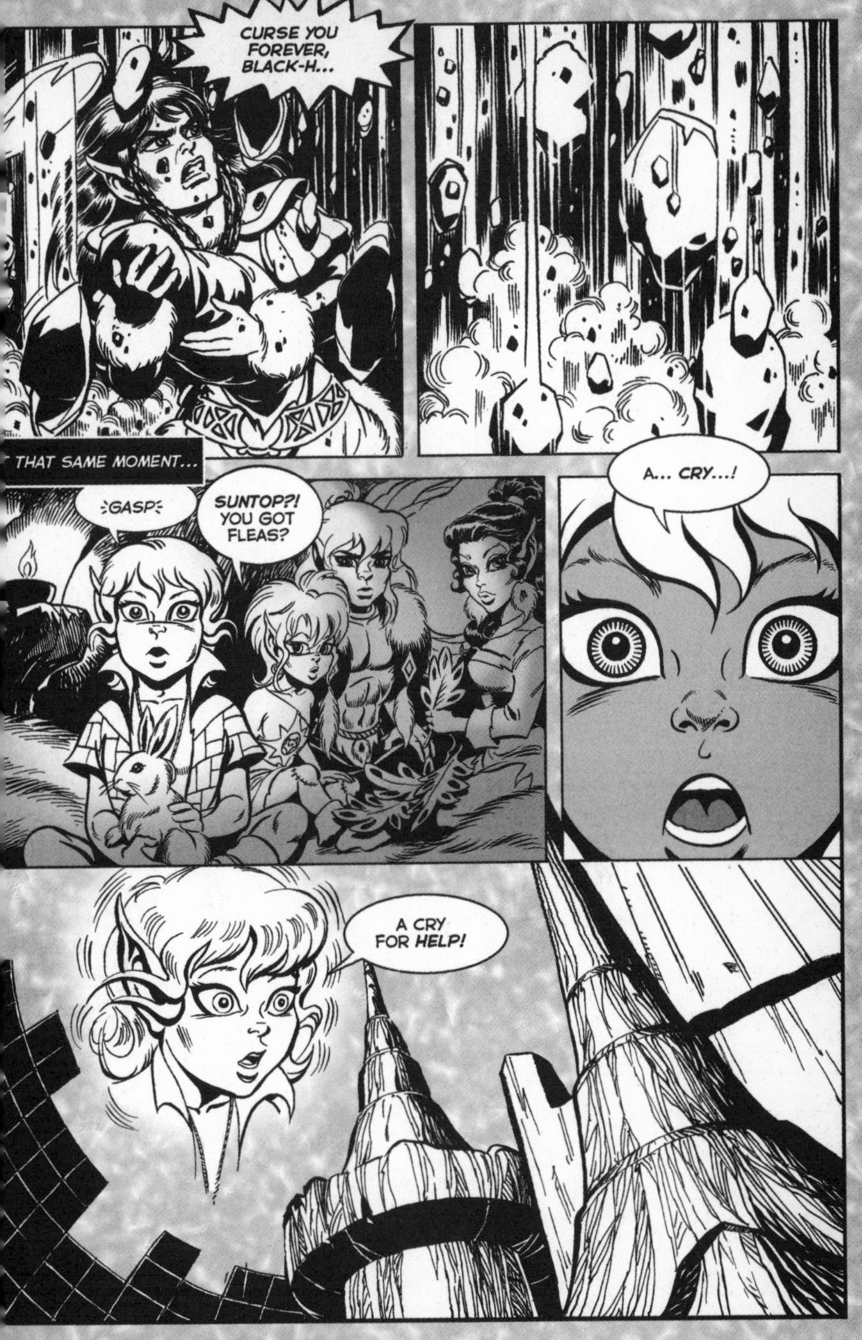
CURSE YOU FOREVER, BLACK-H...
THAT SAME MOMENT...
GASP
SUNTOP?! YOU GOT FLEAS?
A... CRY...!
A CRY FOR HELP!

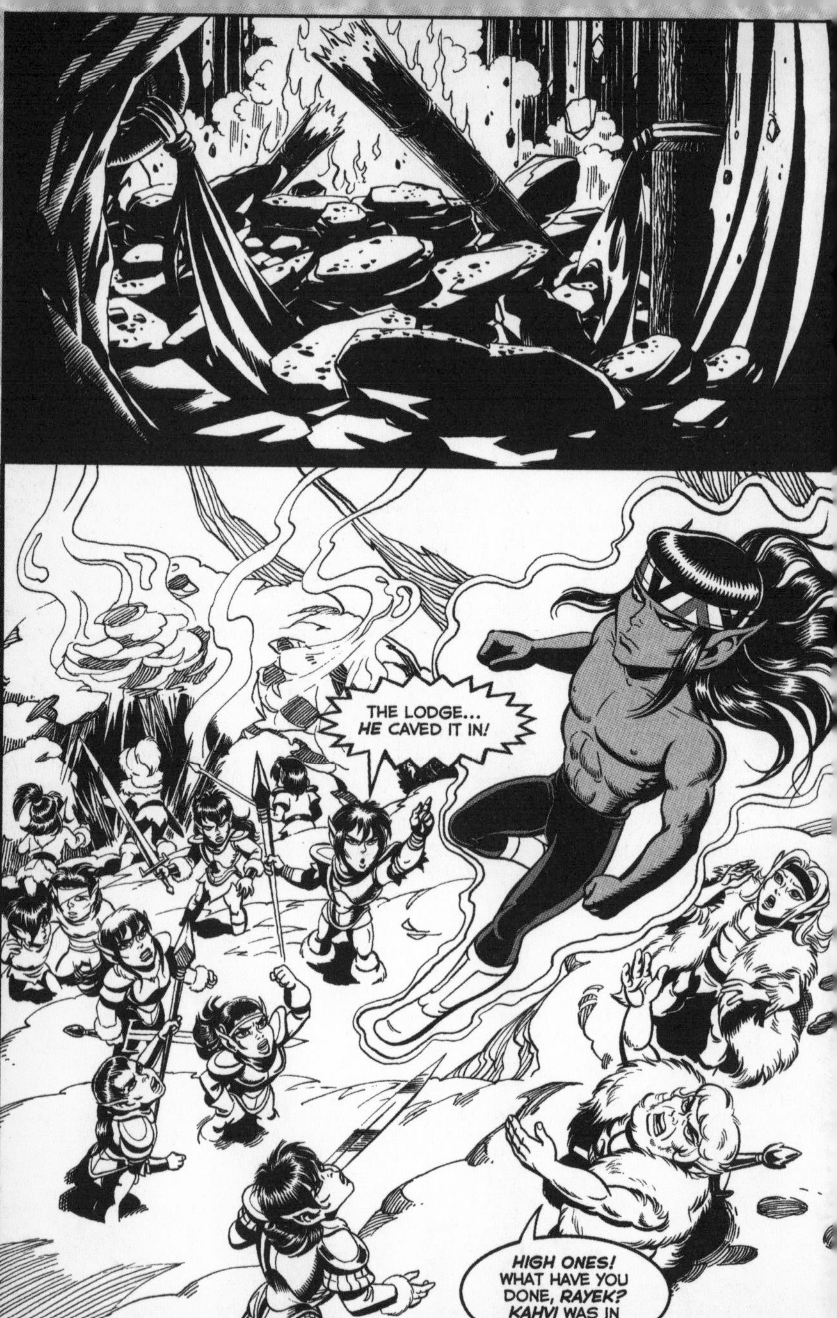
THE LODGE... HE CAVED IT IN!
HIGH ONES! WHAT HAVE YOU DONE, RAYEK? KAHVI WAS IN THERE!

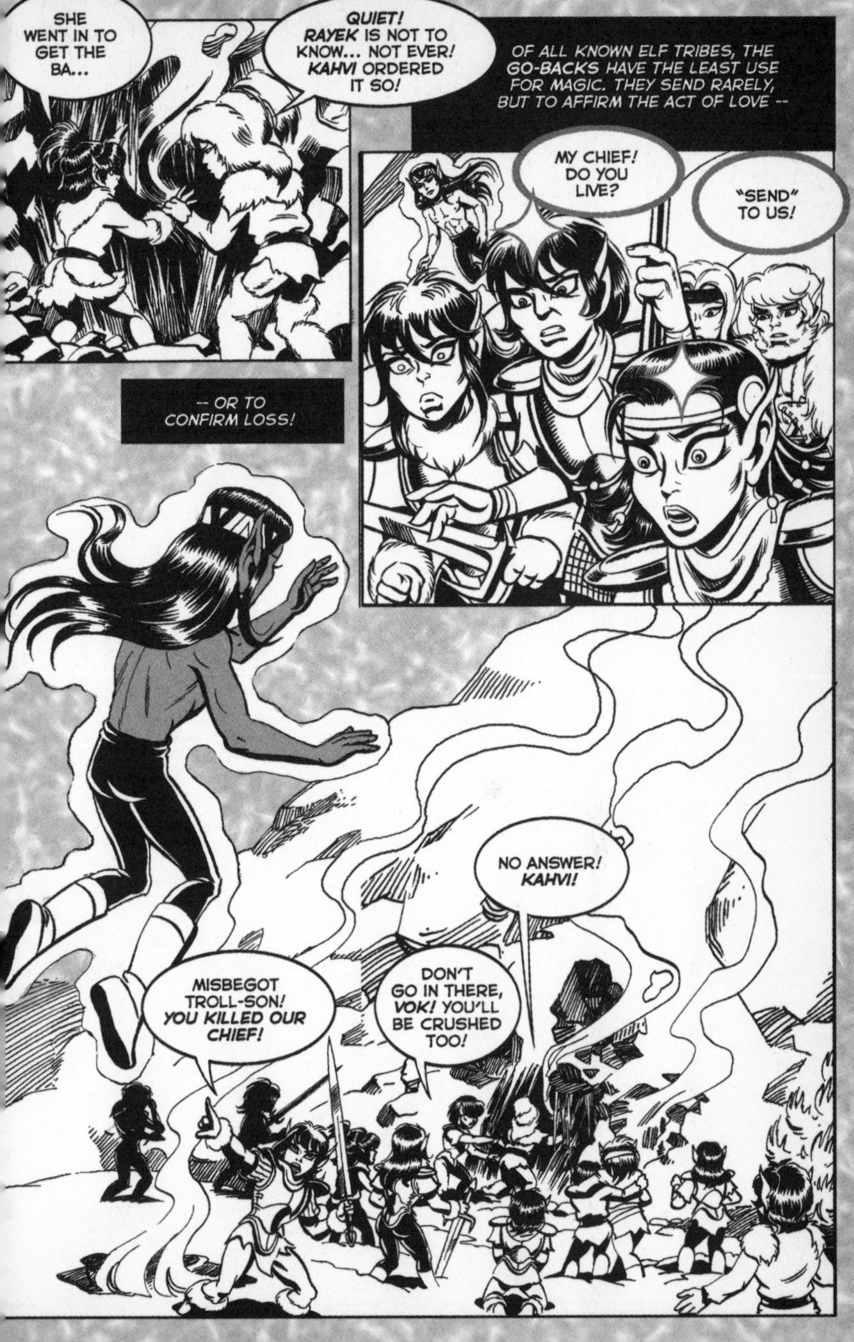
SHE WENT IN TO GET THE BA...
QUIET! RAYEK IS NOT TO KNOW... NOT EVER! KAHVI ORDERED IT SO!
OF ALL KNOWN ELF TRIBES, THE GO-BACKS HAVE THE LEAST USE FOR MAGIC. THEY SEND RARELY, BUT TO AFFIRM THE ACT OF LOVE --
MY CHIEF! DO YOU LIVE?
"SEND" TO US!
-- OR TO CONFIRM LOSS!
NO ANSWER! KAHVI!
MISBEGOT TROLL-SON! YOU KILLED OUR CHIEF!
DON'T GO IN THERE, VOK! YOU'LL BE CRUSHED TOO!

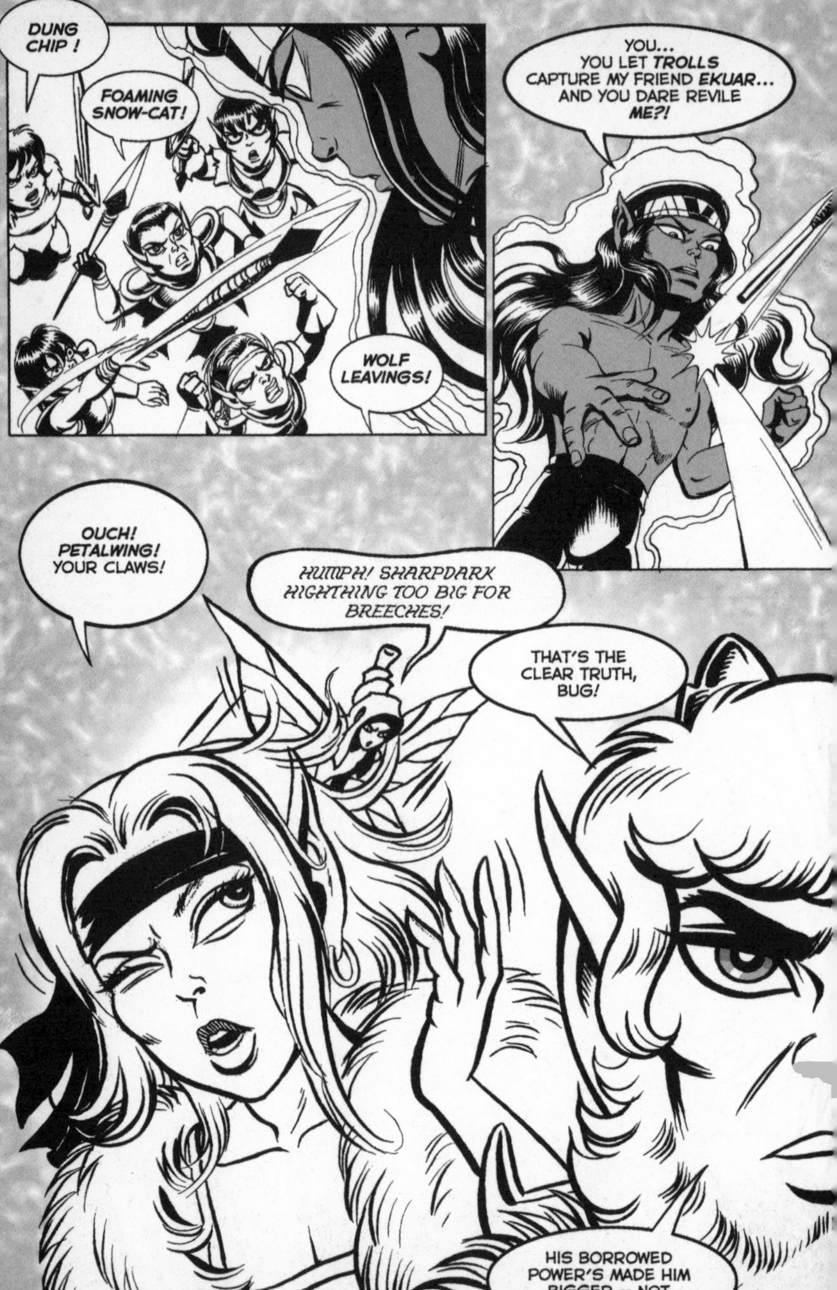
DUNG CHIP!
FOAMING SNOW-CAT!
WOLF LEAVINGS!
YOU... YOU LET TROLLS CAPTURE MY FRIEND EKUAR... AND YOU DARE REVILE ME?!
OUCH! PETALWING! YOUR CLAWS!
HUMPH! SHARPDARK HIGHTHING TOO BIG FOR BREECHES!
THAT'S THE CLEAR TRUTH, BUG!
HIS BORROWED POWER'S MADE HIM BIGGER -- NOT BETTER!

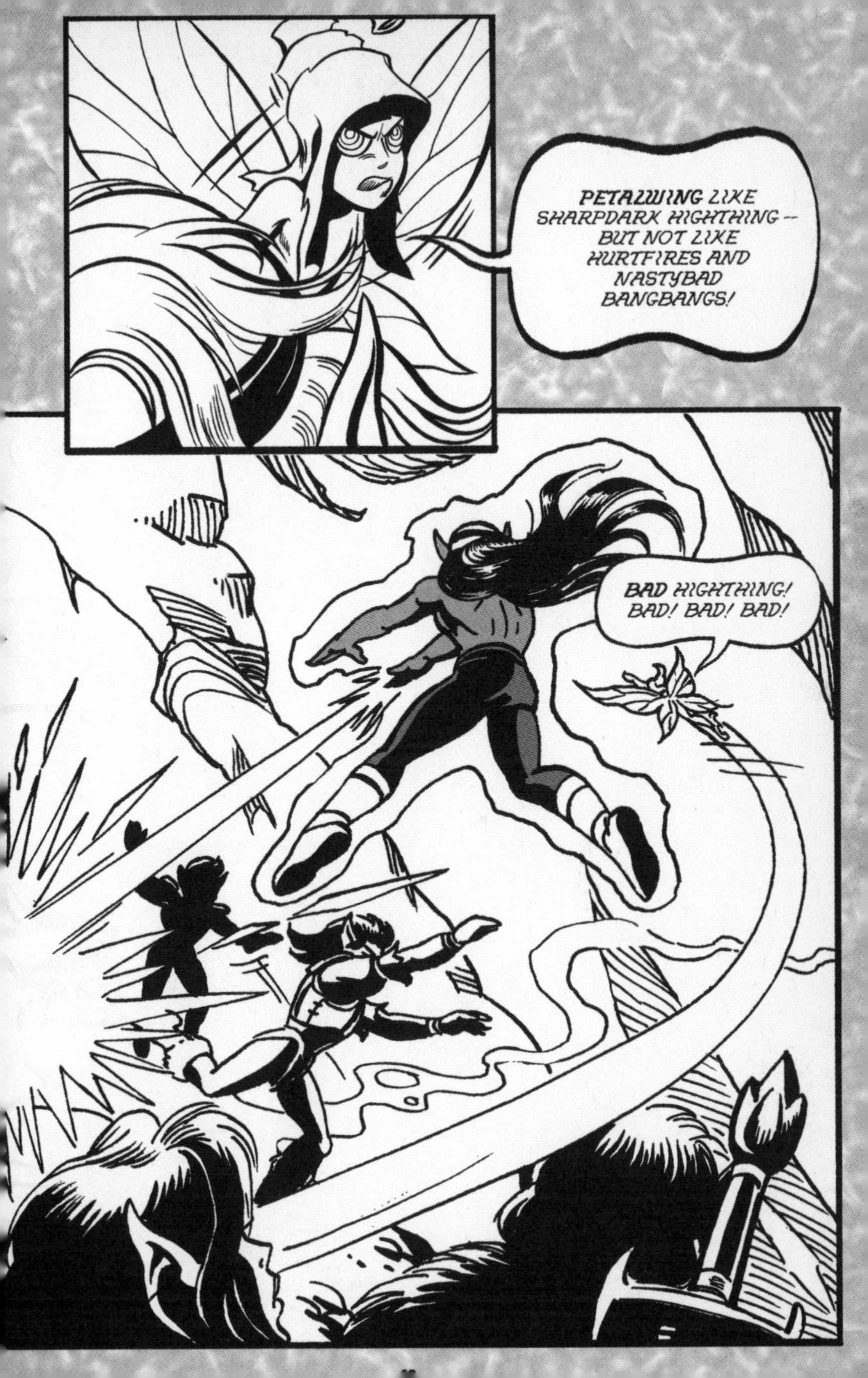
PETALWING LIKE SHARPDARK HIGHTHING -- BUT NOT LIKE HURTFIRES AND NASTYBAD BANGBANGS!
BAD HIGHTHING! BAD! BAD! BAD!

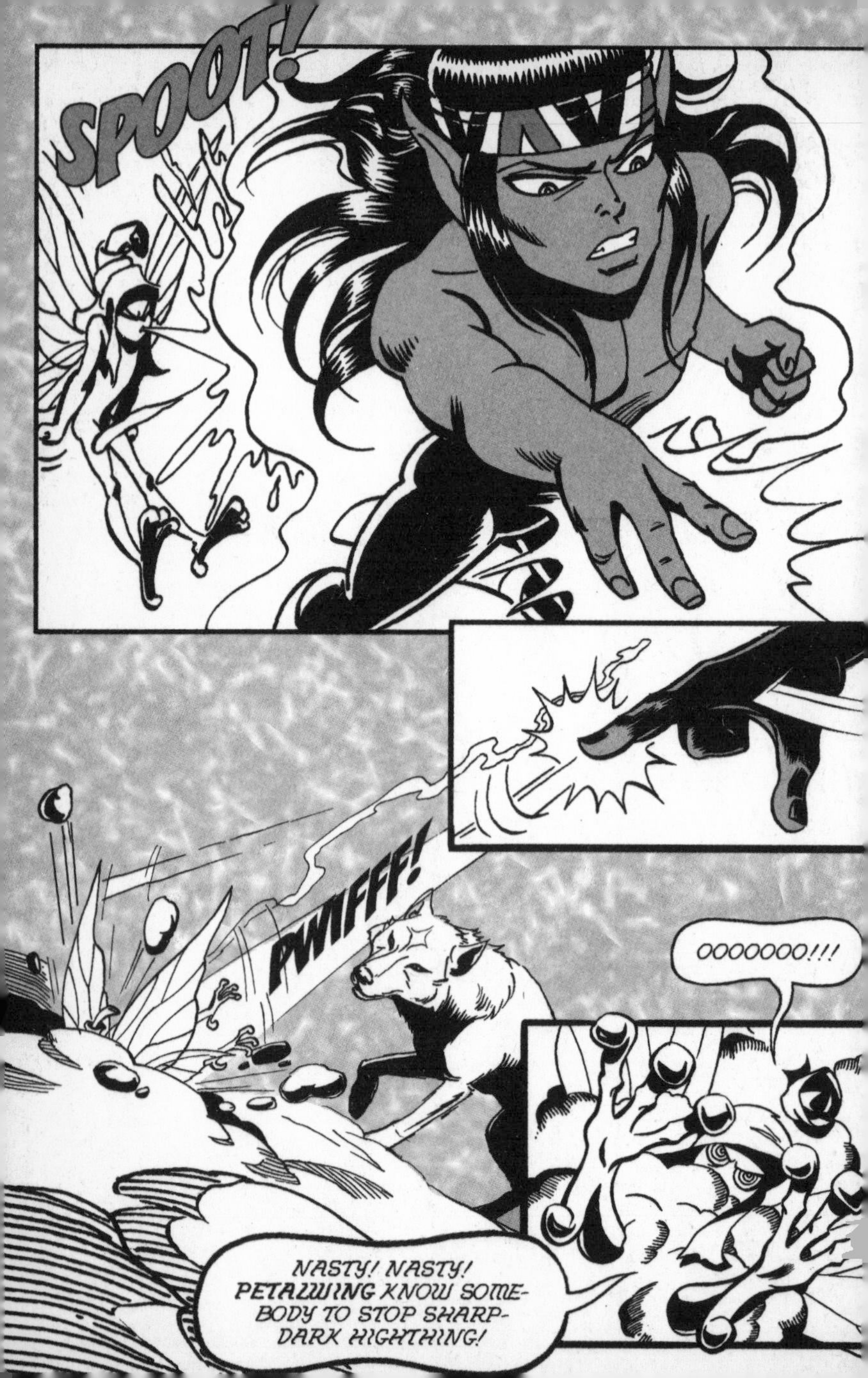
SPOOT!
PWIFFF!
OOOOOOO!!!
NASTY! NASTY! PETALWING KNOW SOME-BODY TO STOP SHARP-DARK HIGHTHING!

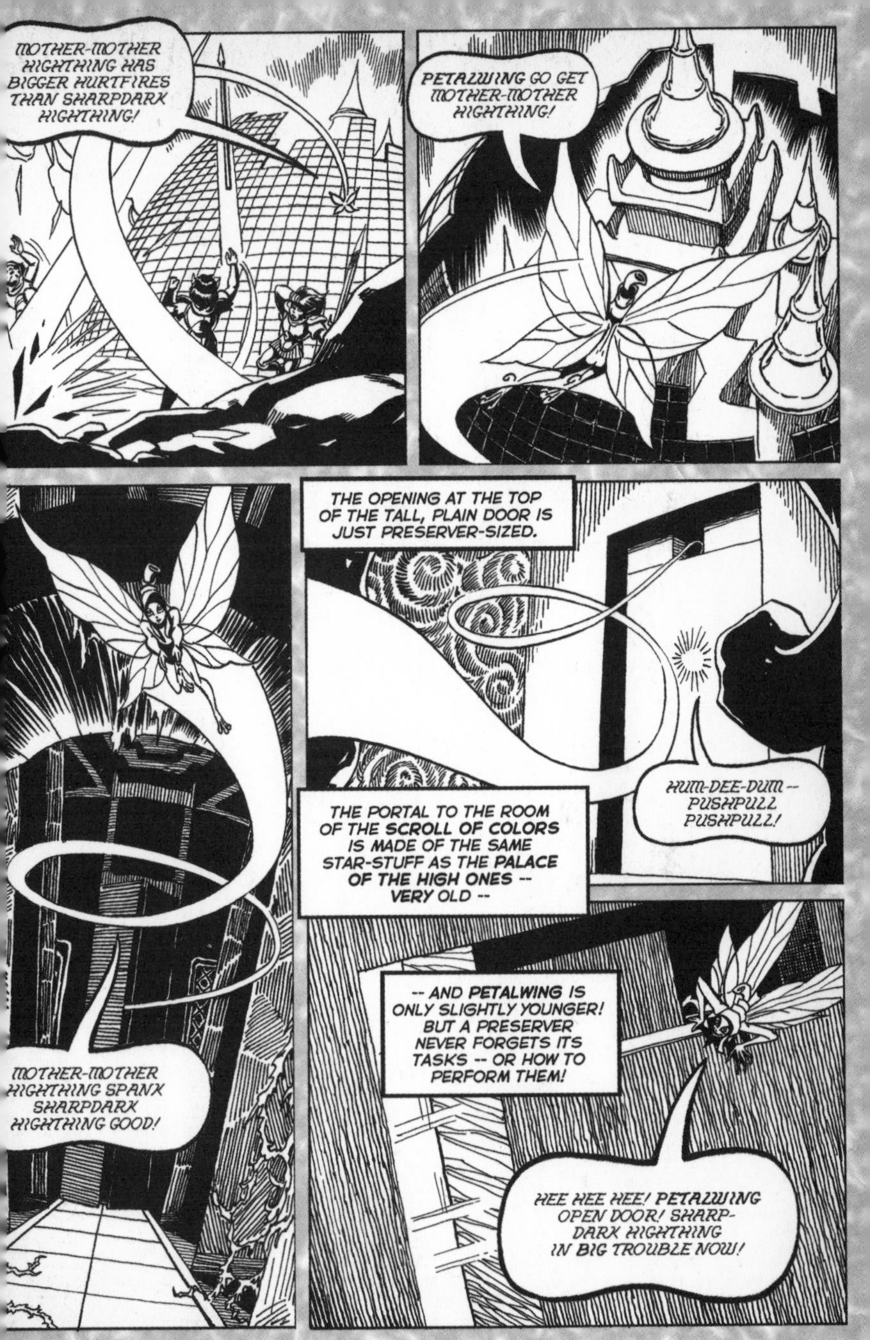
MOTHER-MOTHER HIGHTHING HAS BIGGER HURTFIRES THAN SHARPDARK HIGHTHING!
PETALWING GO GET MOTHER-MOTHER HIGHTHING!
THE OPENING AT THE TOP OF THE TALL, PLAIN DOOR IS JUST PRESERVER-SIZED.
HUM-DEE-DUM -- PUSHPULL PUSHPULL!
MOTHER-MOTHER HIGHTHING SPANK SHARPDARK HIGHTHING GOOD!
THE PORTAL TO THE ROOM OF THE SCROLL OF COLORS IS MADE OF THE SAME STAR-STUFF AS THE PALACE OF THE HIGH ONES -- VERY OLD --
-- AND PETALWING IS ONLY SLIGHTLY YOUNGER! BUT A PRESERVER NEVER FORGETS ITS TASKS -- OR HOW TO PERFORM THEM!
HEE HEE HEE! PETALWING OPEN DOOR! SHARP-DARK HIGHTHING IN BIG TROUBLE NOW!

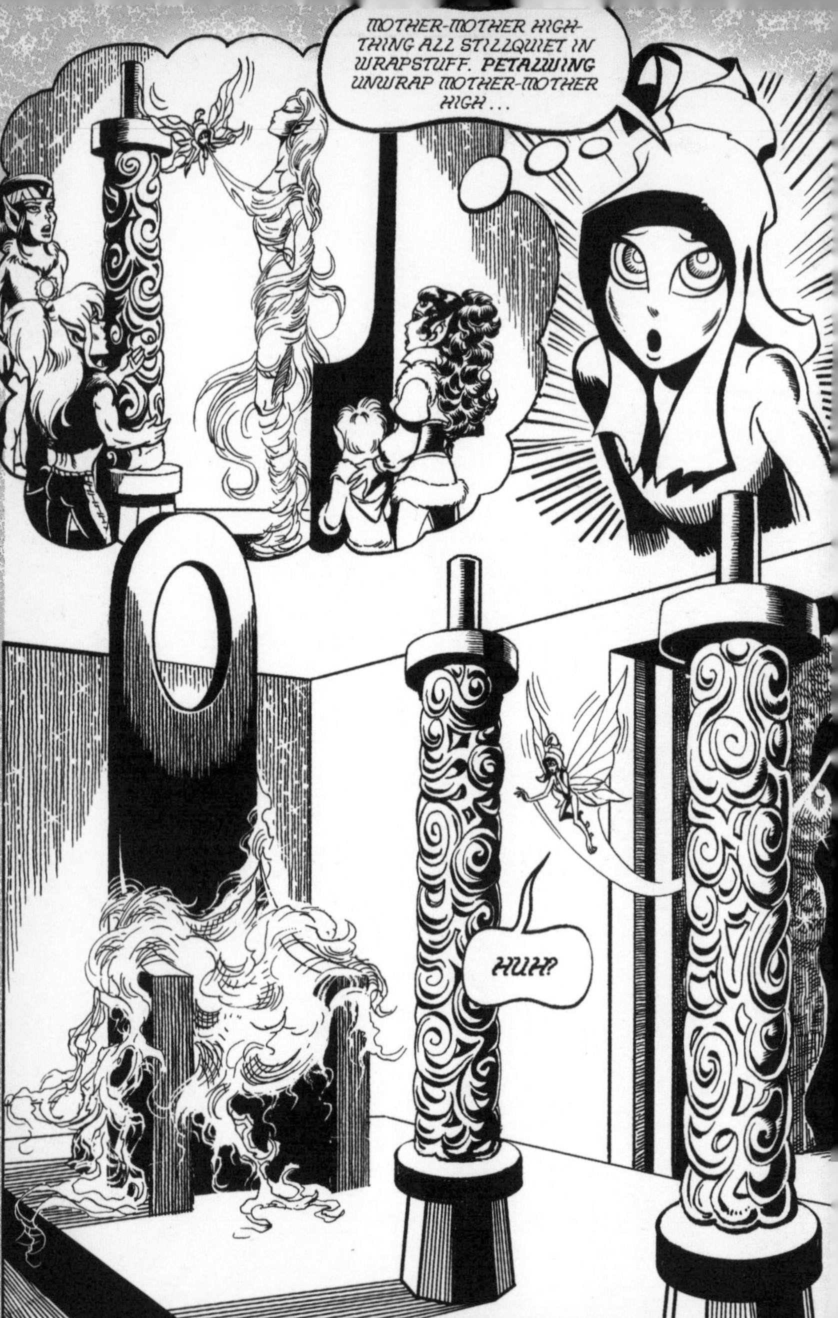
MOTHER-MOTHER HIGH-THING ALL STILLQUIET IN WRAPSTUFF. PETALWING UNWRAP MOTHER-MOTHER HIGH...
HUH?

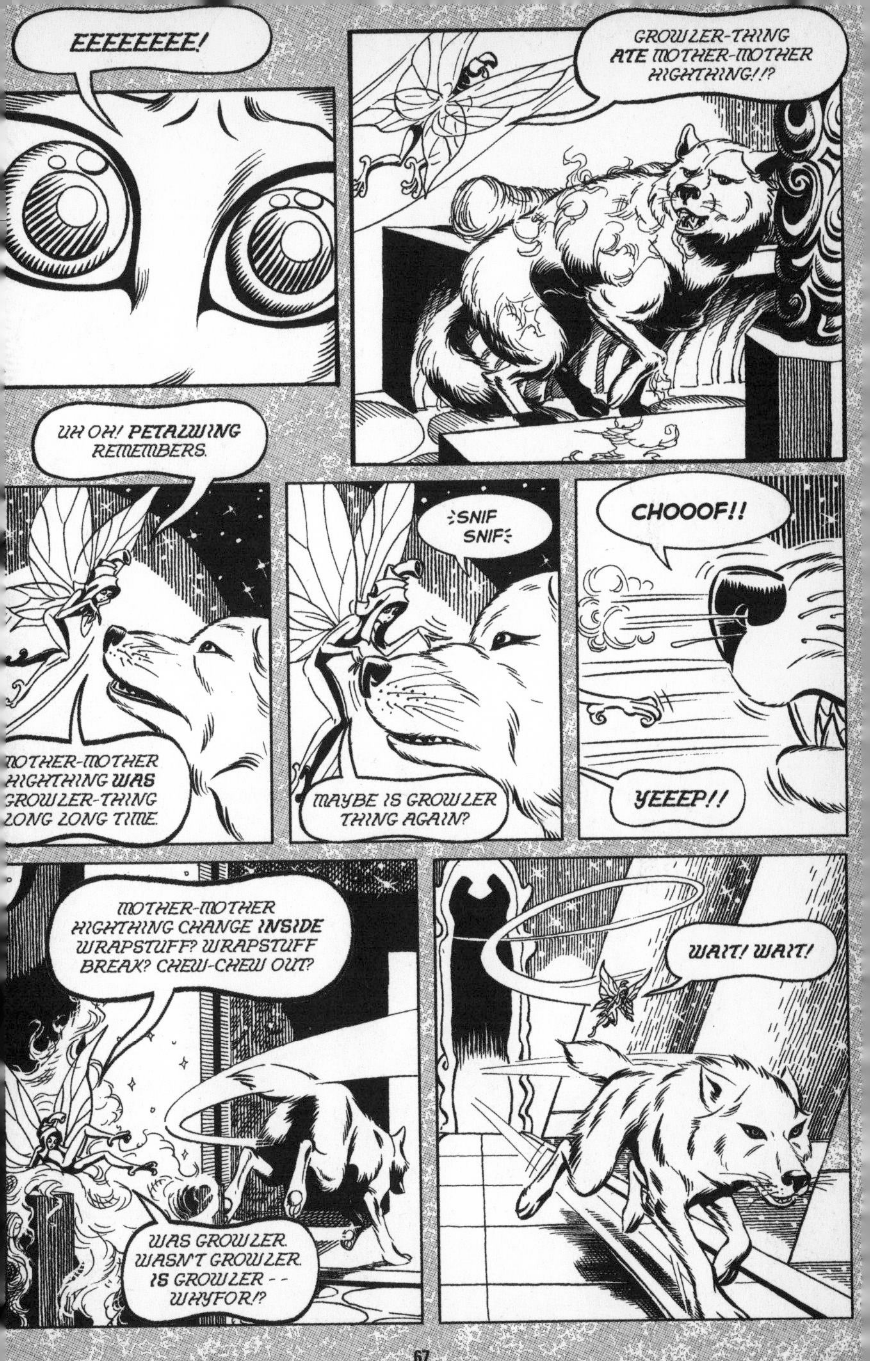
EEEEEEEE!
GROWLER-THING ATE MOTHER-MOTHER HIGHTHING!!?
UH OH! PETALWING REMEMBERS.
MOTHER-MOTHER HIGHTHING WAS GROWLER-THING LONG LONG TIME.
SNIF SNIF
MAYBE IS GROWLER THING AGAIN?
CHOOOF!!
YEEEP!!
MOTHER-MOTHER HIGHTHING CHANGE INSIDE WRAPSTUFF? WRAPSTUFF BREAK? CHEW-CHEW OUT?
WAS GROWLER. WASN'T GROWLER. IS GROWLER -- WHYFOR!?
WAIT! WAIT!

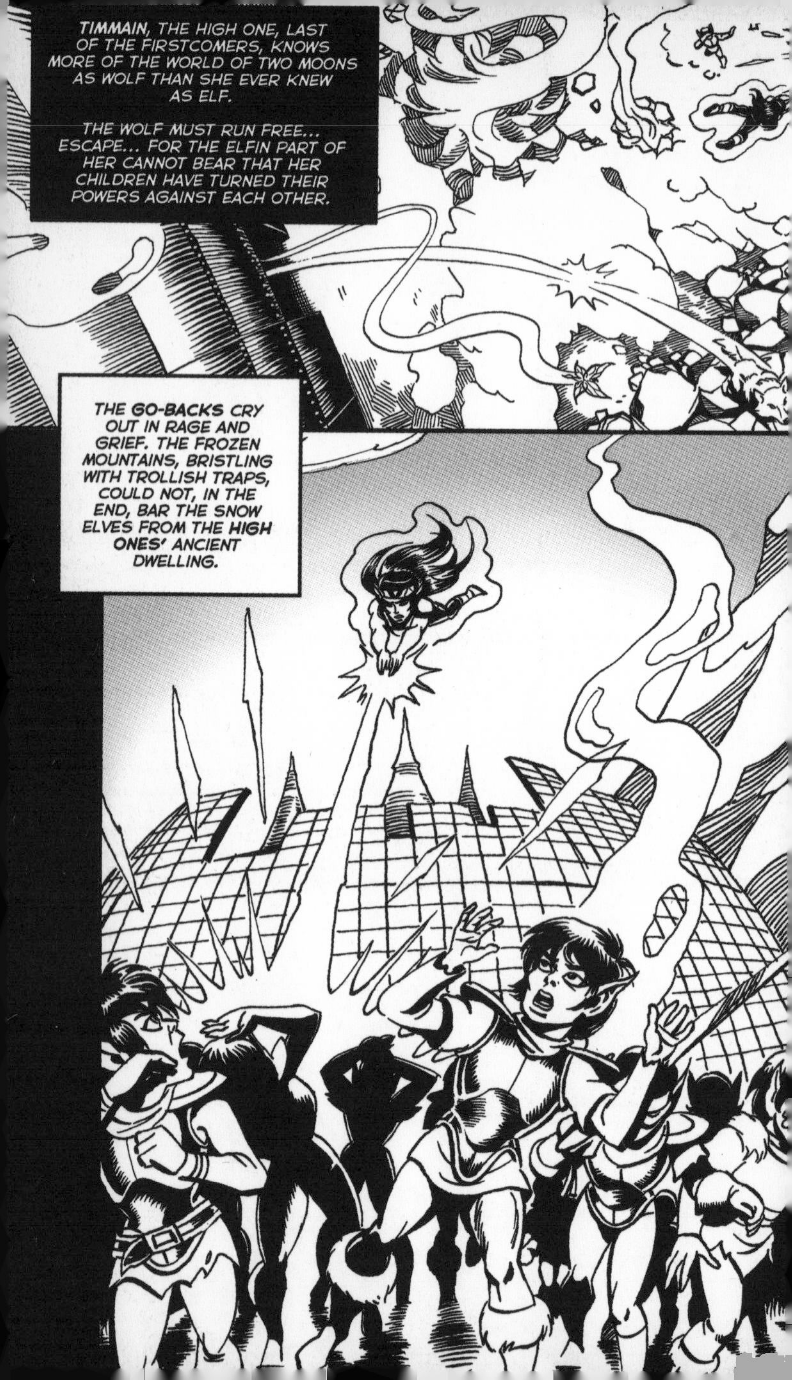
TIMMAIN, THE HIGH ONE, LAST OF THE FIRSTCOMERS, KNOWS MORE OF THE WORLD OF TWO MOONS AS WOLF THAN SHE EVER KNEW AS ELF.
THE WOLF MUST RUN FREE... ESCAPE... FOR THE ELFIN PART OF HER CANNOT BEAR THAT HER CHILDREN HAVE TURNED THEIR POWERS AGAINST EACH OTHER.
THE GO-BACKS CRY OUT IN RAGE AND GRIEF. THE FROZEN MOUNTAINS, BRISTLING WITH TROLLISH TRAPS, COULD NOT, IN THE END, BAR THE SNOW ELVES FROM THE HIGH ONES' ANCIENT DWELLING.

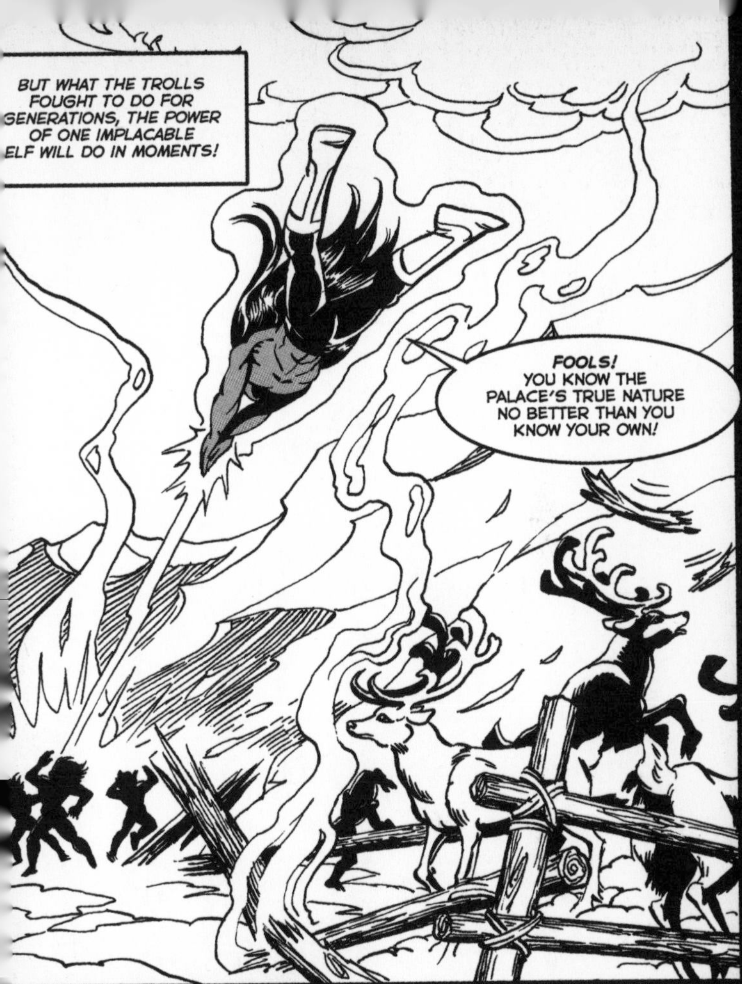
BUT WHAT THE TROLLS FOUGHT TO DO FOR GENERATIONS, THE POWER OF ONE IMPLACABLE ELF WILL DO IN MOMENTS!
FOOLS! YOU KNOW THE PALACE'S TRUE NATURE NO BETTER THAN YOU KNOW YOUR OWN!

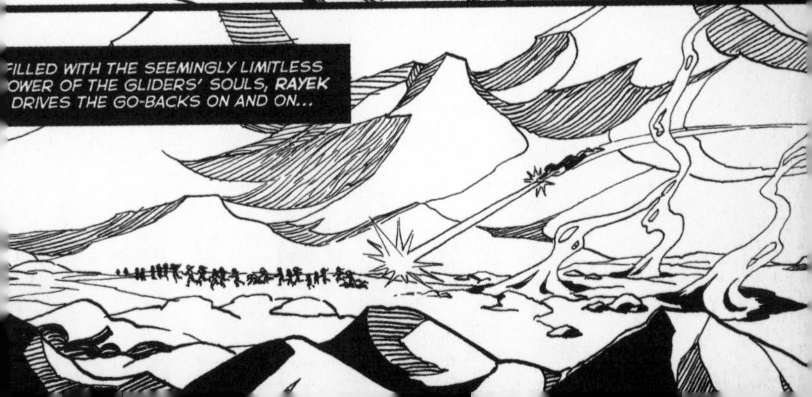
FILLED WITH THE SEEMINGLY LIMITLESS POWER OF THE GLIDERS' SOULS, RAYEK DRIVES THE GO-BACKS ON AND ON...

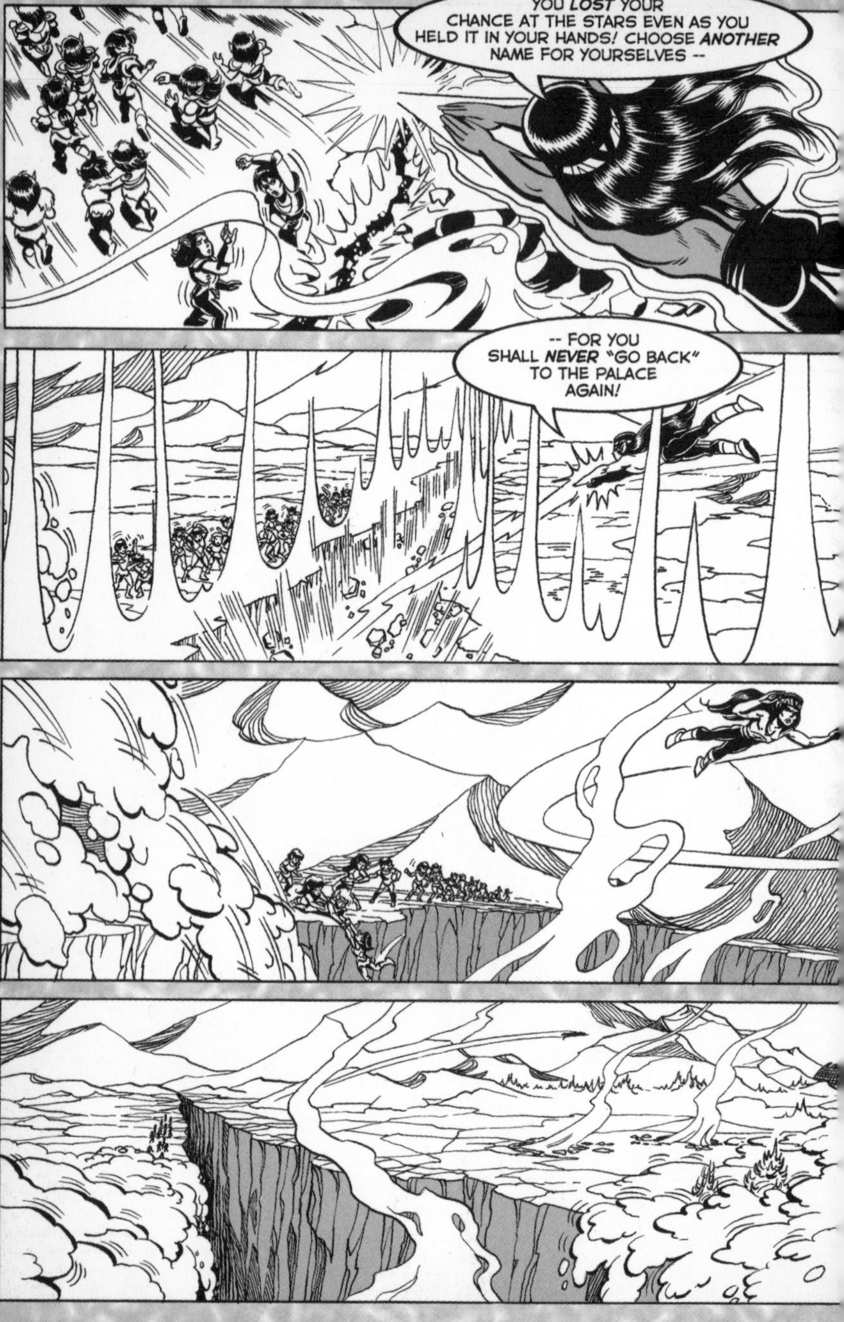
YOU *LOST* YOUR CHANCE AT THE STARS EVEN AS YOU HELD IT IN YOUR HANDS! CHOOSE *ANOTHER* NAME FOR YOURSELVES --
-- FOR YOU SHALL *NEVER* "GO BACK" TO THE PALACE AGAIN!

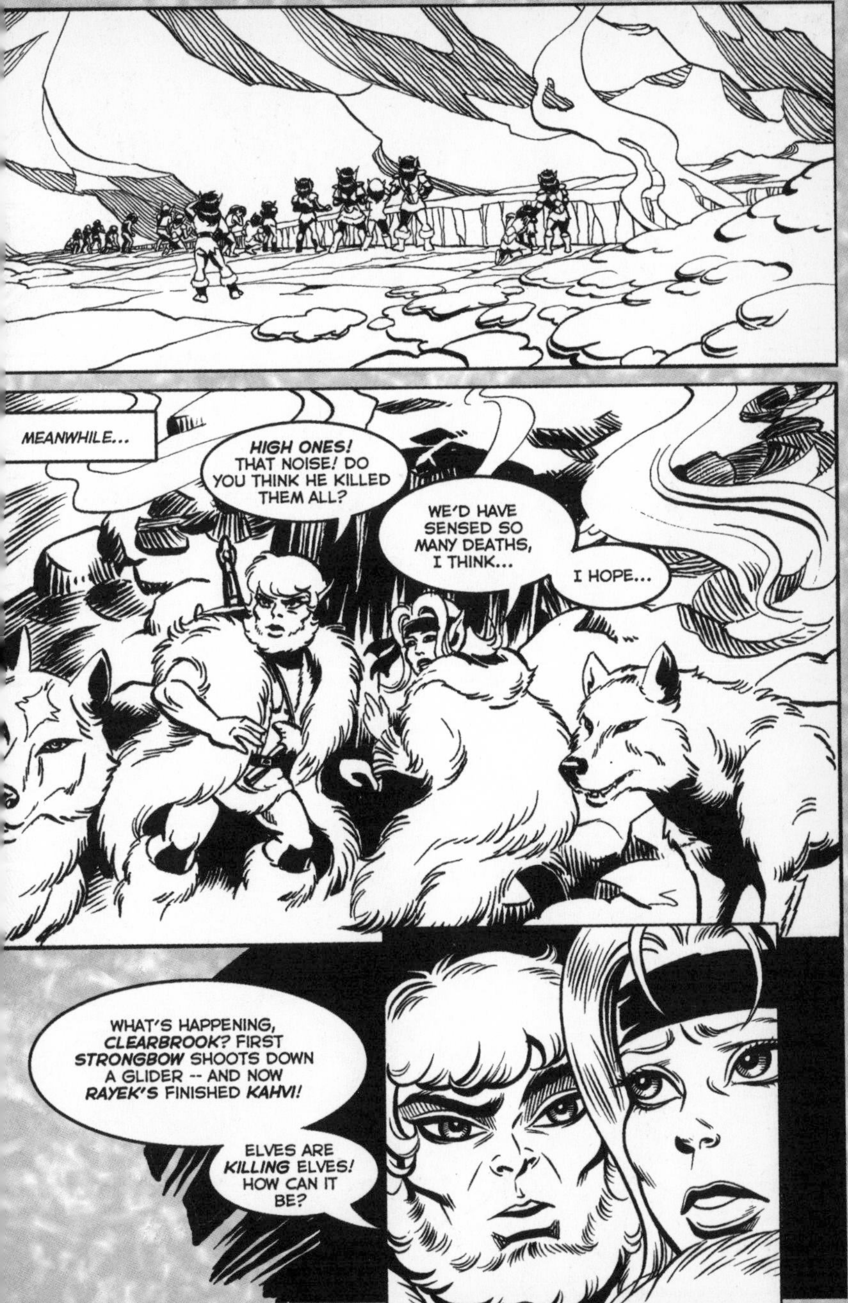
MEANWHILE...
HIGH ONES! THAT NOISE! DO YOU THINK HE KILLED THEM ALL?
WE'D HAVE SENSED SO MANY DEATHS, I THINK...
I HOPE...
WHAT'S HAPPENING, CLEARBROOK? FIRST STRONGBOW SHOOTS DOWN A GLIDER -- AND NOW RAYEK'S FINISHED KAHVI!
ELVES ARE KILLING ELVES! HOW CAN IT BE?

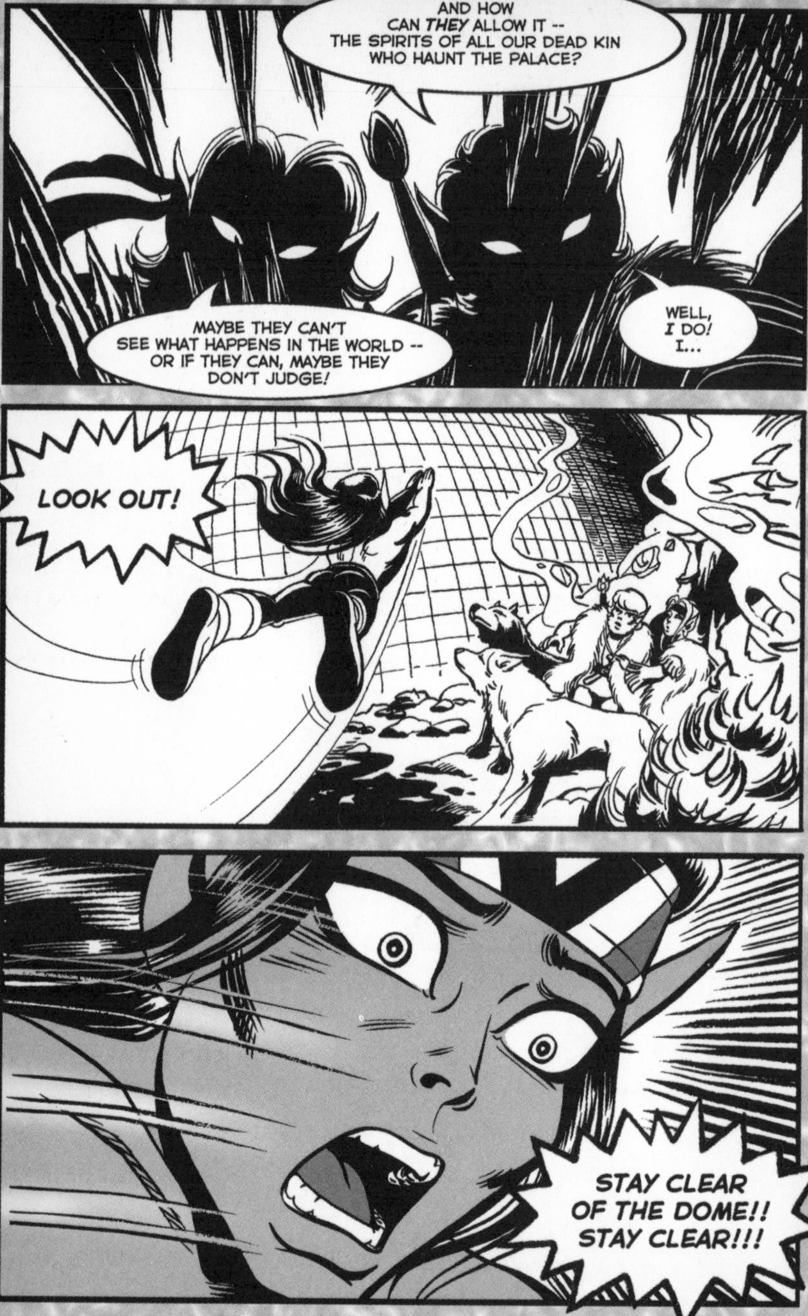
AND HOW CAN *THEY* ALLOW IT -- THE SPIRITS OF ALL OUR DEAD KIN WHO HAUNT THE PALACE?
MAYBE THEY CAN'T SEE WHAT HAPPENS IN THE WORLD -- OR IF THEY CAN, MAYBE THEY DON'T JUDGE!
WELL, *I* DO! I...
LOOK OUT!
STAY CLEAR OF THE DOME!! STAY CLEAR!!!

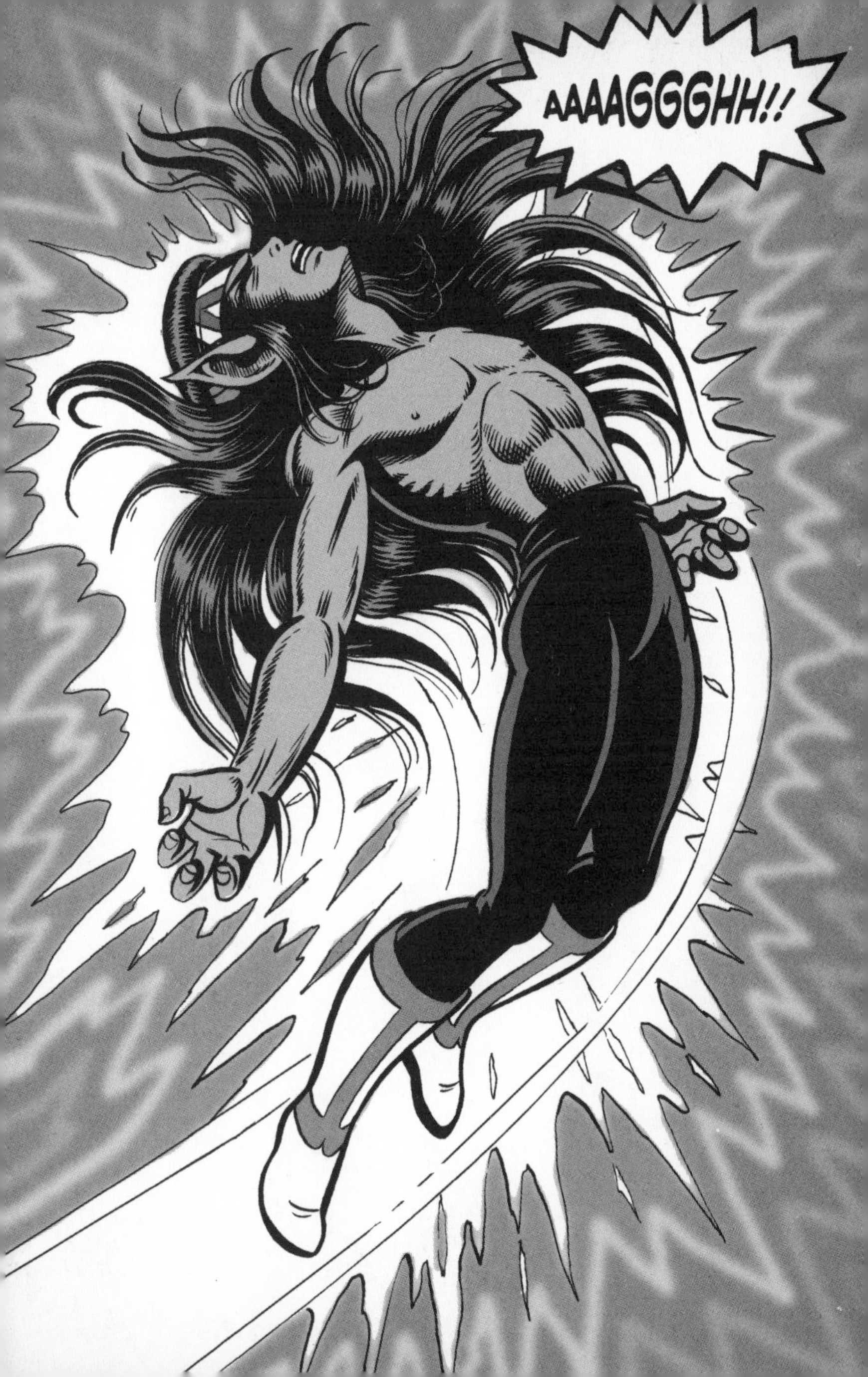
AAAAGGGHH!!

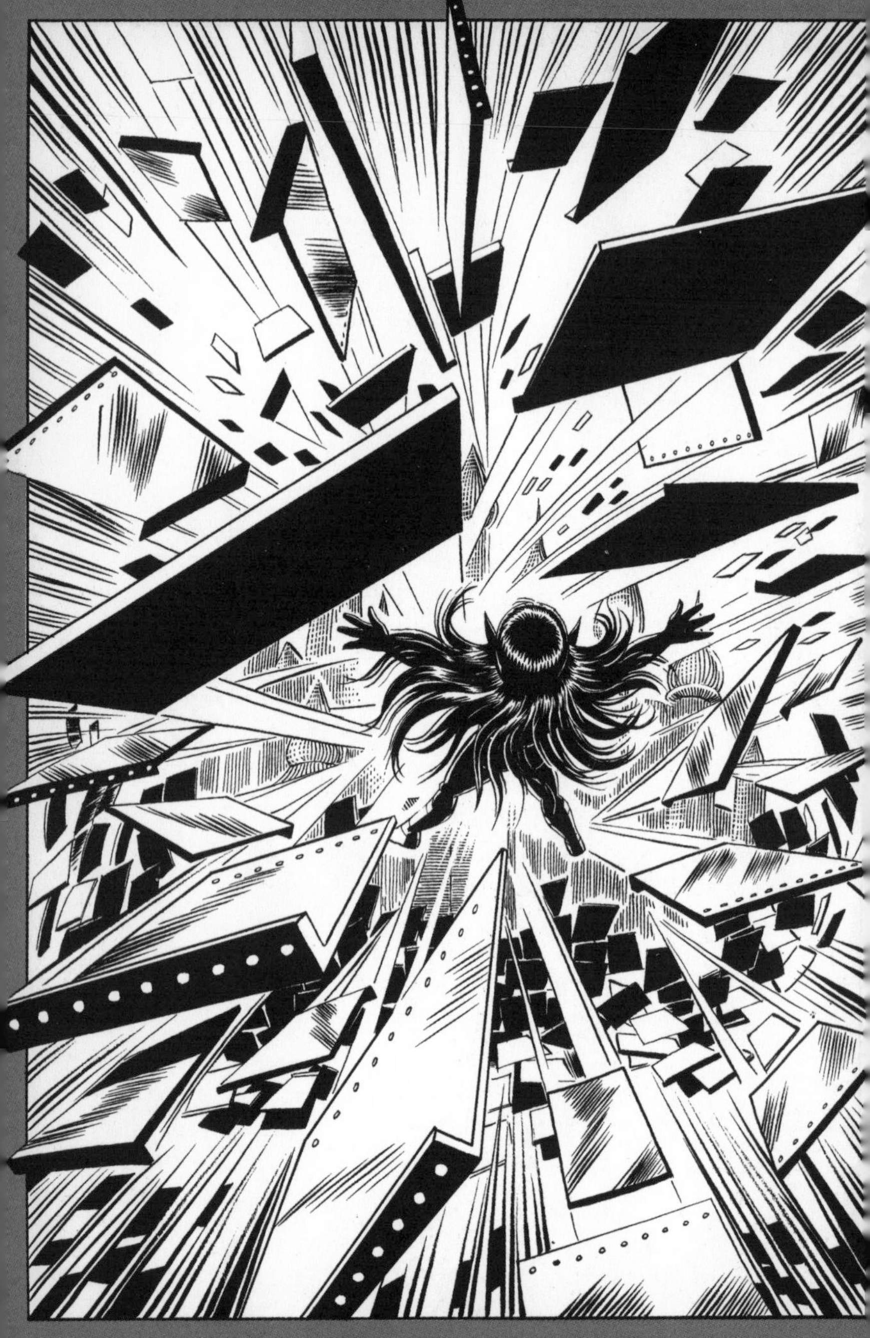

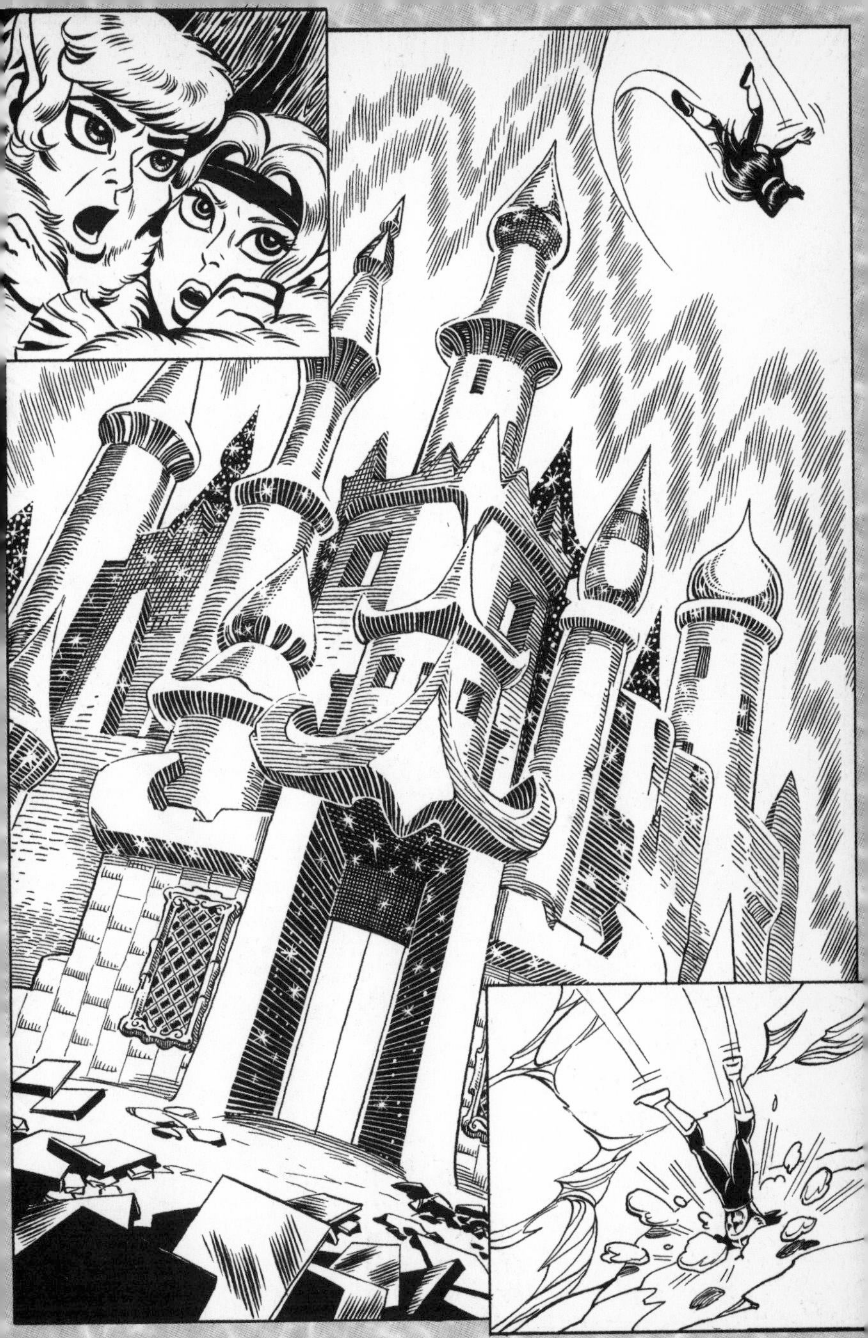

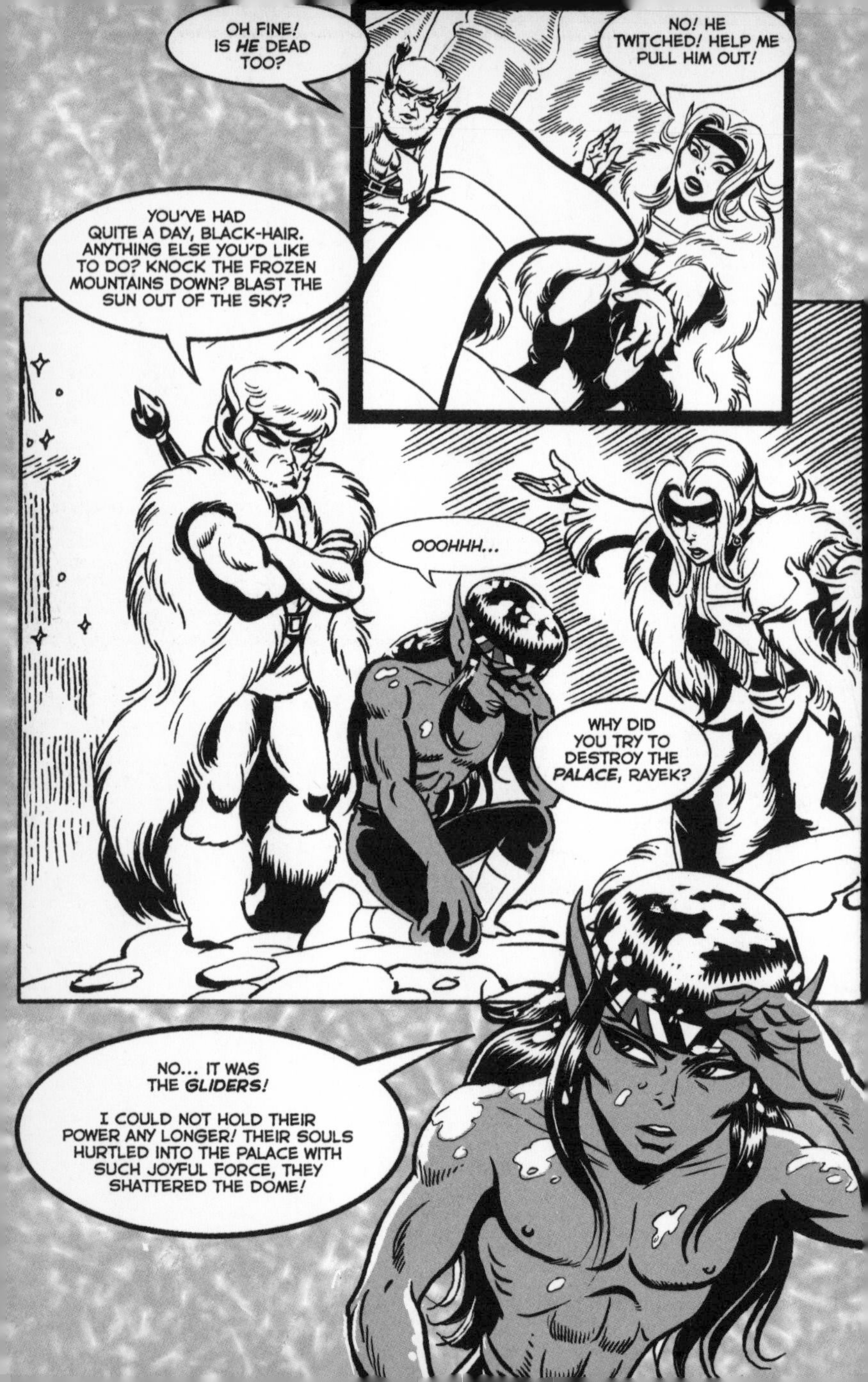
OH FINE! IS HE DEAD TOO?
NO! HE TWITCHED! HELP ME PULL HIM OUT!
YOU'VE HAD QUITE A DAY, BLACK-HAIR. ANYTHING ELSE YOU'D LIKE TO DO? KNOCK THE FROZEN MOUNTAINS DOWN? BLAST THE SUN OUT OF THE SKY?
OOOHHH...
WHY DID YOU TRY TO DESTROY THE PALACE, RAYEK?
NO... IT WAS THE GLIDERS!
I COULD NOT HOLD THEIR POWER ANY LONGER! THEIR SOULS HURTLED INTO THE PALACE WITH SUCH JOYFUL FORCE, THEY SHATTERED THE DOME!

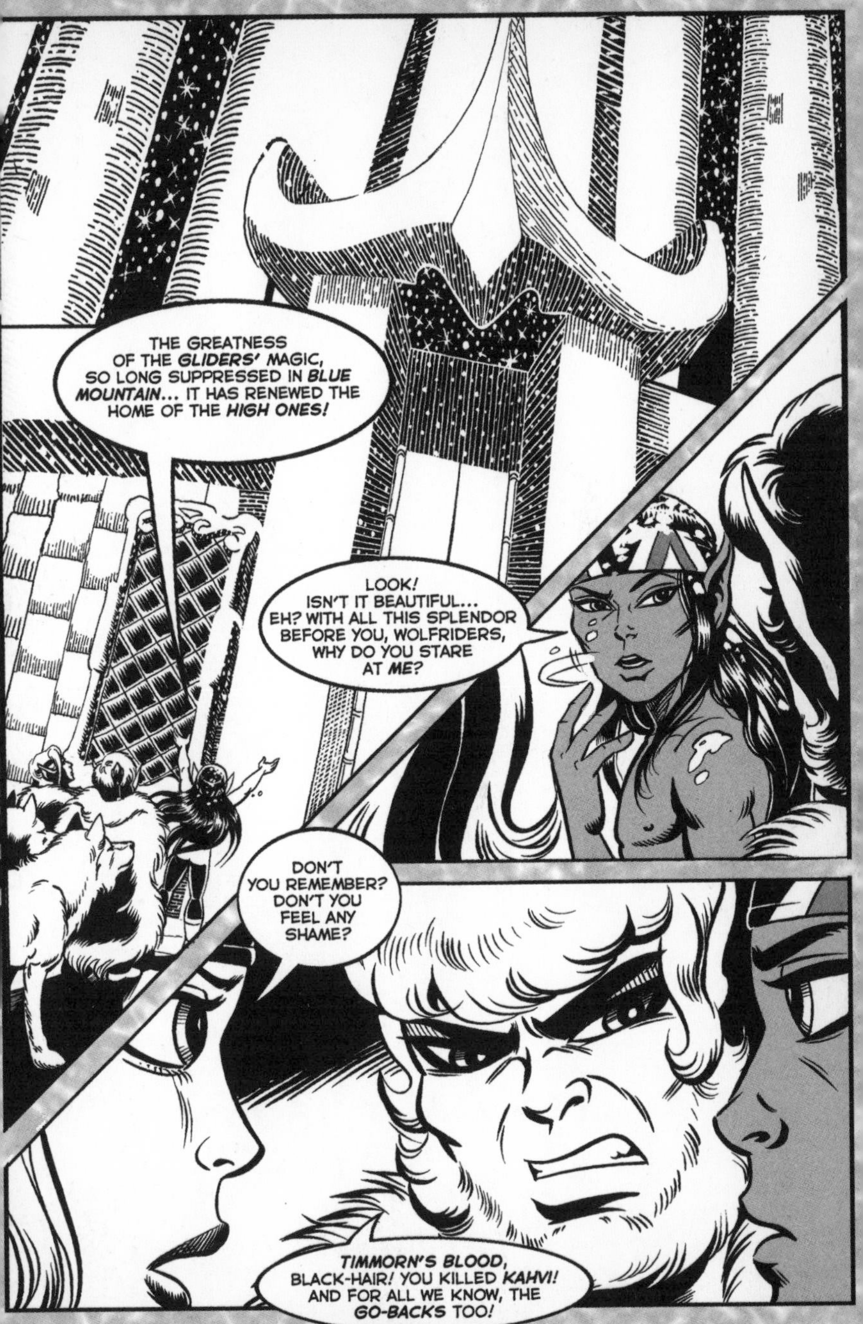
THE GREATNESS OF THE GLIDERS' MAGIC, SO LONG SUPPRESSED IN BLUE MOUNTAIN... IT HAS RENEWED THE HOME OF THE HIGH ONES!
LOOK! ISN'T IT BEAUTIFUL... EH? WITH ALL THIS SPLENDOR BEFORE YOU, WOLFRIDERS, WHY DO YOU STARE AT ME?
DON'T YOU REMEMBER? DON'T YOU FEEL ANY SHAME?
TIMMORN'S BLOOD, BLACK-HAIR! YOU KILLED KAHVI! AND FOR ALL WE KNOW, THE GO-BACKS TOO!

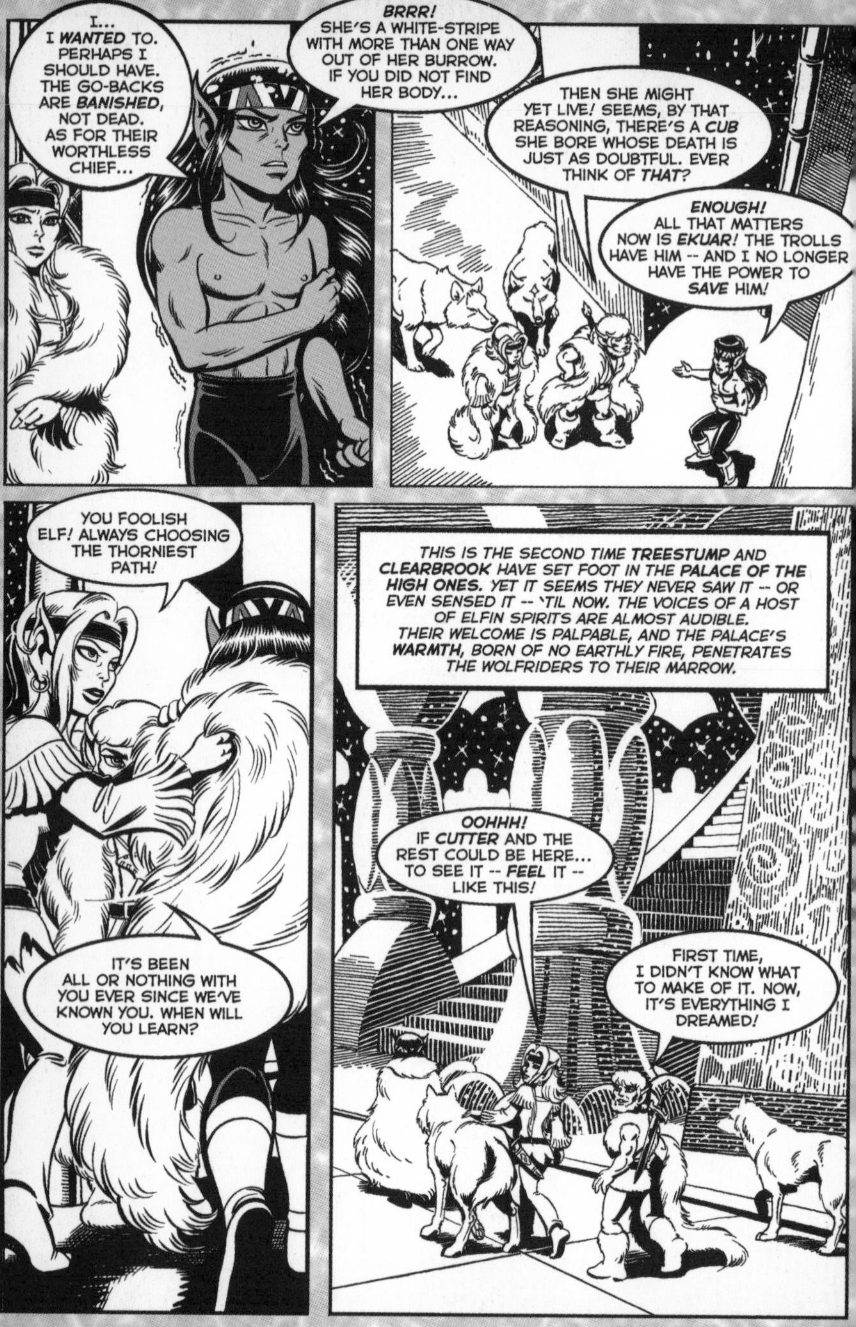

I... I WANTED TO. PERHAPS I SHOULD HAVE. THE GO-BACKS ARE BANISHED, NOT DEAD. AS FOR THEIR WORTHLESS CHIEF...
BRRR! SHE'S A WHITE-STRIPE WITH MORE THAN ONE WAY OUT OF HER BURROW. IF YOU DID NOT FIND HER BODY...
THEN SHE MIGHT YET LIVE! SEEMS, BY THAT REASONING, THERE'S A CUB SHE BORE WHOSE DEATH IS JUST AS DOUBTFUL. EVER THINK OF THAT?
ENOUGH! ALL THAT MATTERS NOW IS EKUAR! THE TROLLS HAVE HIM -- AND I NO LONGER HAVE THE POWER TO SAVE HIM!
YOU FOOLISH ELF! ALWAYS CHOOSING THE THORNIEST PATH!
IT'S BEEN ALL OR NOTHING WITH YOU EVER SINCE WE'VE KNOWN YOU. WHEN WILL YOU LEARN?
THIS IS THE SECOND TIME TREESTUMP AND CLEARBROOK HAVE SET FOOT IN THE PALACE OF THE HIGH ONES. YET IT SEEMS THEY NEVER SAW IT -- OR EVEN SENSED IT -- 'TIL NOW. THE VOICES OF A HOST OF ELFIN SPIRITS ARE ALMOST AUDIBLE. THEIR WELCOME IS PALPABLE, AND THE PALACE'S WARMTH, BORN OF NO EARTHLY FIRE, PENETRATES THE WOLFRIDERS TO THEIR MARROW.
OOHHH! IF CUTTER AND THE REST COULD BE HERE... TO SEE IT -- FEEL IT -- LIKE THIS!
FIRST TIME, I DIDN'T KNOW WHAT TO MAKE OF IT. NOW, IT'S EVERYTHING I DREAMED!

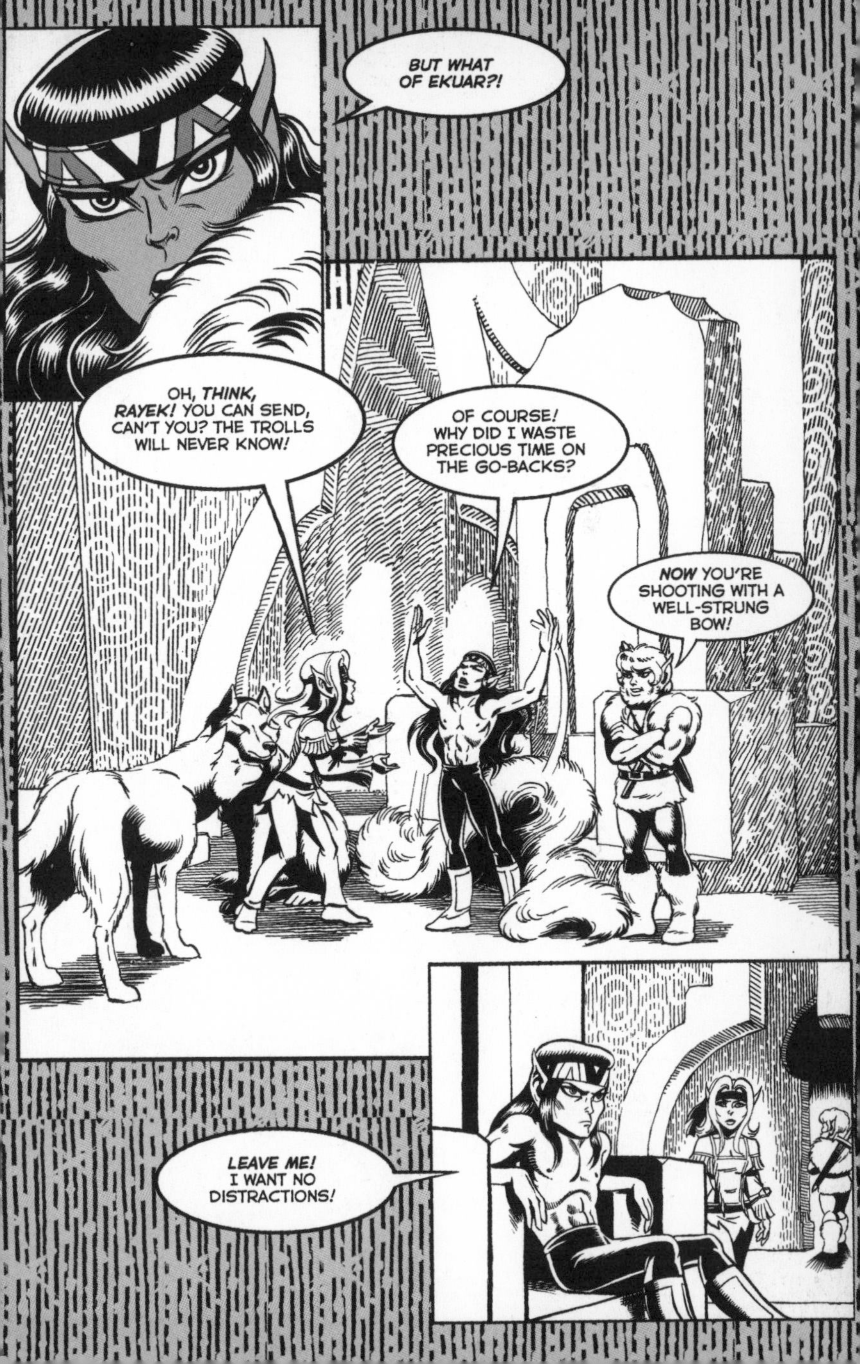
BUT WHAT OF EKUAR?!
OH, THINK, RAYEK! YOU CAN SEND, CAN'T YOU? THE TROLLS WILL NEVER KNOW!
OF COURSE! WHY DID I WASTE PRECIOUS TIME ON THE GO-BACKS?
NOW YOU'RE SHOOTING WITH A WELL-STRUNG BOW!
LEAVE ME! I WANT NO DISTRACTIONS!

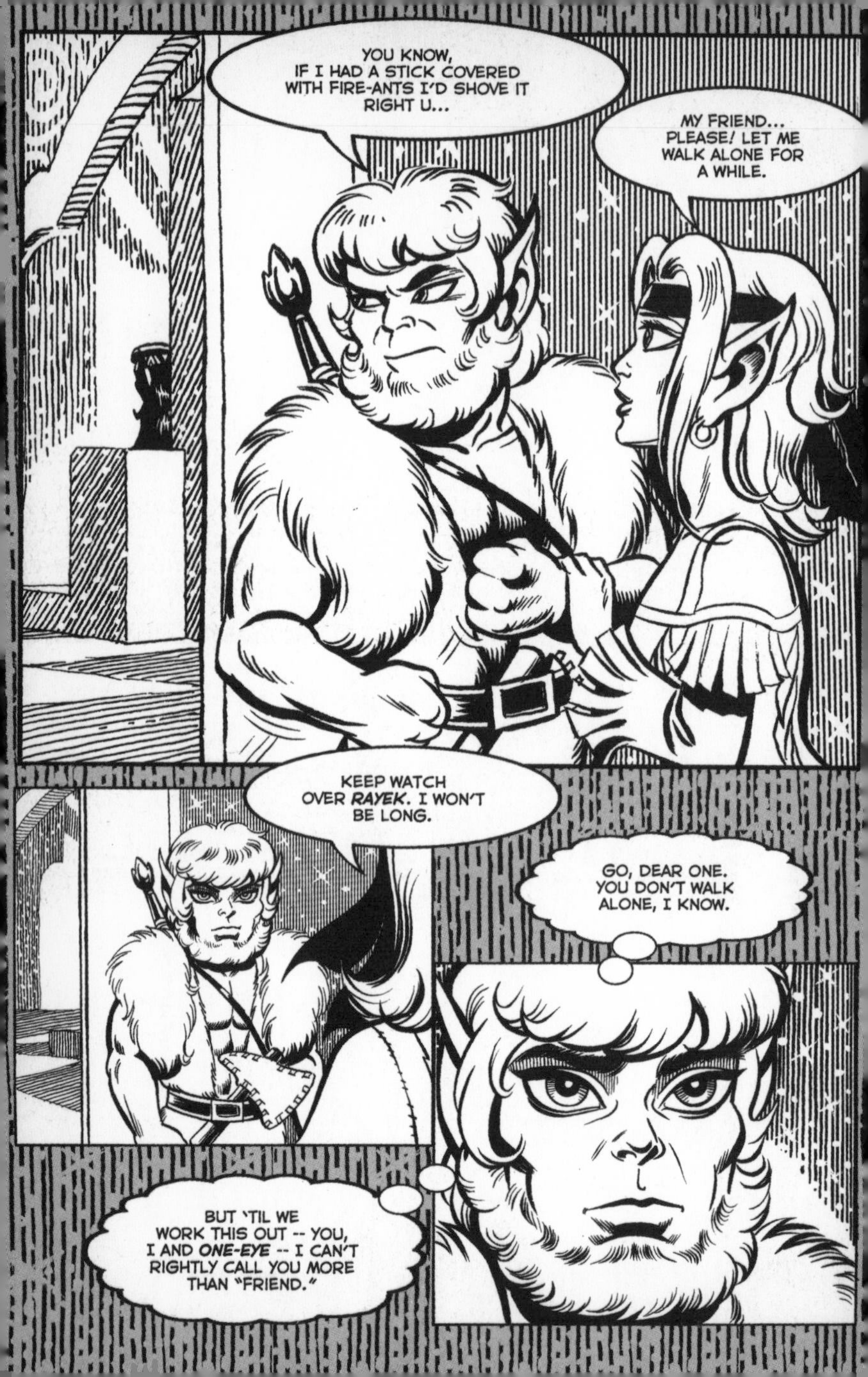
YOU KNOW, IF I HAD A STICK COVERED WITH FIRE-ANTS I'D SHOVE IT RIGHT U...
MY FRIEND... PLEASE! LET ME WALK ALONE FOR A WHILE.
KEEP WATCH OVER RAYEK. I WON'T BE LONG.
GO, DEAR ONE. YOU DON'T WALK ALONE, I KNOW.
BUT 'TIL WE WORK THIS OUT -- YOU, I AND ONE-EYE -- I CAN'T RIGHTLY CALL YOU MORE THAN "FRIEND."

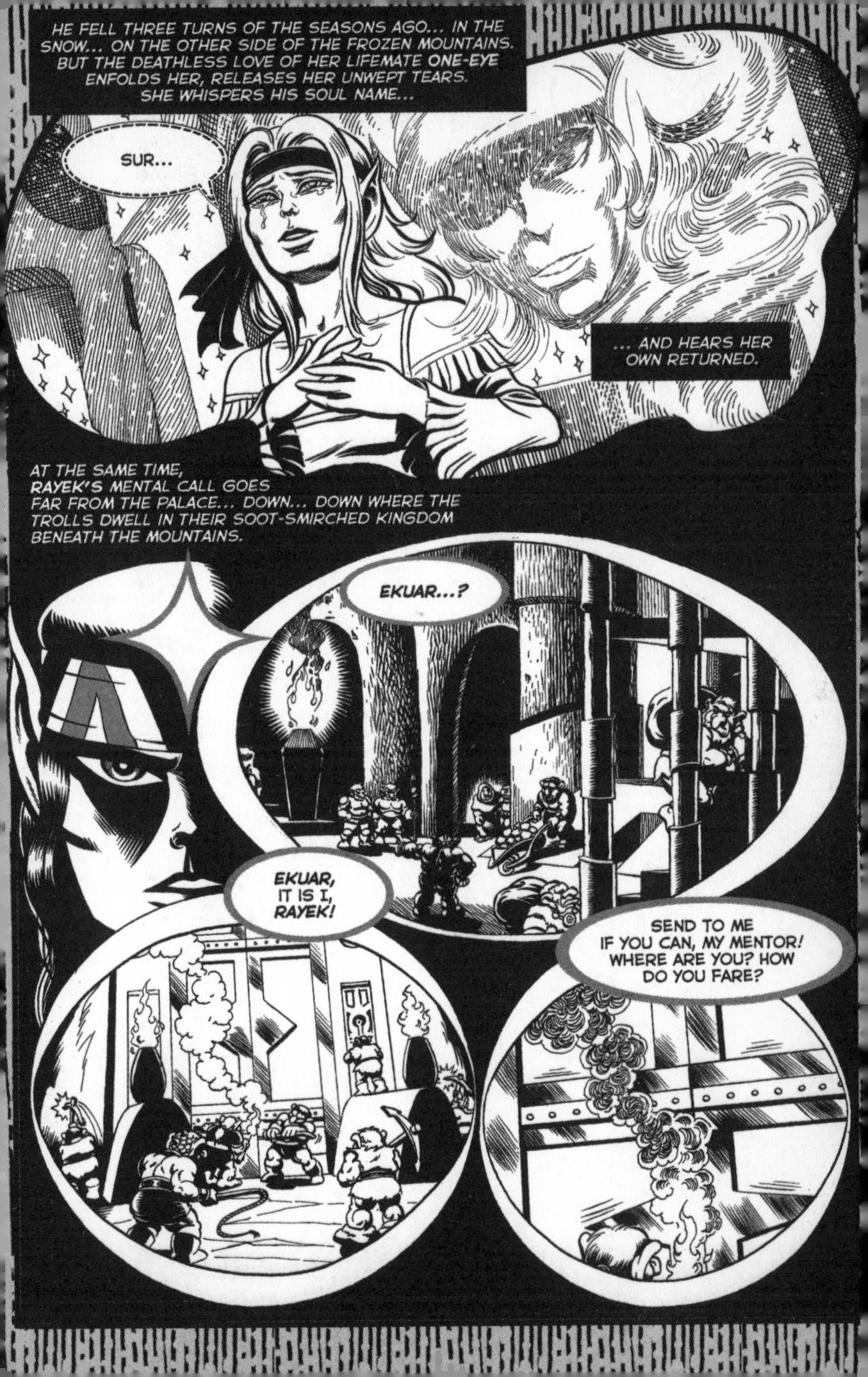
HE FELL THREE TURNS OF THE SEASONS AGO... IN THE SNOW... ON THE OTHER SIDE OF THE FROZEN MOUNTAINS. BUT THE DEATHLESS LOVE OF HER LIFEMATE ONE-EYE ENFOLDS HER, RELEASES HER UNWEPT TEARS. SHE WHISPERS HIS SOUL NAME...
SUR...
... AND HEARS HER OWN RETURNED.
AT THE SAME TIME, RAYEK'S MENTAL CALL GOES FAR FROM THE PALACE... DOWN... DOWN WHERE THE TROLLS DWELL IN THEIR SOOT-SMIRCHED KINGDOM BENEATH THE MOUNTAINS.
EKUAR...?
EKUAR, IT IS I, RAYEK!
SEND TO ME IF YOU CAN, MY MENTOR! WHERE ARE YOU? HOW DO YOU FARE?

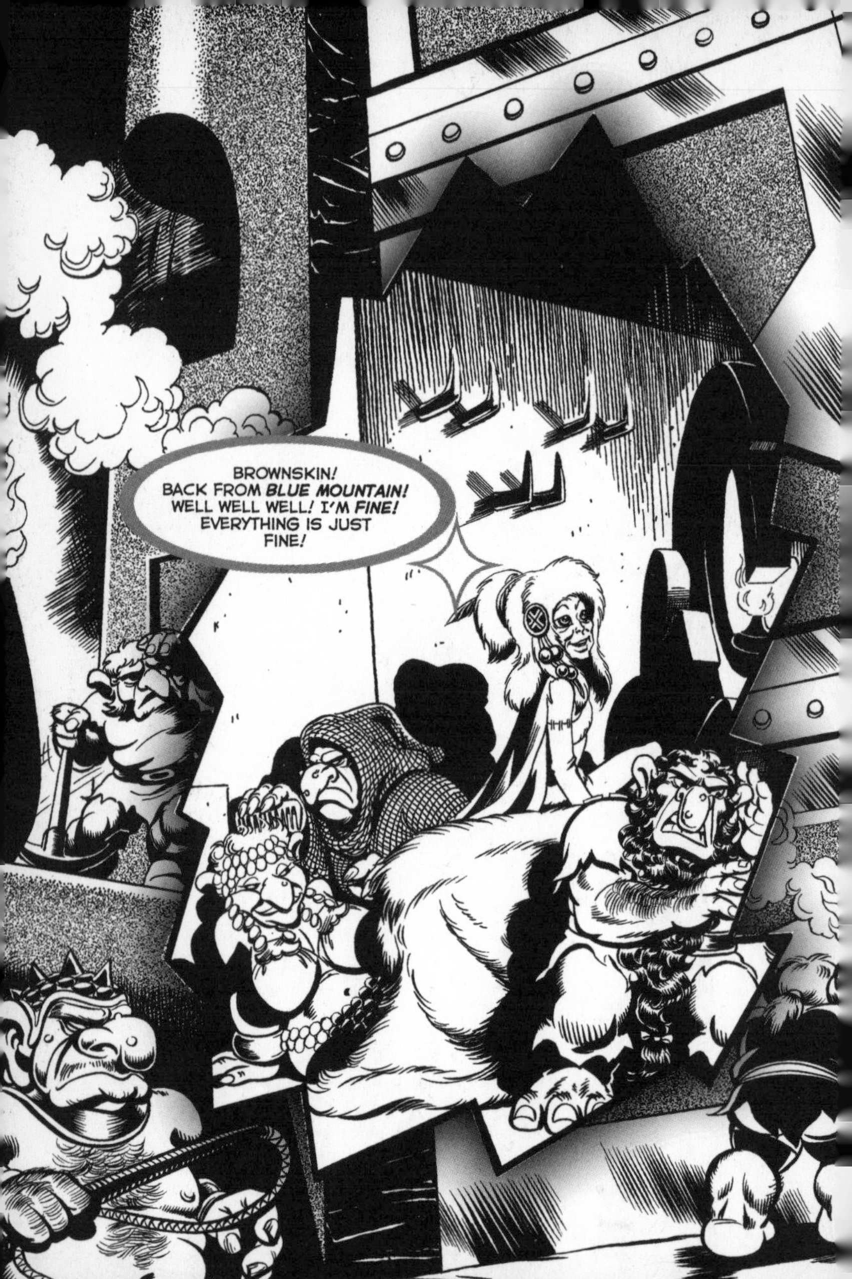
BROWNSKIN! BACK FROM *BLUE MOUNTAIN!* WELL WELL WELL! I'M *FINE!* EVERYTHING IS JUST FINE!

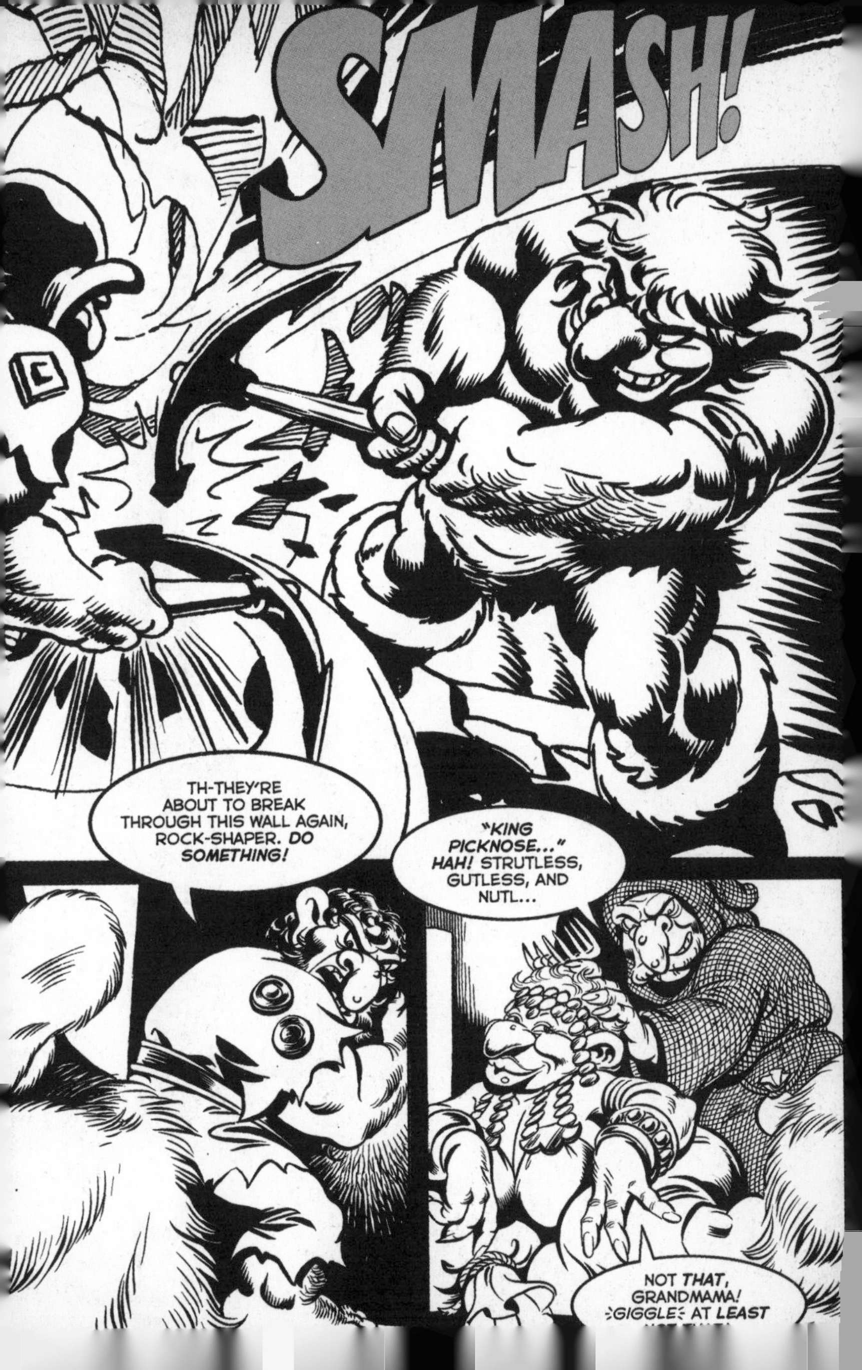
SMASH!
TH-THEY'RE ABOUT TO BREAK THROUGH THIS WALL AGAIN, ROCK-SHAPER. *DO SOMETHING!*
"KING PICKNOSE..." HAH! STRUTLESS, GUTLESS, AND NUTL...
NOT *THAT*, GRANDMAMA! ≈GIGGLE≈ AT *LEAST*

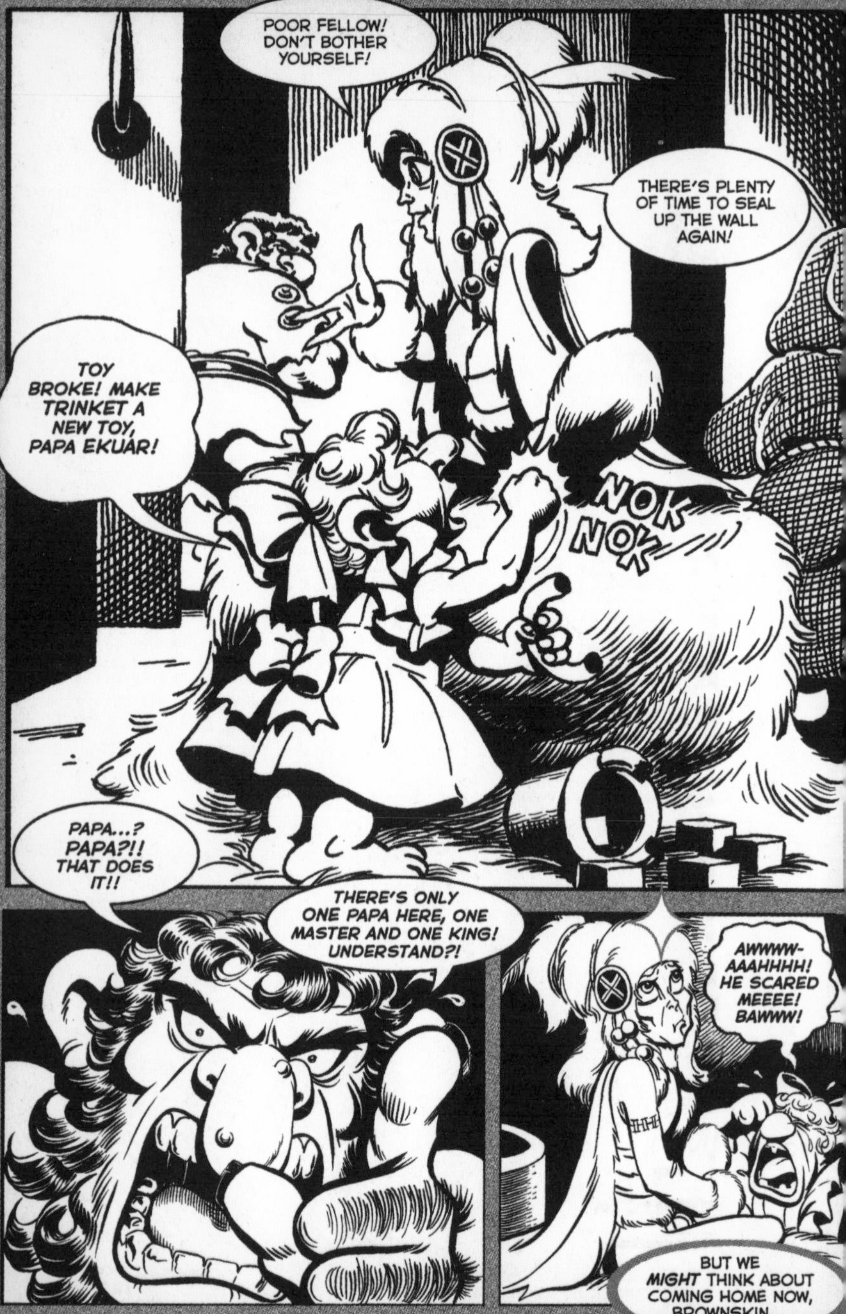
POOR FELLOW! DON'T BOTHER YOURSELF!
THERE'S PLENTY OF TIME TO SEAL UP THE WALL AGAIN!
TOY BROKE! MAKE TRINKET A NEW TOY, PAPA EKUÁR!
NOK NOK
PAPA...? PAPA?!! THAT DOES IT!!
THERE'S ONLY ONE PAPA HERE, ONE MASTER AND ONE KING! UNDERSTAND?!
AWWWW-AAAHHHH! HE SCARED MEEEE! BAWWW!
BUT WE *MIGHT* THINK ABOUT COMING HOME NOW, BROWNSKIN...

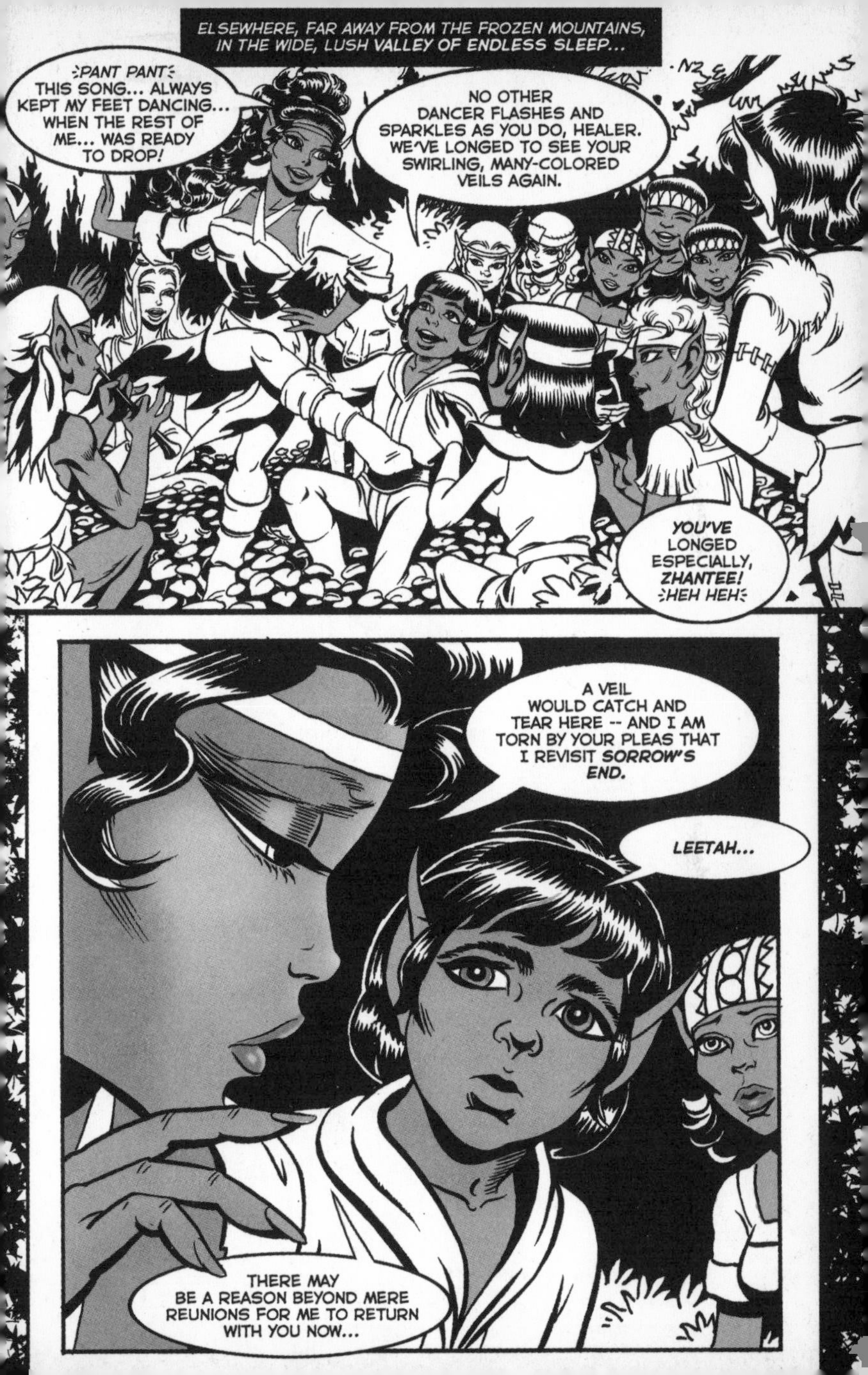
ELSEWHERE, FAR AWAY FROM THE FROZEN MOUNTAINS, IN THE WIDE, LUSH VALLEY OF ENDLESS SLEEP...
PANT PANT THIS SONG... ALWAYS KEPT MY FEET DANCING... WHEN THE REST OF ME... WAS READY TO DROP!
NO OTHER DANCER FLASHES AND SPARKLES AS YOU DO, HEALER. WE'VE LONGED TO SEE YOUR SWIRLING, MANY-COLORED VEILS AGAIN.
YOU'VE LONGED ESPECIALLY, ZHANTEE! HEH HEH
A VEIL WOULD CATCH AND TEAR HERE -- AND I AM TORN BY YOUR PLEAS THAT I REVISIT SORROW'S END.
LEETAH...
THERE MAY BE A REASON BEYOND MERE REUNIONS FOR ME TO RETURN WITH YOU NOW...

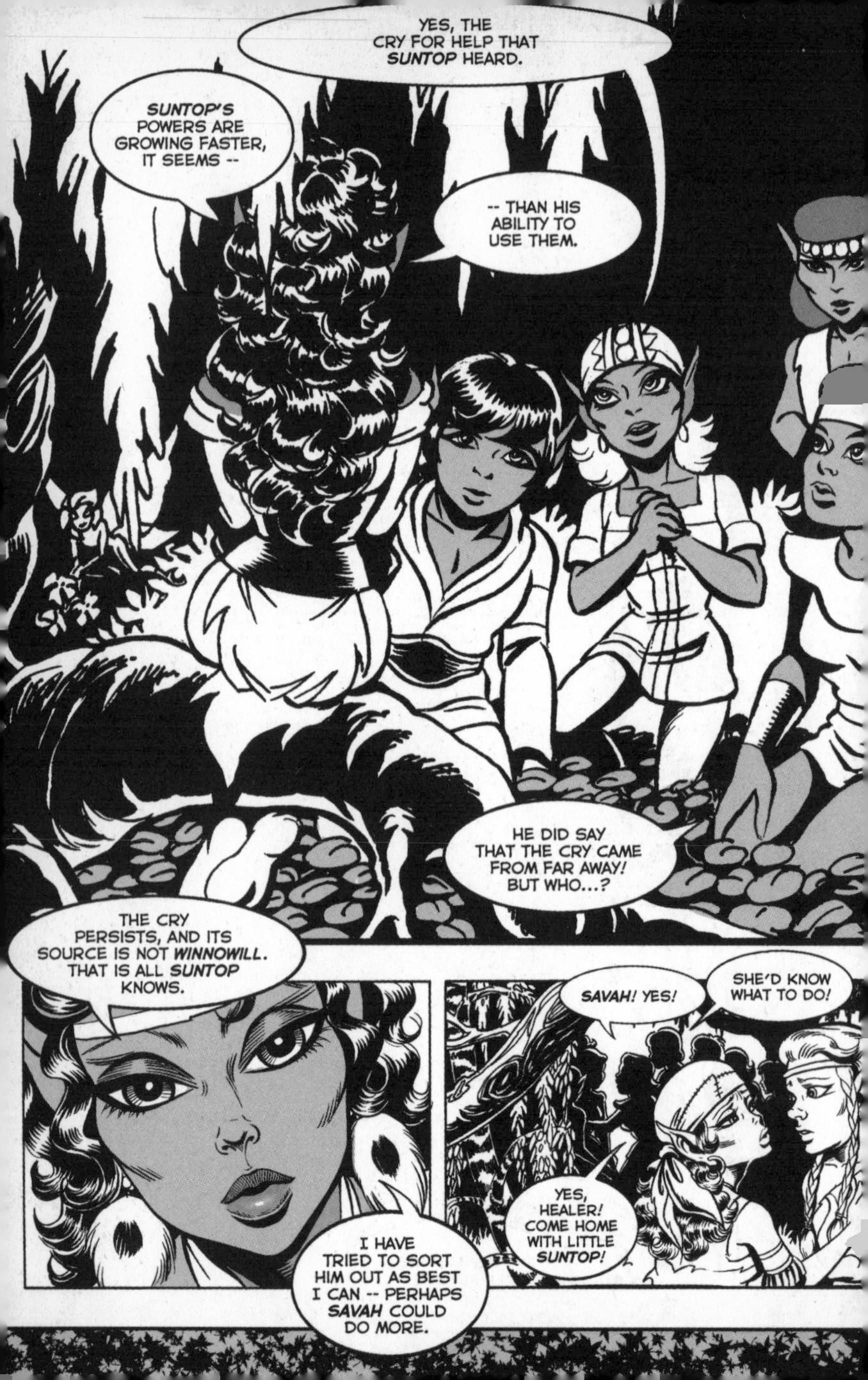
YES, THE CRY FOR HELP THAT SUNTOP HEARD.
SUNTOP'S POWERS ARE GROWING FASTER, IT SEEMS --
-- THAN HIS ABILITY TO USE THEM.
HE DID SAY THAT THE CRY CAME FROM FAR AWAY! BUT WHO...?
THE CRY PERSISTS, AND ITS SOURCE IS NOT WINNOWILL. THAT IS ALL SUNTOP KNOWS.
I HAVE TRIED TO SORT HIM OUT AS BEST I CAN -- PERHAPS SAVAH COULD DO MORE.
SAVAH! YES!
SHE'D KNOW WHAT TO DO!
YES, HEALER! COME HOME WITH LITTLE SUNTOP!

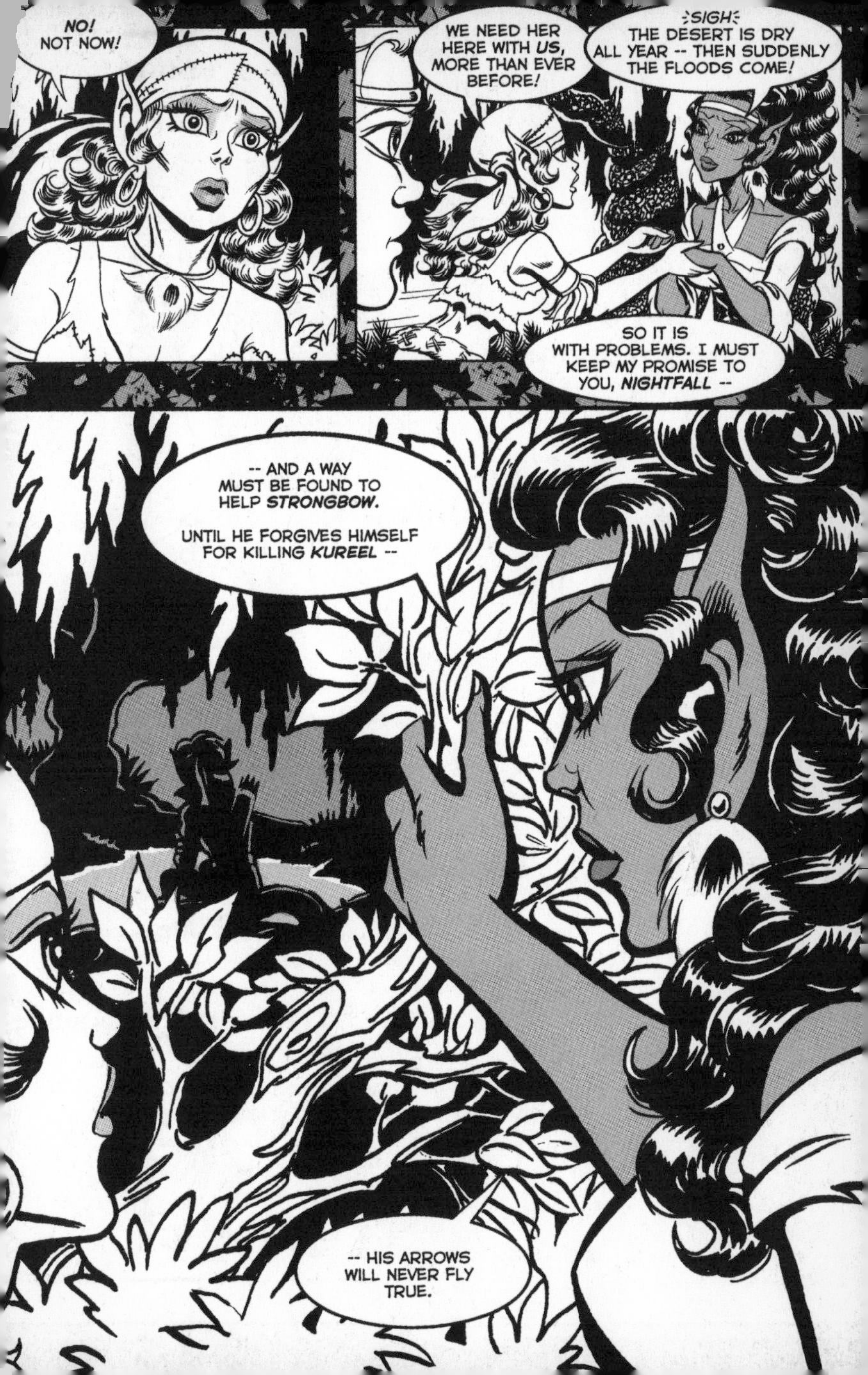
NO! NOT NOW!
WE NEED HER HERE WITH US, MORE THAN EVER BEFORE!
:SIGH: THE DESERT IS DRY ALL YEAR -- THEN SUDDENLY THE FLOODS COME!
SO IT IS WITH PROBLEMS. I MUST KEEP MY PROMISE TO YOU, NIGHTFALL --
-- AND A WAY MUST BE FOUND TO HELP STRONGBOW.
UNTIL HE FORGIVES HIMSELF FOR KILLING KUREEL --
-- HIS ARROWS WILL NEVER FLY TRUE.

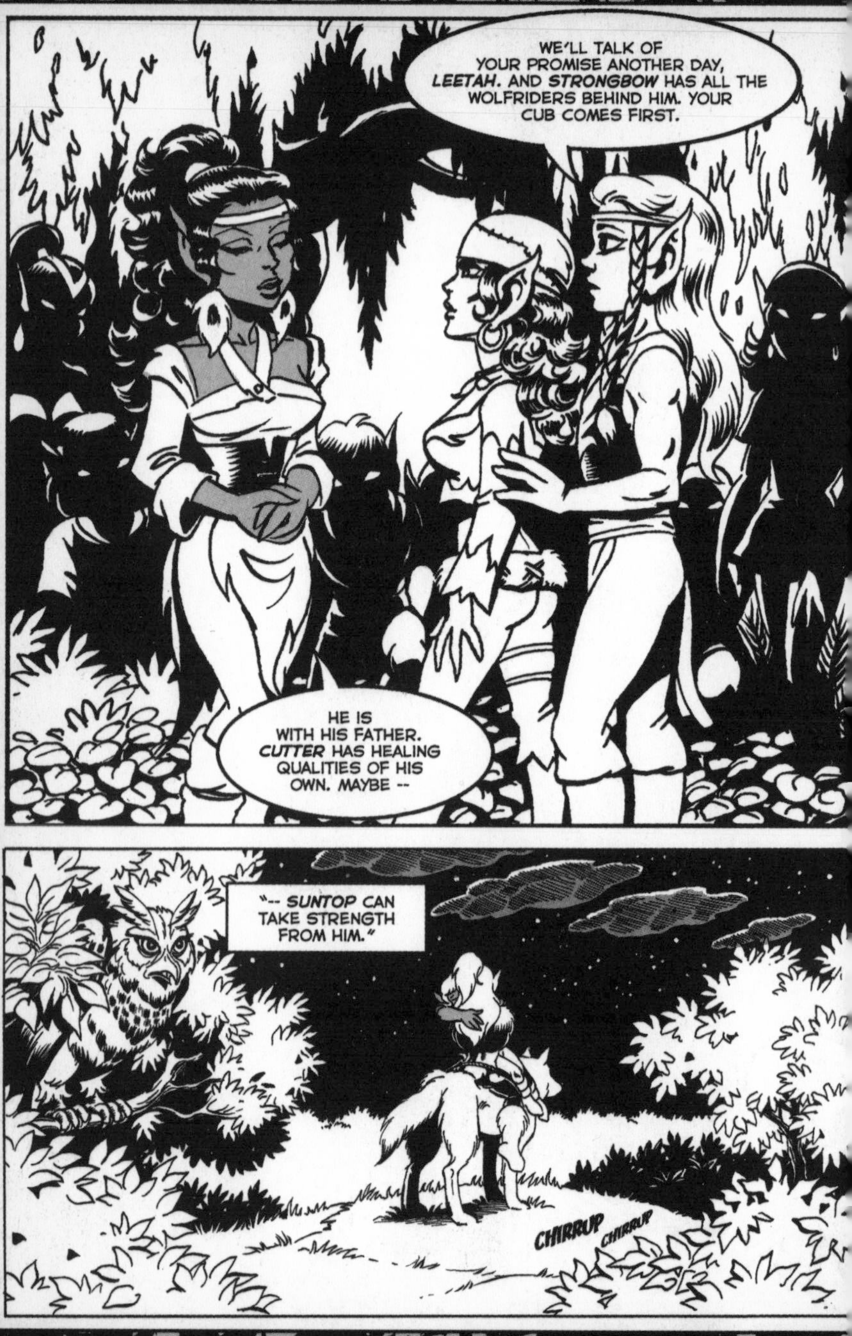
WE'LL TALK OF YOUR PROMISE ANOTHER DAY, LEETAH. AND STRONGBOW HAS ALL THE WOLFRIDERS BEHIND HIM. YOUR CUB COMES FIRST.
HE IS WITH HIS FATHER. CUTTER HAS HEALING QUALITIES OF HIS OWN. MAYBE --
"-- SUNTOP CAN TAKE STRENGTH FROM HIM."
CHIRRUP
CHIRRUP

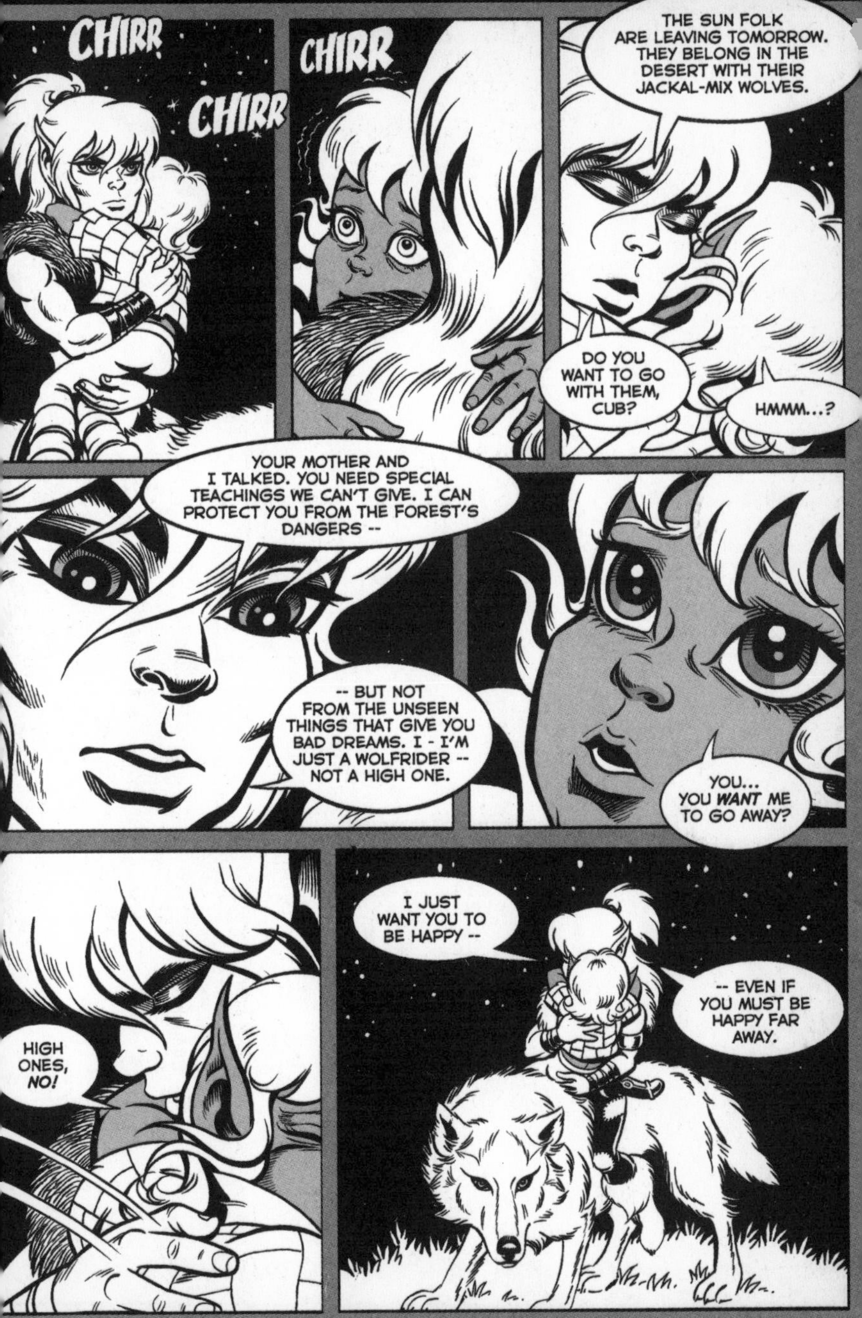
CHIRR
CHIRR
CHIRR
THE SUN FOLK ARE LEAVING TOMORROW. THEY BELONG IN THE DESERT WITH THEIR JACKAL-MIX WOLVES.
DO YOU WANT TO GO WITH THEM, CUB?
HMMM...?
YOUR MOTHER AND I TALKED. YOU NEED SPECIAL TEACHINGS WE CAN'T GIVE. I CAN PROTECT YOU FROM THE FOREST'S DANGERS --
-- BUT NOT FROM THE UNSEEN THINGS THAT GIVE YOU BAD DREAMS. I - I'M JUST A WOLFRIDER -- NOT A HIGH ONE.
YOU... YOU *WANT* ME TO GO AWAY?
HIGH ONES, *NO!*
I JUST WANT YOU TO BE HAPPY --
-- EVEN IF YOU MUST BE HAPPY FAR AWAY.

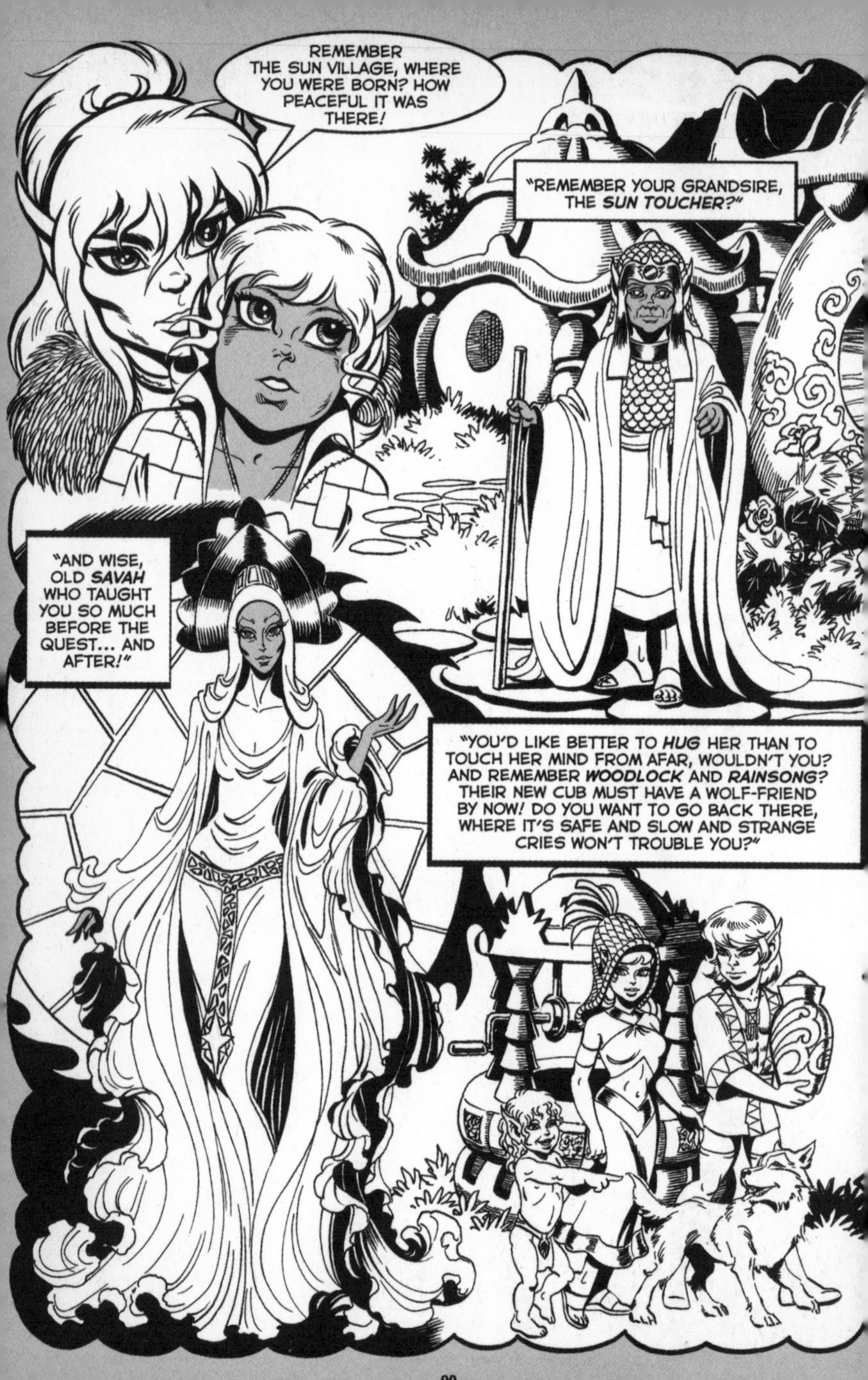

REMEMBER THE SUN VILLAGE, WHERE YOU WERE BORN? HOW PEACEFUL IT WAS THERE!
"REMEMBER YOUR GRANDSIRE, THE SUN TOUCHER?"
"AND WISE, OLD SAVAH WHO TAUGHT YOU SO MUCH BEFORE THE QUEST... AND AFTER!"
"YOU'D LIKE BETTER TO HUG HER THAN TO TOUCH HER MIND FROM AFAR, WOULDN'T YOU? AND REMEMBER WOODLOCK AND RAINSONG? THEIR NEW CUB MUST HAVE A WOLF-FRIEND BY NOW! DO YOU WANT TO GO BACK THERE, WHERE IT'S SAFE AND SLOW AND STRANGE CRIES WON'T TROUBLE YOU?"

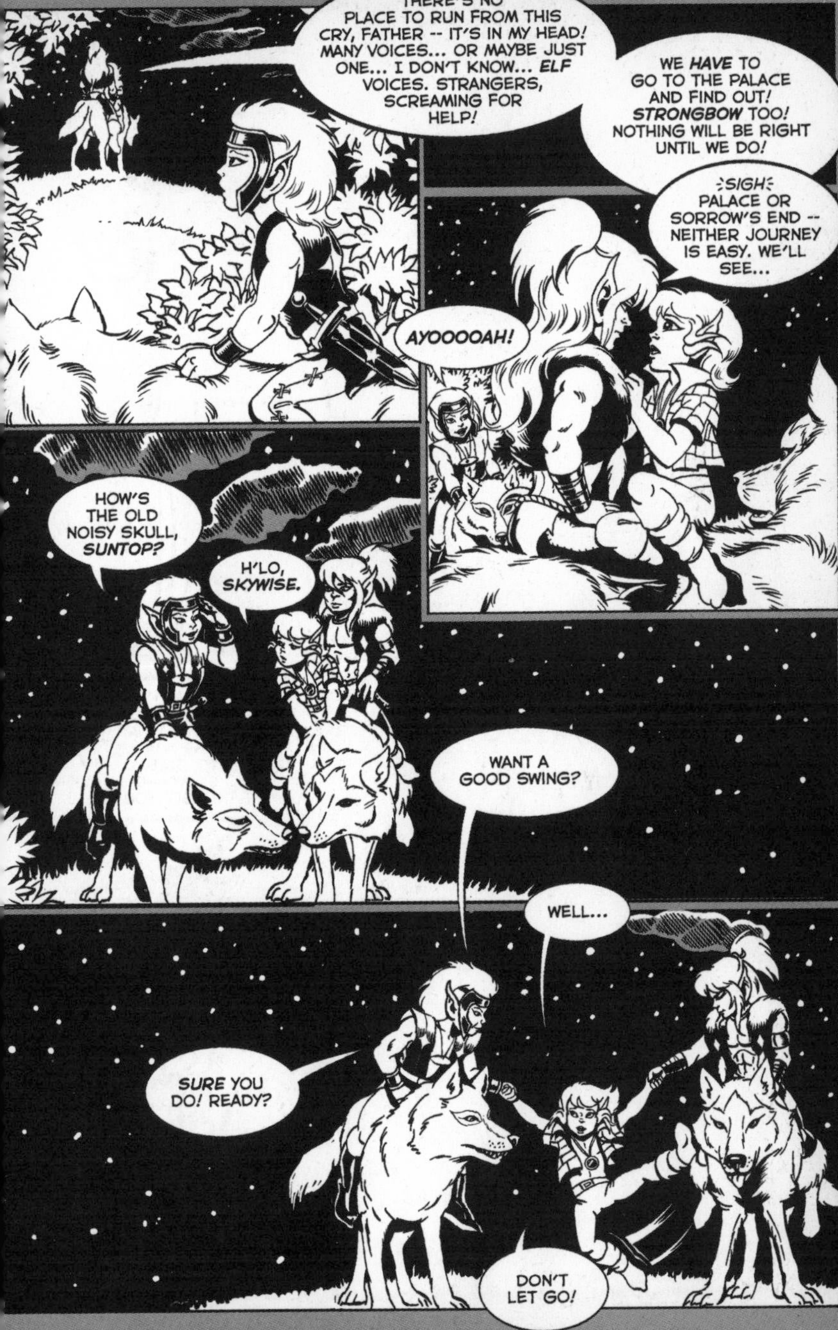
THERE'S NO PLACE TO RUN FROM THIS CRY, FATHER -- IT'S IN MY HEAD! MANY VOICES... OR MAYBE JUST ONE... I DON'T KNOW... ELF VOICES. STRANGERS, SCREAMING FOR HELP!
WE HAVE TO GO TO THE PALACE AND FIND OUT! STRONGBOW TOO! NOTHING WILL BE RIGHT UNTIL WE DO!
SIGH PALACE OR SORROW'S END -- NEITHER JOURNEY IS EASY. WE'LL SEE...
AYOOOOAH!
HOW'S THE OLD NOISY SKULL, SUNTOP?
H'LO, SKYWISE.
WANT A GOOD SWING?
WELL...
SURE YOU DO! READY?
DON'T LET GO!

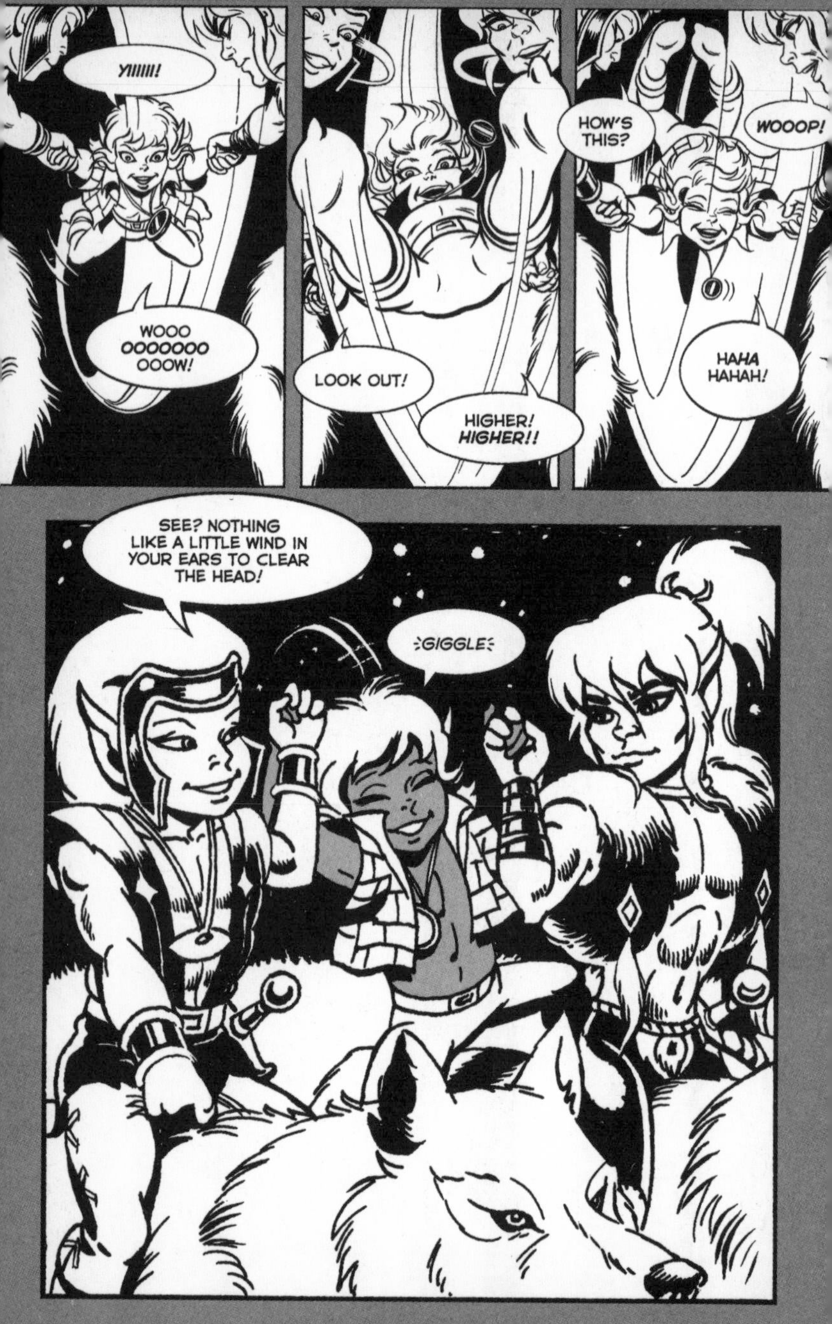
YIIIII!
WOOO OOOOOOO OOOW!
LOOK OUT!
HIGHER! HIGHER!!
HOW'S THIS?
WOOOP!
HAHA HAHAH!
SEE? NOTHING LIKE A LITTLE WIND IN YOUR EARS TO CLEAR THE HEAD!
GIGGLE

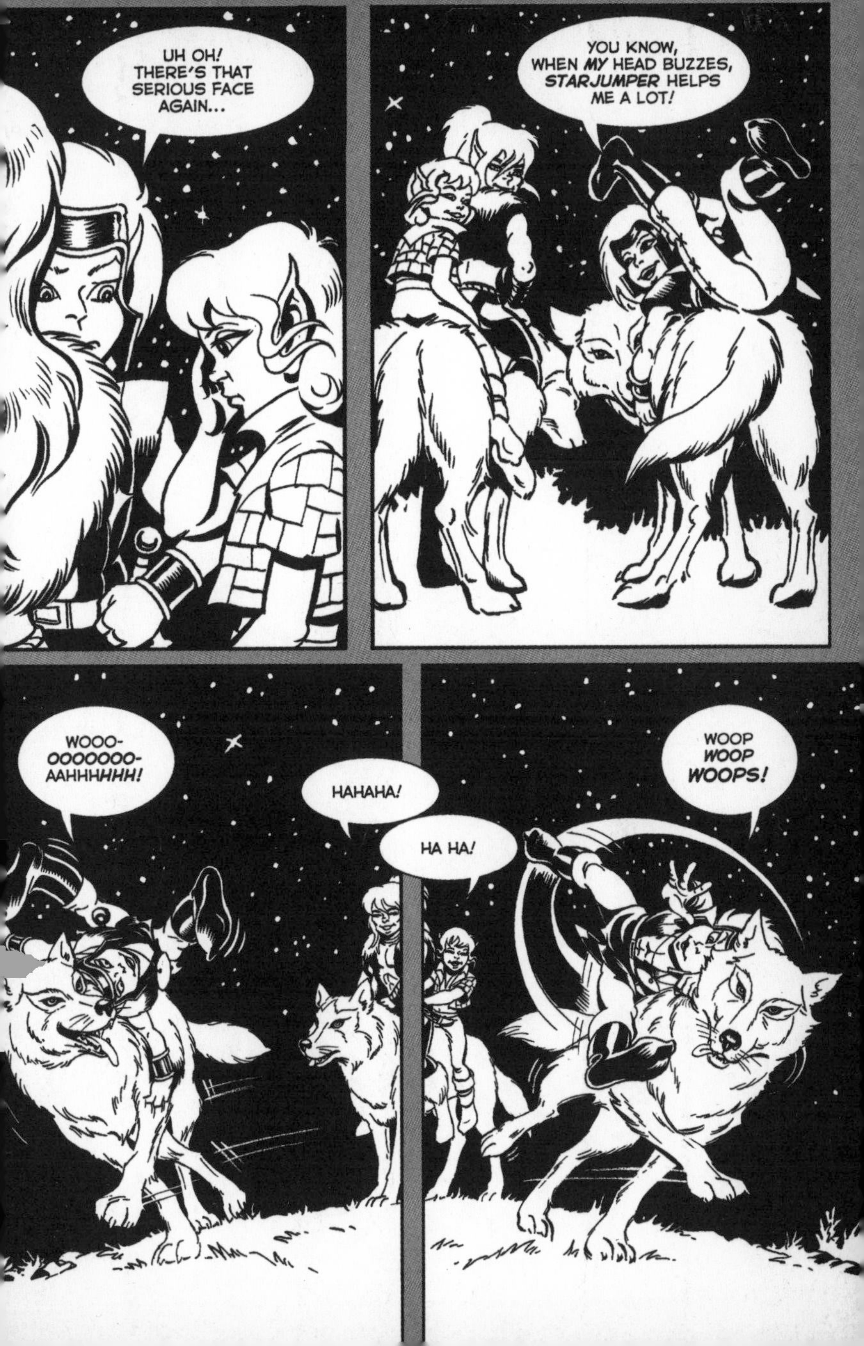
UH OH! THERE'S THAT SERIOUS FACE AGAIN...
YOU KNOW, WHEN *MY* HEAD BUZZES, *STARJUMPER* HELPS ME A LOT!
WOOO-OOOOOOO-AAHHHHHH!
HAHAHA!
HA HA!
WOOP *WOOP* ***WOOPS!***

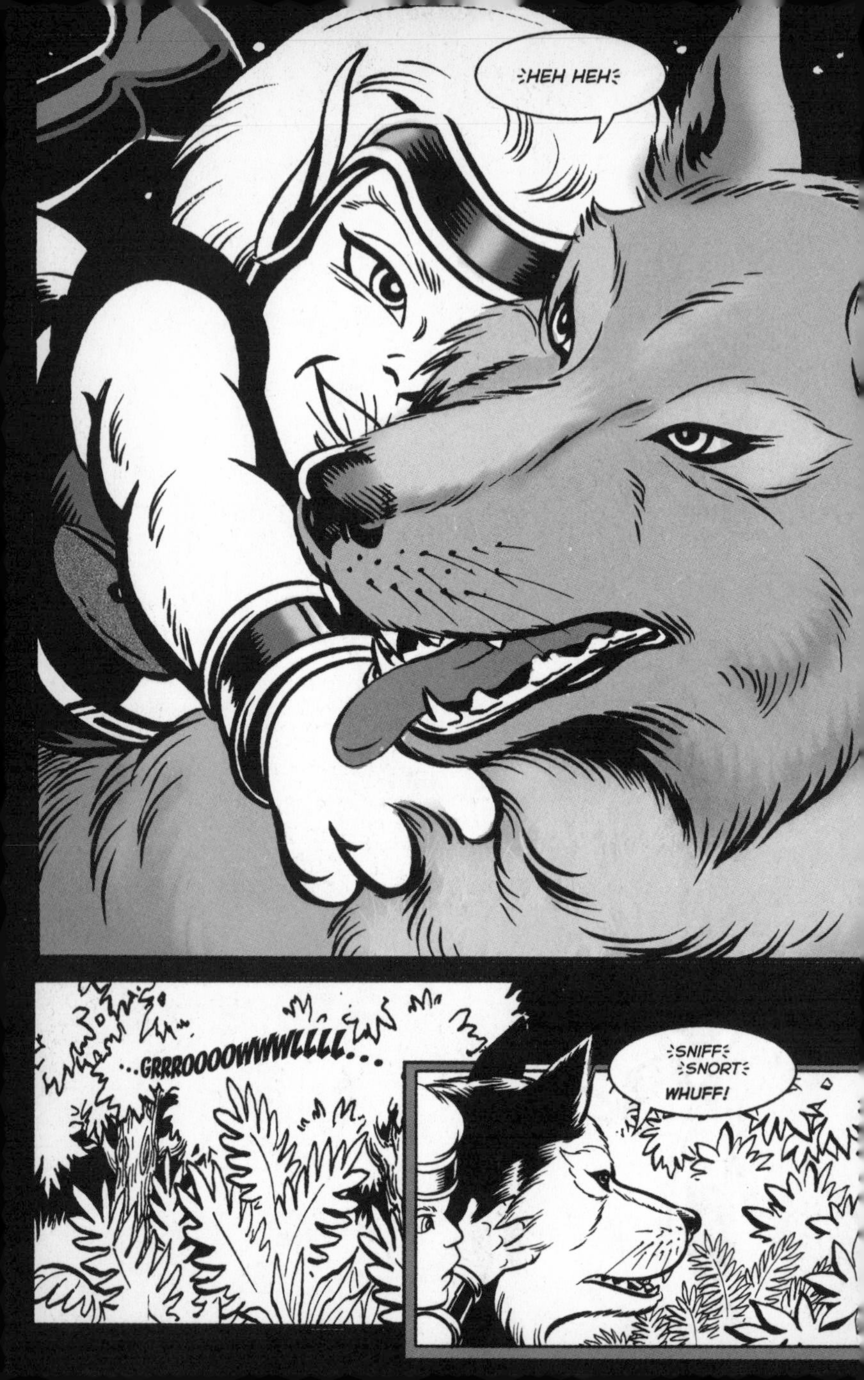
HEH HEH
...GRRROOOOWWWLLLLL...
SNIFF
SNORT
WHUFF!

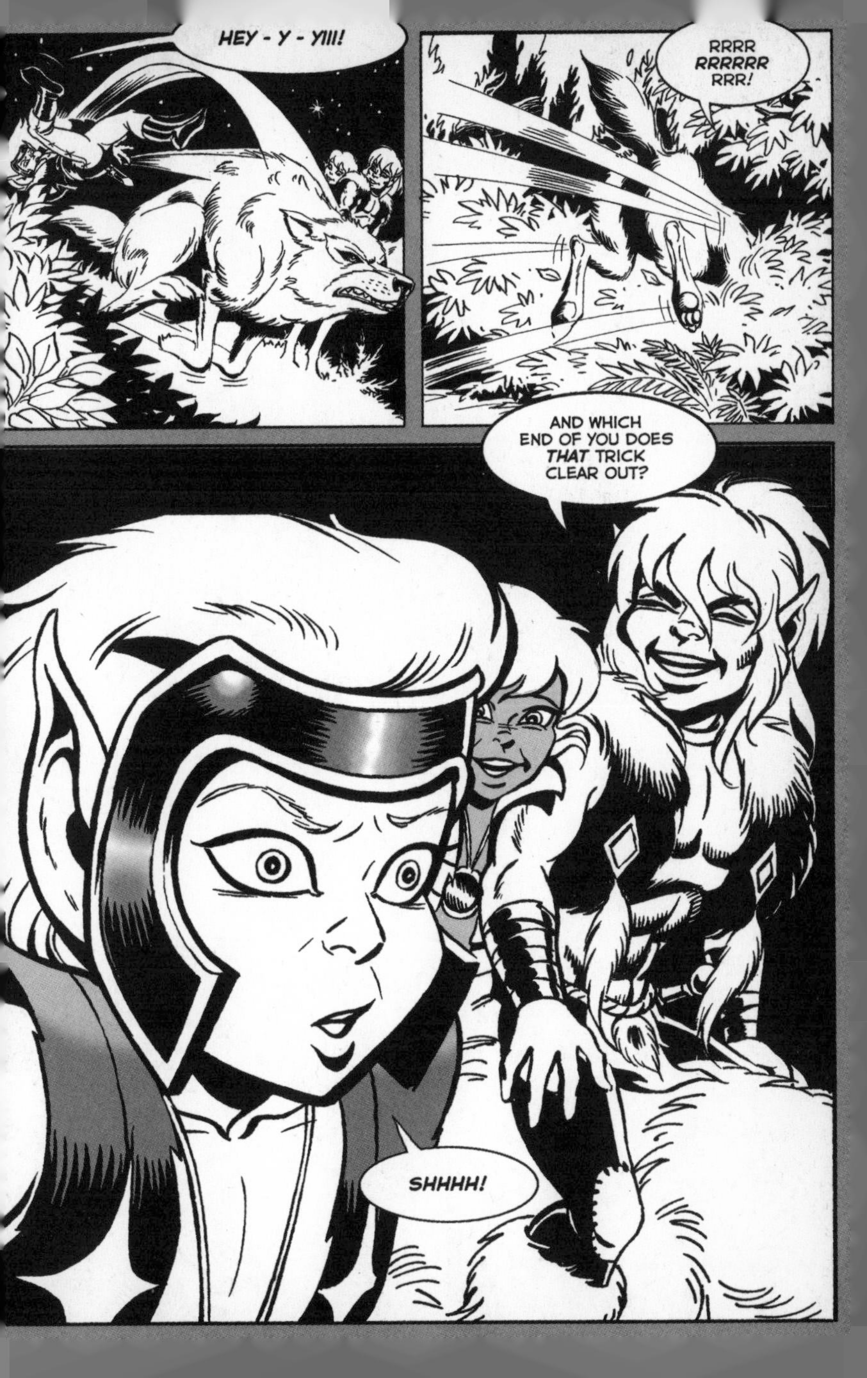

HEY - Y - YIII!
RRRR RRRRRR RRR!
AND WHICH END OF YOU DOES THAT TRICK CLEAR OUT?
SHHHH!

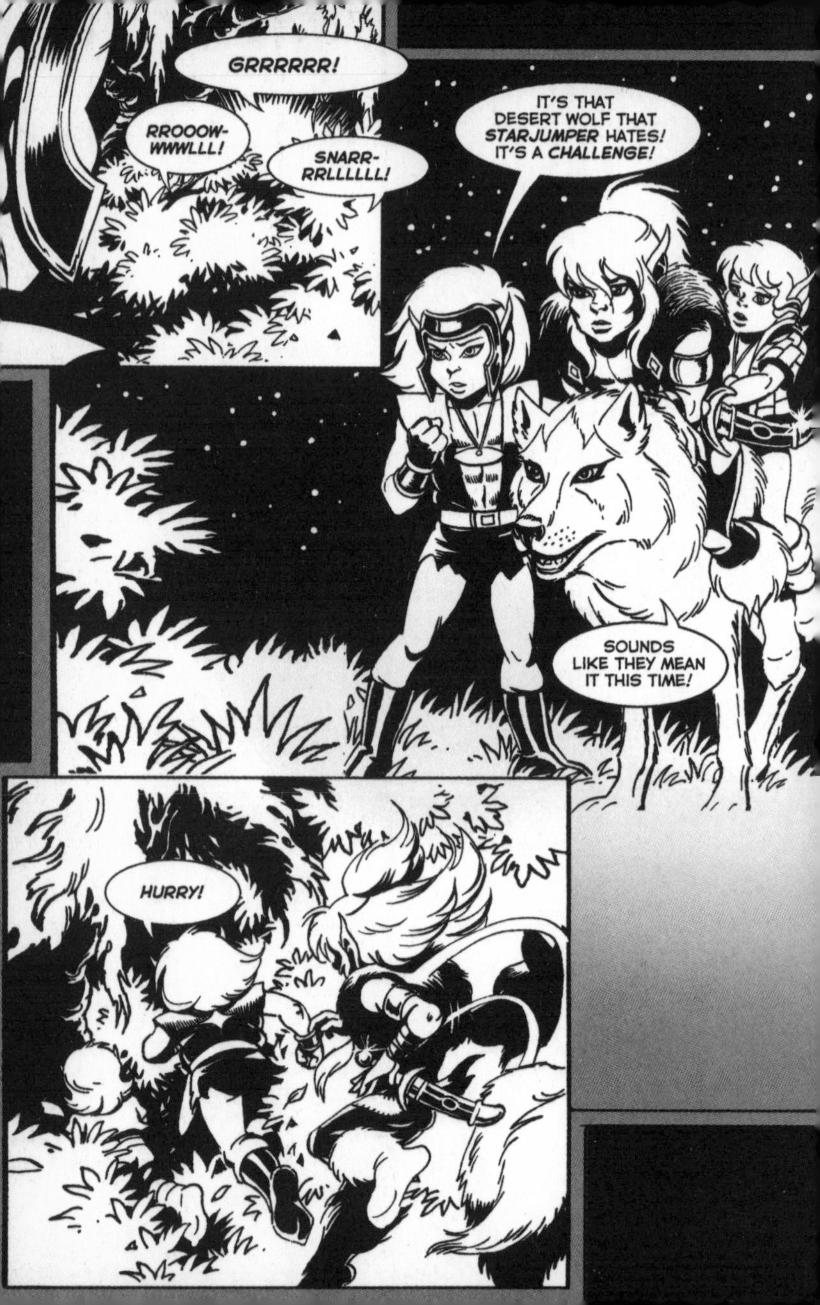

GRRRRRR!
RROOOW-WWWLLL!
SNARR-RRLLLLLLL!
IT'S THAT DESERT WOLF THAT STARJUMPER HATES! IT'S A CHALLENGE!
SOUNDS LIKE THEY MEAN IT THIS TIME!
HURRY!

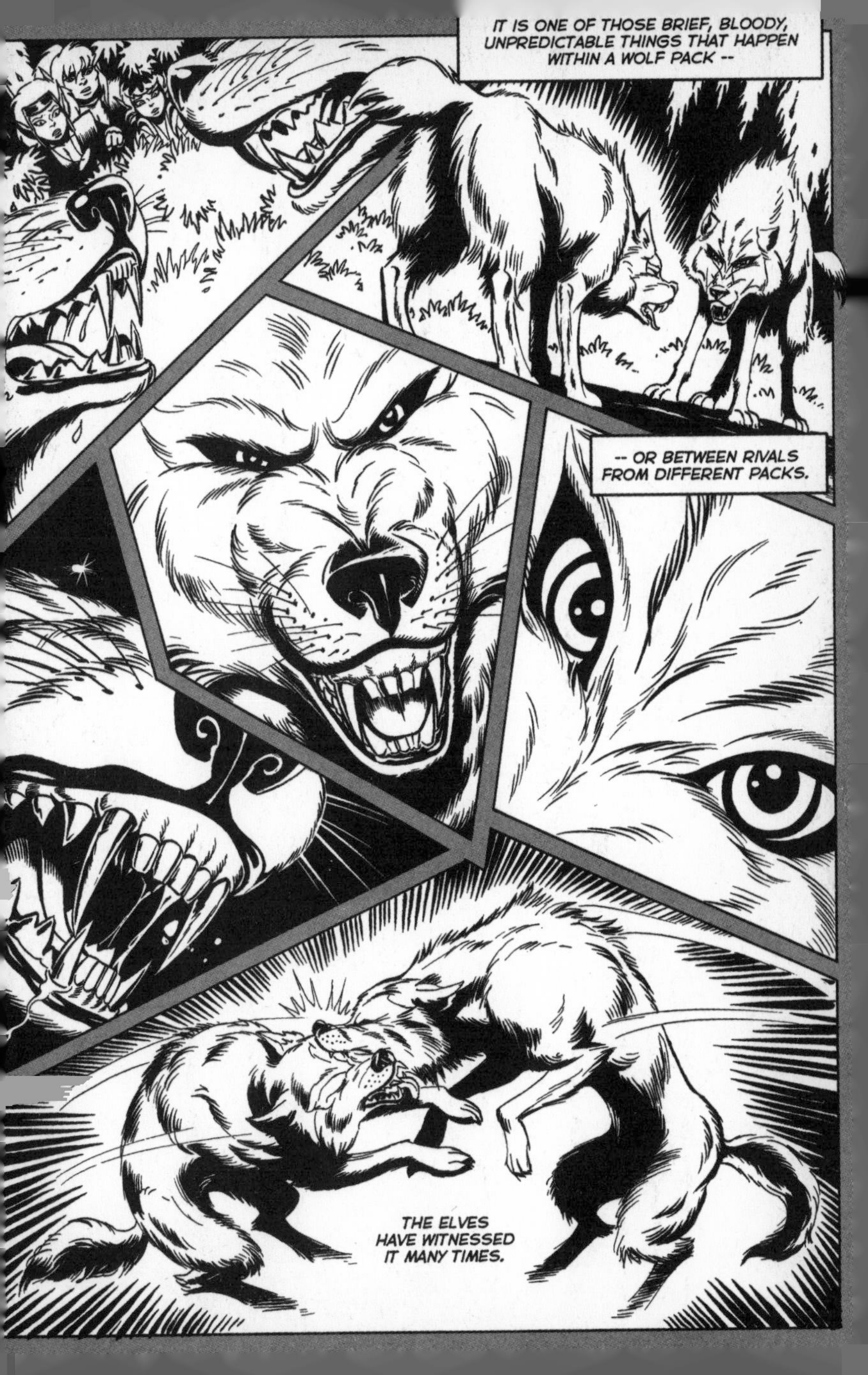
IT IS ONE OF THOSE BRIEF, BLOODY, UNPREDICTABLE THINGS THAT HAPPEN WITHIN A WOLF PACK --
-- OR BETWEEN RIVALS FROM DIFFERENT PACKS.
THE ELVES HAVE WITNESSED IT MANY TIMES.

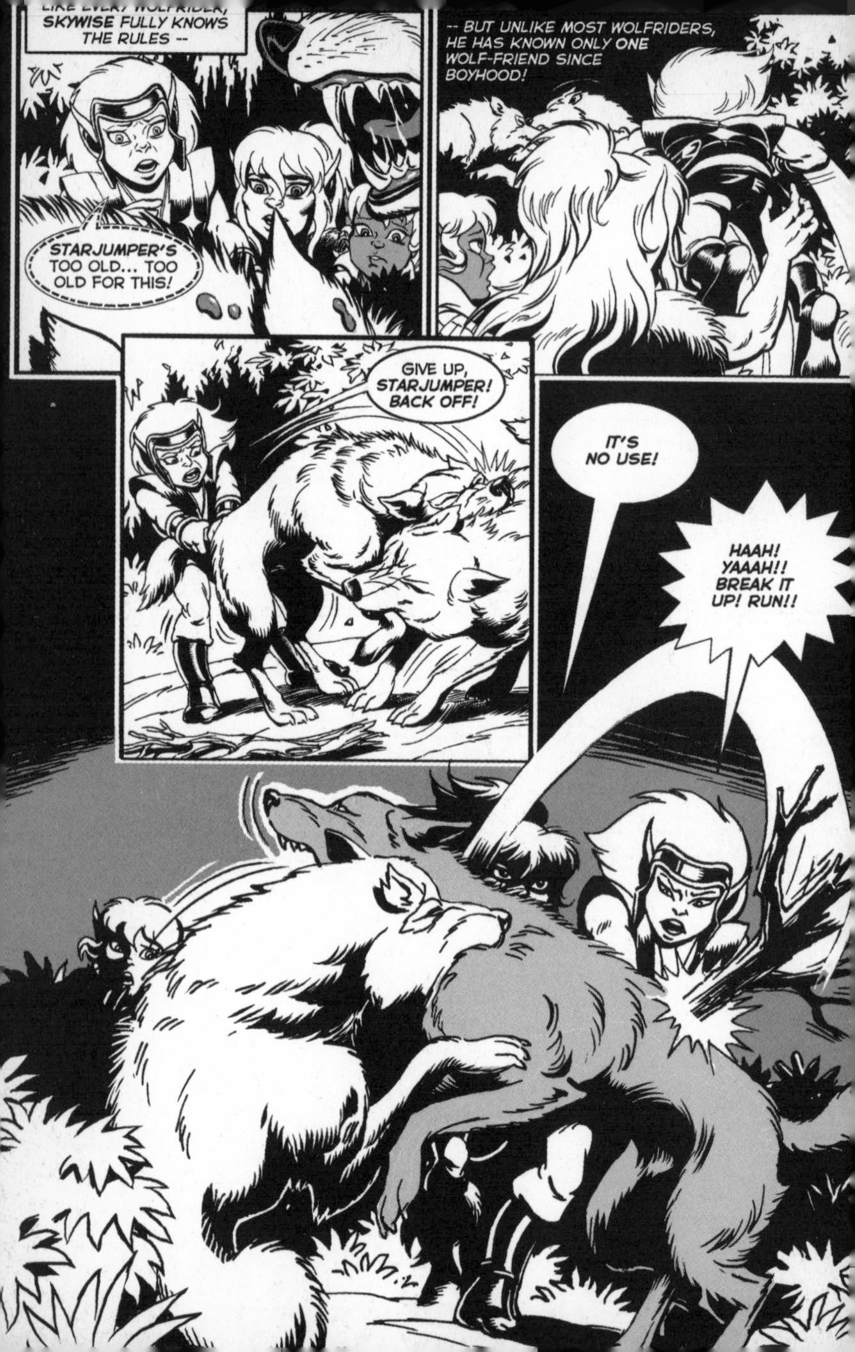
LIKE EVERY WOLFRIDER, SKYWISE FULLY KNOWS THE RULES --
STARJUMPER'S TOO OLD... TOO OLD FOR THIS!
-- BUT UNLIKE MOST WOLFRIDERS, HE HAS KNOWN ONLY ONE WOLF-FRIEND SINCE BOYHOOD!
GIVE UP, STARJUMPER! BACK OFF!
IT'S NO USE!
HAAH! YAAAH!! BREAK IT UP! RUN!!

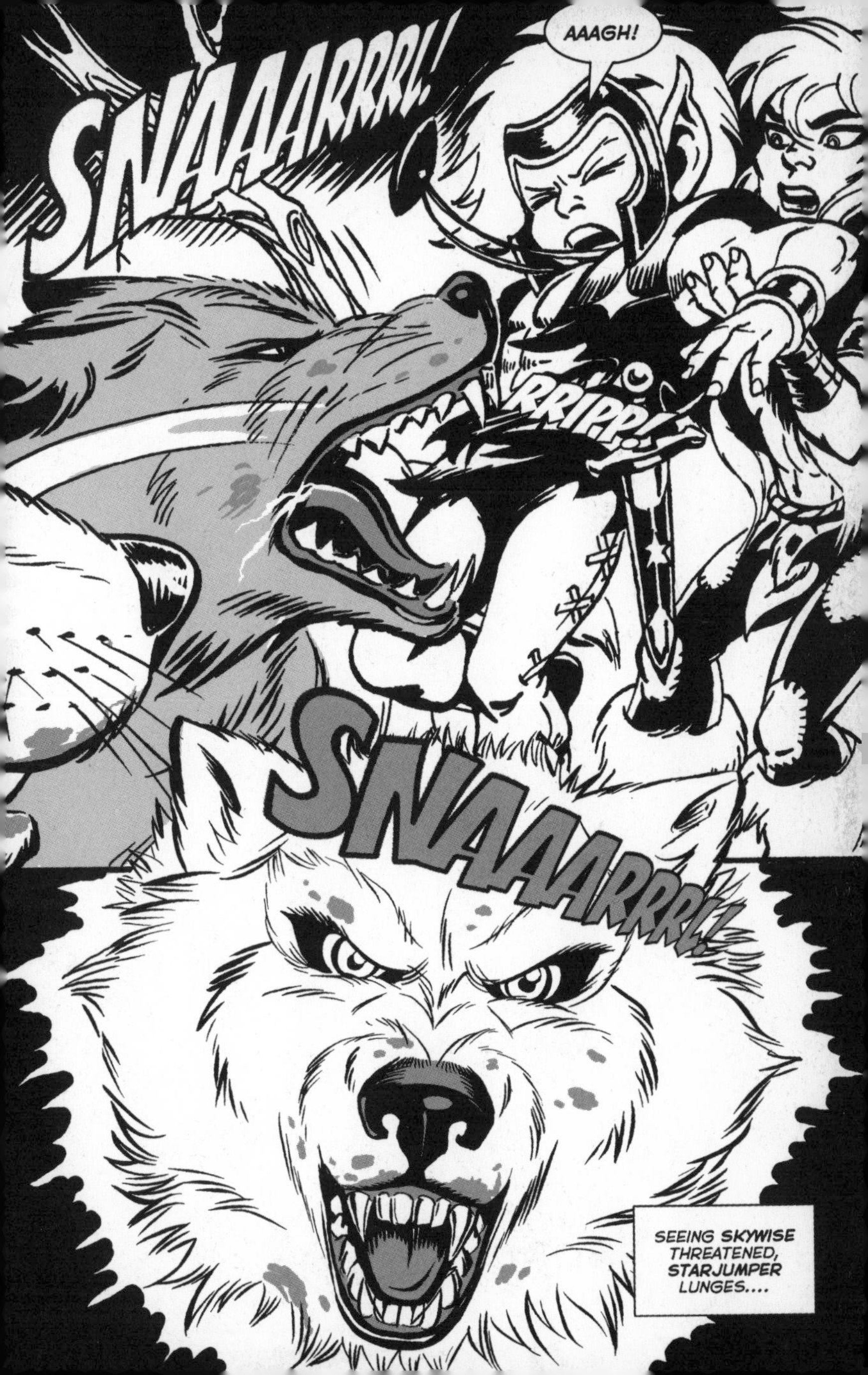
SNAAARRRL!
AAAGH!
RRIPP!
SNAAARRRL!
SEEING SKYWISE THREATENED, STARJUMPER LUNGES....

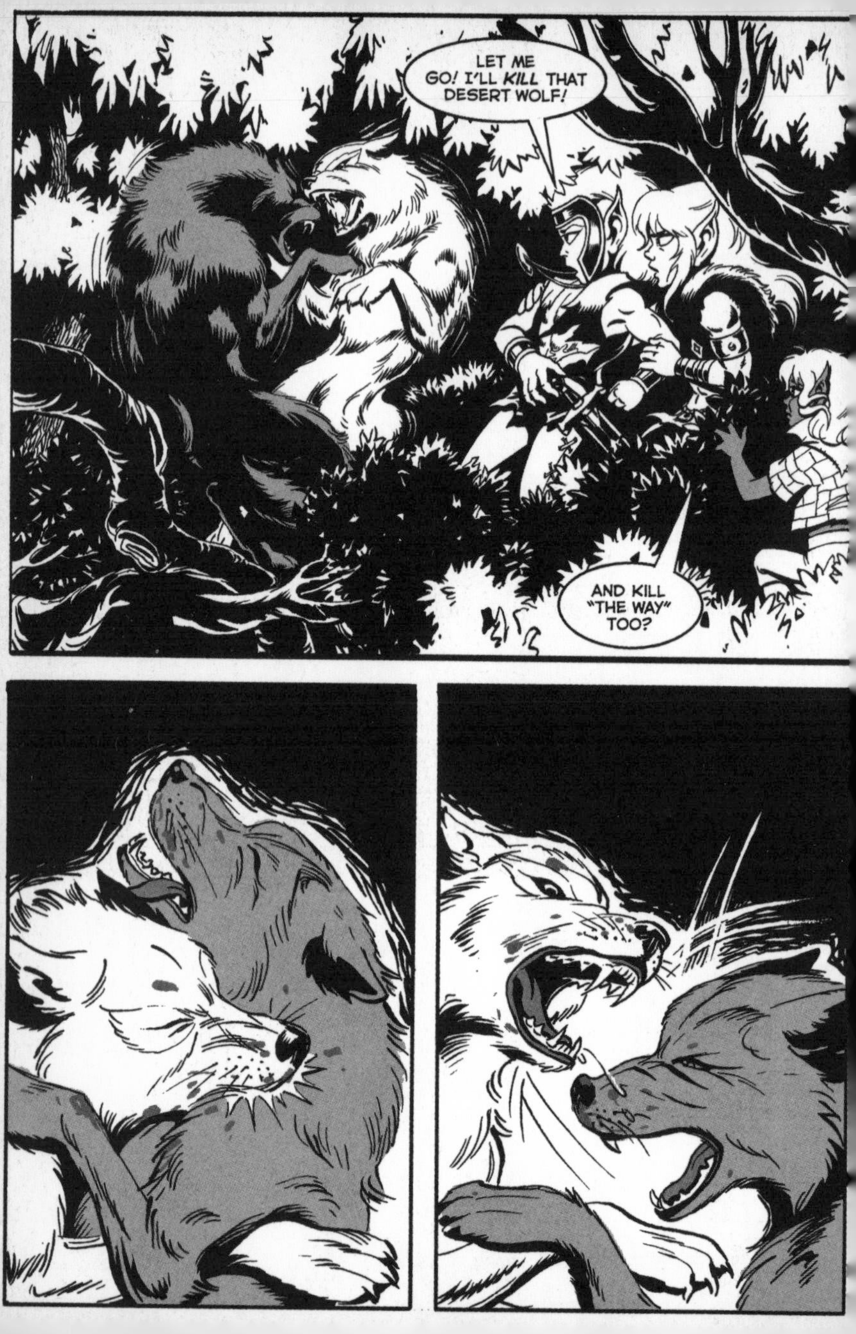
LET ME GO! I'LL *KILL* THAT DESERT WOLF!
AND KILL "THE WAY" TOO?

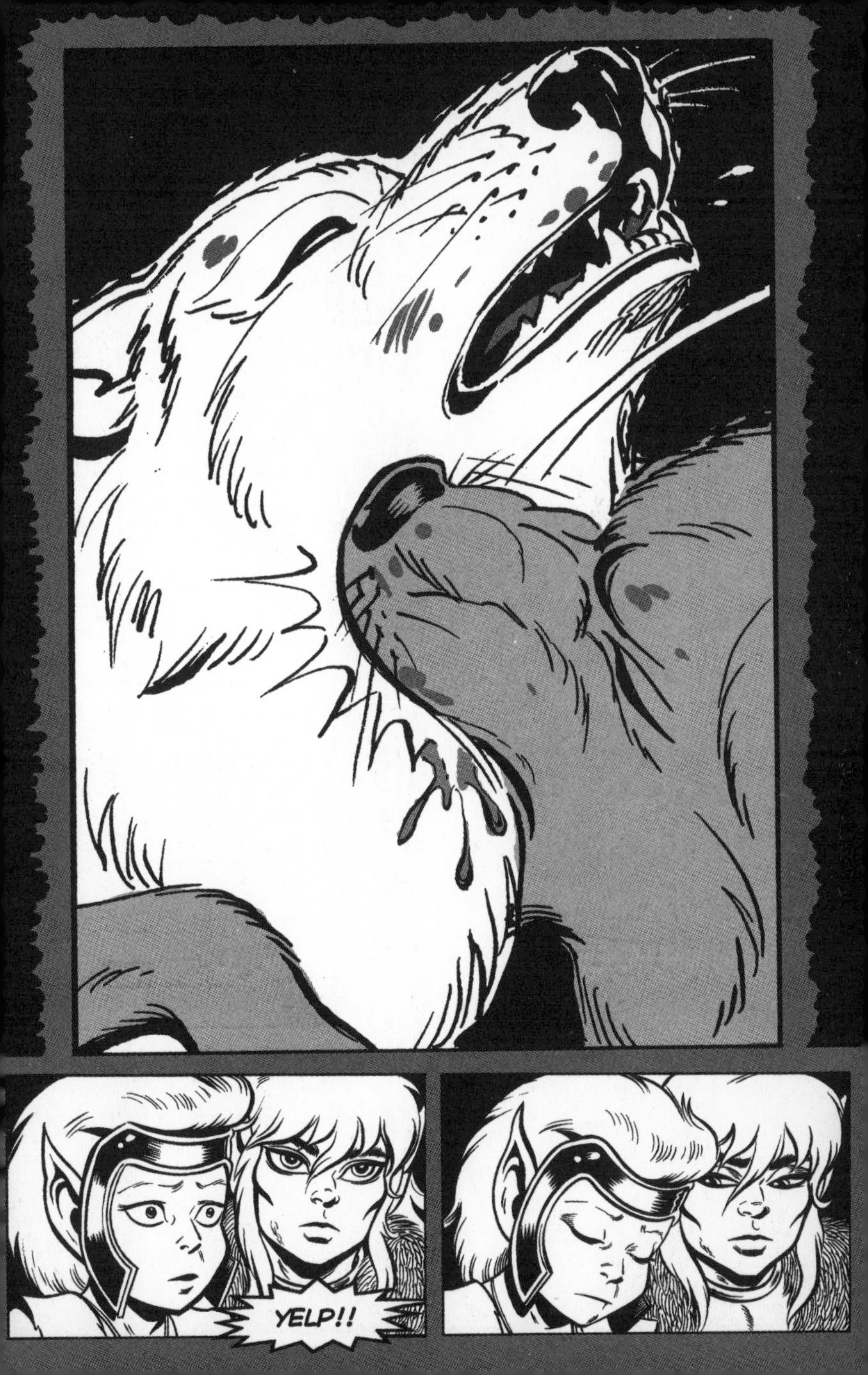
YELP!!

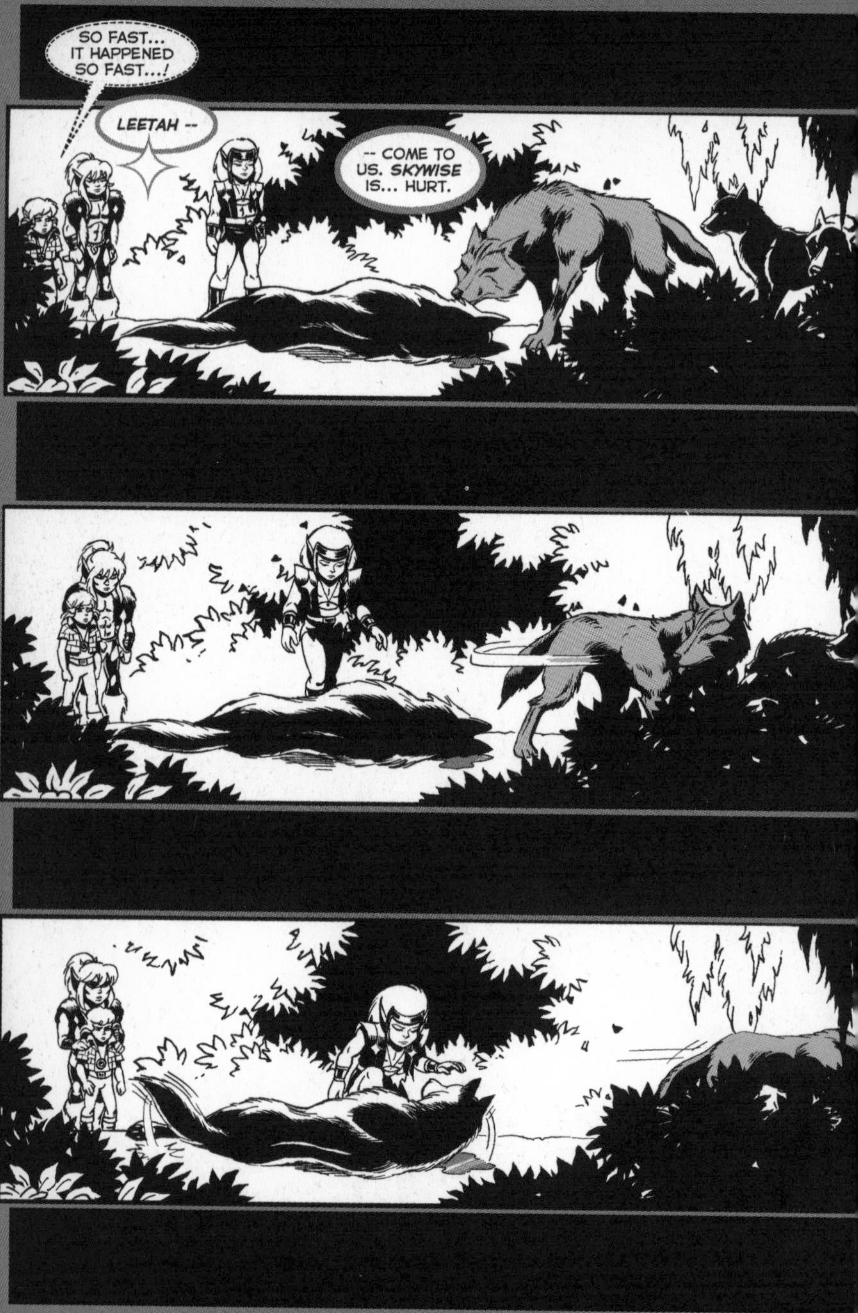
SO FAST... IT HAPPENED SO FAST...!
LEETAH --
-- COME TO US. SKYWISE IS... HURT.

IT'S HIS THROAT...

LEETAH'S COMING. SHE KNOWS. SHE'LL BE HERE IN A HEART-BEAT.

YOU CAN SEE... AS WELL AS I...

EVEN THAT'S TOO LONG TO WAIT.

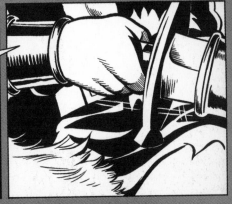

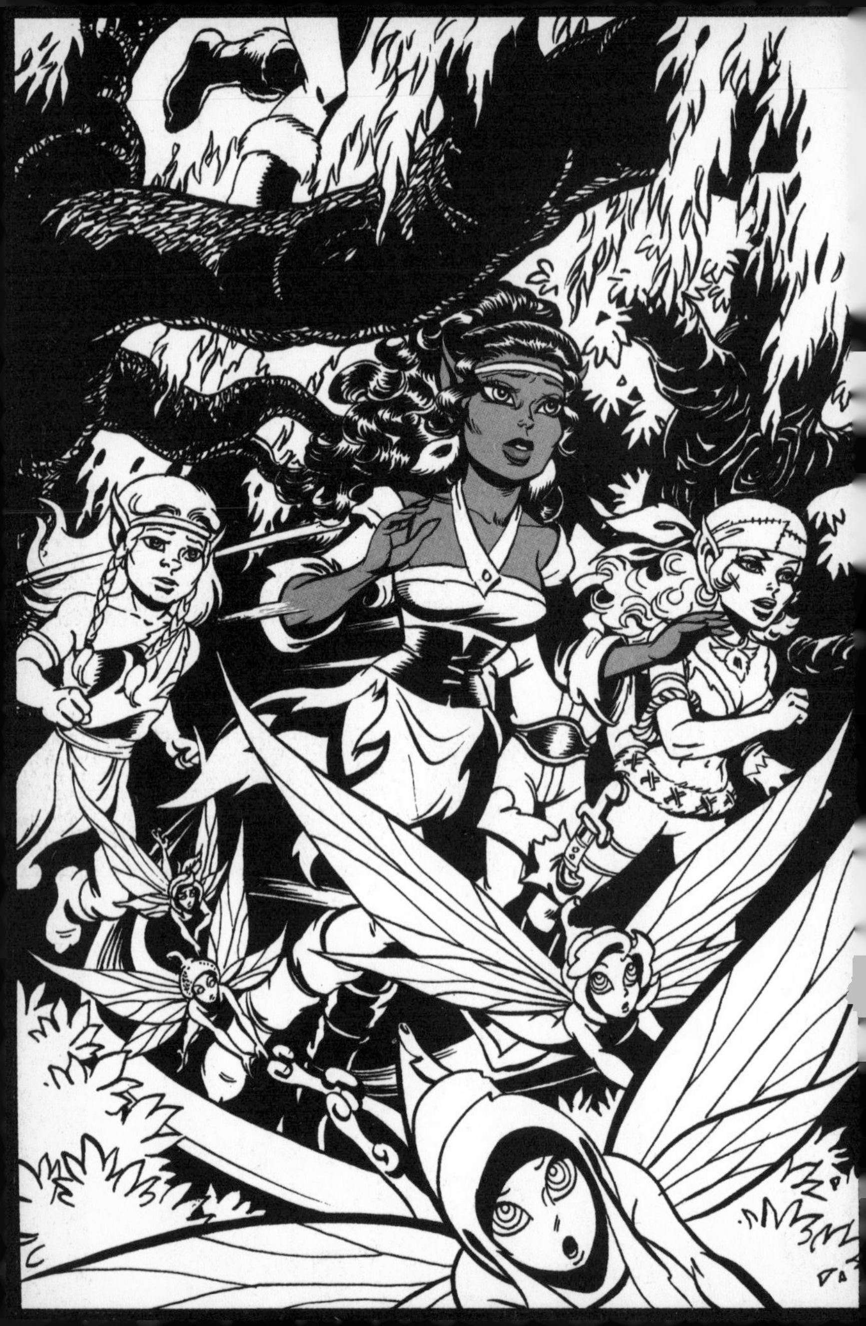

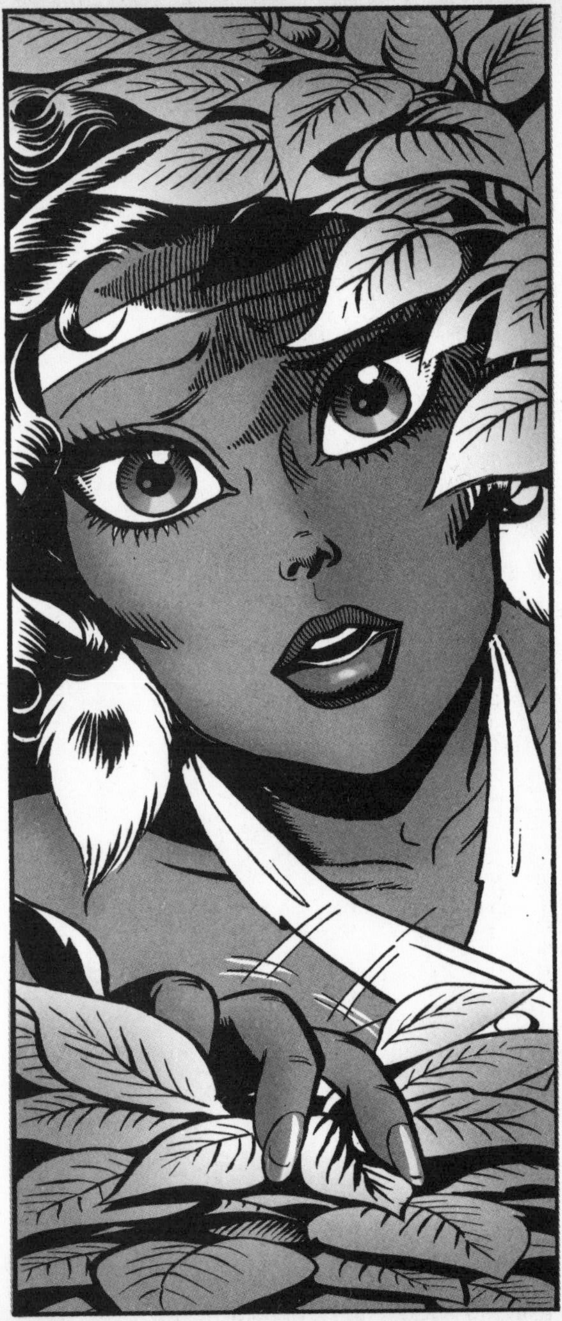

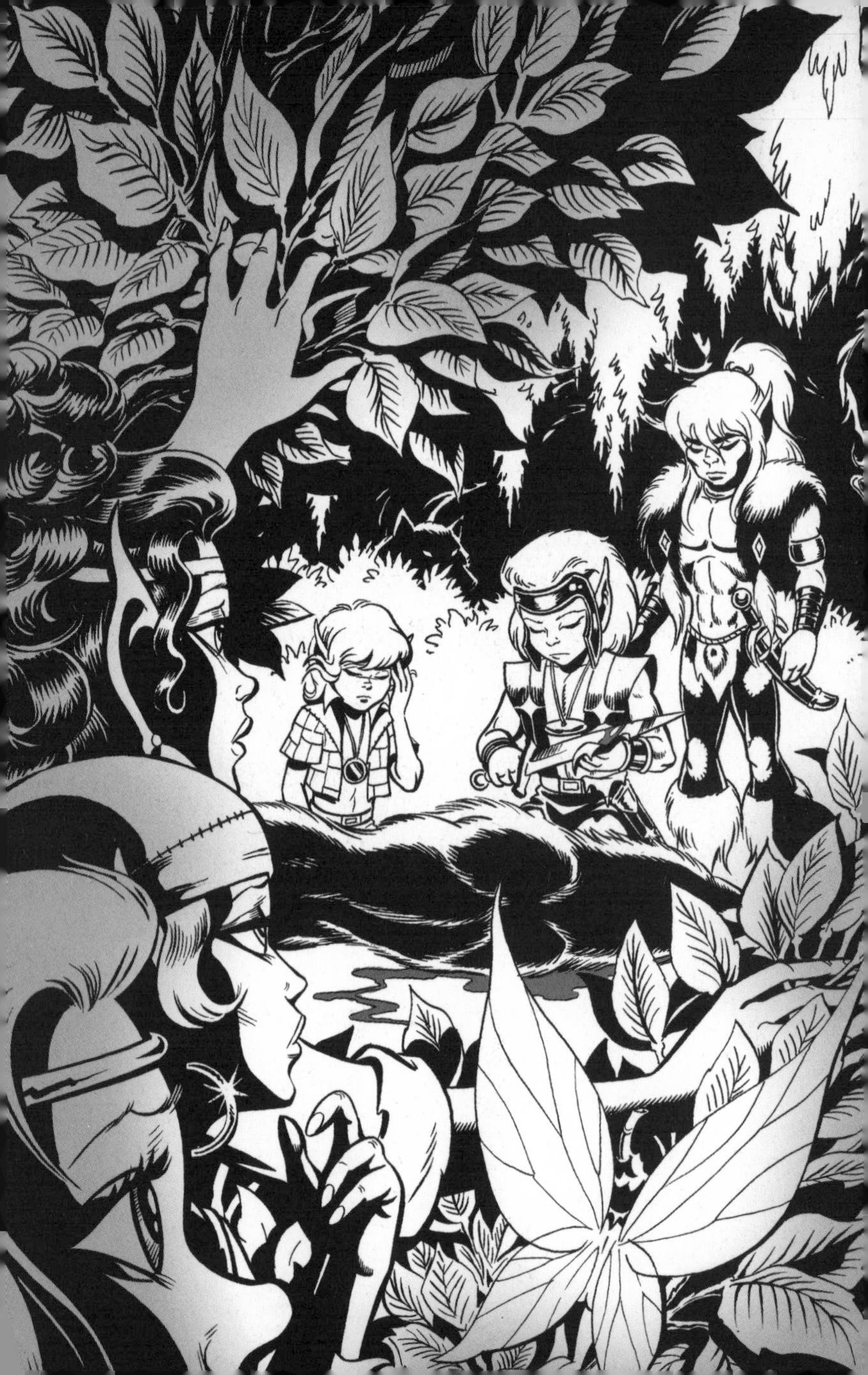

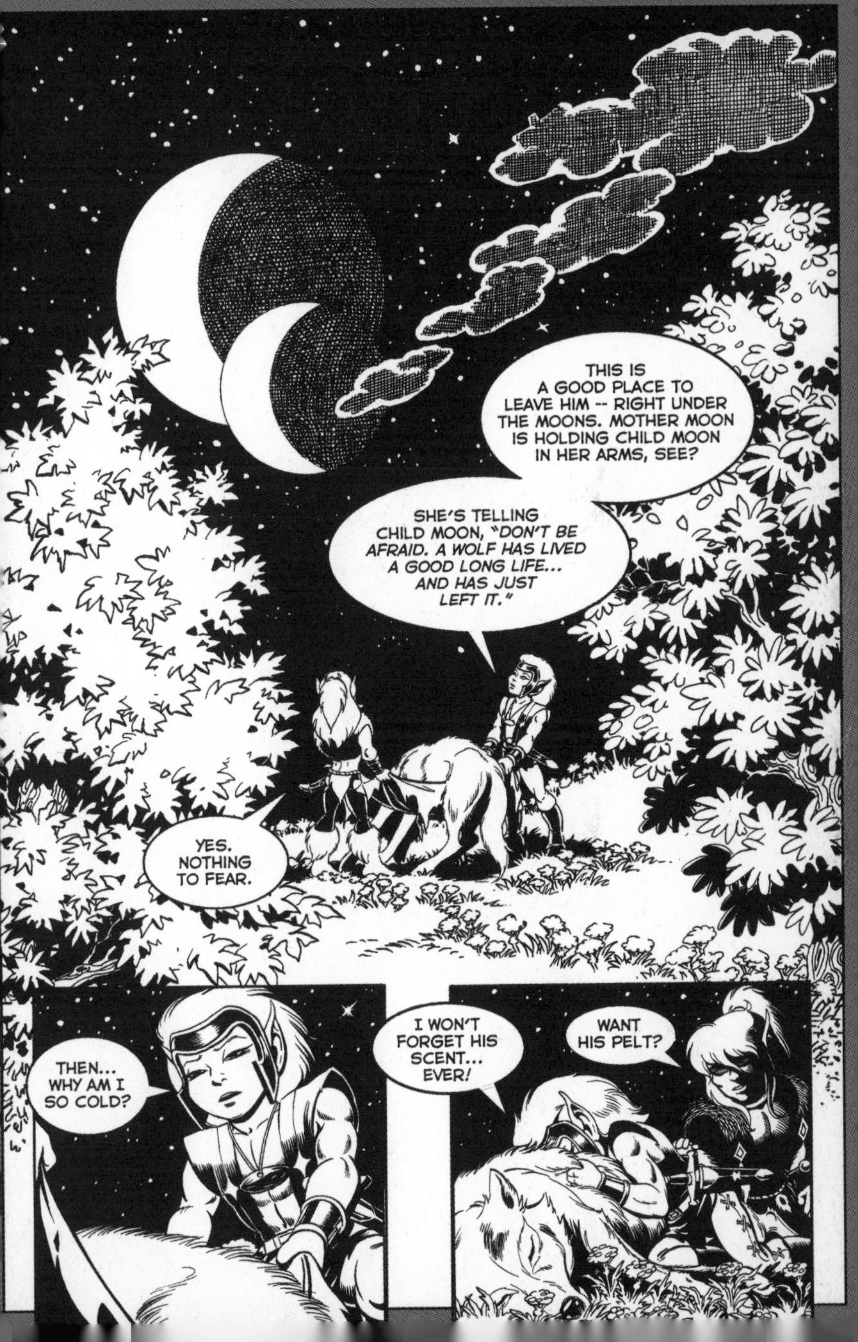

THIS IS A GOOD PLACE TO LEAVE HIM -- RIGHT UNDER THE MOONS. MOTHER MOON IS HOLDING CHILD MOON IN HER ARMS, SEE?
SHE'S TELLING CHILD MOON, "DON'T BE AFRAID. A WOLF HAS LIVED A GOOD LONG LIFE... AND HAS JUST LEFT IT."
YES. NOTHING TO FEAR.
THEN... WHY AM I SO COLD?
I WON'T FORGET HIS SCENT... EVER!
WANT HIS PELT?

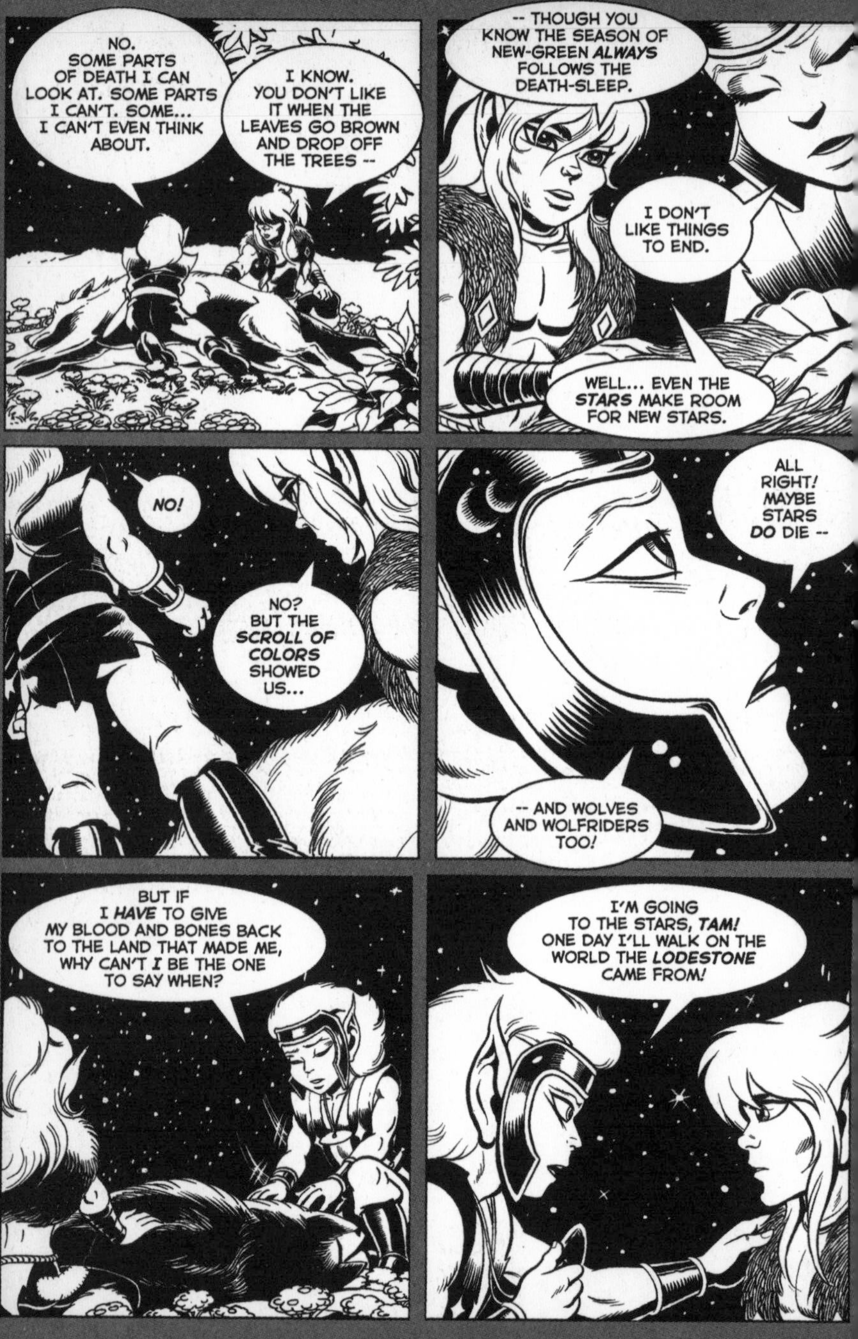
NO. SOME PARTS OF DEATH I CAN LOOK AT. SOME PARTS I CAN'T. SOME... I CAN'T EVEN THINK ABOUT.
I KNOW. YOU DON'T LIKE IT WHEN THE LEAVES GO BROWN AND DROP OFF THE TREES --
-- THOUGH YOU KNOW THE SEASON OF NEW-GREEN ALWAYS FOLLOWS THE DEATH-SLEEP.
I DON'T LIKE THINGS TO END.
WELL... EVEN THE STARS MAKE ROOM FOR NEW STARS.
NO!
NO? BUT THE SCROLL OF COLORS SHOWED US...
ALL RIGHT! MAYBE STARS DO DIE --
-- AND WOLVES AND WOLFRIDERS TOO!
BUT IF I HAVE TO GIVE MY BLOOD AND BONES BACK TO THE LAND THAT MADE ME, WHY CAN'T I BE THE ONE TO SAY WHEN?
I'M GOING TO THE STARS, TAM! ONE DAY I'LL WALK ON THE WORLD THE LODESTONE CAME FROM!

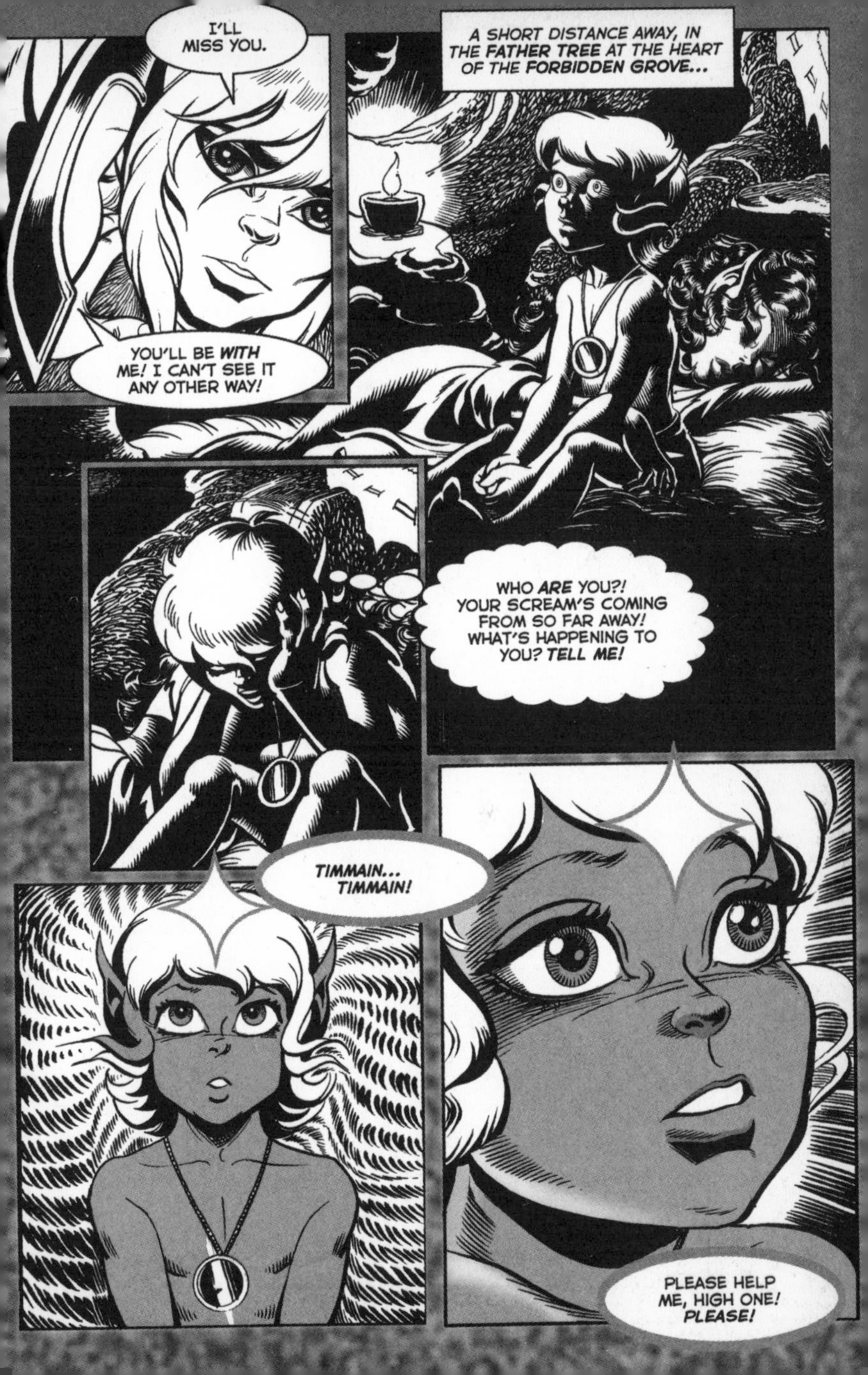
I'LL MISS YOU.
YOU'LL BE WITH ME! I CAN'T SEE IT ANY OTHER WAY!
A SHORT DISTANCE AWAY, IN THE FATHER TREE AT THE HEART OF THE FORBIDDEN GROVE...
WHO ARE YOU?! YOUR SCREAM'S COMING FROM SO FAR AWAY! WHAT'S HAPPENING TO YOU? TELL ME!
TIMMAIN... TIMMAIN!
PLEASE HELP ME, HIGH ONE! PLEASE!

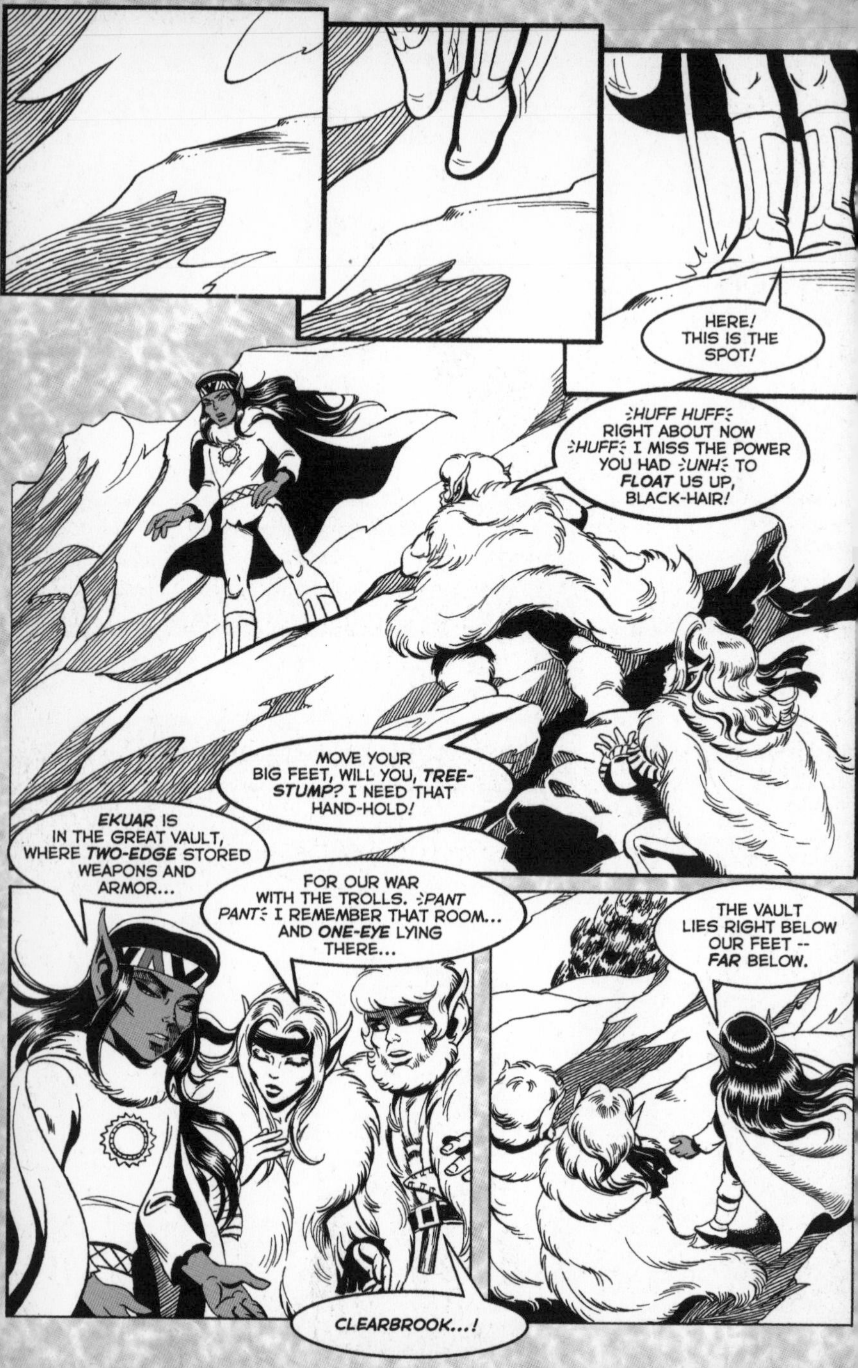
HERE! THIS IS THE SPOT!
HUFF HUFF RIGHT ABOUT NOW HUFF I MISS THE POWER YOU HAD UNH TO FLOAT US UP, BLACK-HAIR!
MOVE YOUR BIG FEET, WILL YOU, TREE-STUMP? I NEED THAT HAND-HOLD!
EKUAR IS IN THE GREAT VAULT, WHERE TWO-EDGE STORED WEAPONS AND ARMOR...
FOR OUR WAR WITH THE TROLLS. PANT PANT I REMEMBER THAT ROOM... AND ONE-EYE LYING THERE...
CLEARBROOK...!
THE VAULT LIES RIGHT BELOW OUR FEET -- FAR BELOW.

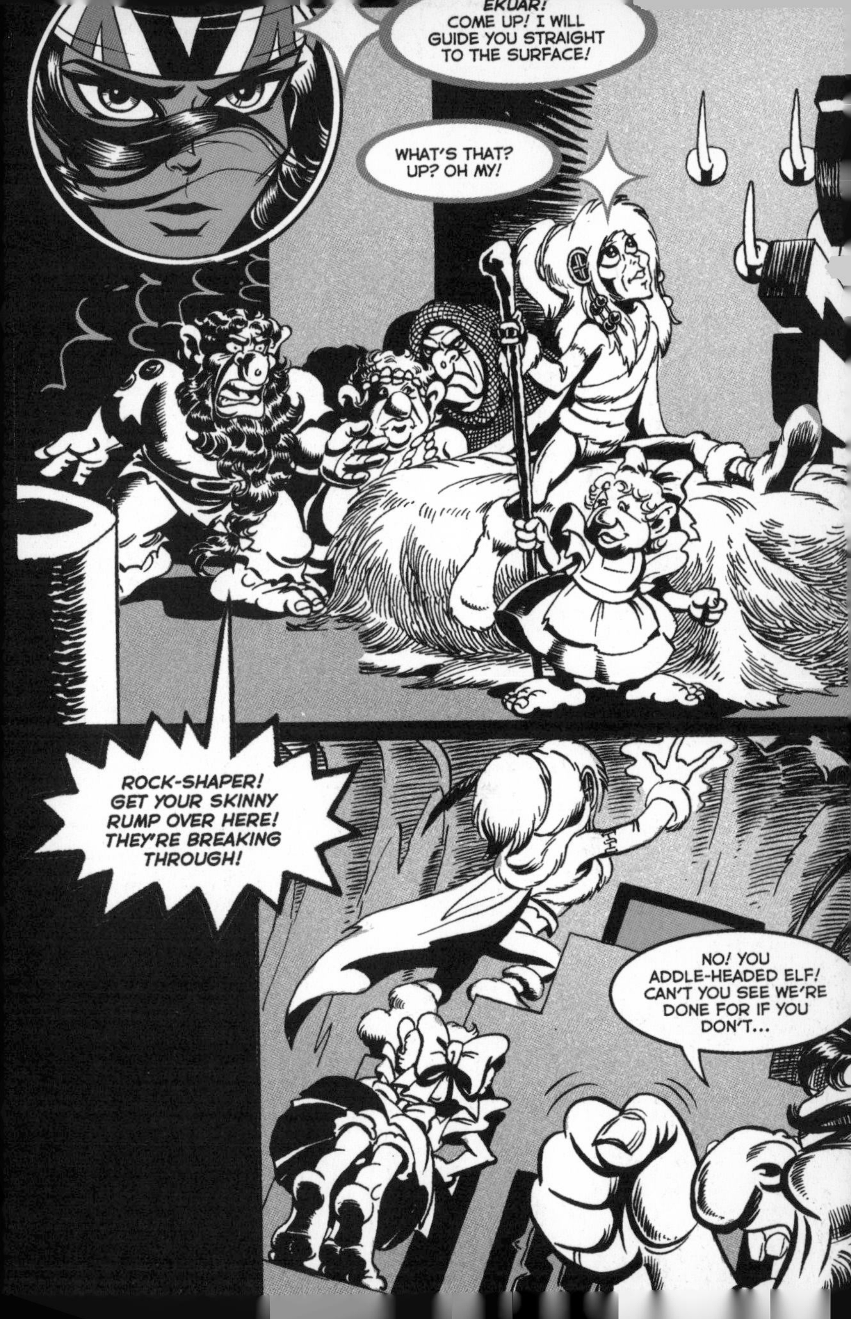
EKUAR! COME UP! I WILL GUIDE YOU STRAIGHT TO THE SURFACE!
WHAT'S THAT? UP? OH MY!
ROCK-SHAPER! GET YOUR SKINNY RUMP OVER HERE! THEY'RE BREAKING THROUGH!
NO! YOU ADDLE-HEADED ELF! CAN'T YOU SEE WE'RE DONE FOR IF YOU DON'T...

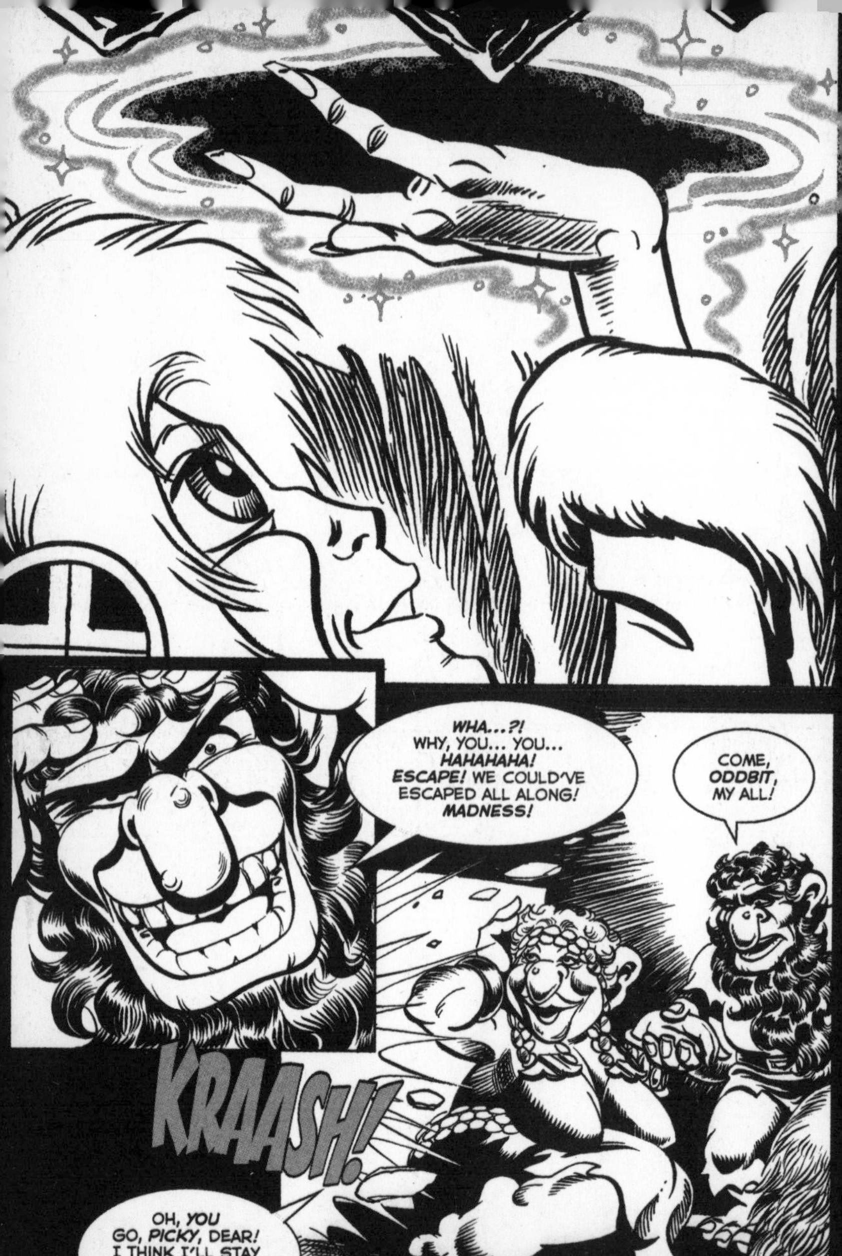
WHA...?! WHY, YOU... YOU... HAHAHAHA! ESCAPE! WE COULD'VE ESCAPED ALL ALONG! MADNESS!
COME, ODDBIT, MY ALL!
KRAASH!
OH, YOU GO, PICKY, DEAR! I THINK I'LL STAY AND TAKE MY

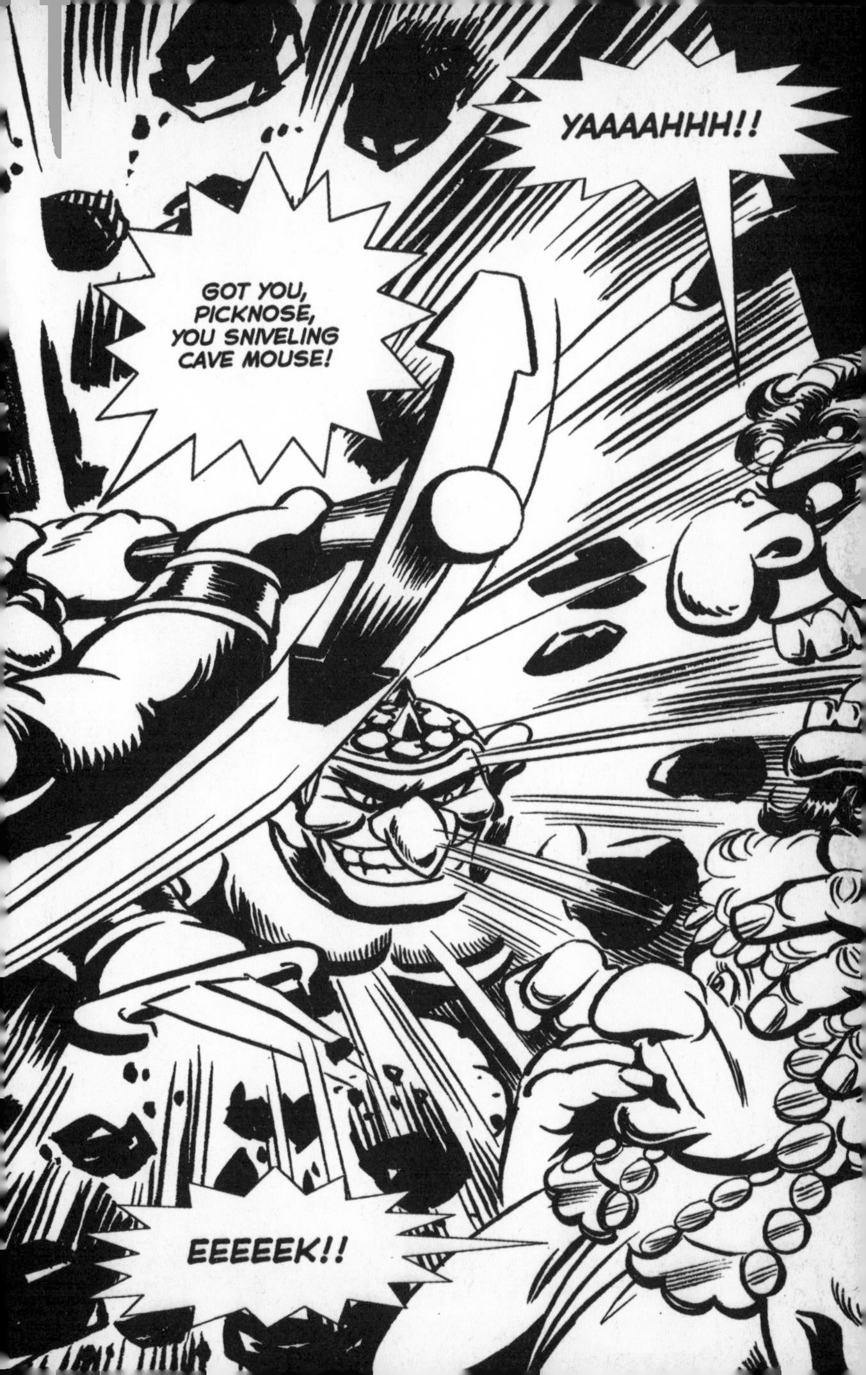
YAAAAHHH!!
GOT YOU, PICKNOSE, YOU SNIVELING CAVE MOUSE!
EEEEEK!!

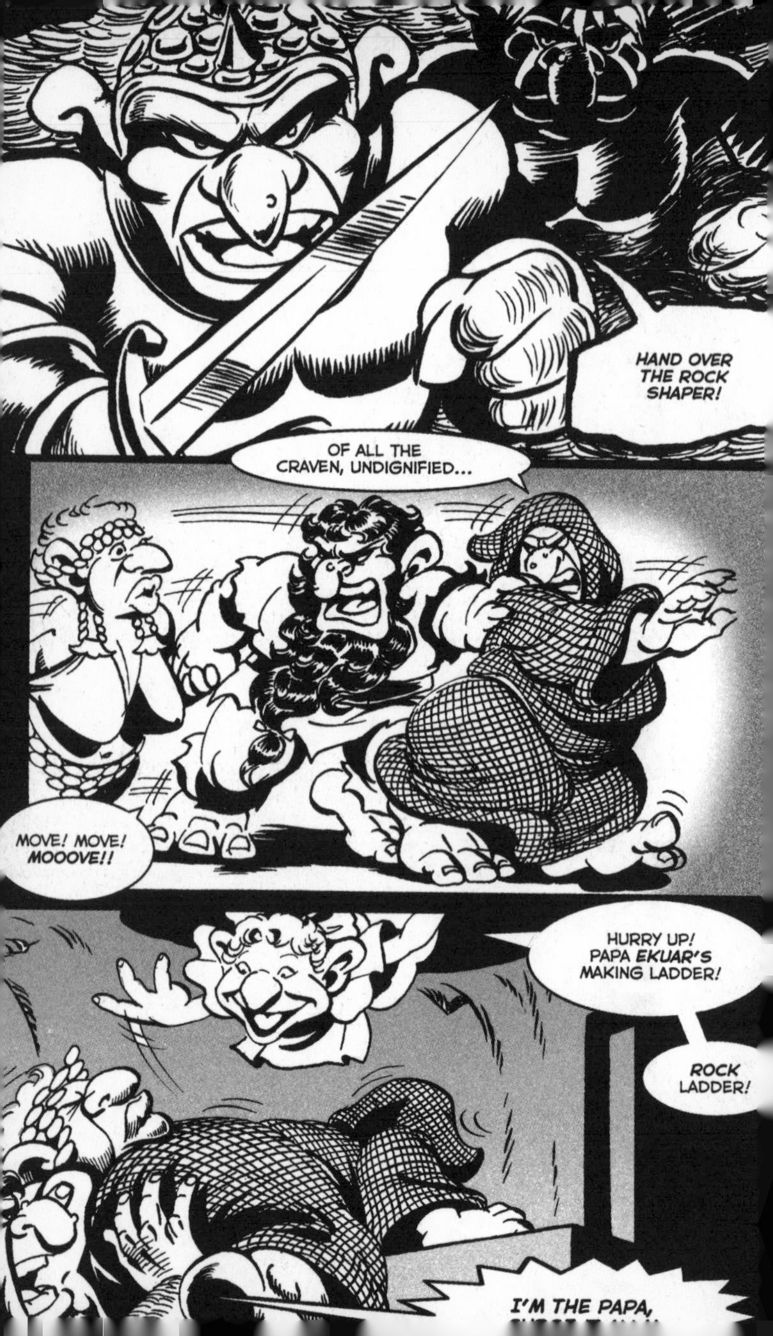
HAND OVER THE ROCK SHAPER!
OF ALL THE CRAVEN, UNDIGNIFIED...
MOVE! MOVE! MOOOVE!!
HURRY UP! PAPA EKUAR'S MAKING LADDER!
ROCK LADDER!
I'M THE PAPA,

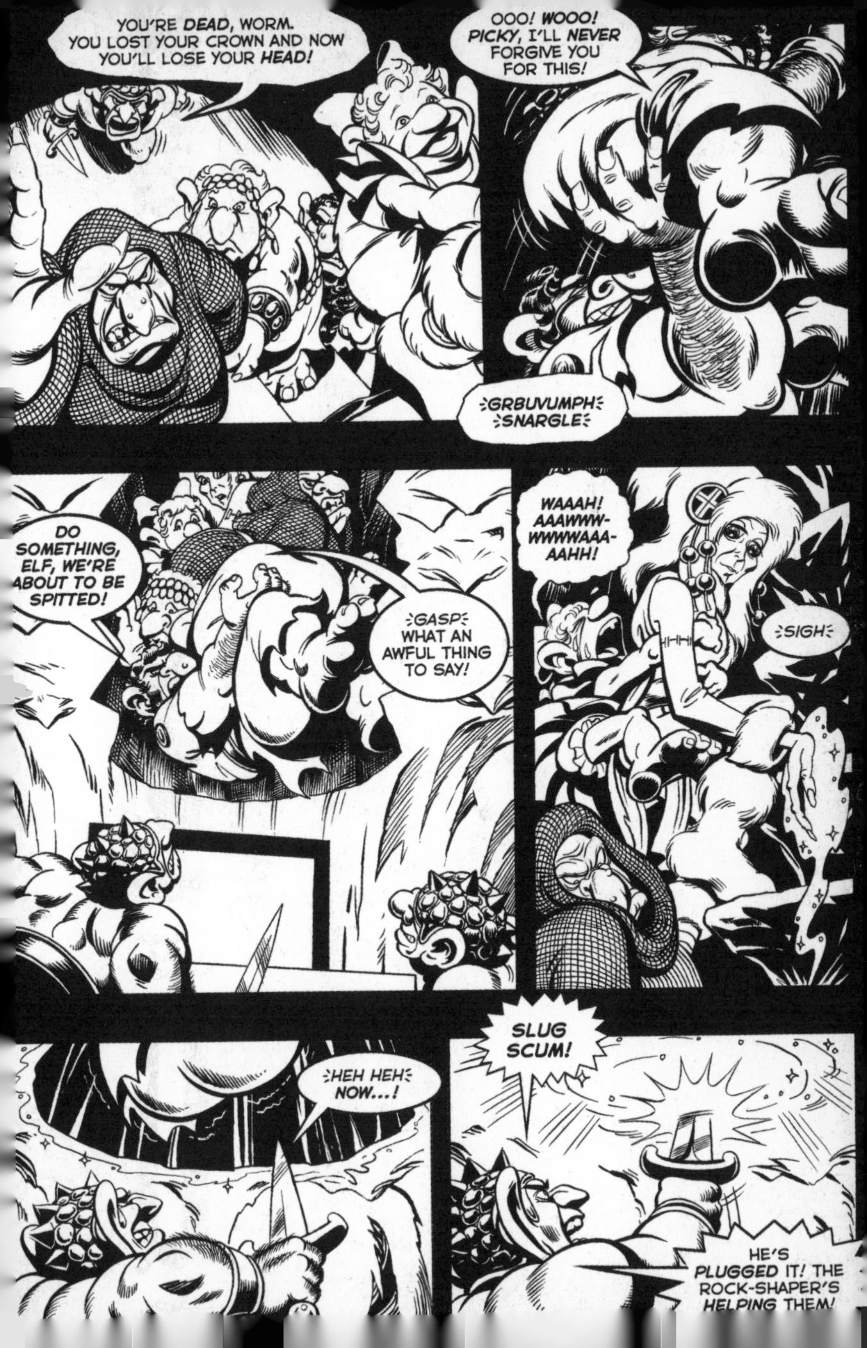
YOU'RE DEAD, WORM. YOU LOST YOUR CROWN AND NOW YOU'LL LOSE YOUR HEAD!
OOO! WOOO! PICKY, I'LL NEVER FORGIVE YOU FOR THIS!
GRBUVUMPH SNARGLE
DO SOMETHING, ELF, WE'RE ABOUT TO BE SPITTED!
GASP WHAT AN AWFUL THING TO SAY!
WAAAH! AAAWWW-WWWWAAA-AAHH!
SIGH
HEH HEH NOW...!
SLUG SCUM!
HE'S PLUGGED IT! THE ROCK-SHAPER'S HELPING THEM!

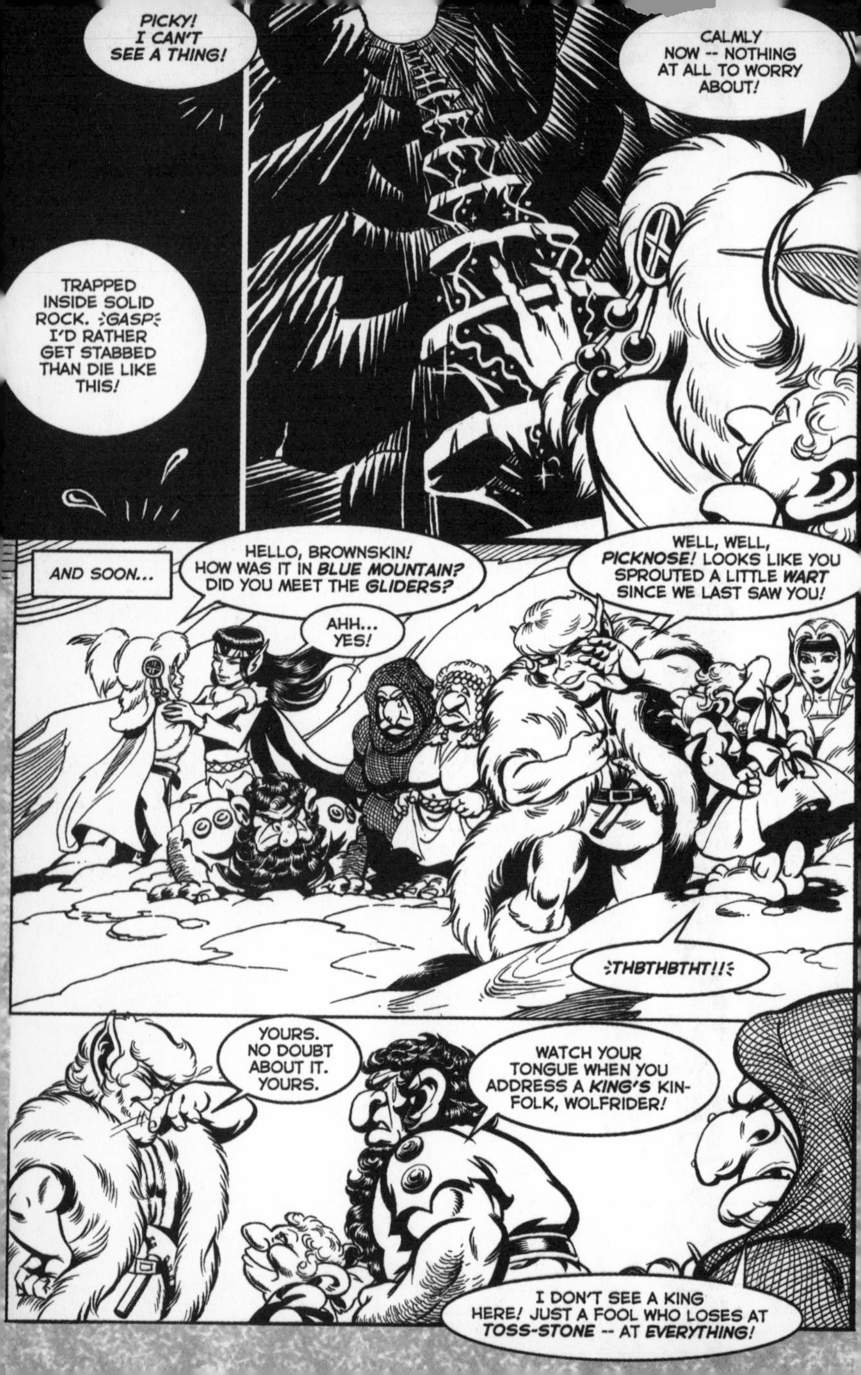
PICKY! I CAN'T SEE A THING!
TRAPPED INSIDE SOLID ROCK. GASP I'D RATHER GET STABBED THAN DIE LIKE THIS!
CALMLY NOW -- NOTHING AT ALL TO WORRY ABOUT!
AND SOON...
HELLO, BROWNSKIN! HOW WAS IT IN BLUE MOUNTAIN? DID YOU MEET THE GLIDERS?
AHH... YES!
WELL, WELL, PICKNOSE! LOOKS LIKE YOU SPROUTED A LITTLE WART SINCE WE LAST SAW YOU!
THBTHBTHT!!
YOURS. NO DOUBT ABOUT IT. YOURS.
WATCH YOUR TONGUE WHEN YOU ADDRESS A KING'S KIN-FOLK, WOLFRIDER!
I DON'T SEE A KING HERE! JUST A FOOL WHO LOSES AT TOSS-STONE -- AT EVERYTHING!

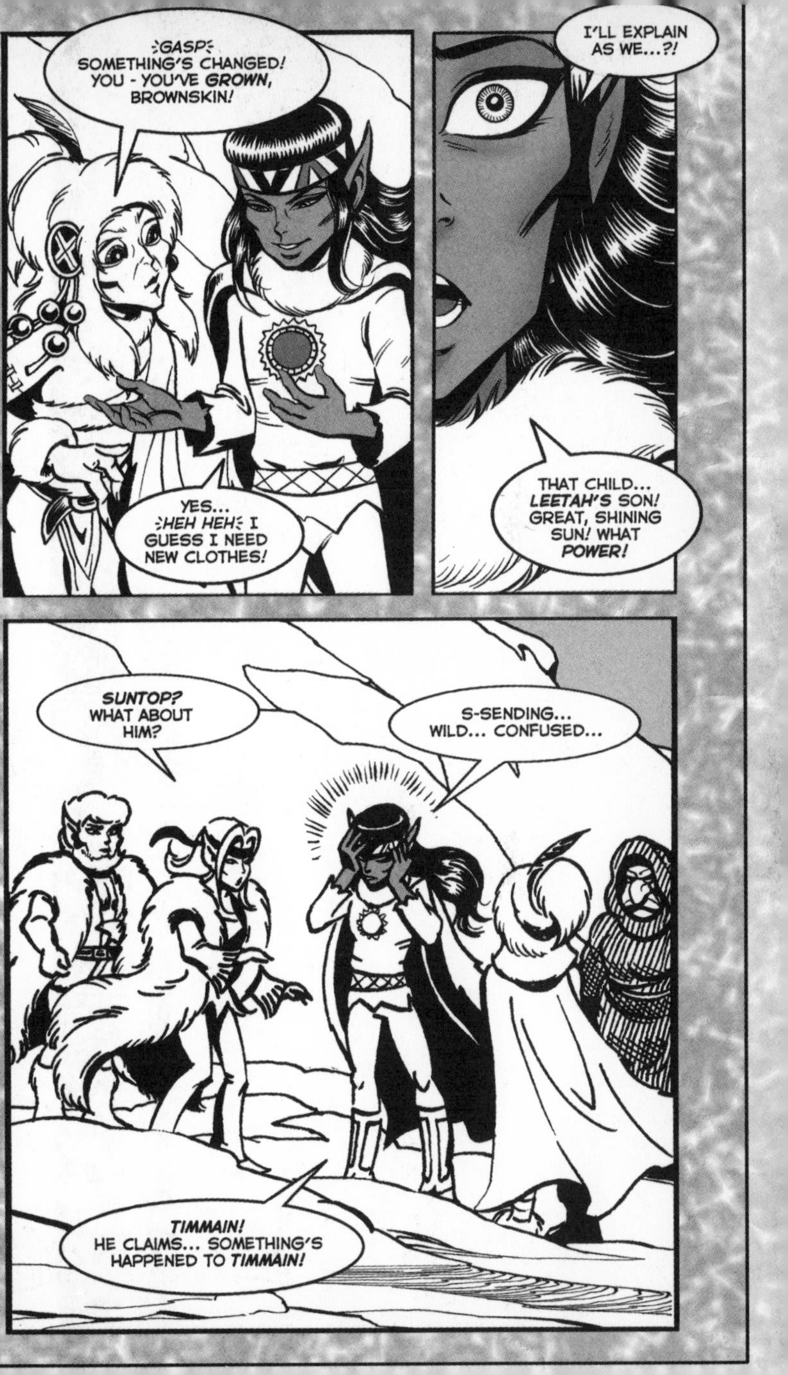

GASP
SOMETHING'S CHANGED! YOU - YOU'VE GROWN, BROWNSKIN!
YES... HEH HEH I GUESS I NEED NEW CLOTHES!
I'LL EXPLAIN AS WE...?!
THAT CHILD... LEETAH'S SON! GREAT, SHINING SUN! WHAT POWER!
SUNTOP? WHAT ABOUT HIM?
S-SENDING... WILD... CONFUSED...
TIMMAIN! HE CLAIMS... SOMETHING'S HAPPENED TO TIMMAIN!

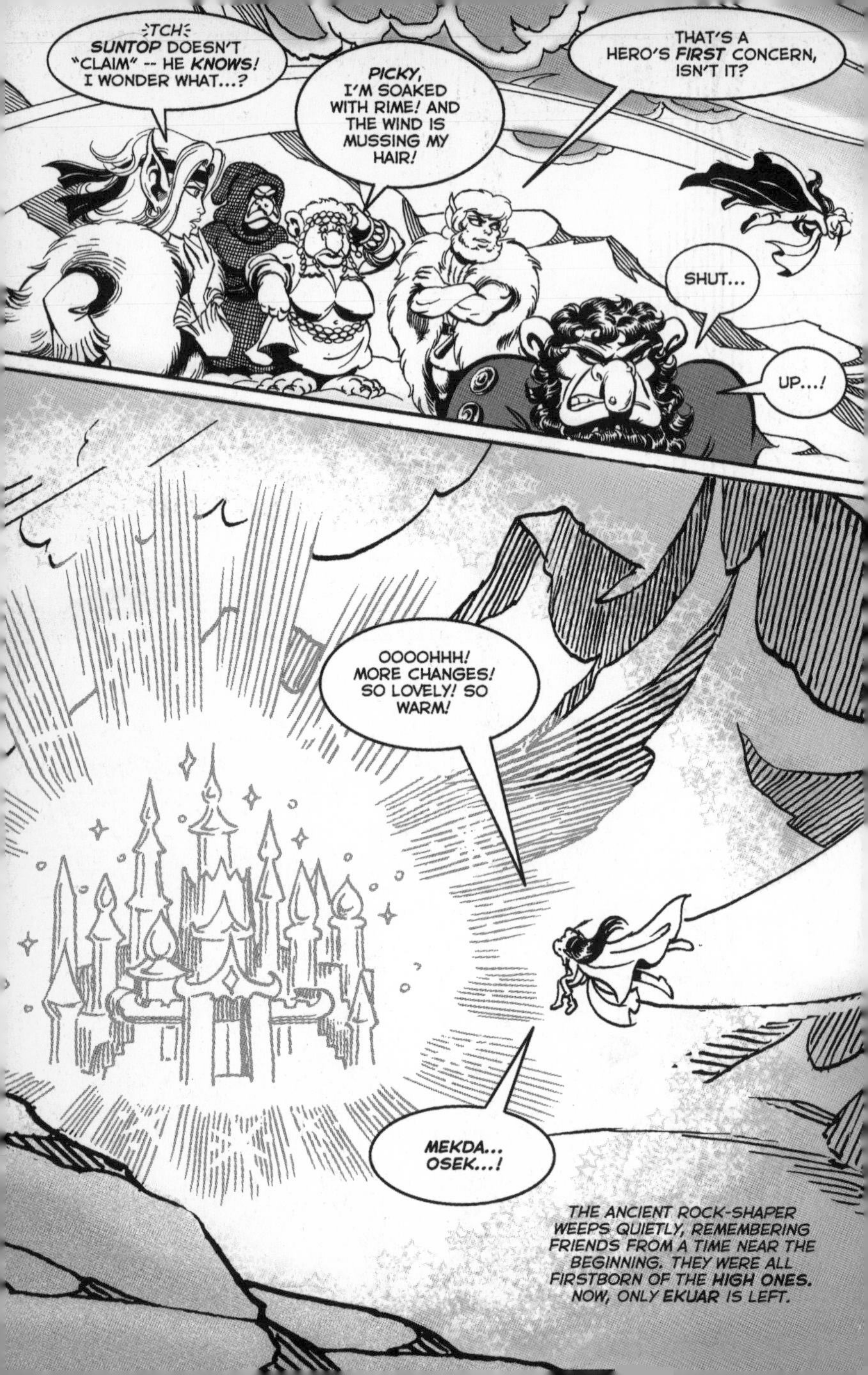
TCH
SUNTOP DOESN'T "CLAIM" -- HE KNOWS! I WONDER WHAT...?
PICKY, I'M SOAKED WITH RIME! AND THE WIND IS MUSSING MY HAIR!
THAT'S A HERO'S FIRST CONCERN, ISN'T IT?
SHUT...
UP...!
OOOOHHH! MORE CHANGES! SO LOVELY! SO WARM!
MEKDA... OSEK...!
THE ANCIENT ROCK-SHAPER WEEPS QUIETLY, REMEMBERING FRIENDS FROM A TIME NEAR THE BEGINNING. THEY WERE ALL FIRSTBORN OF THE HIGH ONES. NOW, ONLY EKUAR IS LEFT.

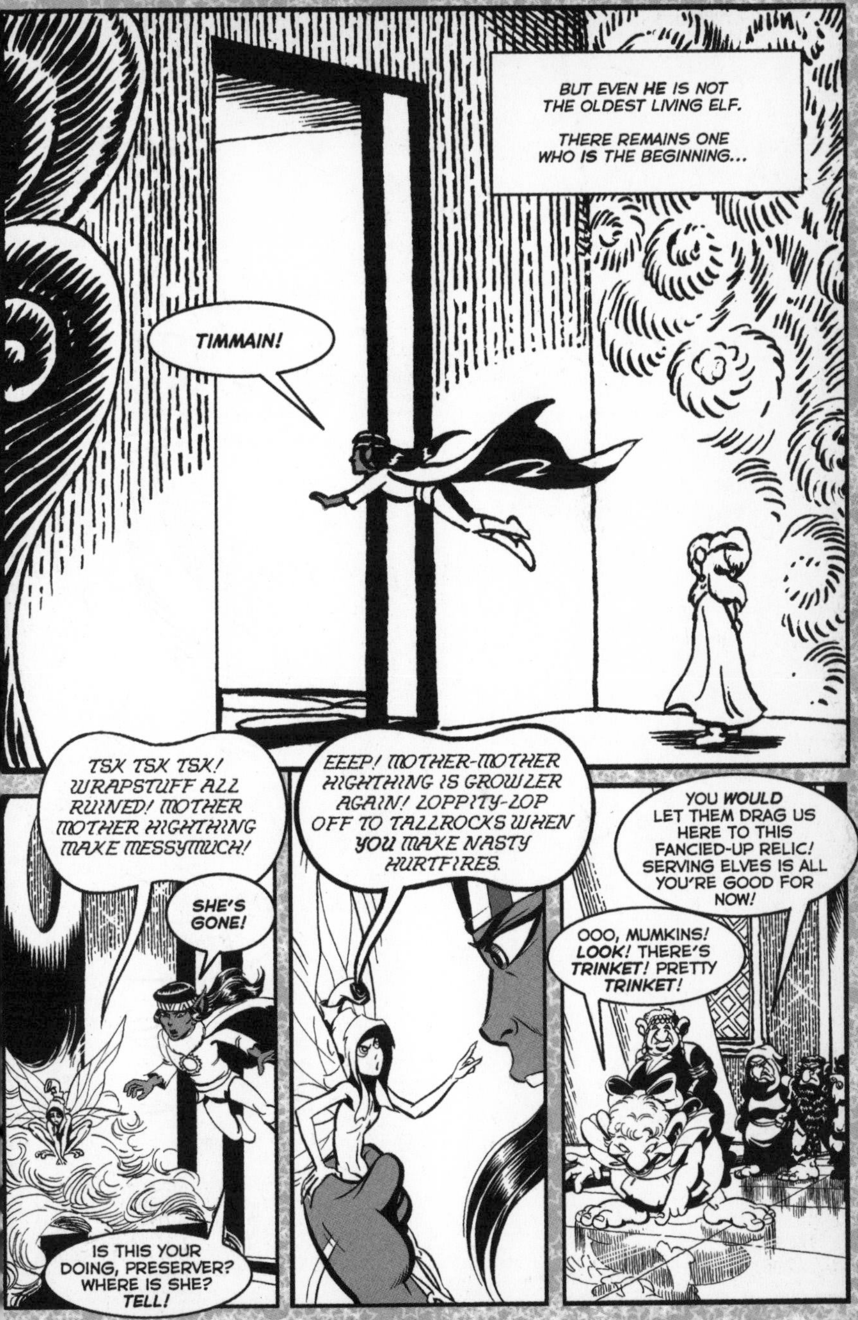
BUT EVEN HE IS NOT THE OLDEST LIVING ELF.

THERE REMAINS ONE WHO IS THE BEGINNING...
TIMMAIN!
TSK TSK TSK! WRAPSTUFF ALL RUINED! MOTHER MOTHER HIGHTHING MAKE MESSYMUCH!
SHE'S GONE!
IS THIS YOUR DOING, PRESERVER? WHERE IS SHE? TELL!
EEEP! MOTHER-MOTHER HIGHTHING IS GROWLER AGAIN! ZOPPITY-ZOP OFF TO TALLROCKS WHEN YOU MAKE NASTY HURTFIRES.
YOU WOULD LET THEM DRAG US HERE TO THIS FANCIED-UP RELIC! SERVING ELVES IS ALL YOU'RE GOOD FOR NOW!
OOO, MUMKINS! LOOK! THERE'S TRINKET! PRETTY TRINKET!

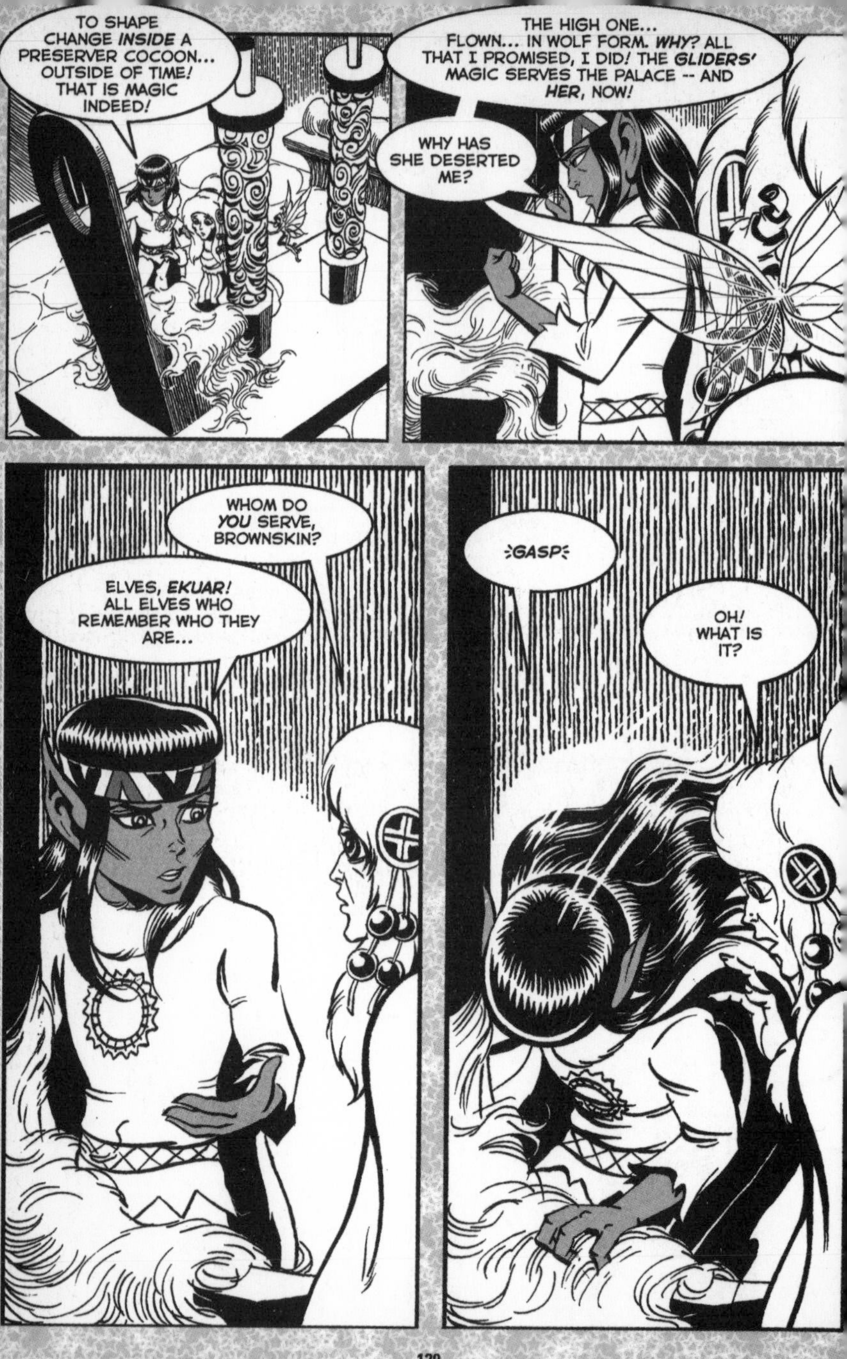
TO SHAPE CHANGE *INSIDE* A PRESERVER COCOON... OUTSIDE OF TIME! THAT IS MAGIC INDEED!
THE HIGH ONE... FLOWN... IN WOLF FORM. *WHY?* ALL THAT I PROMISED, I DID! THE *GLIDERS'* MAGIC SERVES THE PALACE -- AND *HER*, NOW!
WHY HAS SHE DESERTED ME?
WHOM DO *YOU* SERVE, BROWNSKIN?
ELVES, *EKUAR!* ALL ELVES WHO REMEMBER WHO THEY ARE...
GASP
OH! WHAT IS IT?

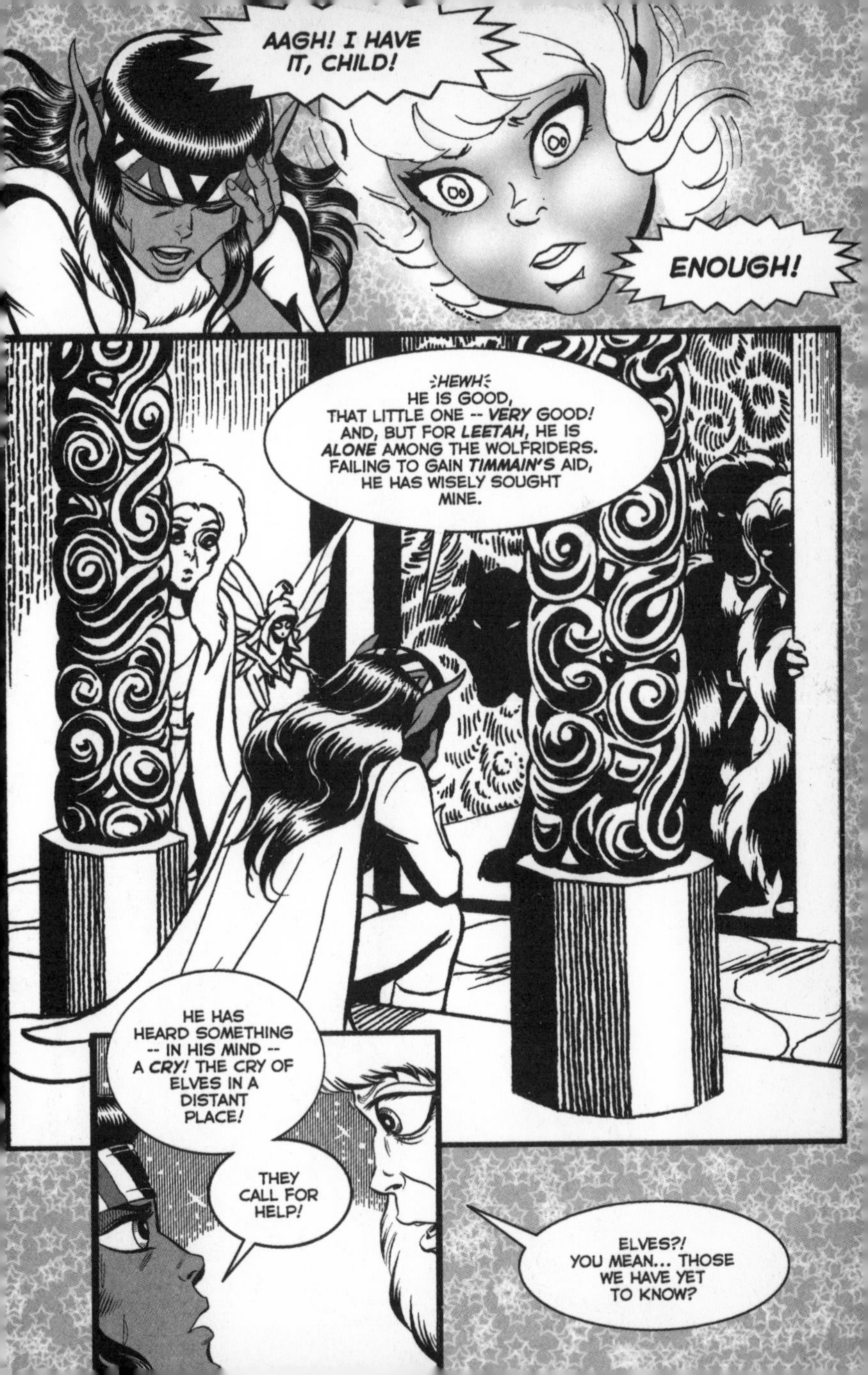
AAGH! I HAVE IT, CHILD!
ENOUGH!
HEWH
HE IS GOOD, THAT LITTLE ONE -- VERY GOOD! AND, BUT FOR LEETAH, HE IS ALONE AMONG THE WOLFRIDERS. FAILING TO GAIN TIMMAIN'S AID, HE HAS WISELY SOUGHT MINE.
HE HAS HEARD SOMETHING -- IN HIS MIND -- A CRY! THE CRY OF ELVES IN A DISTANT PLACE!
THEY CALL FOR HELP!
ELVES?! YOU MEAN... THOSE WE HAVE YET TO KNOW?

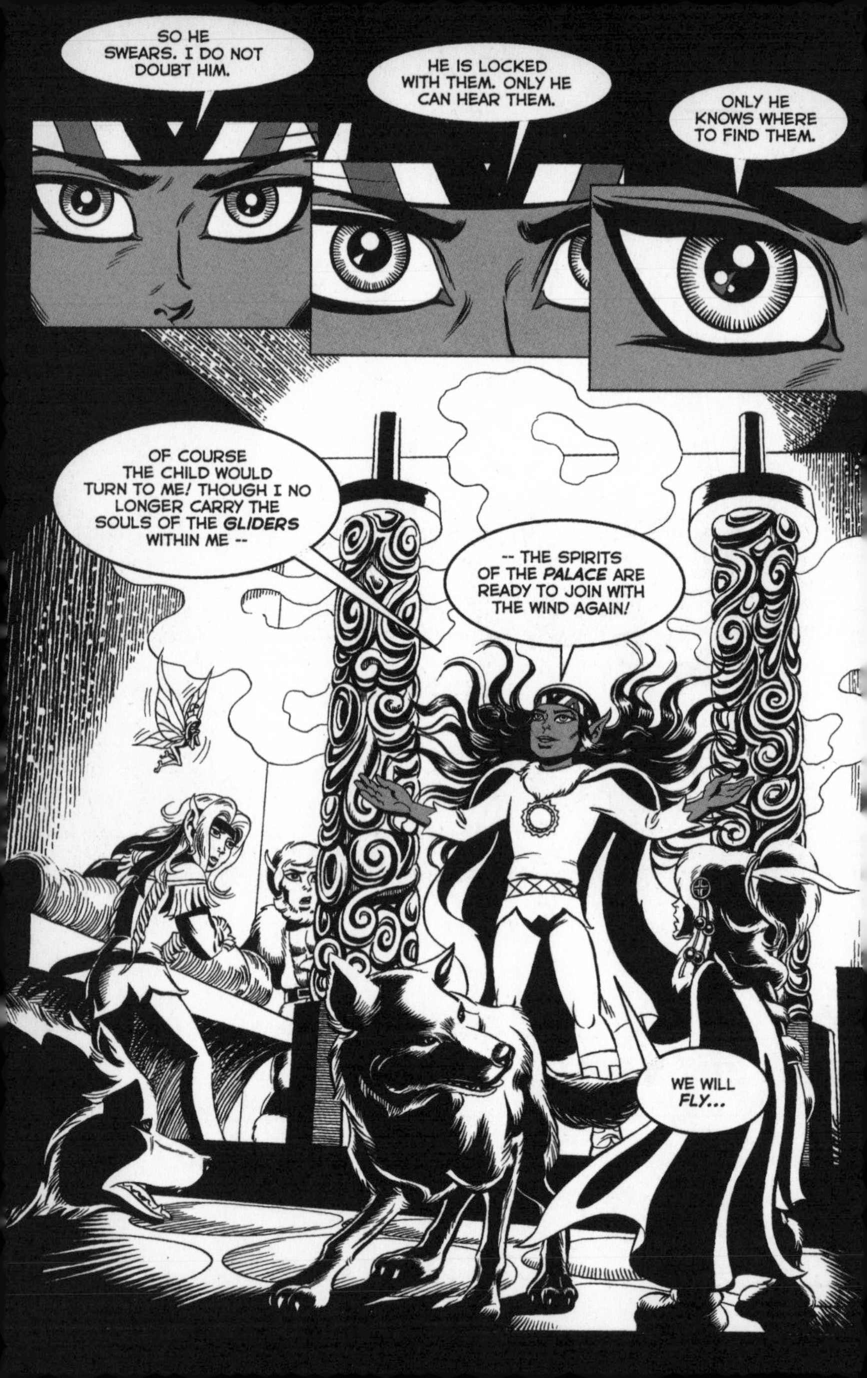
SO HE SWEARS. I DO NOT DOUBT HIM.
HE IS LOCKED WITH THEM. ONLY HE CAN HEAR THEM.
ONLY HE KNOWS WHERE TO FIND THEM.
OF COURSE THE CHILD WOULD TURN TO ME! THOUGH I NO LONGER CARRY THE SOULS OF THE GLIDERS WITHIN ME --
-- THE SPIRITS OF THE PALACE ARE READY TO JOIN WITH THE WIND AGAIN!
WE WILL FLY...

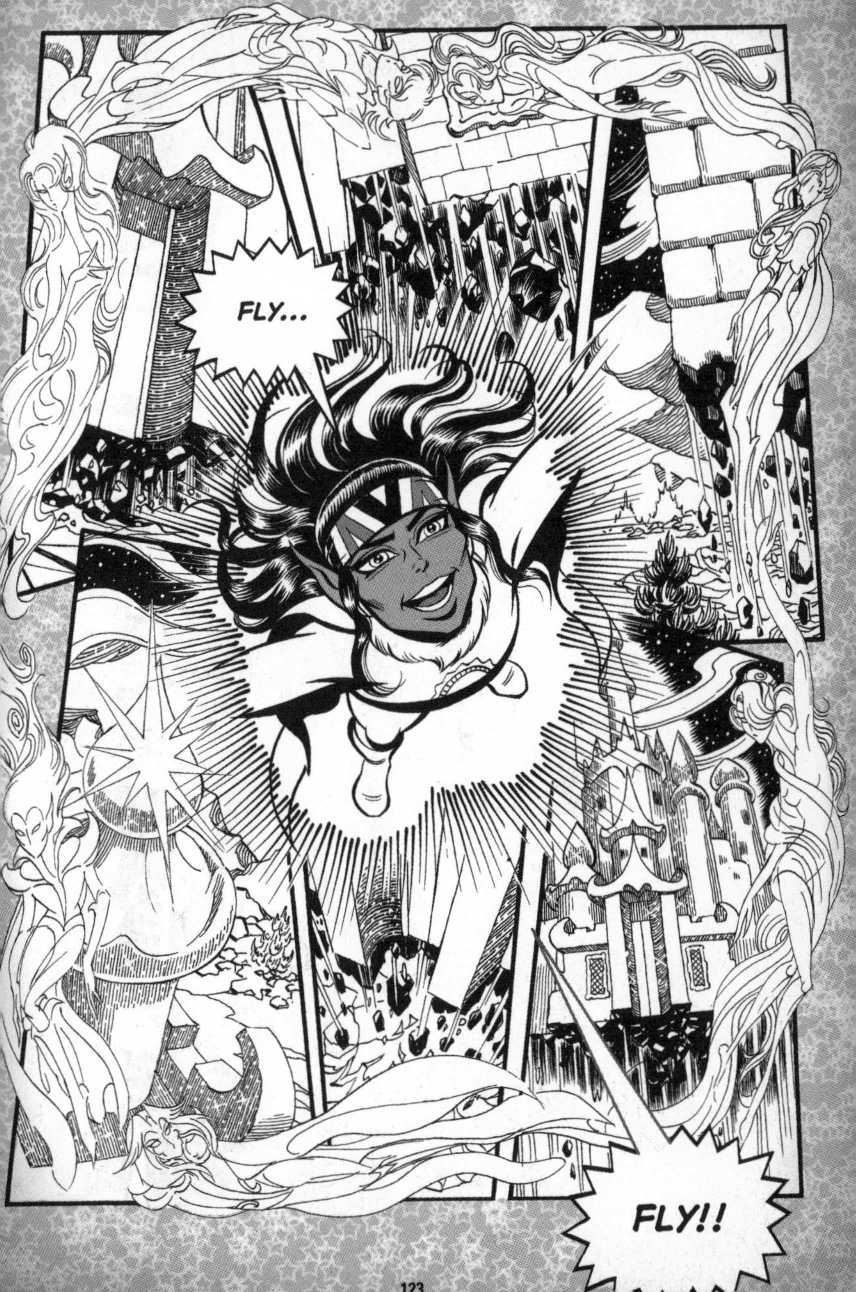
FLY...
FLY!!

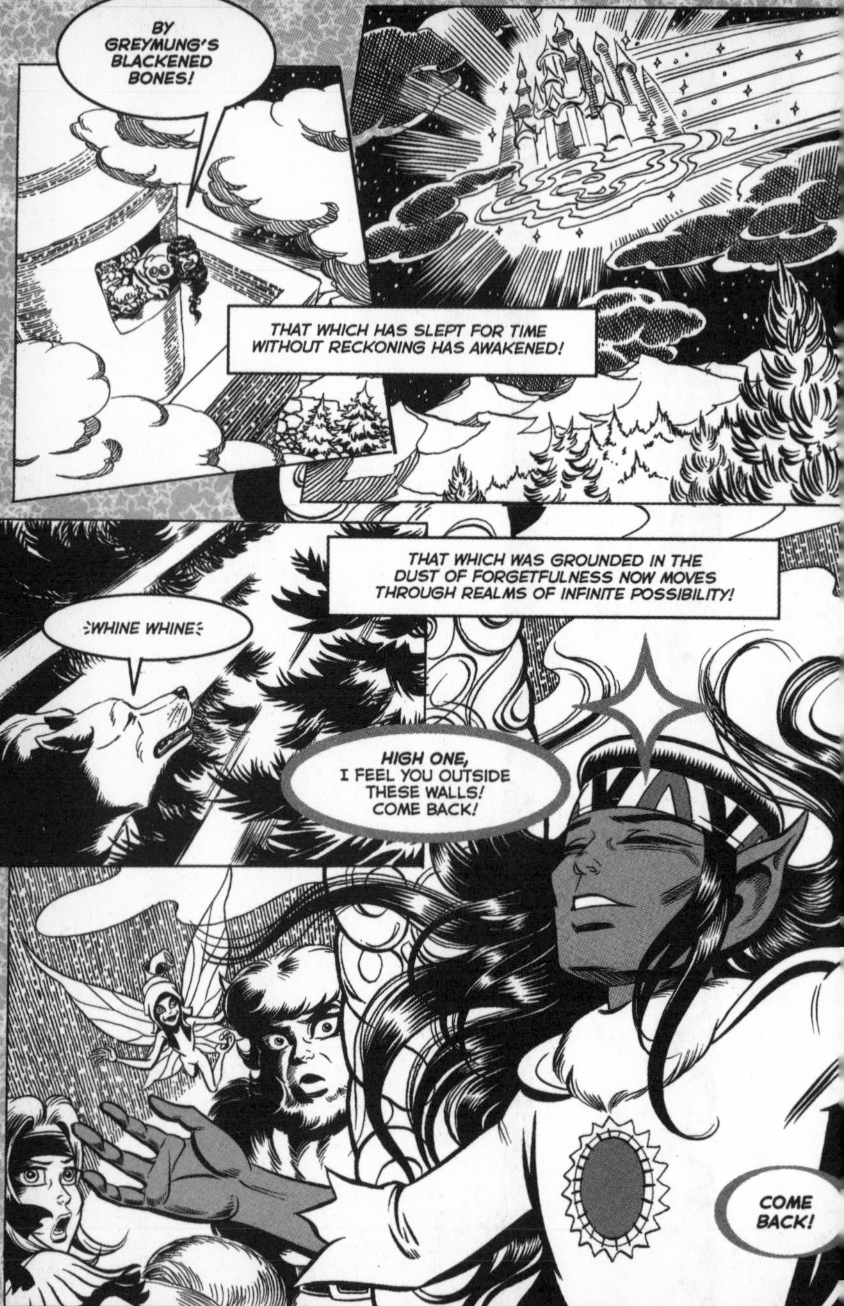
BY GREYMUNG'S BLACKENED BONES!
THAT WHICH HAS SLEPT FOR TIME WITHOUT RECKONING HAS AWAKENED!
THAT WHICH WAS GROUNDED IN THE DUST OF FORGETFULNESS NOW MOVES THROUGH REALMS OF INFINITE POSSIBILITY!
WHINE WHINE
HIGH ONE, I FEEL YOU OUTSIDE THESE WALLS! COME BACK!
COME BACK!

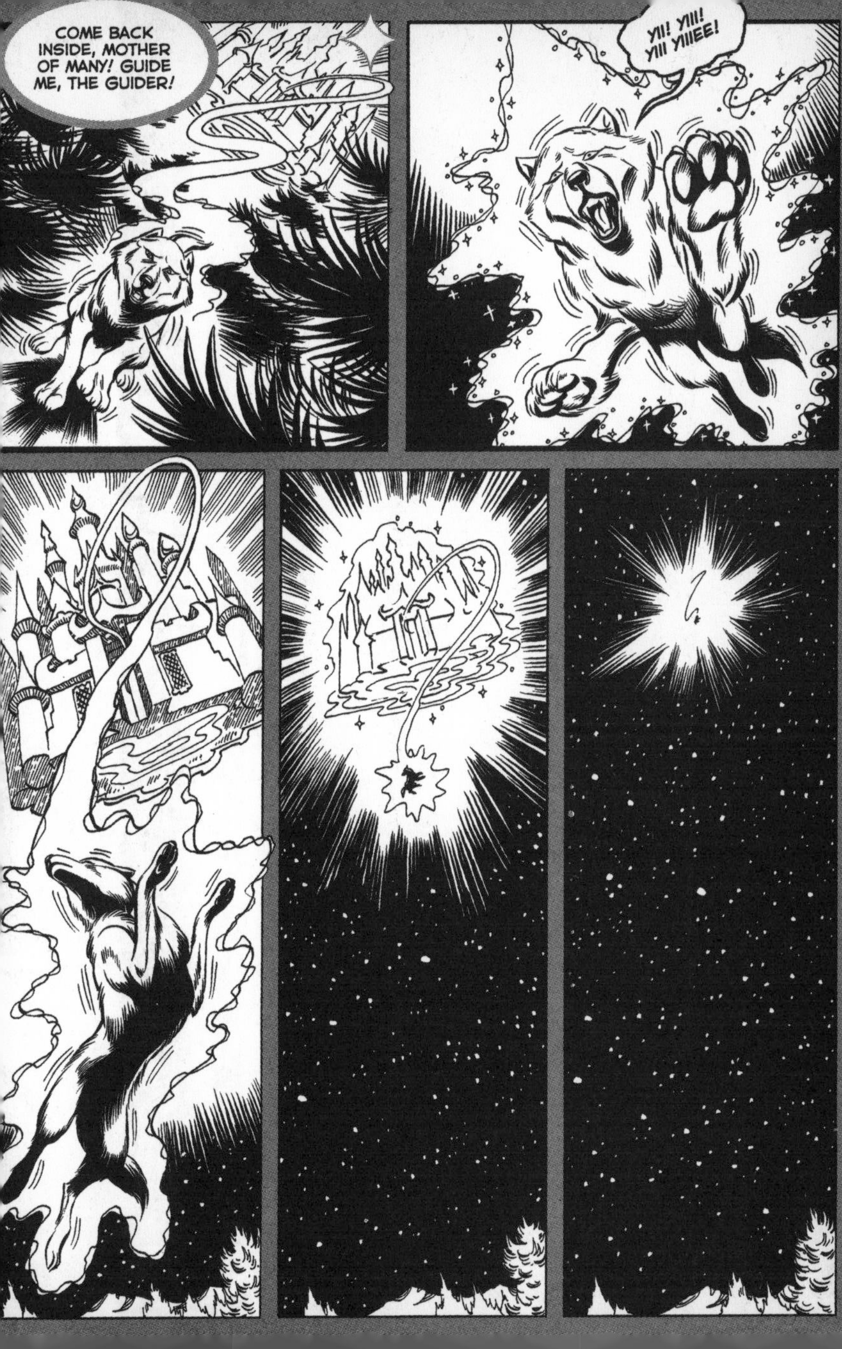
COME BACK INSIDE, MOTHER OF MANY! GUIDE ME, THE GUIDER!
YII! YIII! YIII YIIIEE!

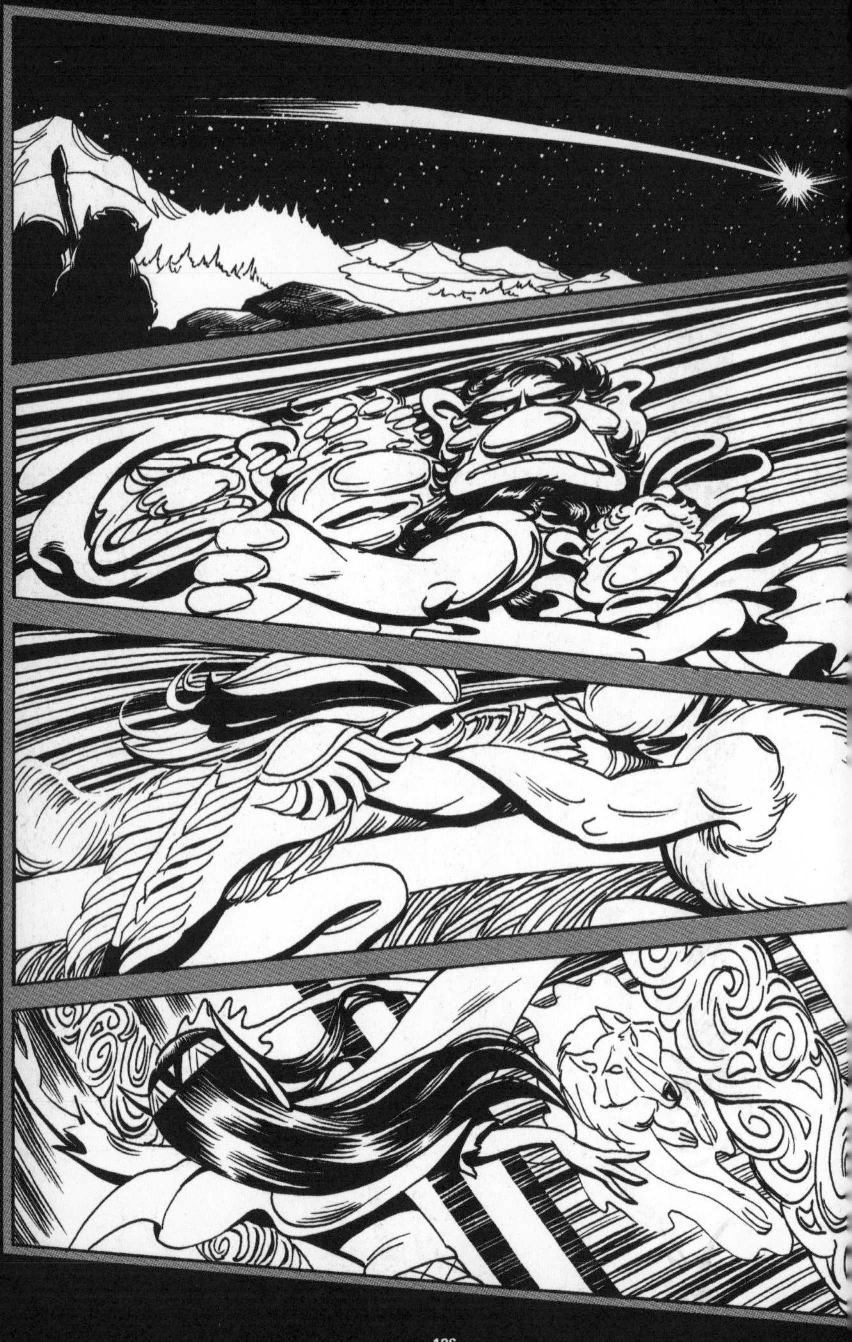

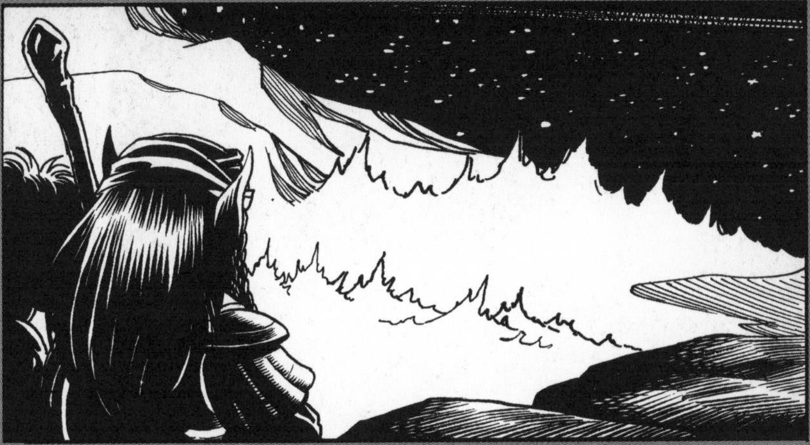

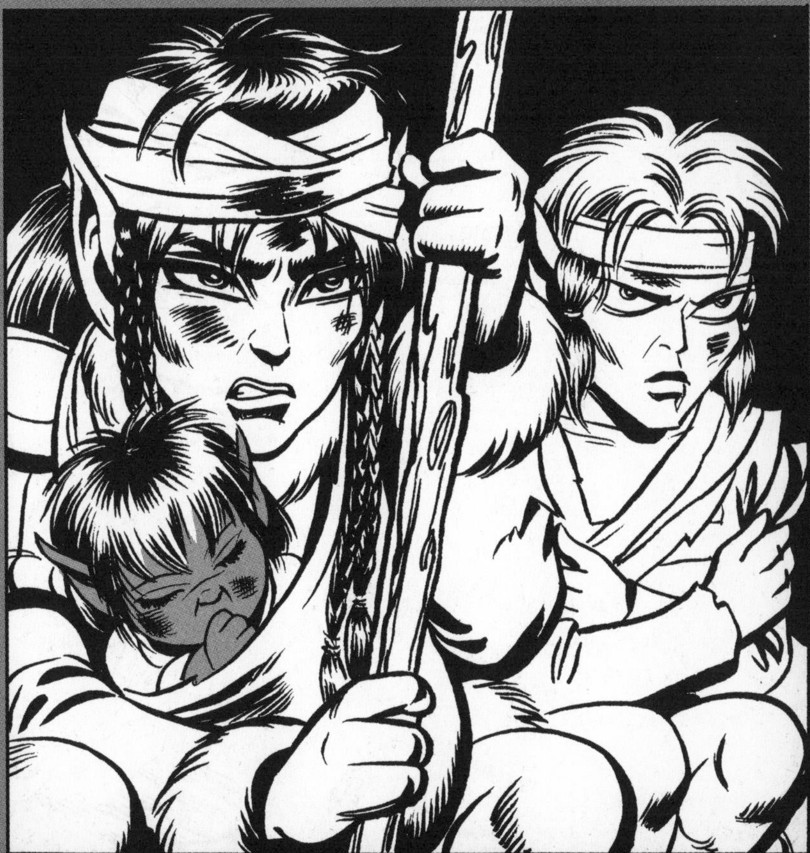

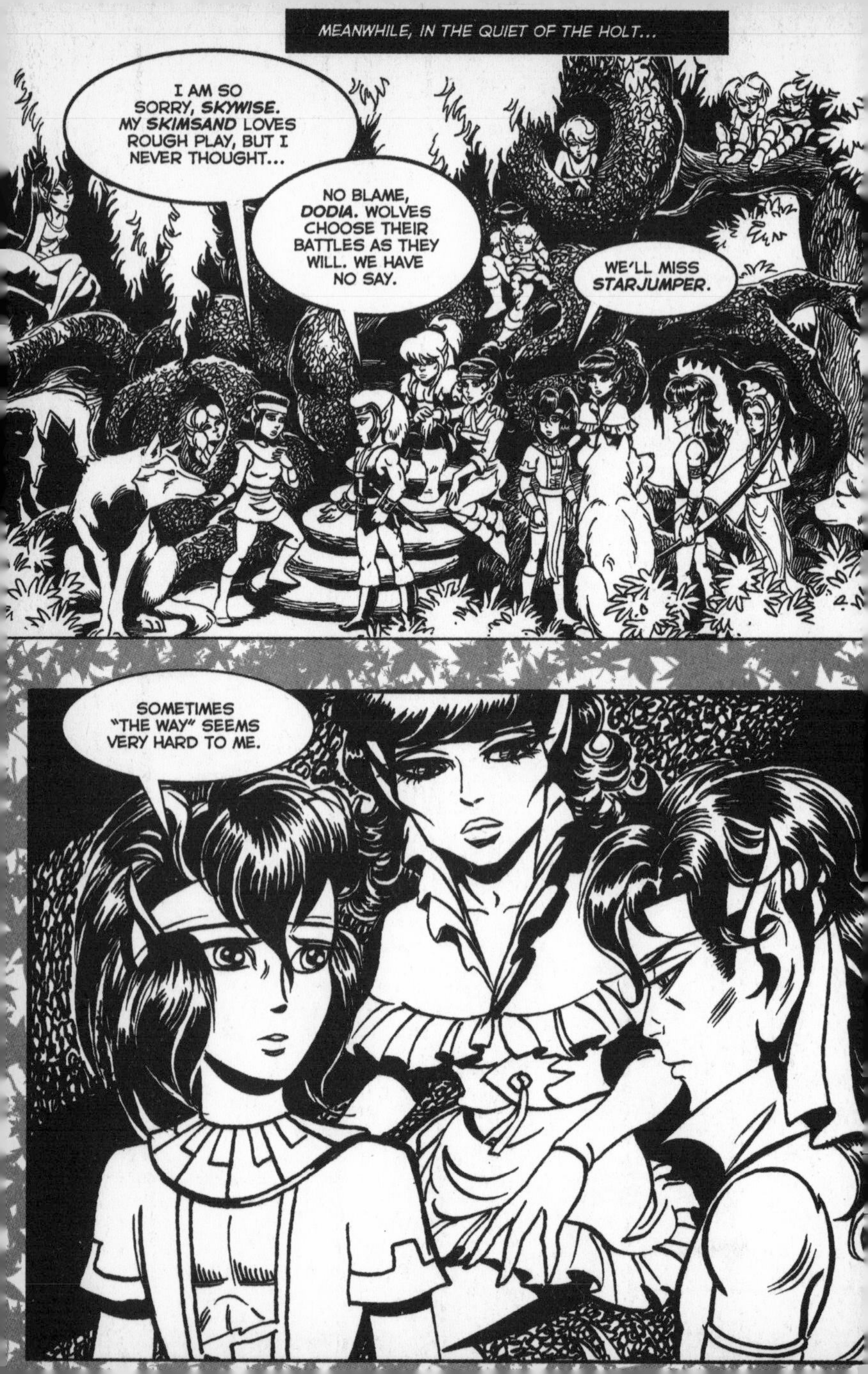
MEANWHILE, IN THE QUIET OF THE HOLT...
I AM SO SORRY, SKYWISE. MY SKIMSAND LOVES ROUGH PLAY, BUT I NEVER THOUGHT...
NO BLAME, DODIA. WOLVES CHOOSE THEIR BATTLES AS THEY WILL. WE HAVE NO SAY.
WE'LL MISS STARJUMPER.
SOMETIMES "THE WAY" SEEMS VERY HARD TO ME.

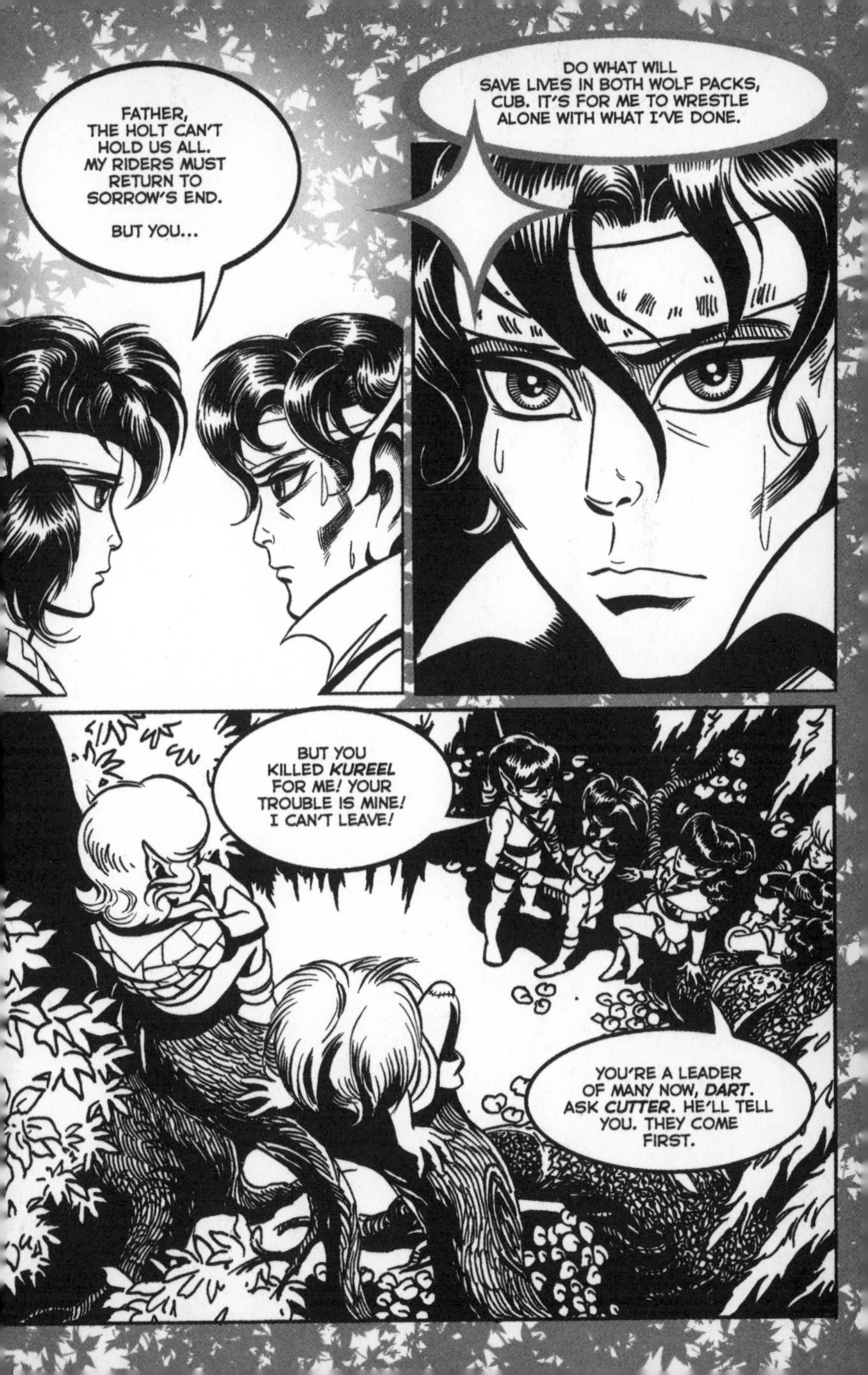
FATHER, THE HOLT CAN'T HOLD US ALL. MY RIDERS MUST RETURN TO SORROW'S END.

BUT YOU...
DO WHAT WILL SAVE LIVES IN BOTH WOLF PACKS, CUB. IT'S FOR ME TO WRESTLE ALONE WITH WHAT I'VE DONE.
BUT YOU KILLED KUREEL FOR ME! YOUR TROUBLE IS MINE! I CAN'T LEAVE!
YOU'RE A LEADER OF MANY NOW, DART. ASK CUTTER. HE'LL TELL YOU. THEY COME FIRST.

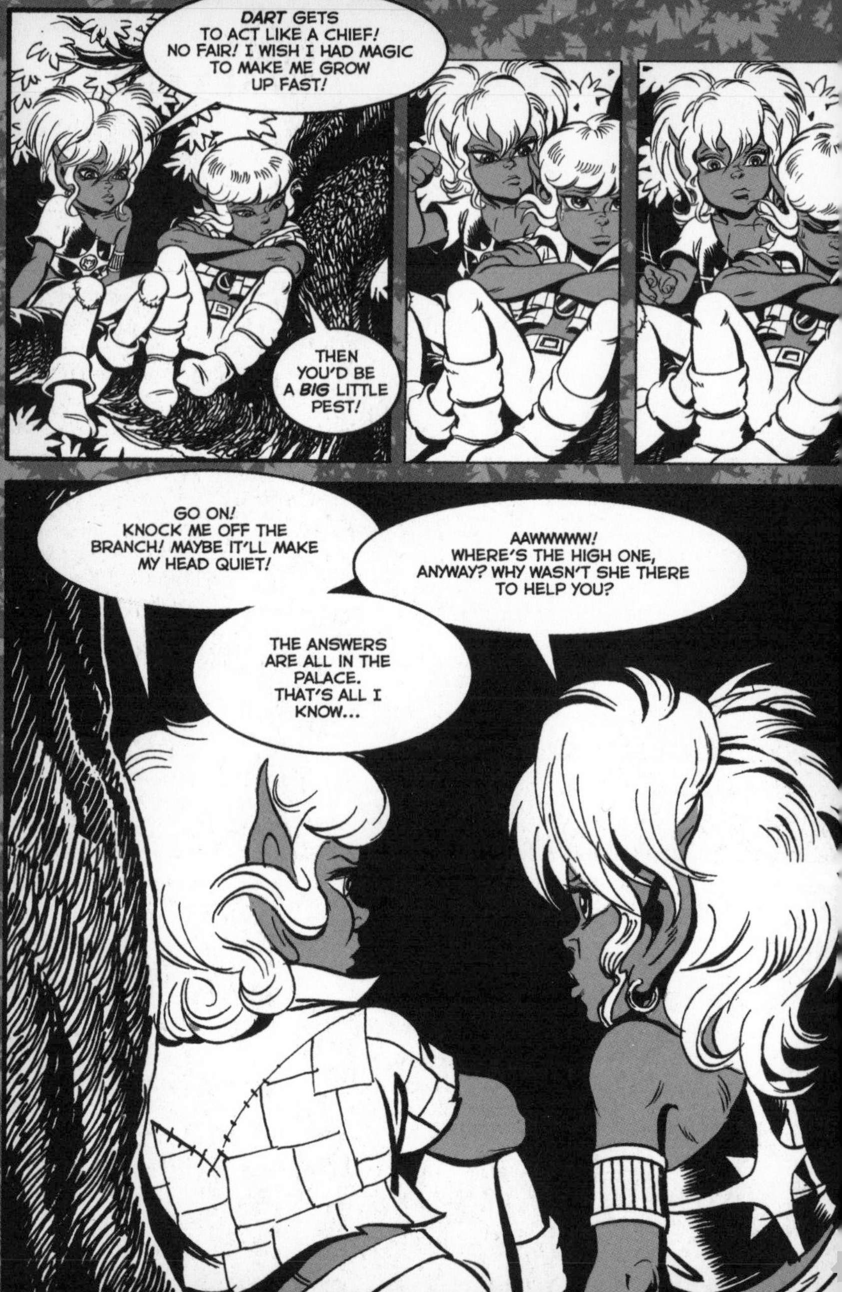
DART GETS TO ACT LIKE A CHIEF! NO FAIR! I WISH I HAD MAGIC TO MAKE ME GROW UP FAST!
THEN YOU'D BE A BIG LITTLE PEST!
GO ON! KNOCK ME OFF THE BRANCH! MAYBE IT'LL MAKE MY HEAD QUIET!
AAWWWWWW! WHERE'S THE HIGH ONE, ANYWAY? WHY WASN'T SHE THERE TO HELP YOU?
THE ANSWERS ARE ALL IN THE PALACE. THAT'S ALL I KNOW...

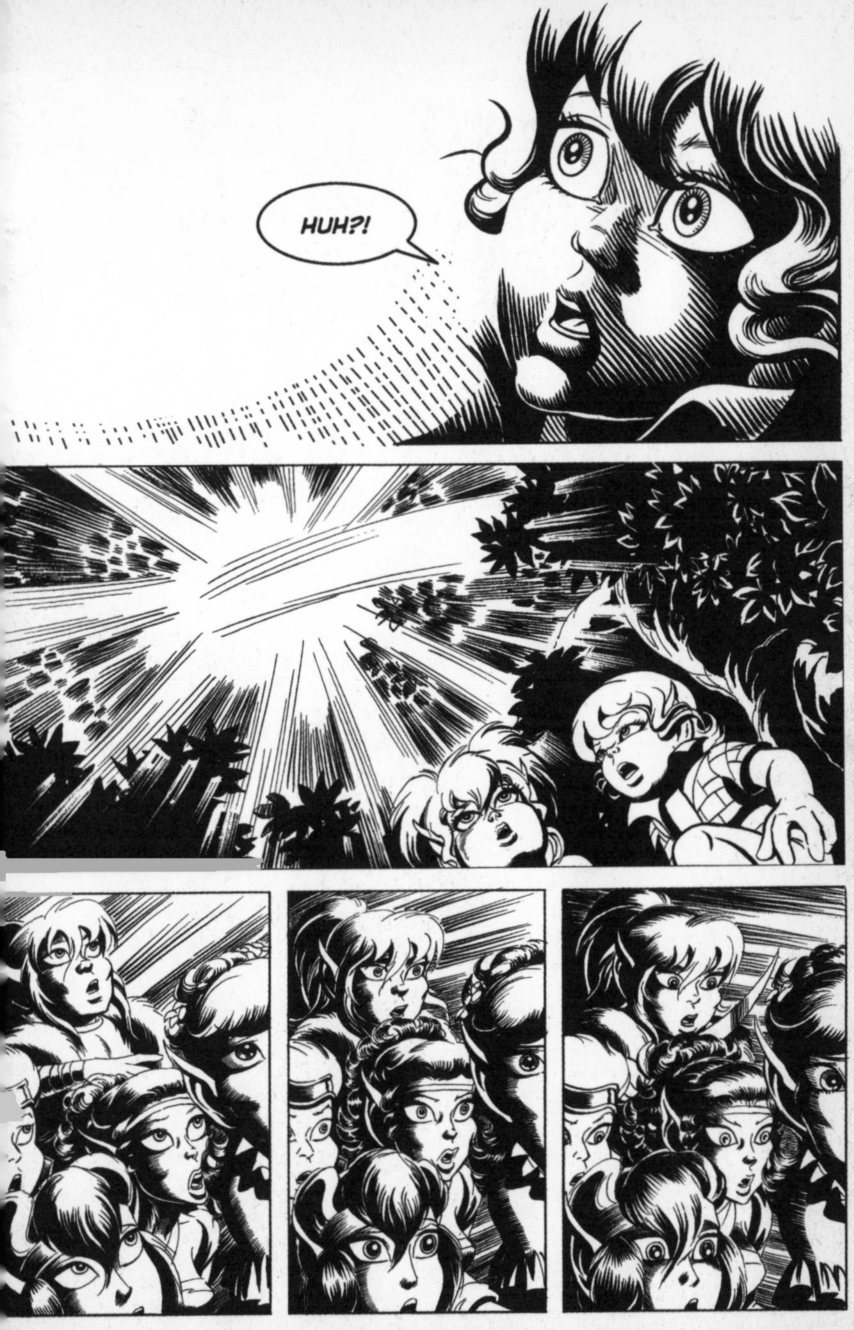
HUH?!

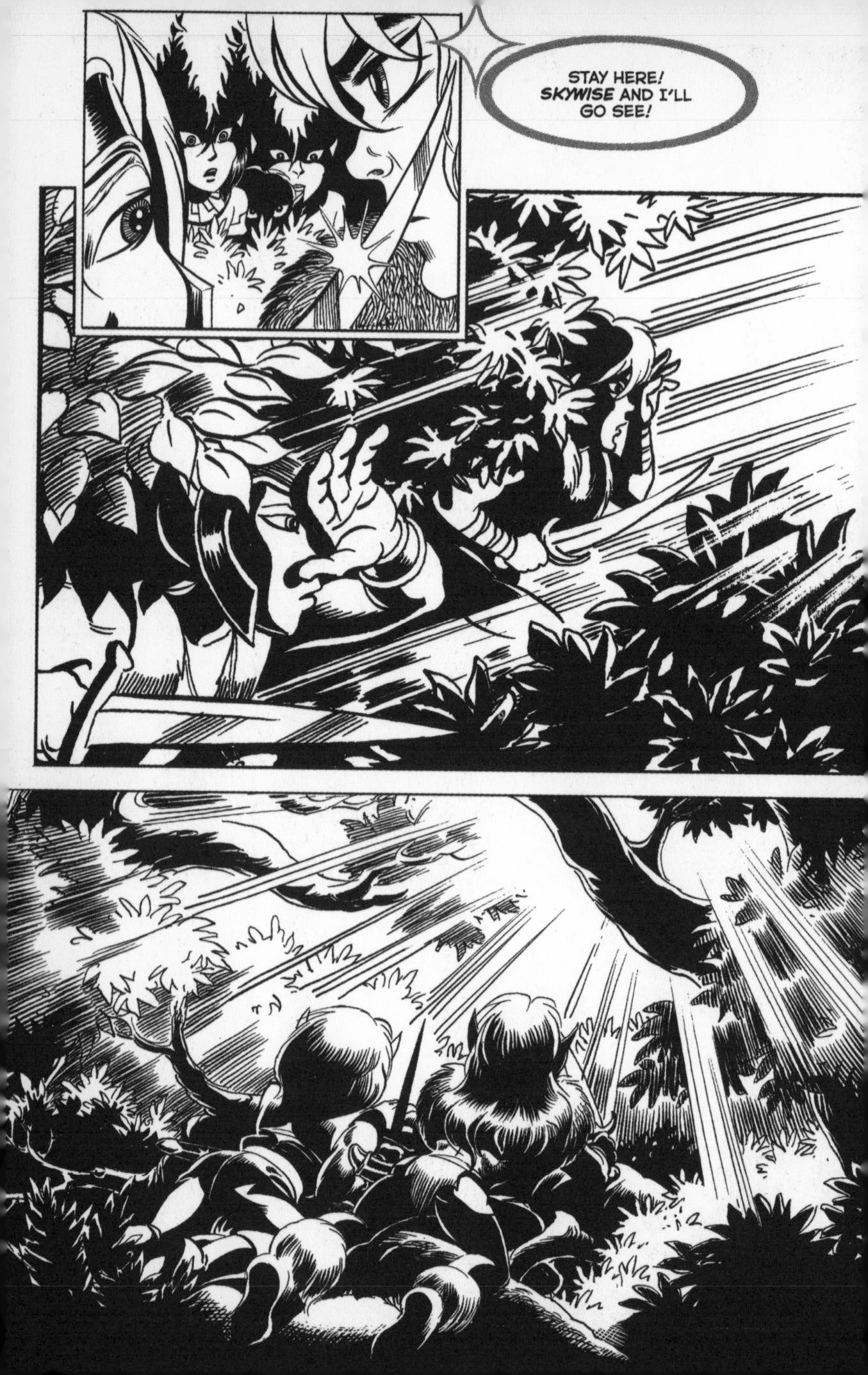
STAY HERE! SKYWISE AND I'LL GO SEE!

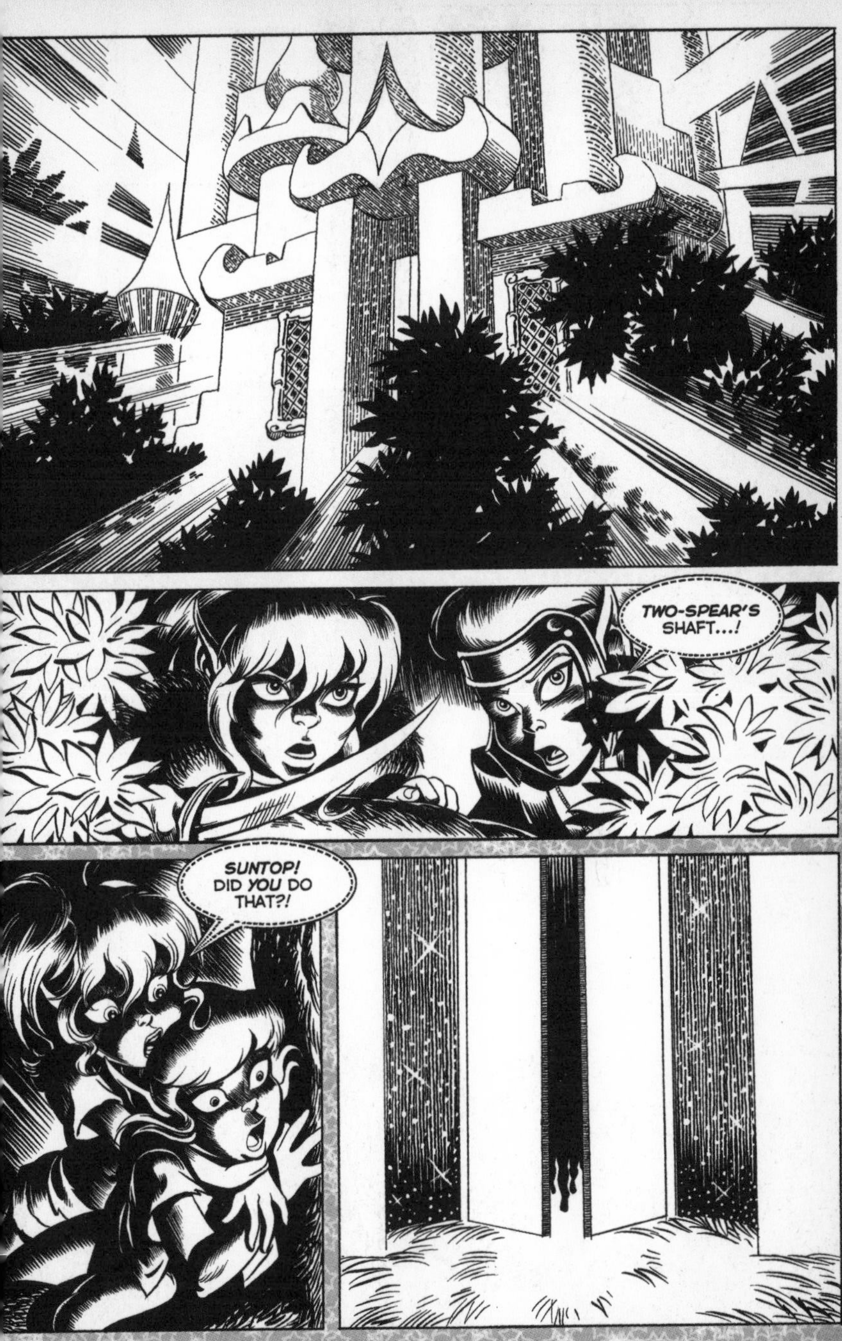
TWO-SPEAR'S SHAFT...!
SUNTOP! DID YOU DO THAT?!

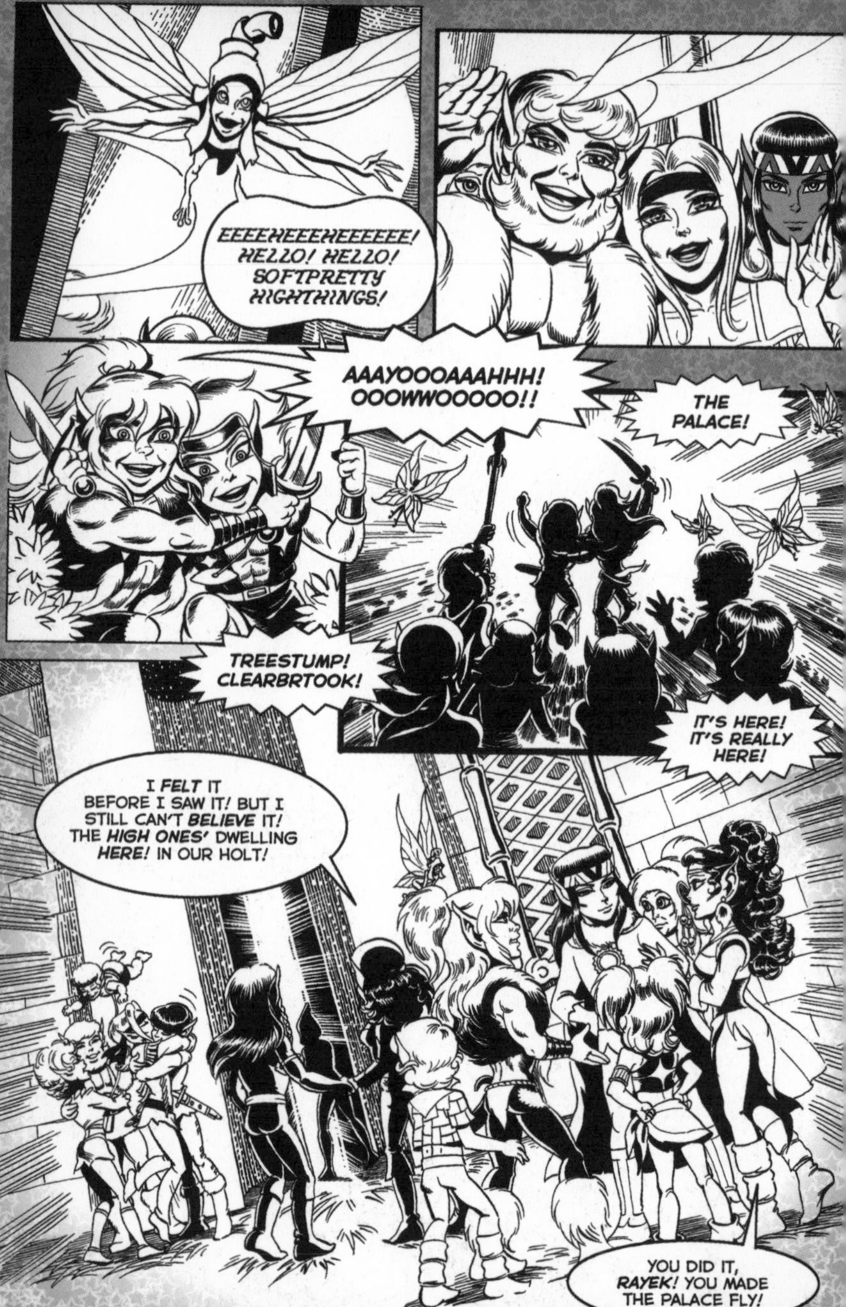
EEEEHEEEEHEEEEEE! HELLO! HELLO! SOFTPRETTY HIGHTHINGS!
AAAYOOOAAAHHH! OOOWWOOOOO!!
THE PALACE!
TREESTUMP! CLEARBRTOOK!
IT'S HERE! IT'S REALLY HERE!
I FELT IT BEFORE I SAW IT! BUT I STILL CAN'T BELIEVE IT! THE HIGH ONES' DWELLING HERE! IN OUR HOLT!
YOU DID IT, RAYEK! YOU MADE THE PALACE FLY!

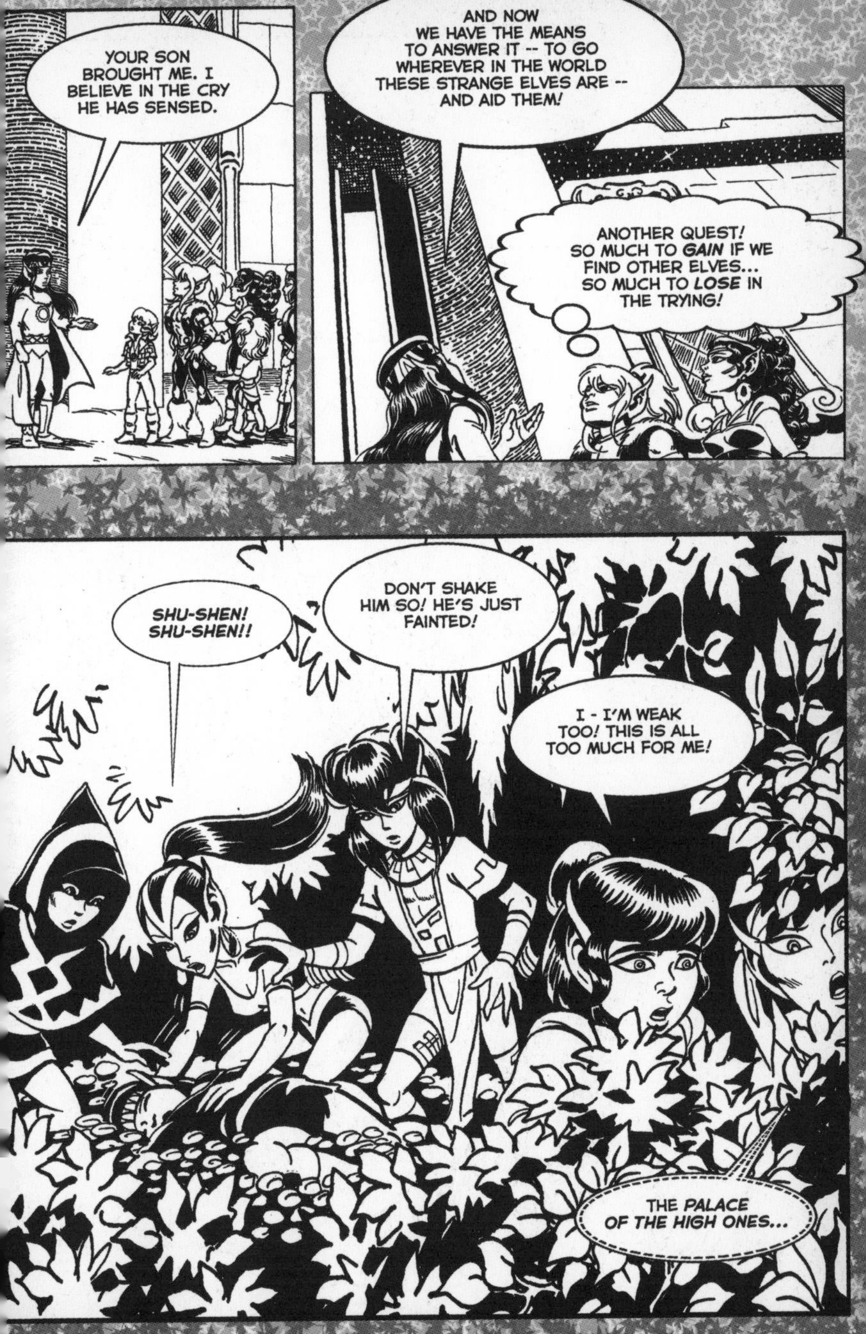
YOUR SON BROUGHT ME. I BELIEVE IN THE CRY HE HAS SENSED.
AND NOW WE HAVE THE MEANS TO ANSWER IT -- TO GO WHEREVER IN THE WORLD THESE STRANGE ELVES ARE -- AND AID THEM!
ANOTHER QUEST! SO MUCH TO GAIN IF WE FIND OTHER ELVES... SO MUCH TO LOSE IN THE TRYING!
SHU-SHEN! SHU-SHEN!!
DON'T SHAKE HIM SO! HE'S JUST FAINTED!
I - I'M WEAK TOO! THIS IS ALL TOO MUCH FOR ME!
THE PALACE OF THE HIGH ONES...

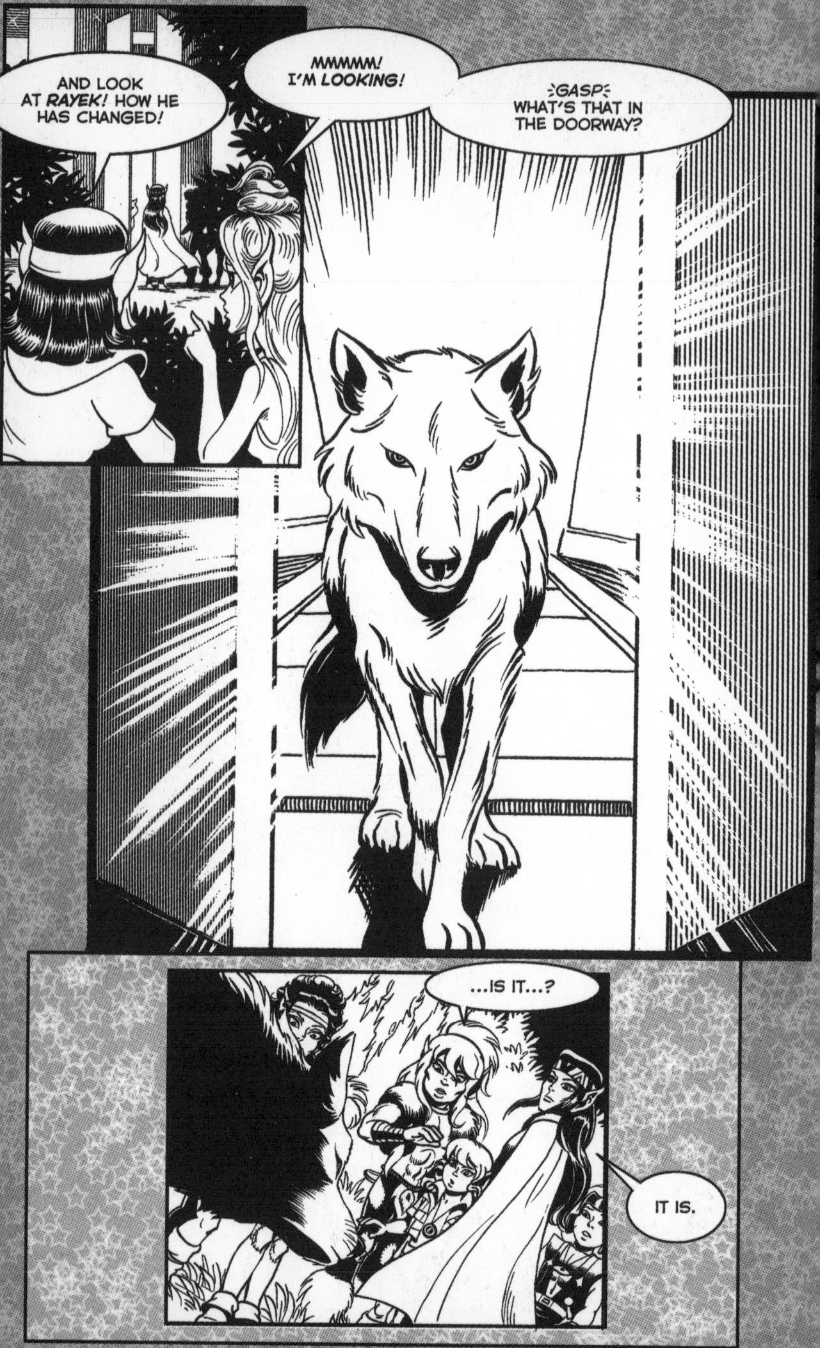
AND LOOK AT RAYEK! HOW HE HAS CHANGED!
MMMMM! I'M LOOKING!
GASP WHAT'S THAT IN THE DOORWAY?
...IS IT...?
IT IS.

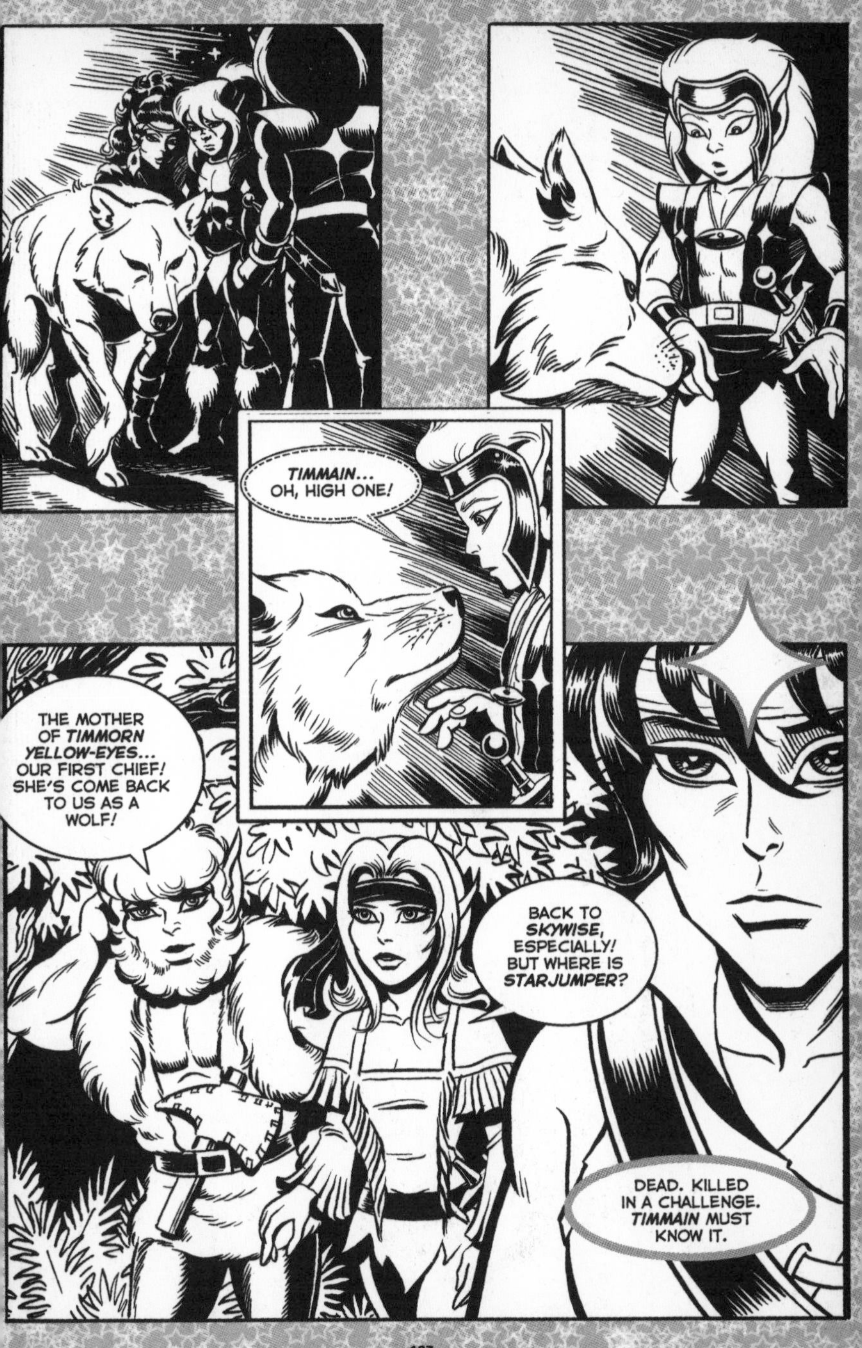
TIMMAIN... OH, HIGH ONE!
THE MOTHER OF TIMMORN YELLOW-EYES... OUR FIRST CHIEF! SHE'S COME BACK TO US AS A WOLF!
BACK TO SKYWISE, ESPECIALLY! BUT WHERE IS STARJUMPER?
DEAD. KILLED IN A CHALLENGE. TIMMAIN MUST KNOW IT.

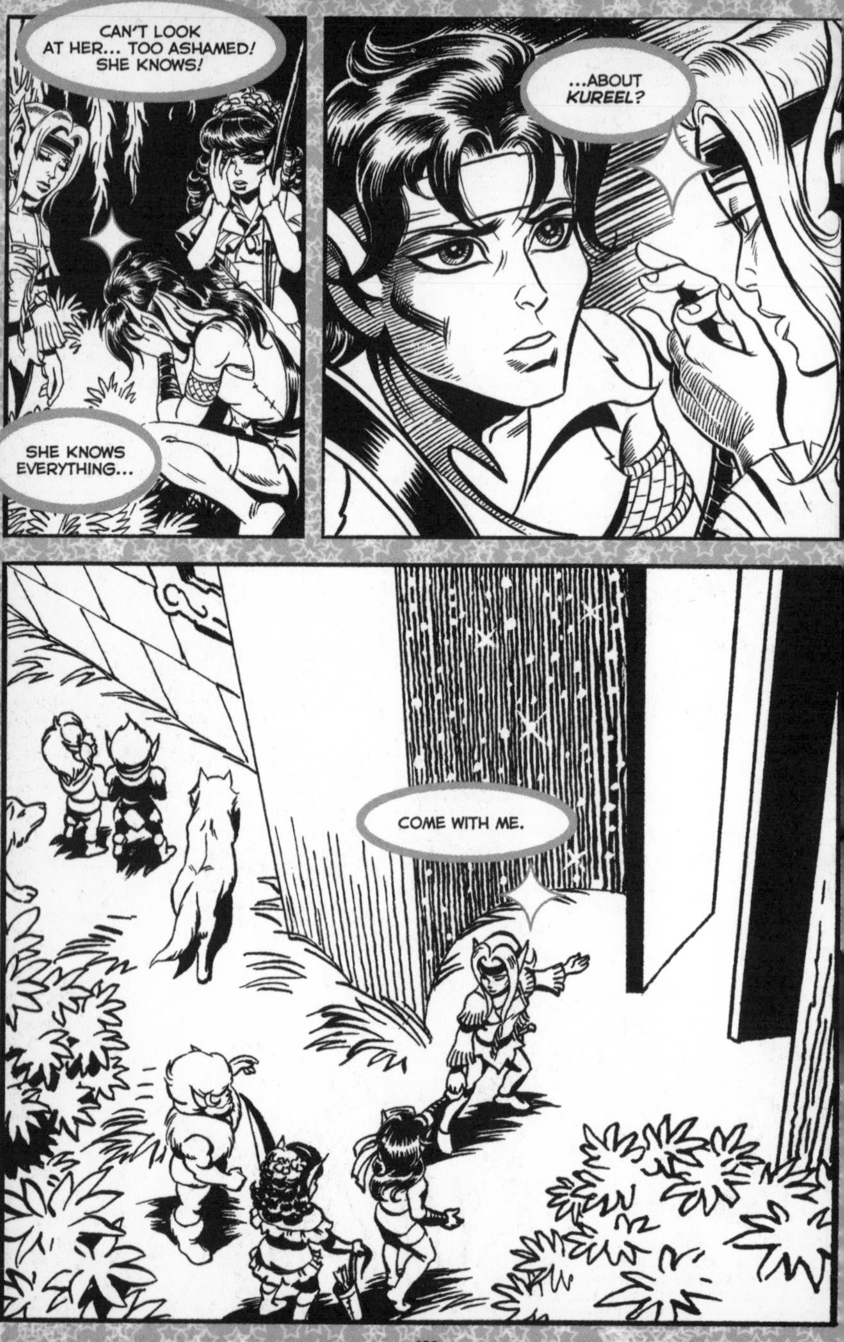
CAN'T LOOK AT HER... TOO ASHAMED! SHE KNOWS!
SHE KNOWS EVERYTHING...
...ABOUT KUREEL?
COME WITH ME.

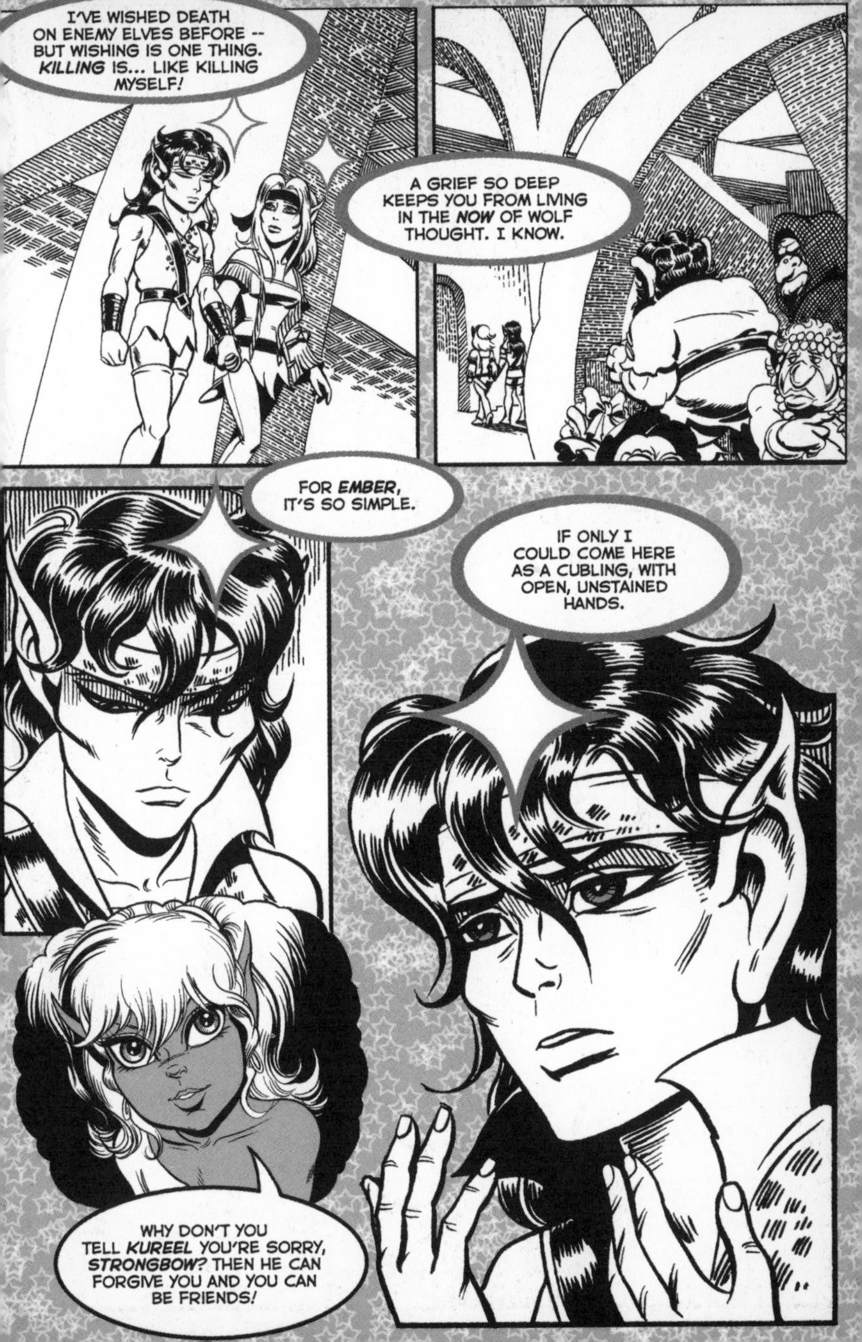
I'VE WISHED DEATH ON ENEMY ELVES BEFORE -- BUT WISHING IS ONE THING. *KILLING* IS... LIKE KILLING MYSELF!
A GRIEF SO DEEP KEEPS YOU FROM LIVING IN THE *NOW* OF WOLF THOUGHT. I KNOW.
FOR *EMBER*, IT'S SO SIMPLE.
IF ONLY I COULD COME HERE AS A CUBLING, WITH OPEN, UNSTAINED HANDS.
WHY DON'T YOU TELL *KUREEL* YOU'RE SORRY, *STRONGBOW?* THEN HE CAN FORGIVE YOU AND YOU CAN BE FRIENDS!

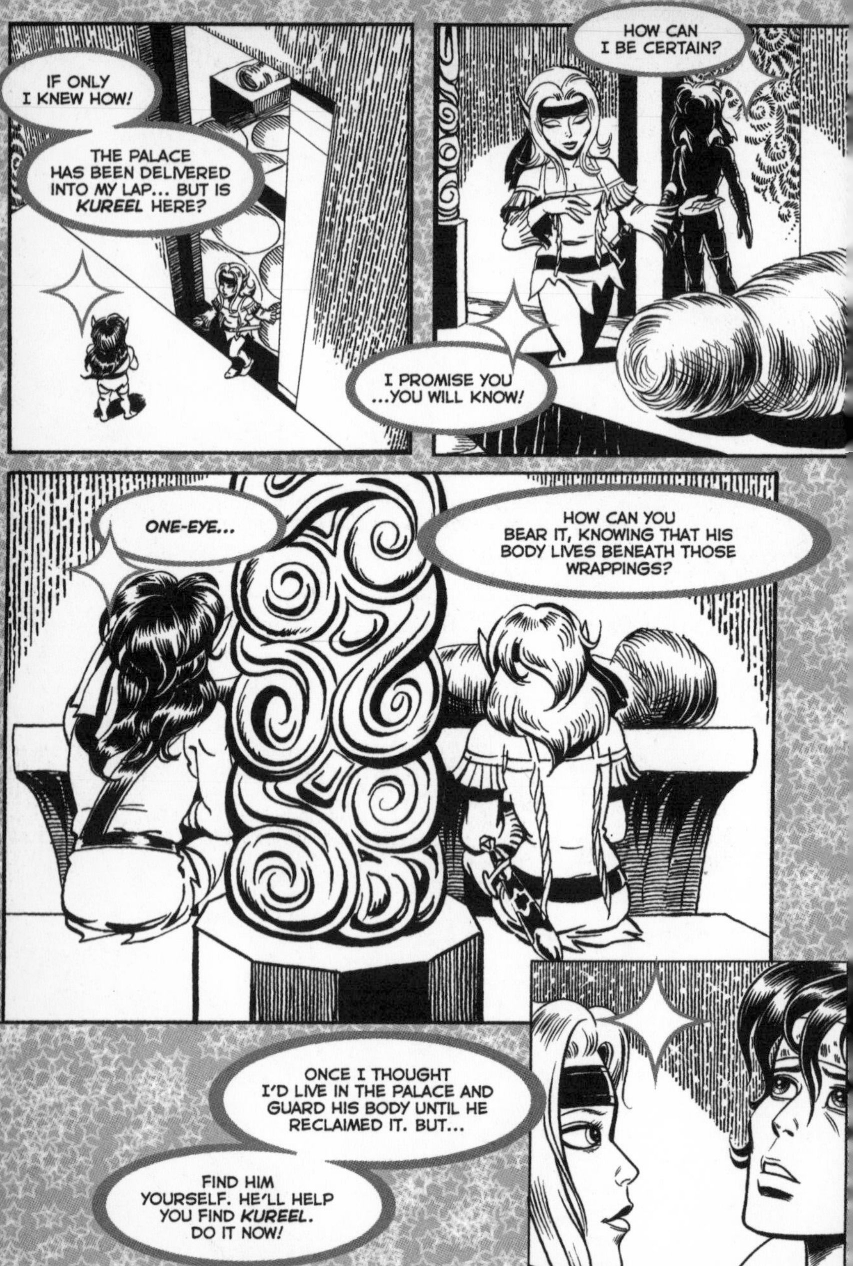

IF ONLY I KNEW HOW!
THE PALACE HAS BEEN DELIVERED INTO MY LAP... BUT IS KUREEL HERE?
HOW CAN I BE CERTAIN?
I PROMISE YOU ...YOU WILL KNOW!
ONE-EYE...
HOW CAN YOU BEAR IT, KNOWING THAT HIS BODY LIVES BENEATH THOSE WRAPPINGS?
ONCE I THOUGHT I'D LIVE IN THE PALACE AND GUARD HIS BODY UNTIL HE RECLAIMED IT. BUT...
FIND HIM YOURSELF. HE'LL HELP YOU FIND KUREEL. DO IT NOW!

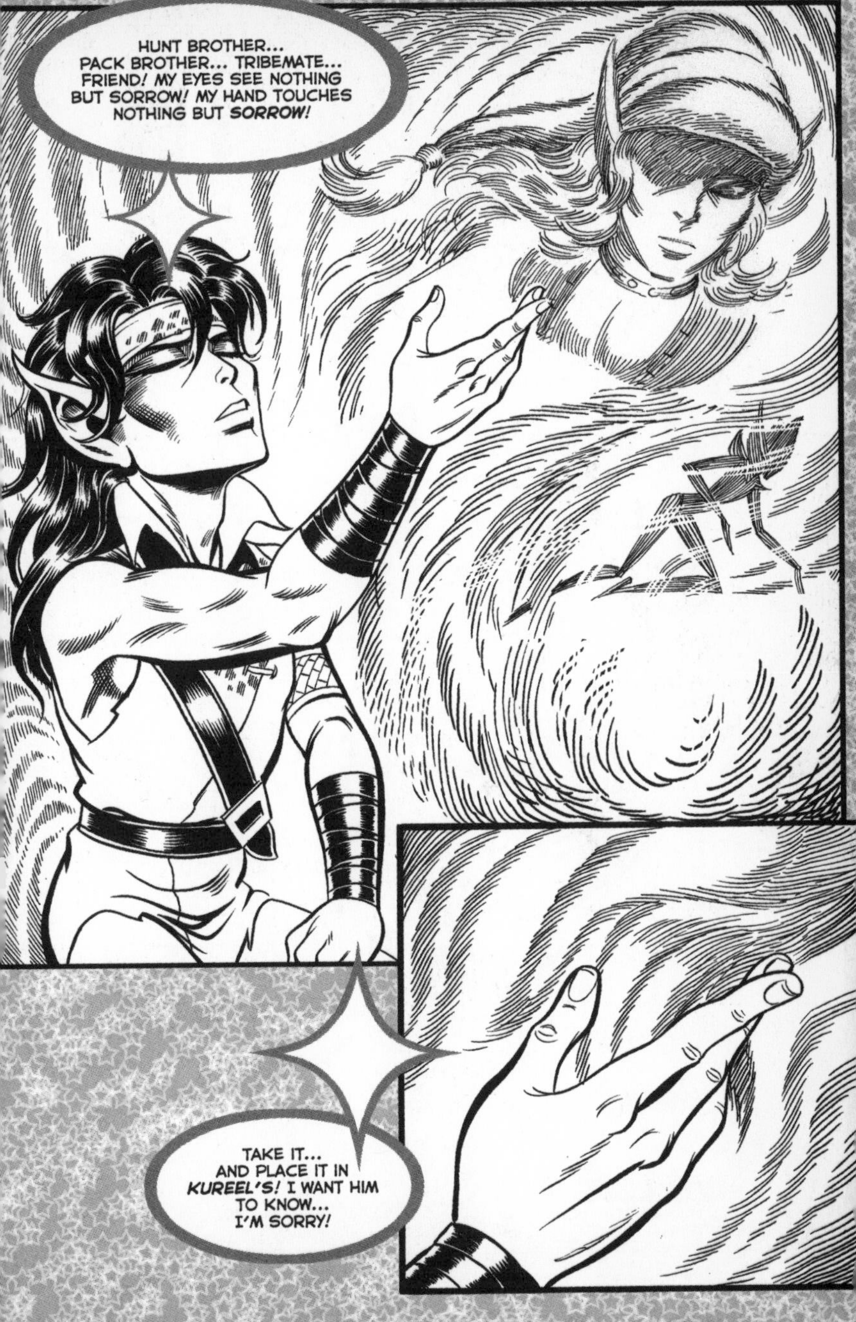
HUNT BROTHER... PACK BROTHER... TRIBEMATE... FRIEND! MY EYES SEE NOTHING BUT SORROW! MY HAND TOUCHES NOTHING BUT *SORROW!*
TAKE IT... AND PLACE IT IN *KUREEL'S!* I WANT HIM TO KNOW... I'M SORRY!

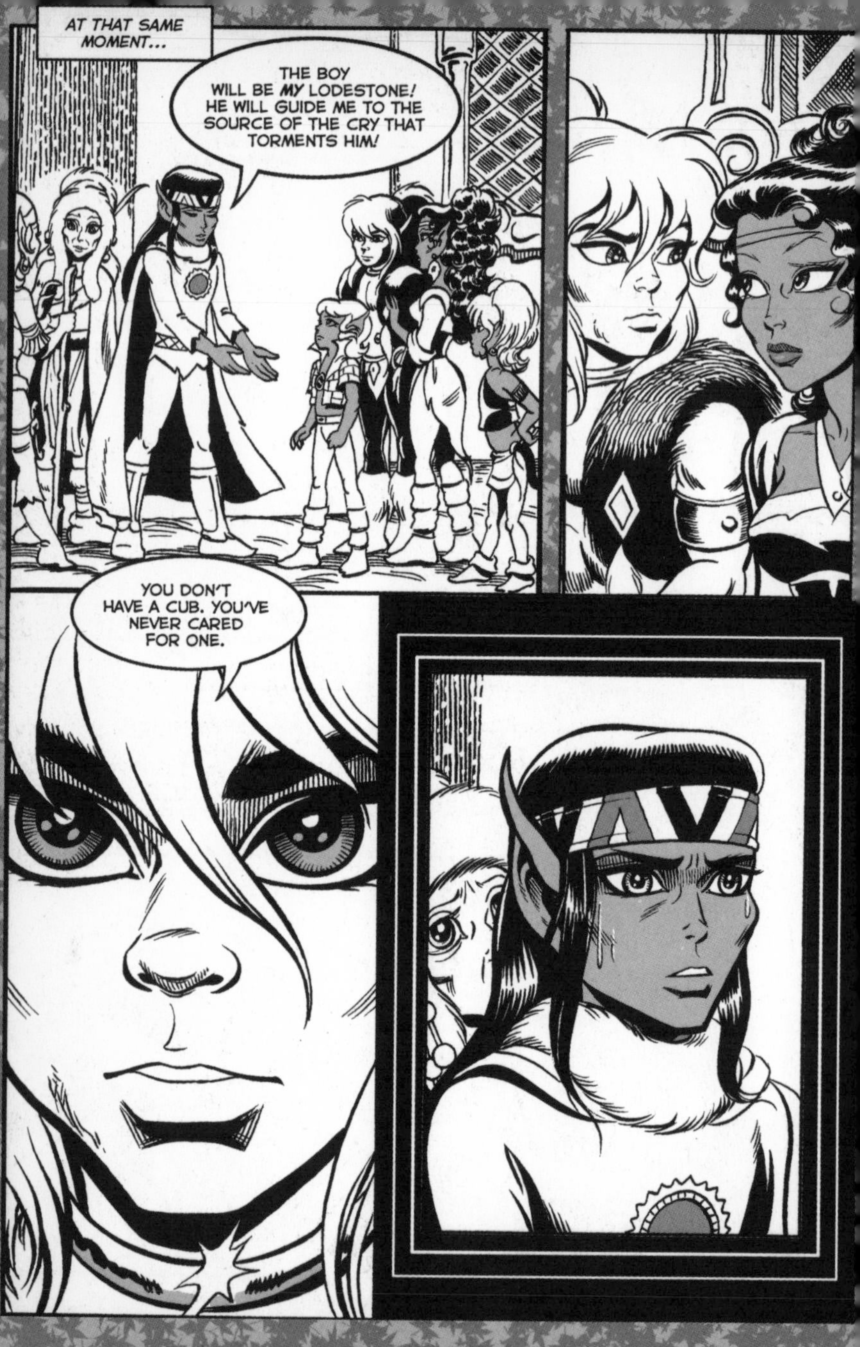
AT THAT SAME MOMENT...
THE BOY WILL BE MY LODESTONE! HE WILL GUIDE ME TO THE SOURCE OF THE CRY THAT TORMENTS HIM!
YOU DON'T HAVE A CUB. YOU'VE NEVER CARED FOR ONE.

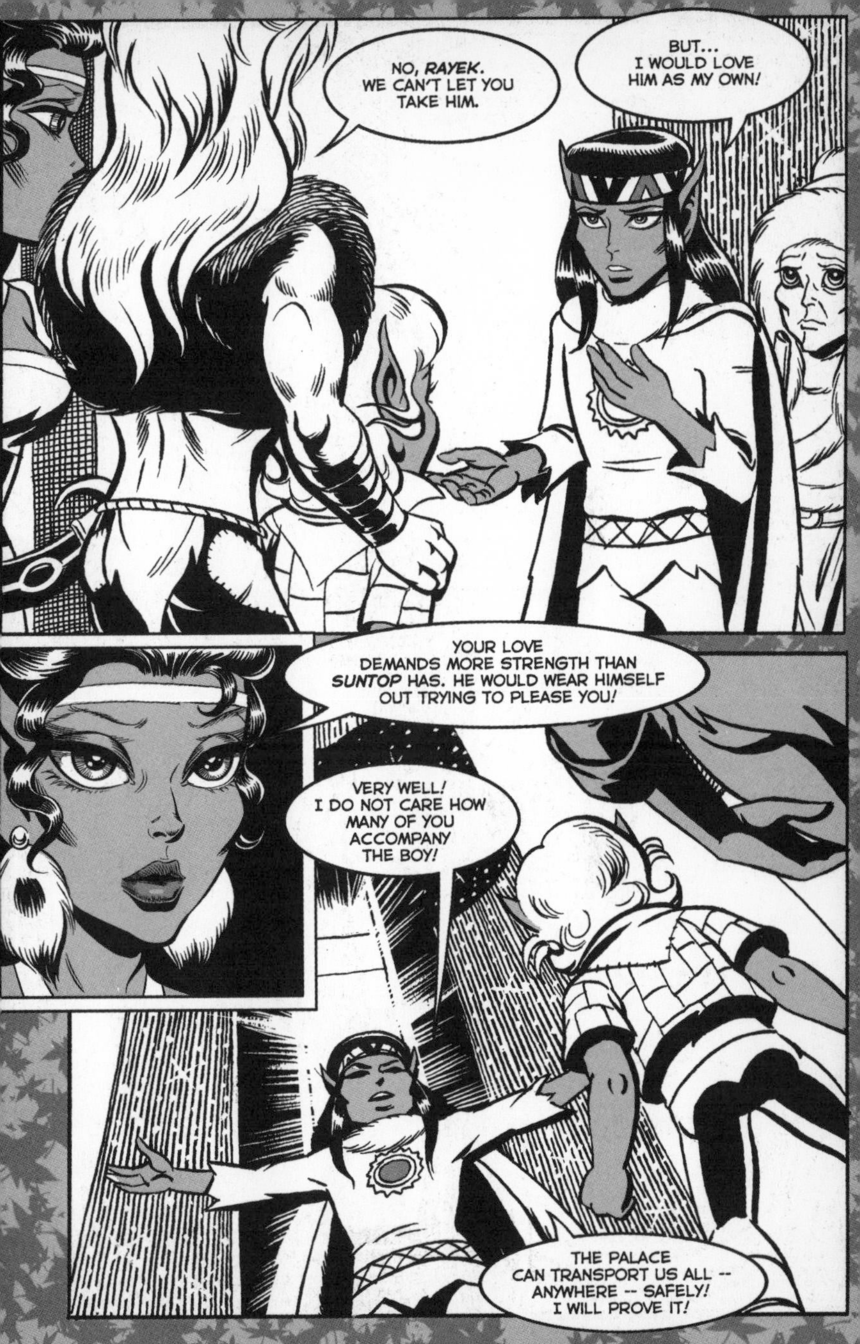
NO, RAYEK. WE CAN'T LET YOU TAKE HIM.
BUT... I WOULD LOVE HIM AS MY OWN!
YOUR LOVE DEMANDS MORE STRENGTH THAN SUNTOP HAS. HE WOULD WEAR HIMSELF OUT TRYING TO PLEASE YOU!
VERY WELL! I DO NOT CARE HOW MANY OF YOU ACCOMPANY THE BOY!
THE PALACE CAN TRANSPORT US ALL -- ANYWHERE -- SAFELY! I WILL PROVE IT!

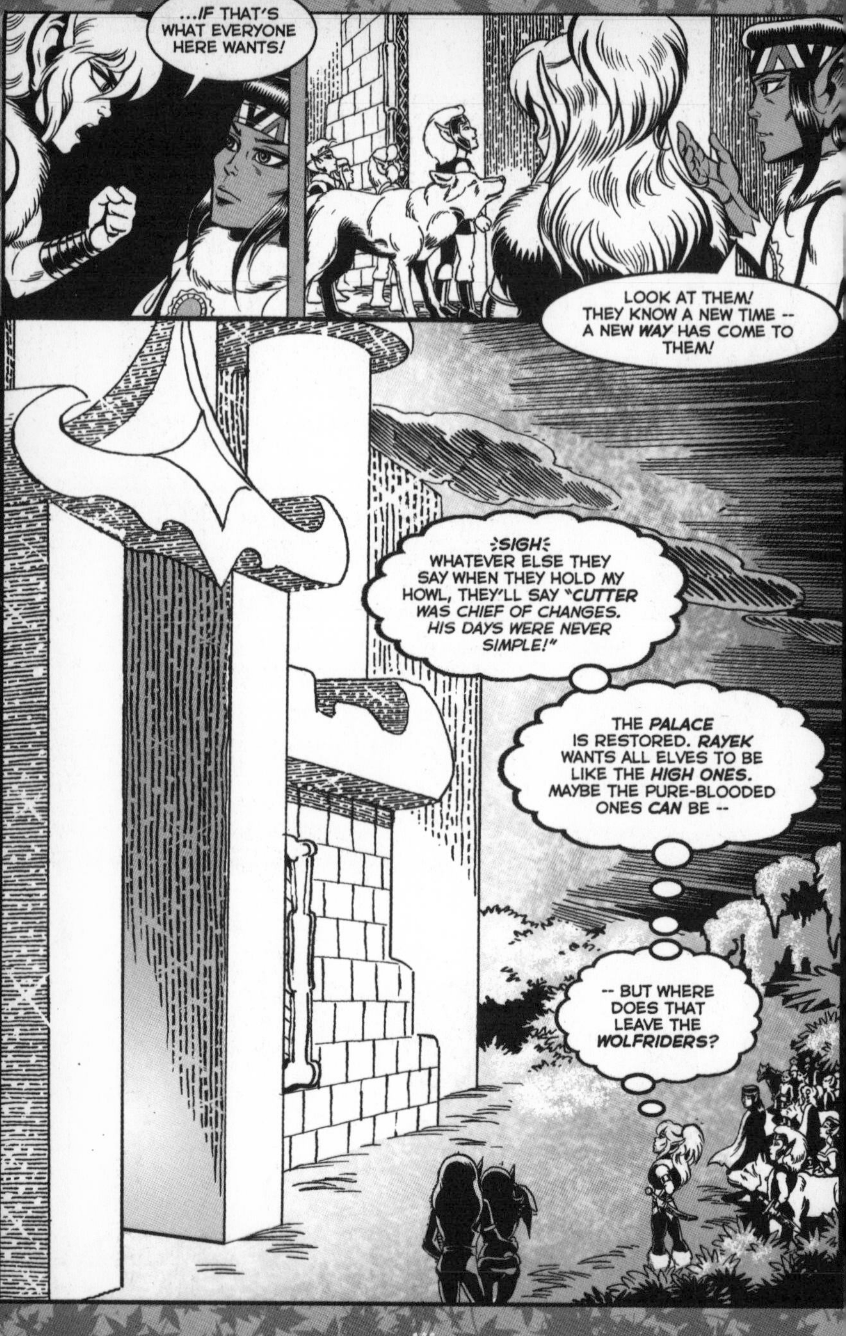
...IF THAT'S WHAT EVERYONE HERE WANTS!
LOOK AT THEM! THEY KNOW A NEW TIME -- A NEW WAY HAS COME TO THEM!
SIGH WHATEVER ELSE THEY SAY WHEN THEY HOLD MY HOWL, THEY'LL SAY "CUTTER WAS CHIEF OF CHANGES. HIS DAYS WERE NEVER SIMPLE!"
THE PALACE IS RESTORED. RAYEK WANTS ALL ELVES TO BE LIKE THE HIGH ONES. MAYBE THE PURE-BLOODED ONES CAN BE --
-- BUT WHERE DOES THAT LEAVE THE WOLFRIDERS?

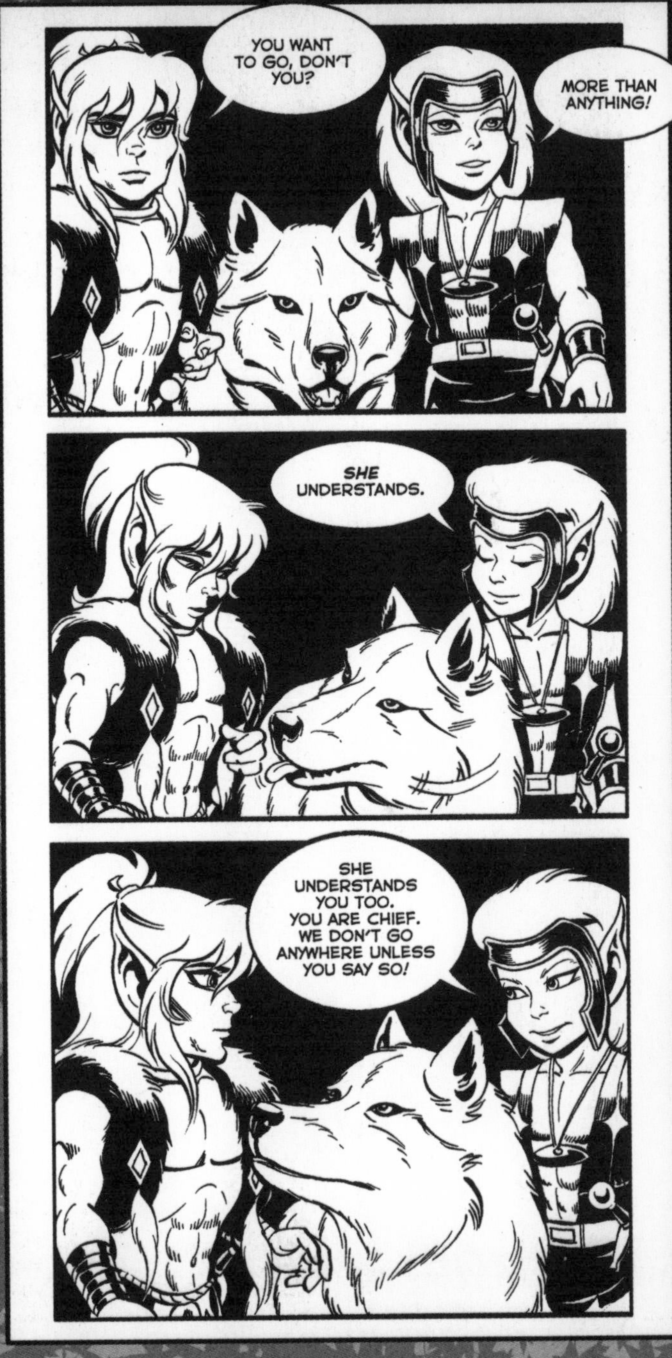
YOU WANT TO GO, DON'T YOU?
MORE THAN ANYTHING!
SHE UNDERSTANDS.
SHE UNDERSTANDS YOU TOO. YOU ARE CHIEF. WE DON'T GO ANYWHERE UNLESS YOU SAY SO!

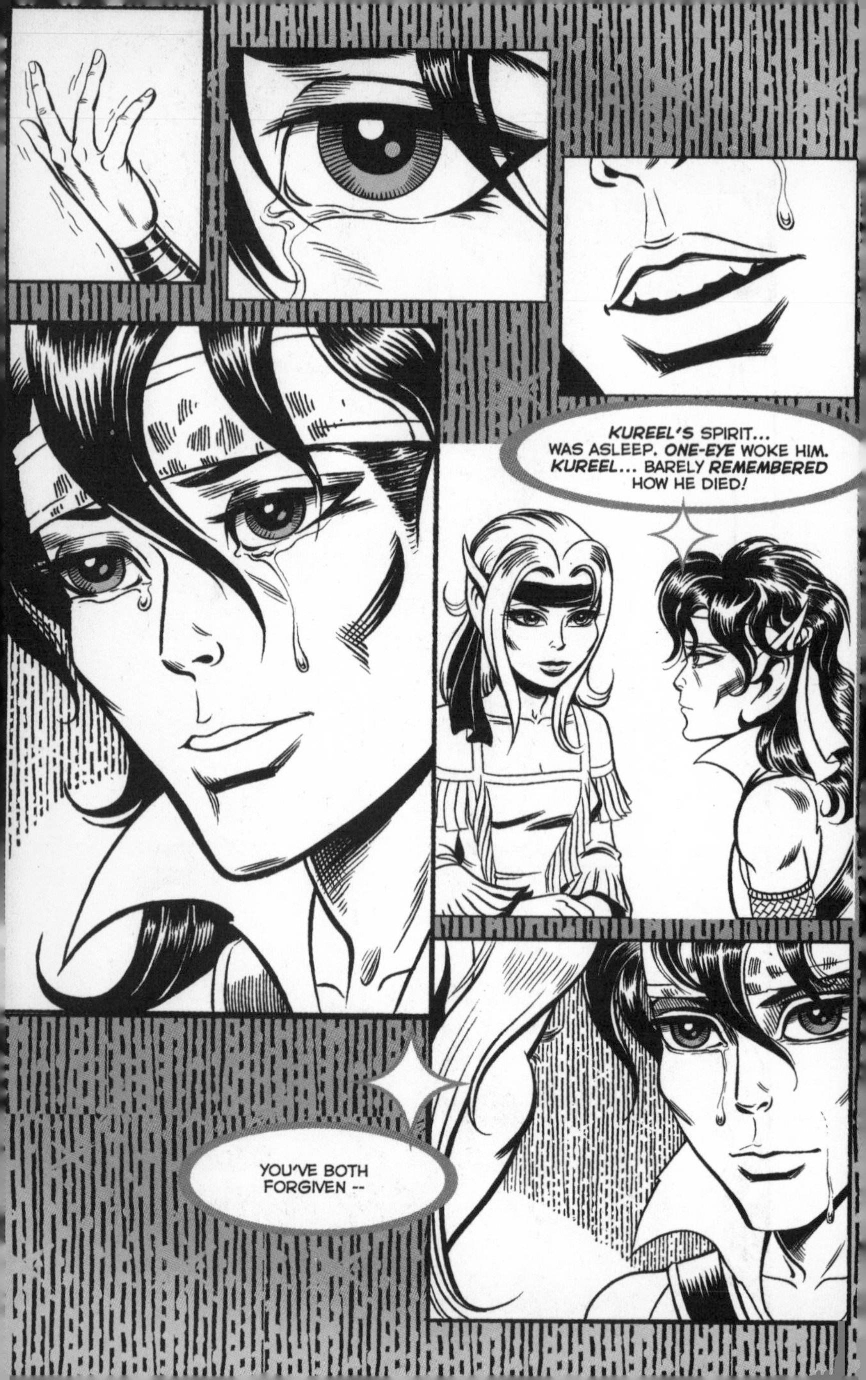
KUREEL'S SPIRIT... WAS ASLEEP. ONE-EYE WOKE HIM. KUREEL... BARELY REMEMBERED HOW HE DIED!
YOU'VE BOTH FORGIVEN --

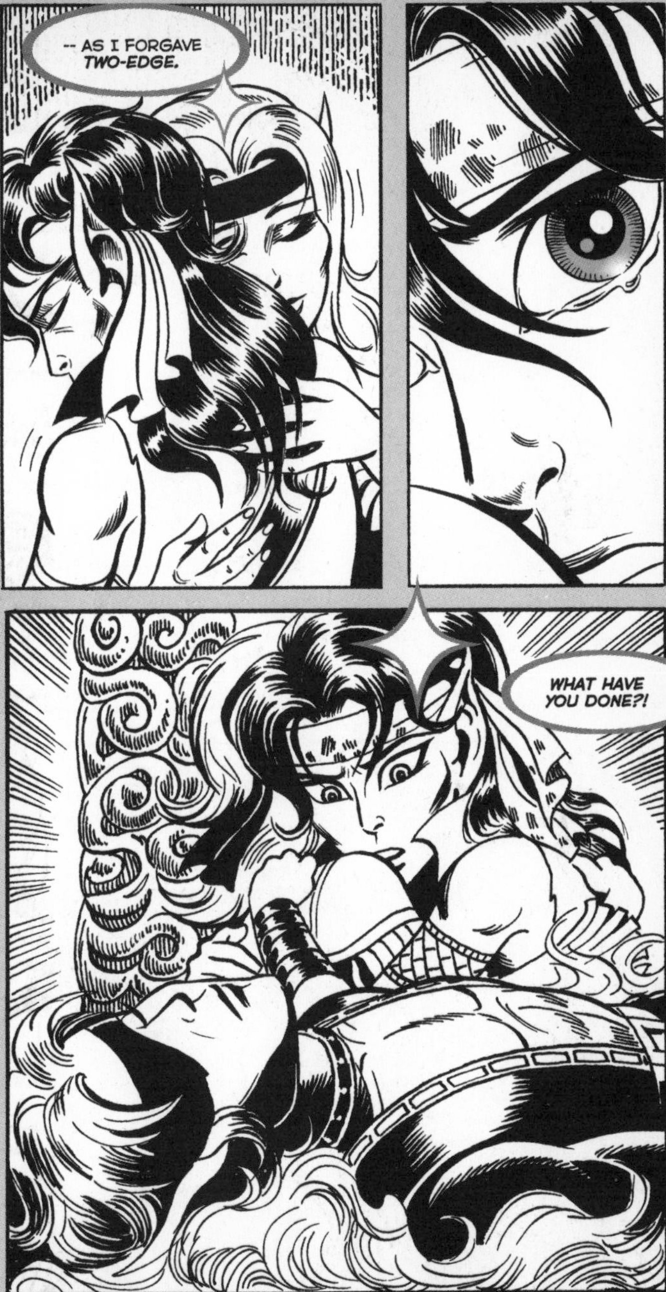

-- AS I FORGAVE TWO-EDGE.
WHAT HAVE YOU DONE?!

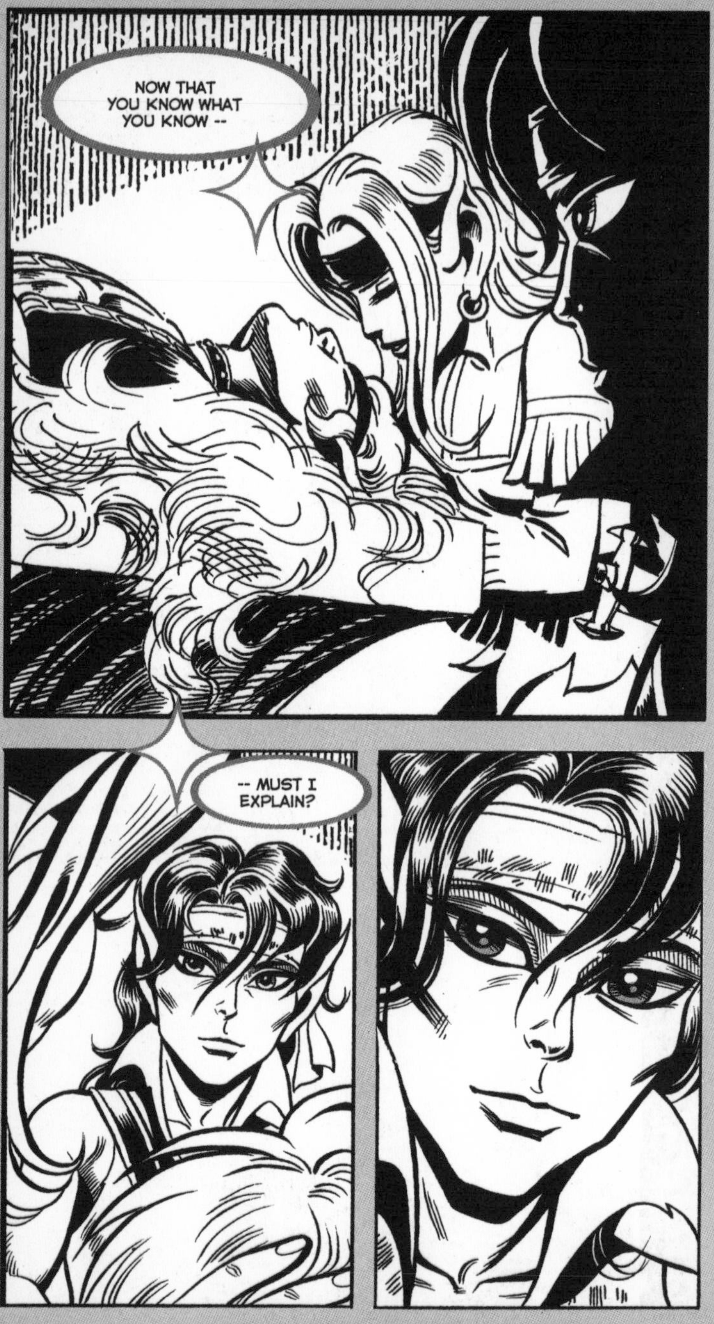
NOW THAT YOU KNOW WHAT YOU KNOW --
-- MUST I EXPLAIN?

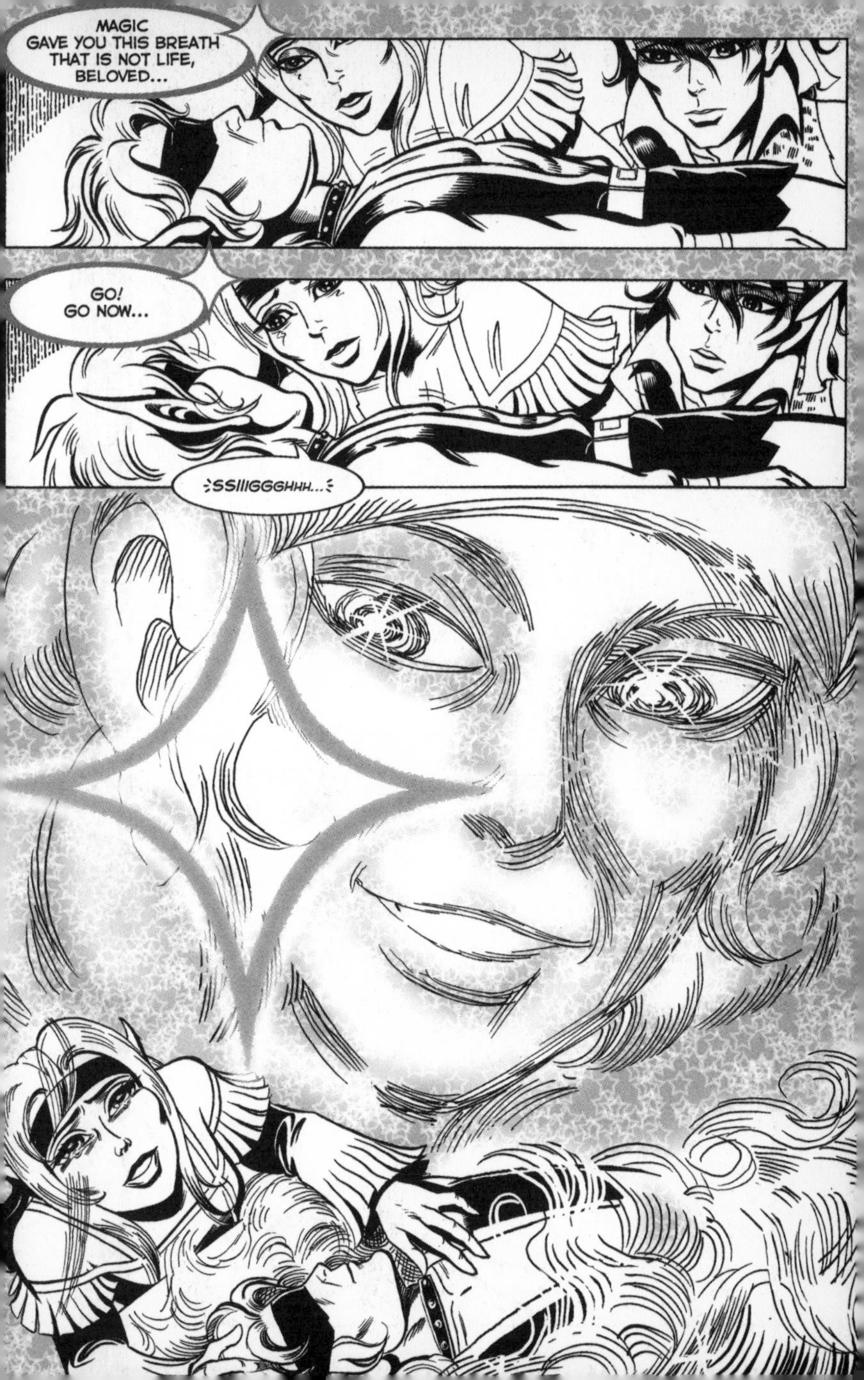
MAGIC GAVE YOU THIS BREATH THAT IS NOT LIFE, BELOVED...
GO! GO NOW...
SSIIIGGGHHH...

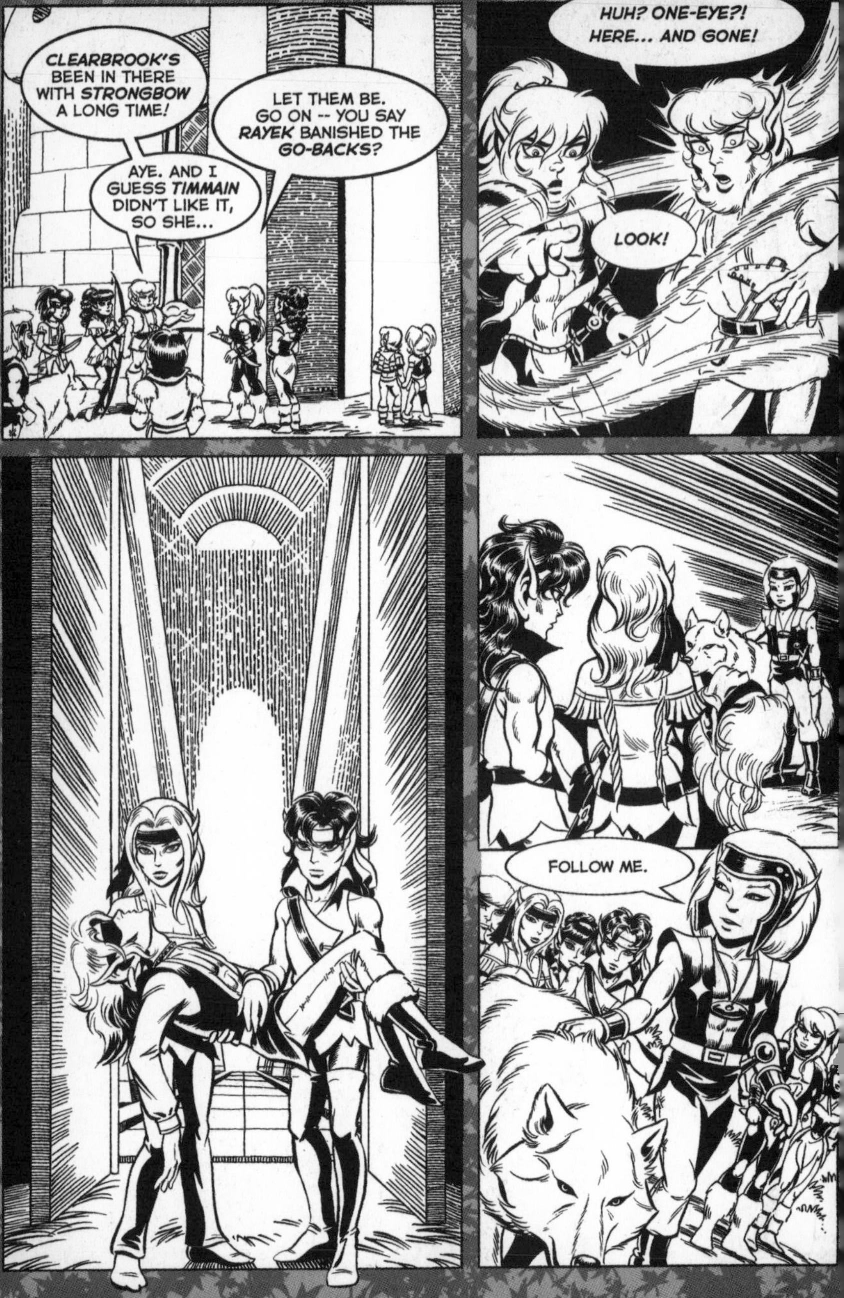
CLEARBROOK'S BEEN IN THERE WITH STRONGBOW A LONG TIME!
LET THEM BE. GO ON -- YOU SAY RAYEK BANISHED THE GO-BACKS?
AYE. AND I GUESS TIMMAIN DIDN'T LIKE IT, SO SHE...
HUH? ONE-EYE?! HERE... AND GONE!
LOOK!
FOLLOW ME.

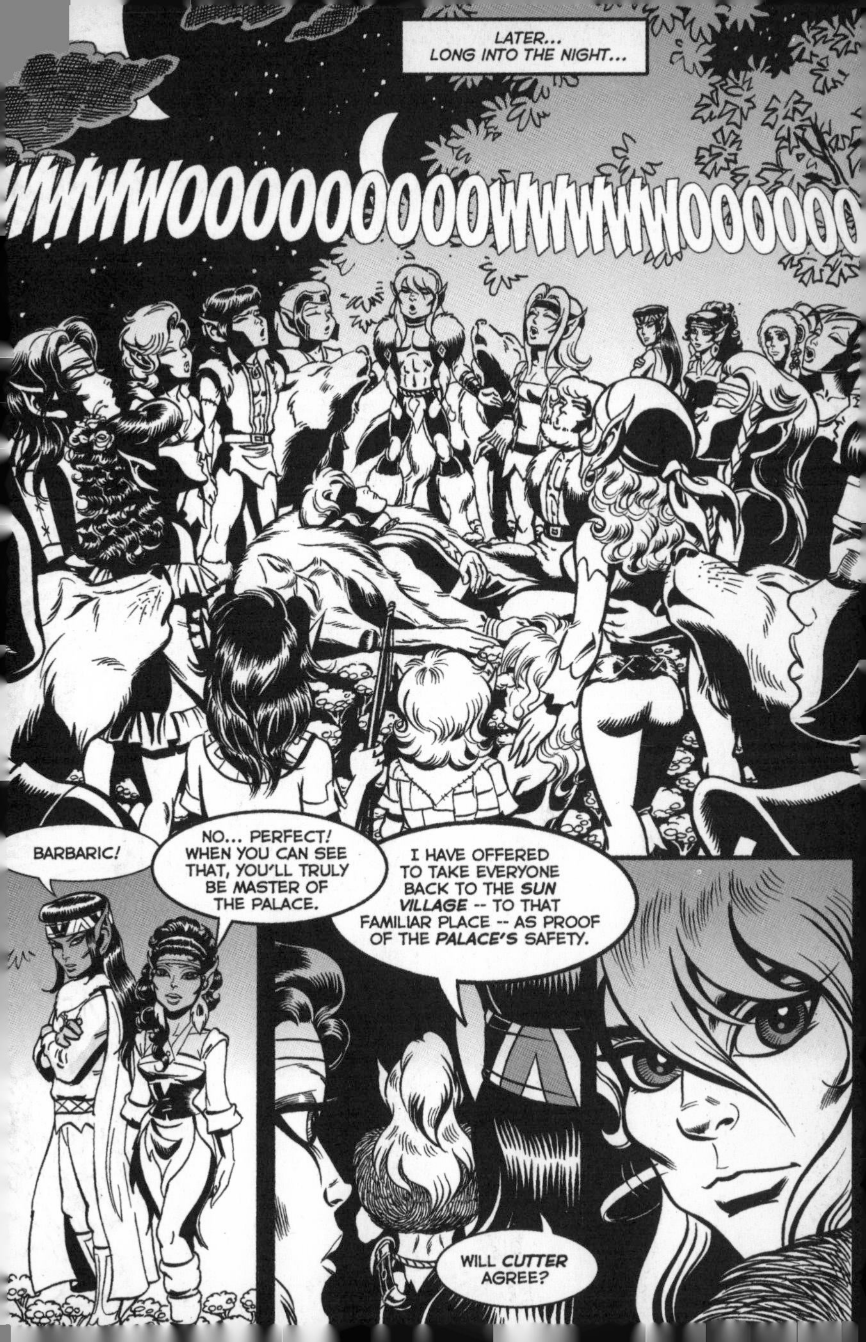
LATER... LONG INTO THE NIGHT...
WWWWOOOOOOOOOOWWWWWOOOOOO
BARBARIC!
NO... PERFECT! WHEN YOU CAN SEE THAT, YOU'LL TRULY BE MASTER OF THE PALACE.
I HAVE OFFERED TO TAKE EVERYONE BACK TO THE SUN VILLAGE -- TO THAT FAMILIAR PLACE -- AS PROOF OF THE PALACE'S SAFETY.
WILL CUTTER AGREE?

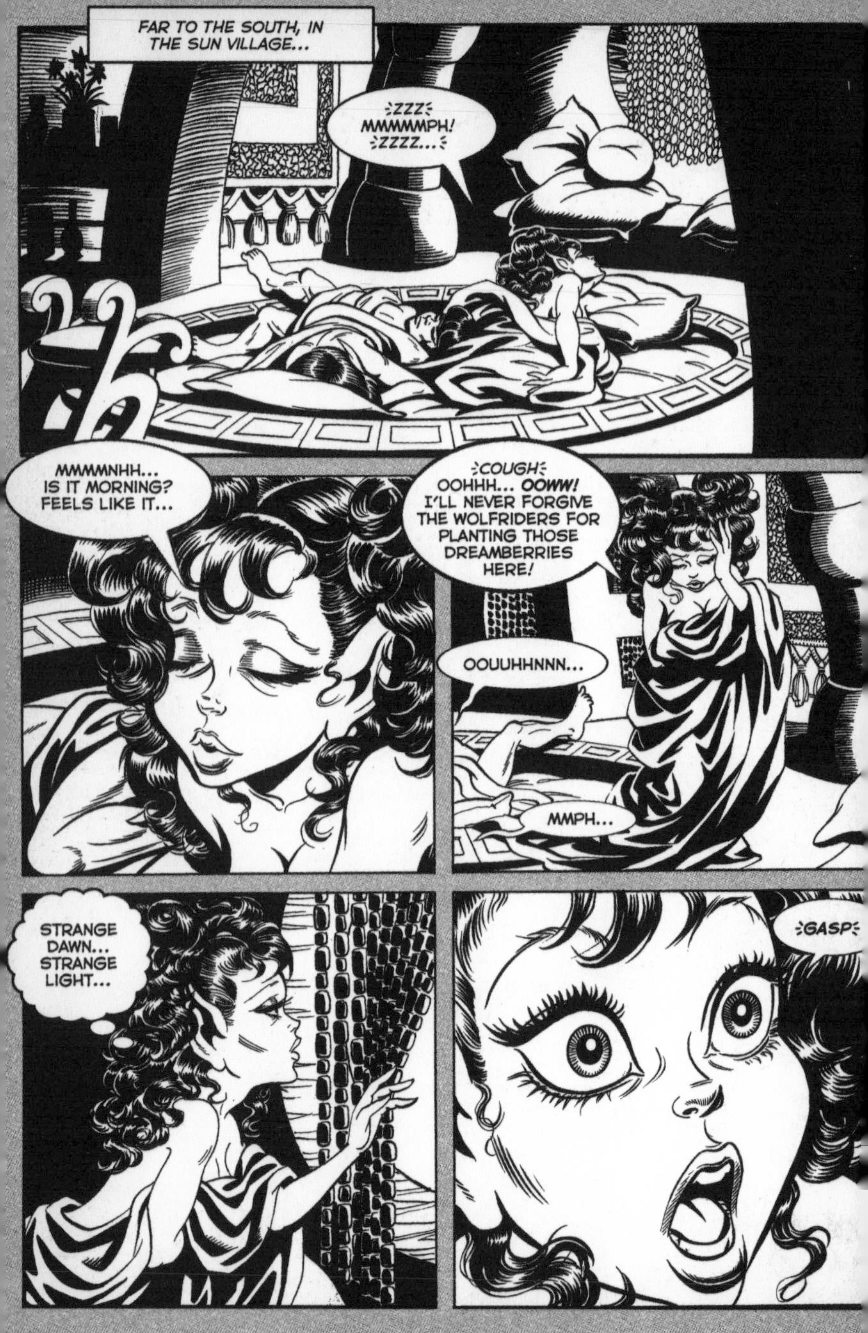
FAR TO THE SOUTH, IN THE SUN VILLAGE...
:ZZZ: MMMMMPH! :ZZZZ...:
MMMMNHH... IS IT MORNING? FEELS LIKE IT...
:COUGH: OOHHH... OOWW! I'LL NEVER FORGIVE THE WOLFRIDERS FOR PLANTING THOSE DREAMBERRIES HERE!
OOUUHHNNN...
MMPH...
STRANGE DAWN... STRANGE LIGHT...
:GASP:

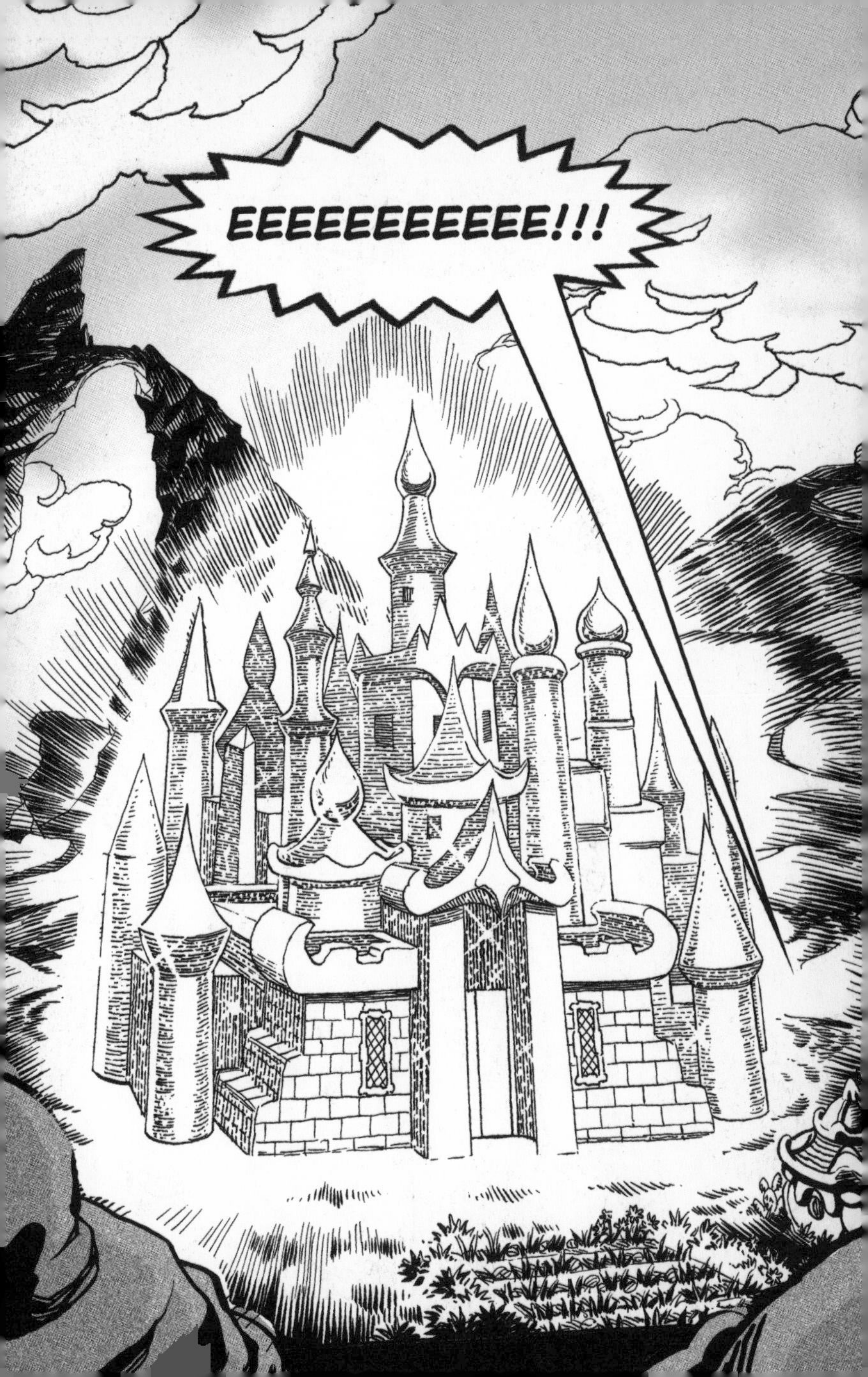
EEEEEEEEEEEEE!!!

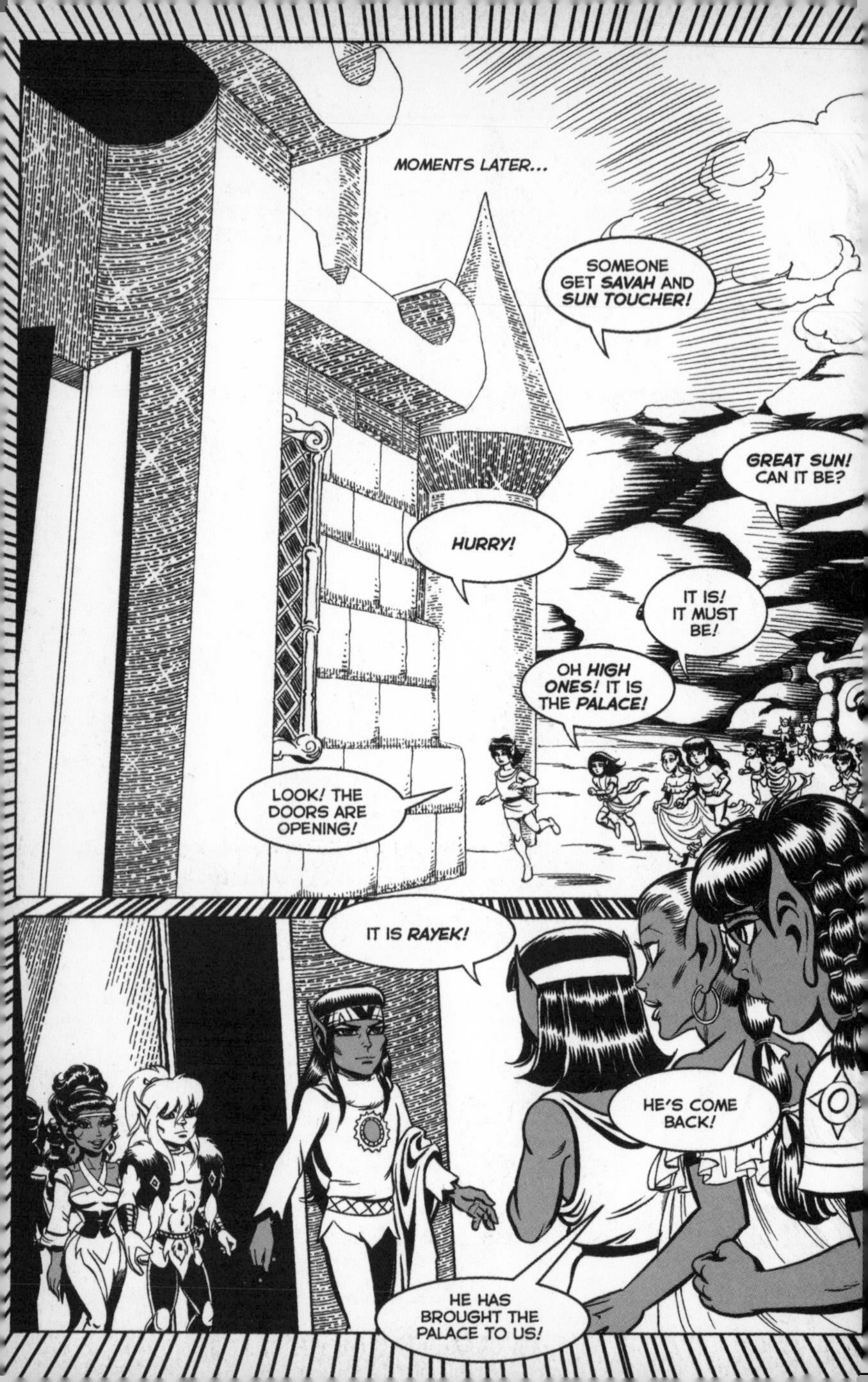
MOMENTS LATER...
SOMEONE GET SAVAH AND SUN TOUCHER!
GREAT SUN! CAN IT BE?
HURRY!
IT IS! IT MUST BE!
OH HIGH ONES! IT IS THE PALACE!
LOOK! THE DOORS ARE OPENING!
IT IS RAYEK!
HE'S COME BACK!
HE HAS BROUGHT THE PALACE TO US!

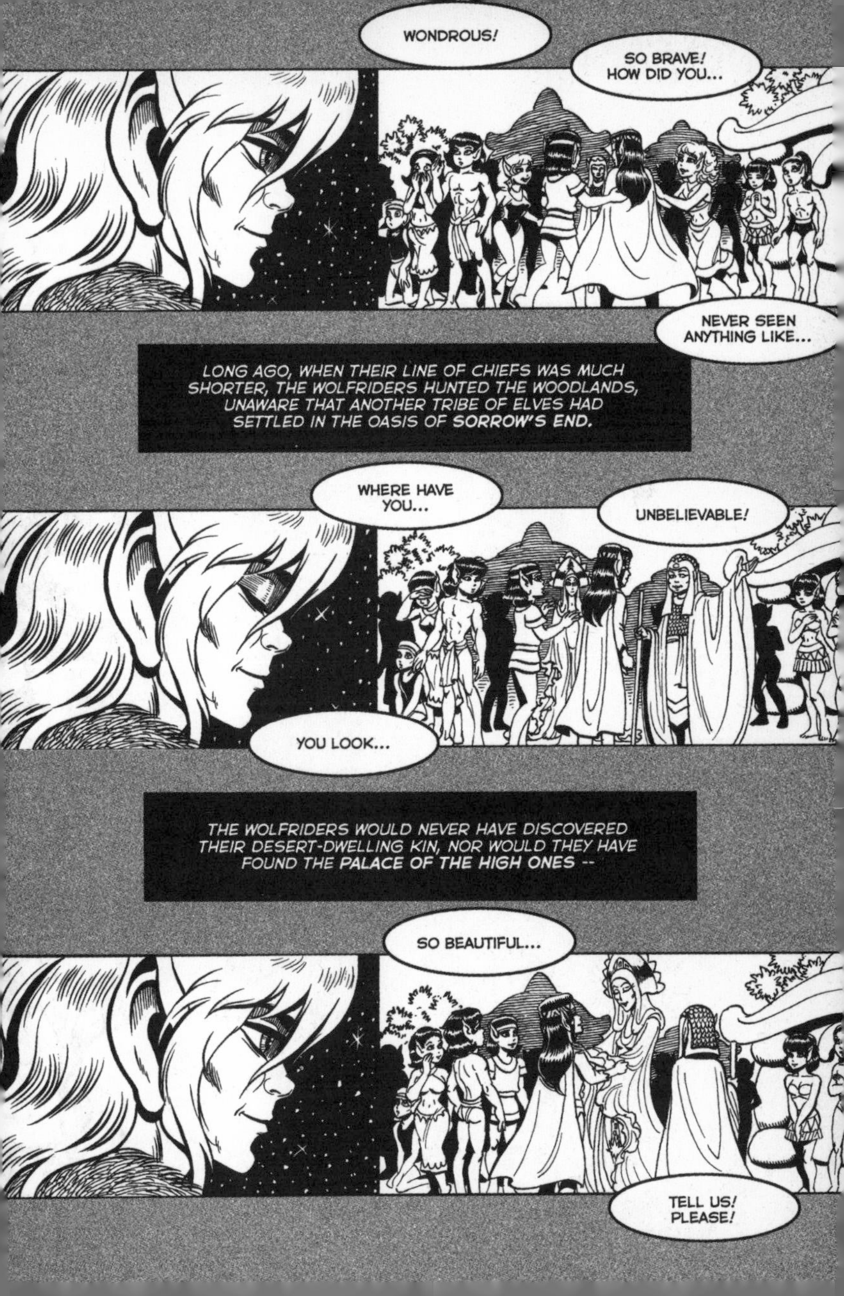
WONDROUS!
SO BRAVE! HOW DID YOU...
NEVER SEEN ANYTHING LIKE...
LONG AGO, WHEN THEIR LINE OF CHIEFS WAS MUCH SHORTER, THE WOLFRIDERS HUNTED THE WOODLANDS, UNAWARE THAT ANOTHER TRIBE OF ELVES HAD SETTLED IN THE OASIS OF SORROW'S END.
WHERE HAVE YOU...
UNBELIEVABLE!
YOU LOOK...
THE WOLFRIDERS WOULD NEVER HAVE DISCOVERED THEIR DESERT-DWELLING KIN, NOR WOULD THEY HAVE FOUND THE PALACE OF THE HIGH ONES --
SO BEAUTIFUL...
TELL US! PLEASE!

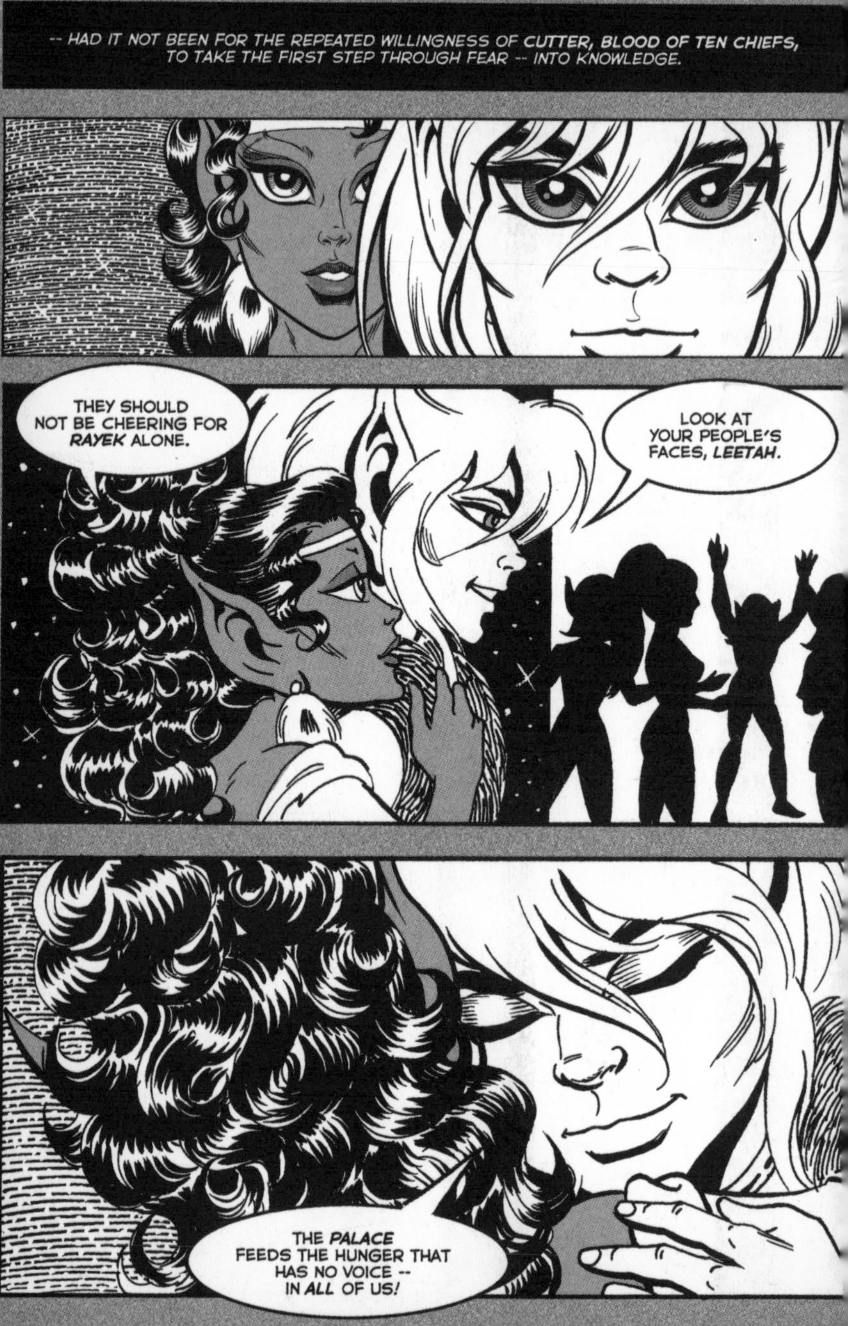
-- HAD IT NOT BEEN FOR THE REPEATED WILLINGNESS OF CUTTER, BLOOD OF TEN CHIEFS, TO TAKE THE FIRST STEP THROUGH FEAR -- INTO KNOWLEDGE.
THEY SHOULD NOT BE CHEERING FOR RAYEK ALONE.
LOOK AT YOUR PEOPLE'S FACES, LEETAH.
THE PALACE FEEDS THE HUNGER THAT HAS NO VOICE -- IN ALL OF US!

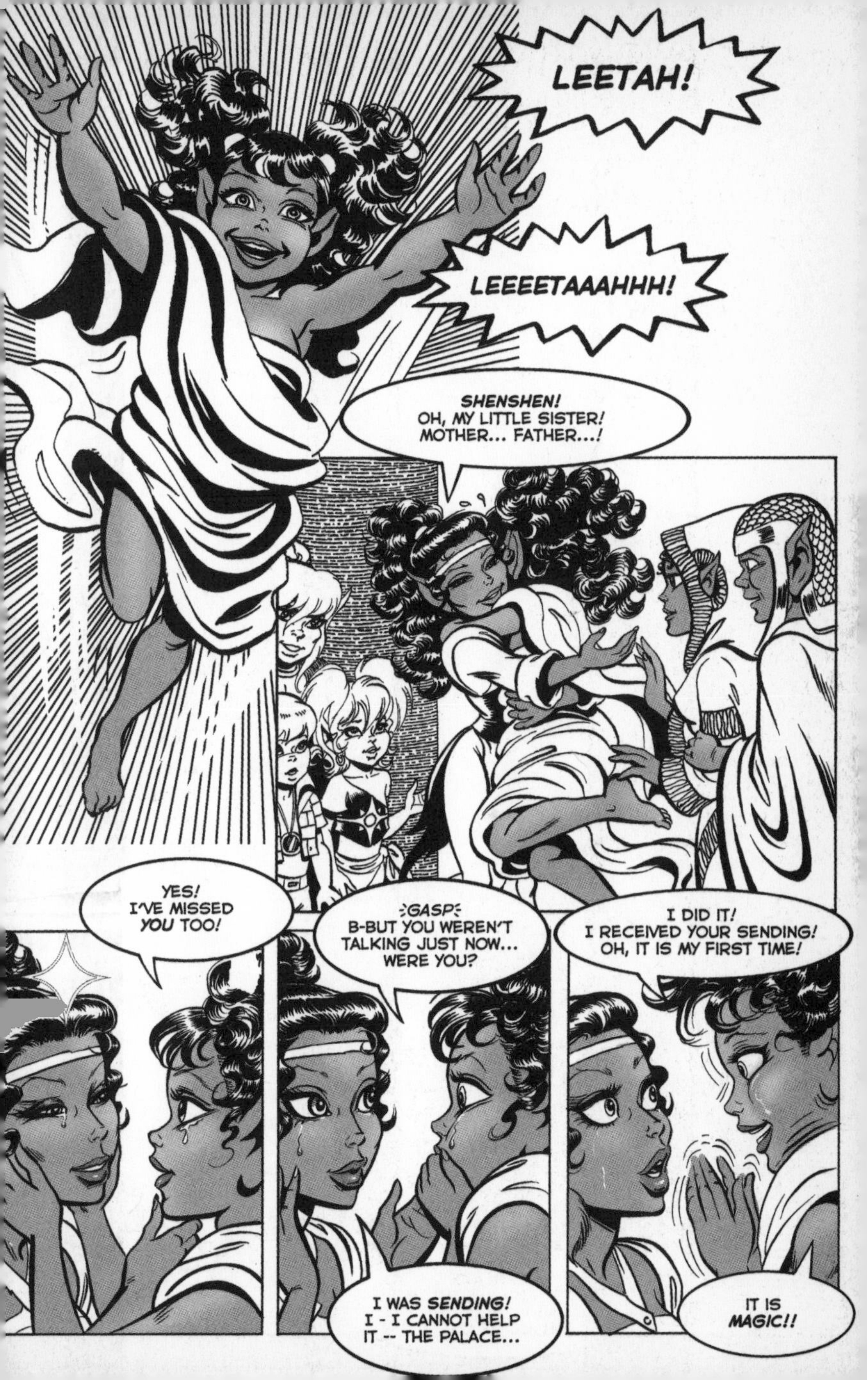
LEETAH!
LEEEETAAAHHH!
SHENSHEN! OH, MY LITTLE SISTER! MOTHER... FATHER...!
YES! I'VE MISSED YOU TOO!
GASP B-BUT YOU WEREN'T TALKING JUST NOW... WERE YOU?
I WAS SENDING! I - I CANNOT HELP IT -- THE PALACE...
I DID IT! I RECEIVED YOUR SENDING! OH, IT IS MY FIRST TIME!
IT IS MAGIC!!

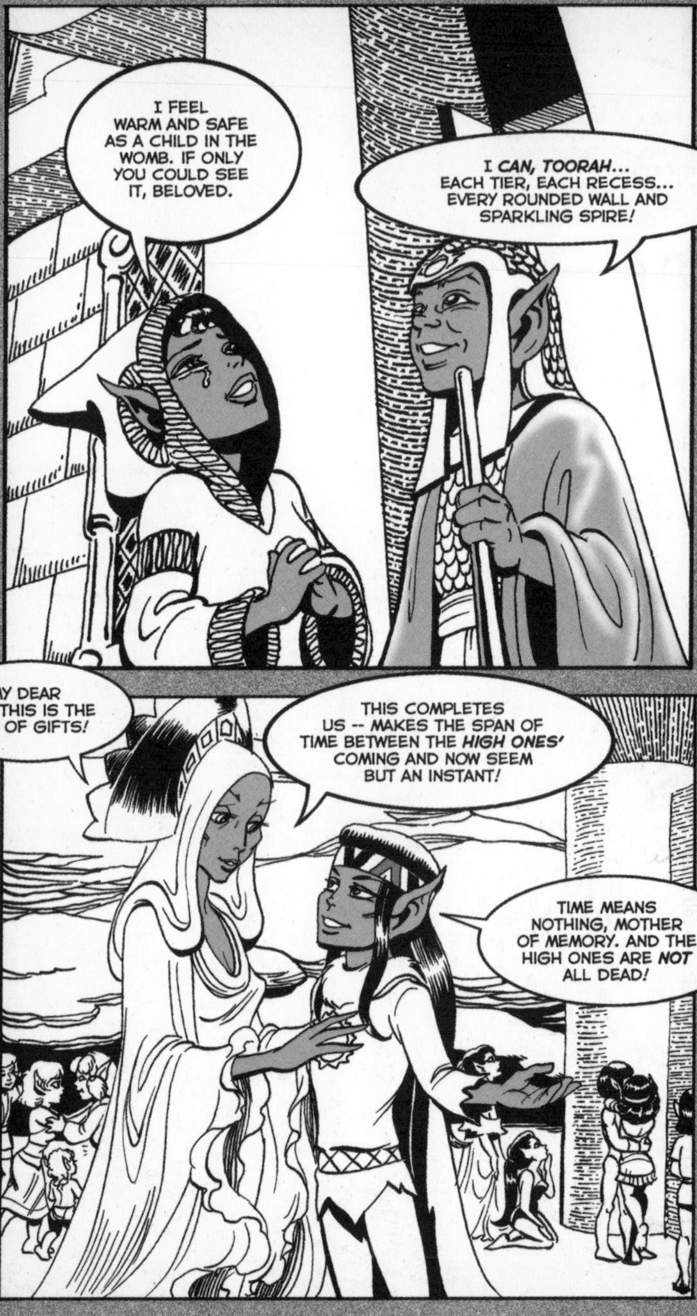

I FEEL WARM AND SAFE AS A CHILD IN THE WOMB. IF ONLY YOU COULD SEE IT, BELOVED.
I *CAN, TOORAH*... EACH TIER, EACH RECESS... EVERY ROUNDED WALL AND SPARKLING SPIRE!
MY DEAR ONE, THIS IS THE GIFT OF GIFTS!
THIS COMPLETES US -- MAKES THE SPAN OF TIME BETWEEN THE *HIGH ONES'* COMING AND NOW SEEM BUT AN INSTANT!
TIME MEANS NOTHING, MOTHER OF MEMORY. AND THE HIGH ONES ARE *NOT* ALL DEAD!

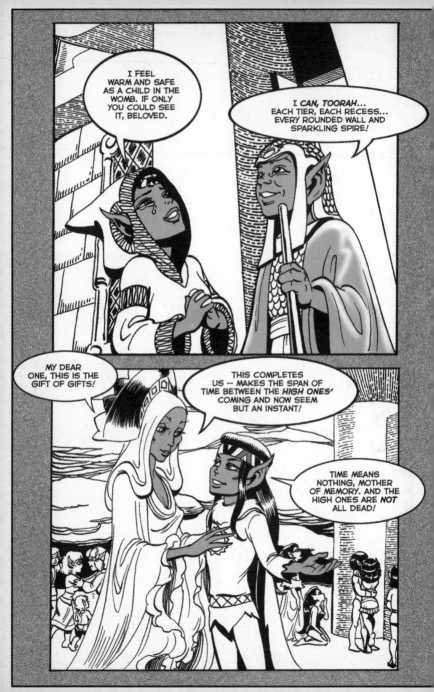

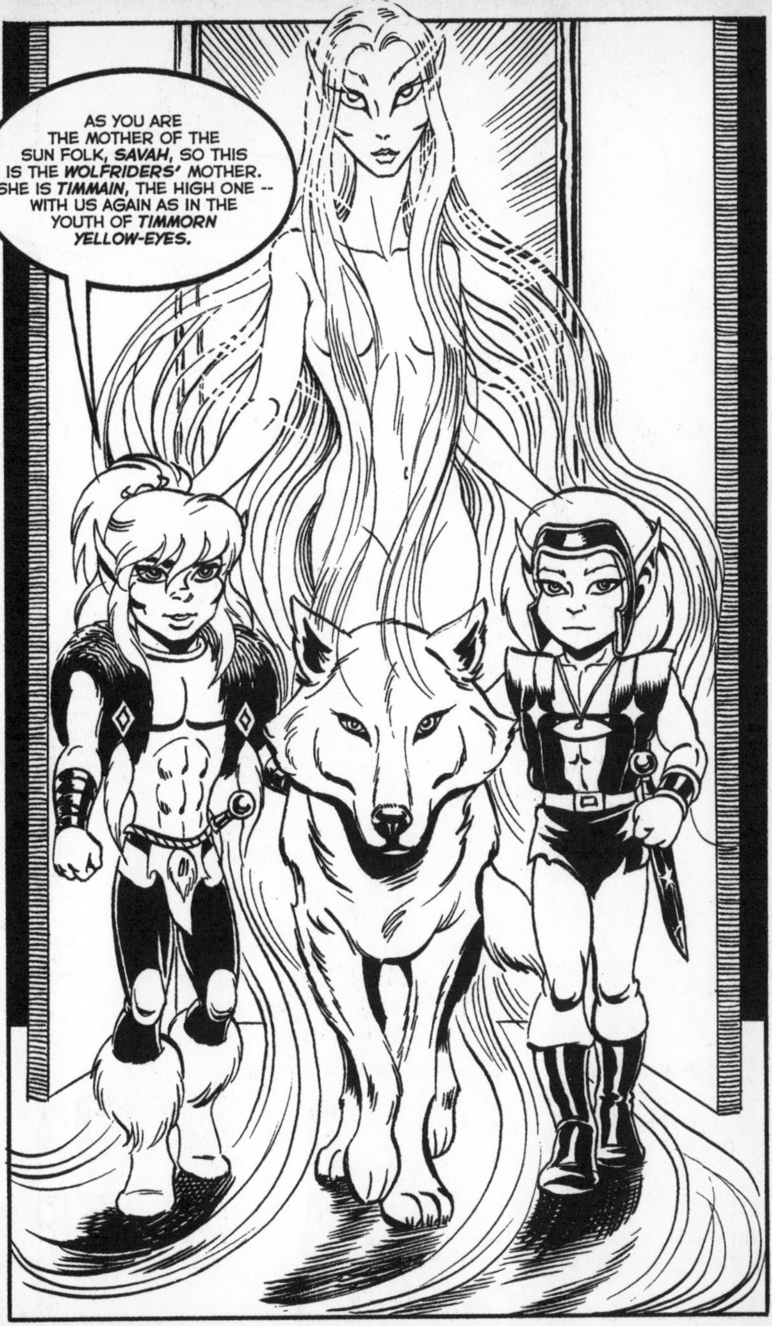
AS YOU ARE THE MOTHER OF THE SUN FOLK, SAVAH, SO THIS IS THE WOLFRIDERS' MOTHER. SHE IS TIMMAIN, THE HIGH ONE -- WITH US AGAIN AS IN THE YOUTH OF TIMMORN YELLOW-EYES.

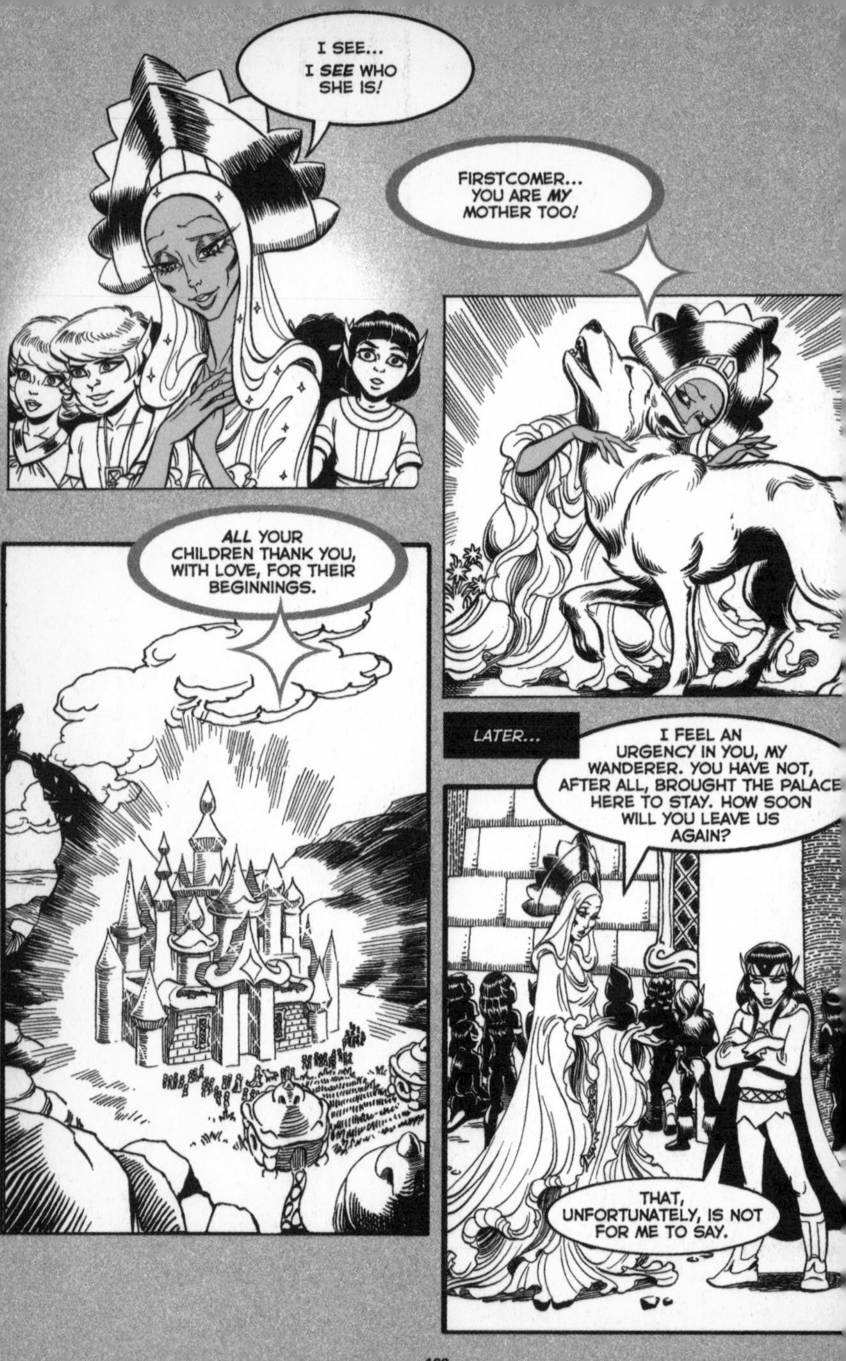
I SEE...
I *SEE* WHO SHE IS!
FIRSTCOMER... YOU ARE *MY* MOTHER TOO!
ALL YOUR CHILDREN THANK YOU, WITH LOVE, FOR THEIR BEGINNINGS.
LATER...
I FEEL AN URGENCY IN YOU, MY WANDERER. YOU HAVE NOT, AFTER ALL, BROUGHT THE PALACE HERE TO STAY. HOW SOON WILL YOU LEAVE US AGAIN?
THAT, UNFORTUNATELY, IS NOT FOR ME TO SAY.

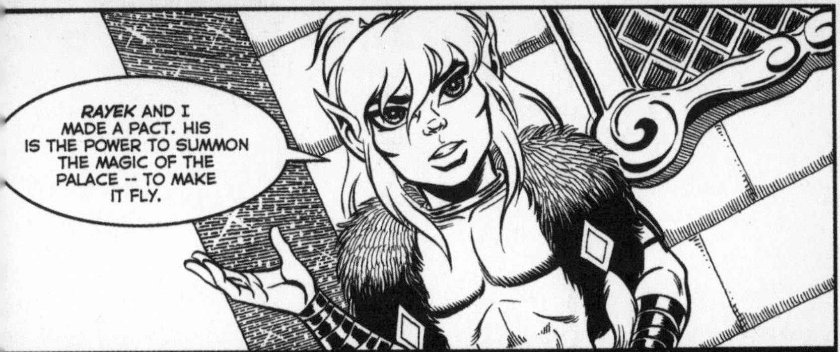
RAYEK AND I MADE A PACT. HIS IS THE POWER TO SUMMON THE MAGIC OF THE PALACE -- TO MAKE IT FLY.

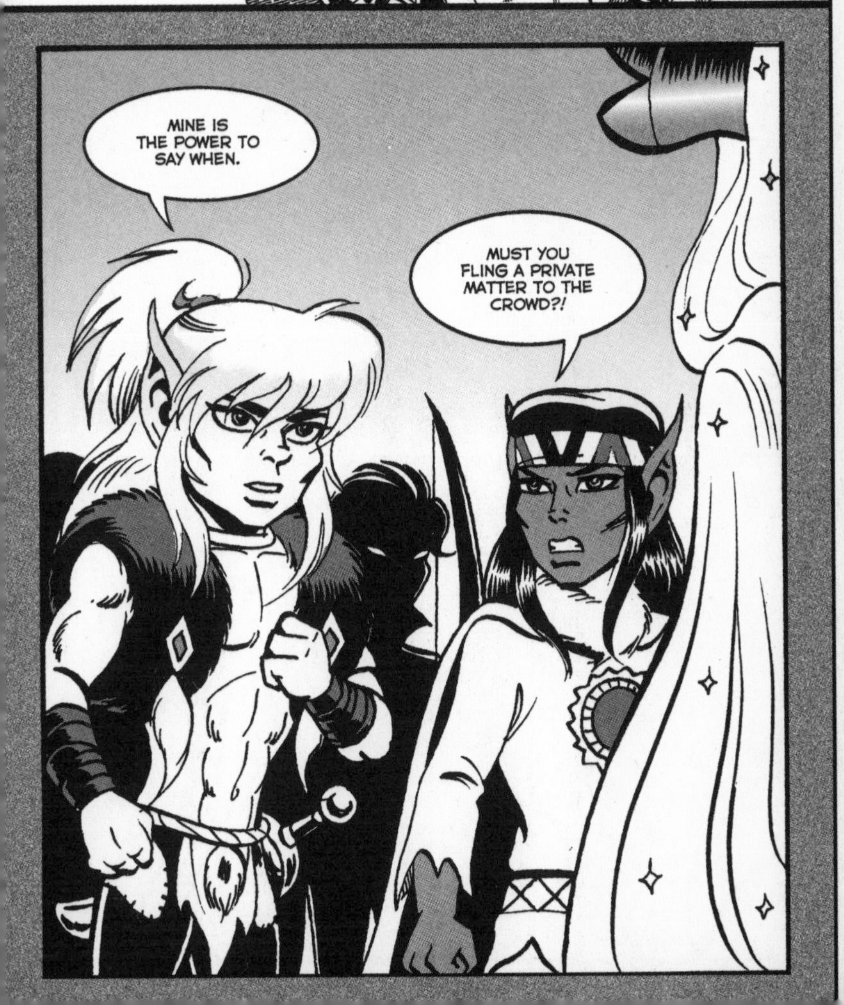
MINE IS THE POWER TO SAY WHEN.
MUST YOU FLING A PRIVATE MATTER TO THE CROWD?!

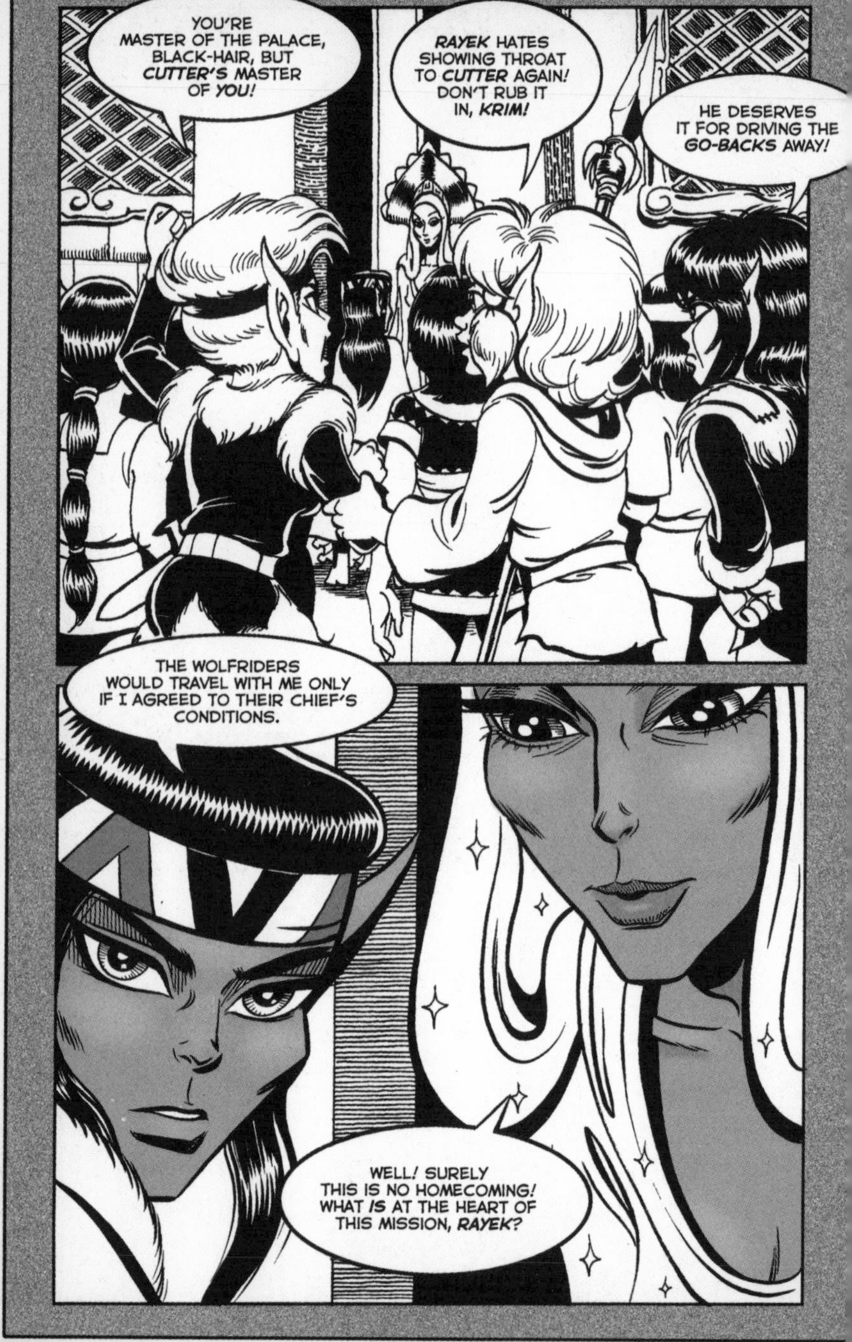
YOU'RE MASTER OF THE PALACE, BLACK-HAIR, BUT CUTTER'S MASTER OF YOU!
RAYEK HATES SHOWING THROAT TO CUTTER AGAIN! DON'T RUB IT IN, KRIM!
HE DESERVES IT FOR DRIVING THE GO-BACKS AWAY!
THE WOLFRIDERS WOULD TRAVEL WITH ME ONLY IF I AGREED TO THEIR CHIEF'S CONDITIONS.
WELL! SURELY THIS IS NO HOMECOMING! WHAT IS AT THE HEART OF THIS MISSION, RAYEK?

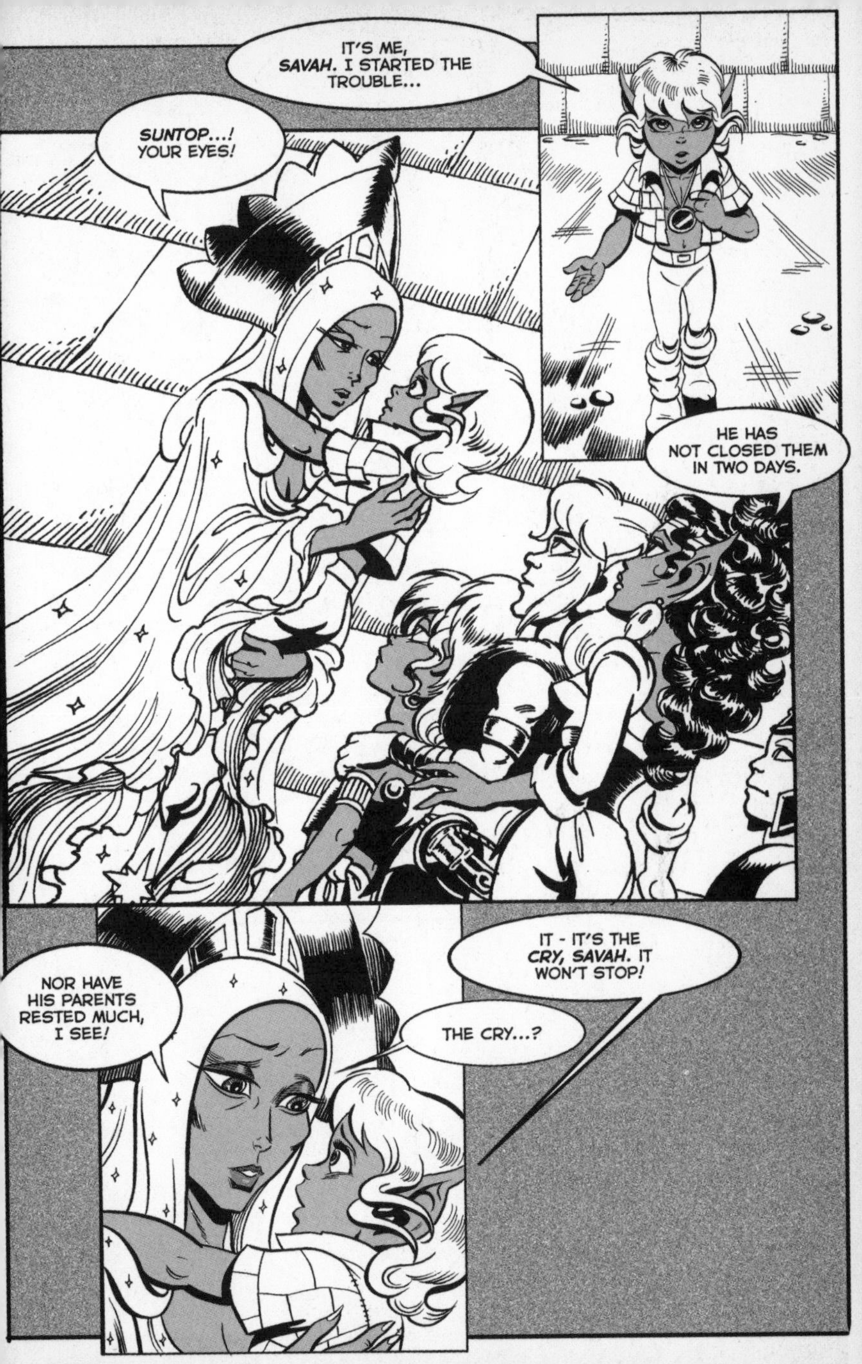
IT'S ME, SAVAH. I STARTED THE TROUBLE...
SUNTOP...! YOUR EYES!
HE HAS NOT CLOSED THEM IN TWO DAYS.
NOR HAVE HIS PARENTS RESTED MUCH, I SEE!
IT - IT'S THE CRY, SAVAH. IT WON'T STOP!
THE CRY...?

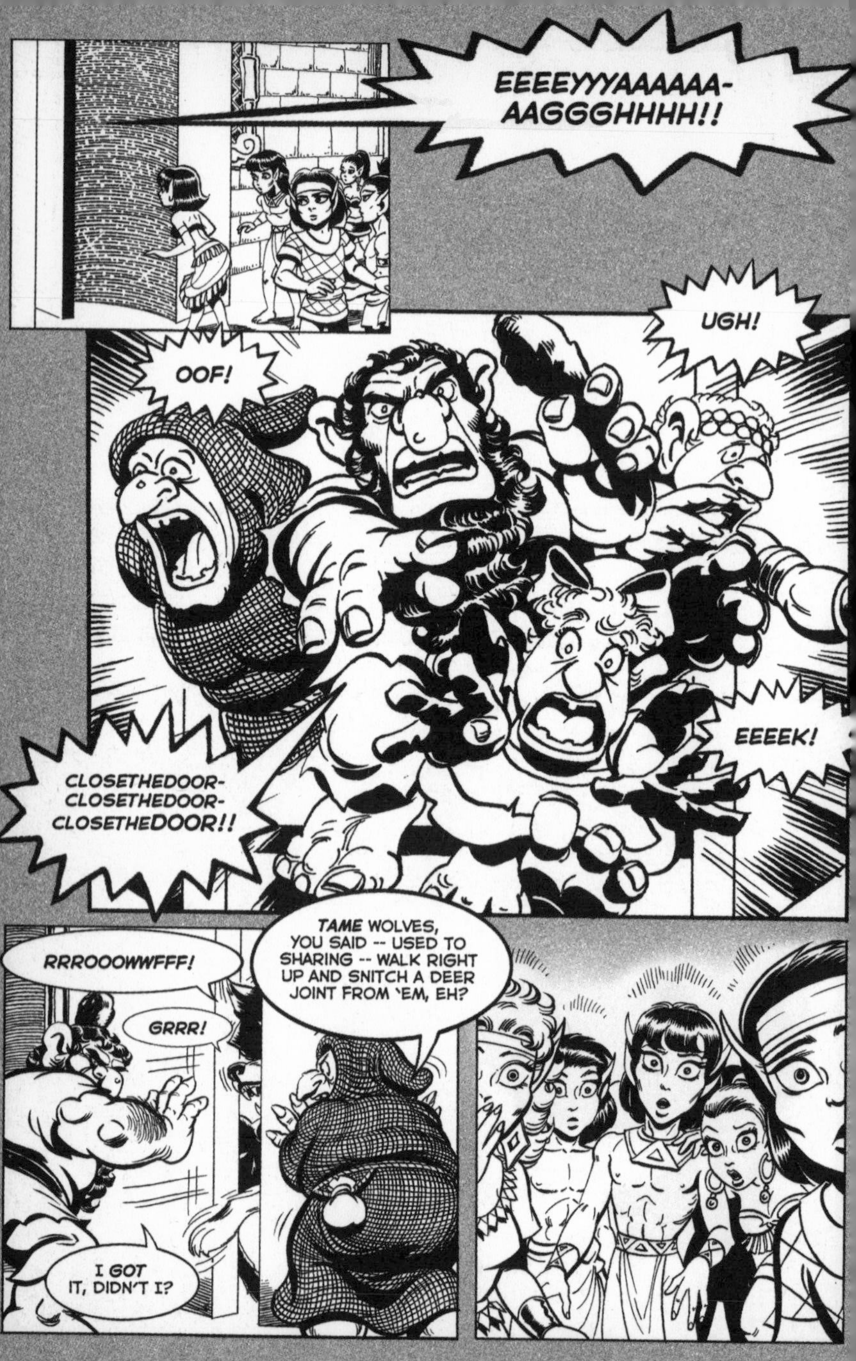
EEEEYYYAAAAAA-
AAGGGHHHH!!
OOF!
UGH!
CLOSETHEDOOR-
CLOSETHEDOOR-
CLOSETHEDOOR!!
EEEEK!
RRROOOWWFFF!
GRRR!
I GOT IT, DIDN'T I?
TAME WOLVES, YOU SAID -- USED TO SHARING -- WALK RIGHT UP AND SNITCH A DEER JOINT FROM 'EM, EH?

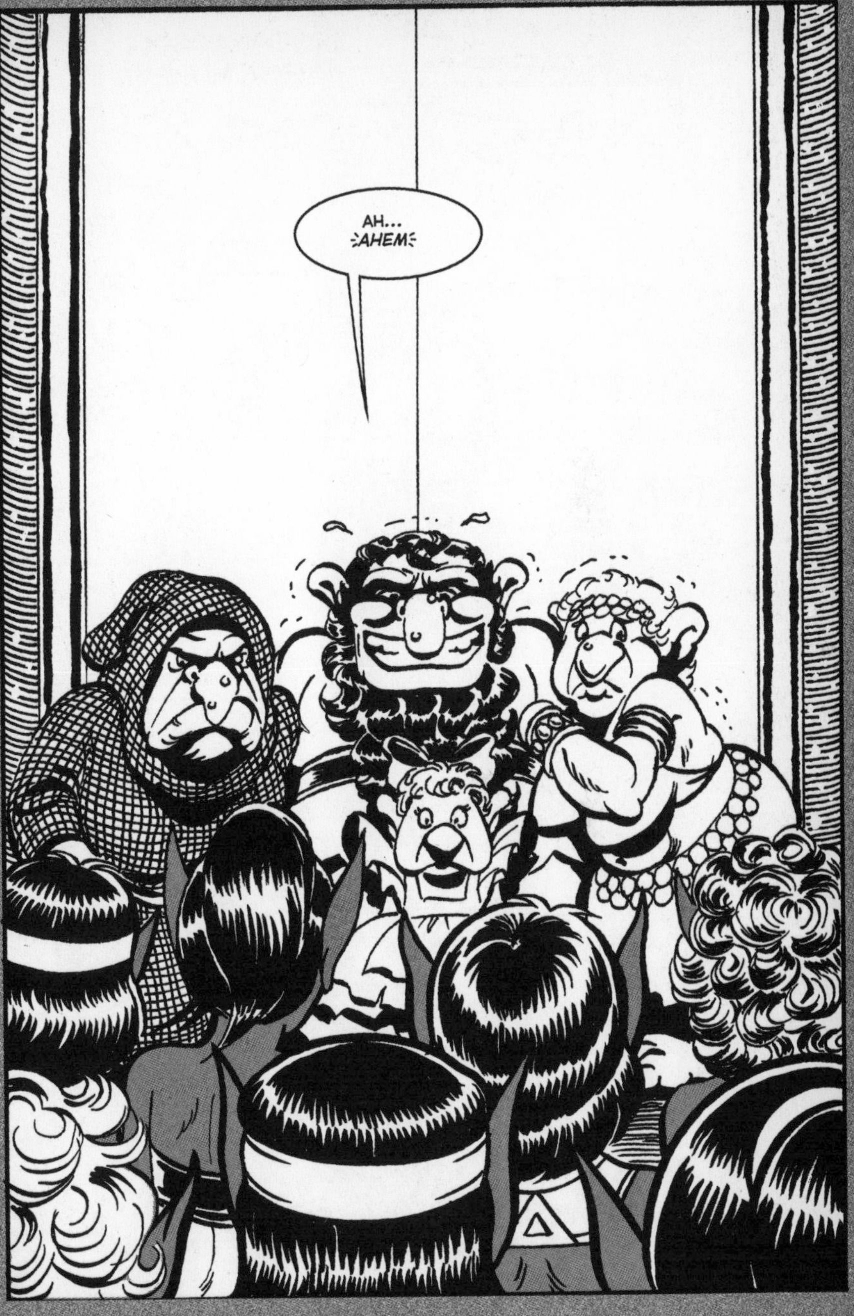
AH... AHEM

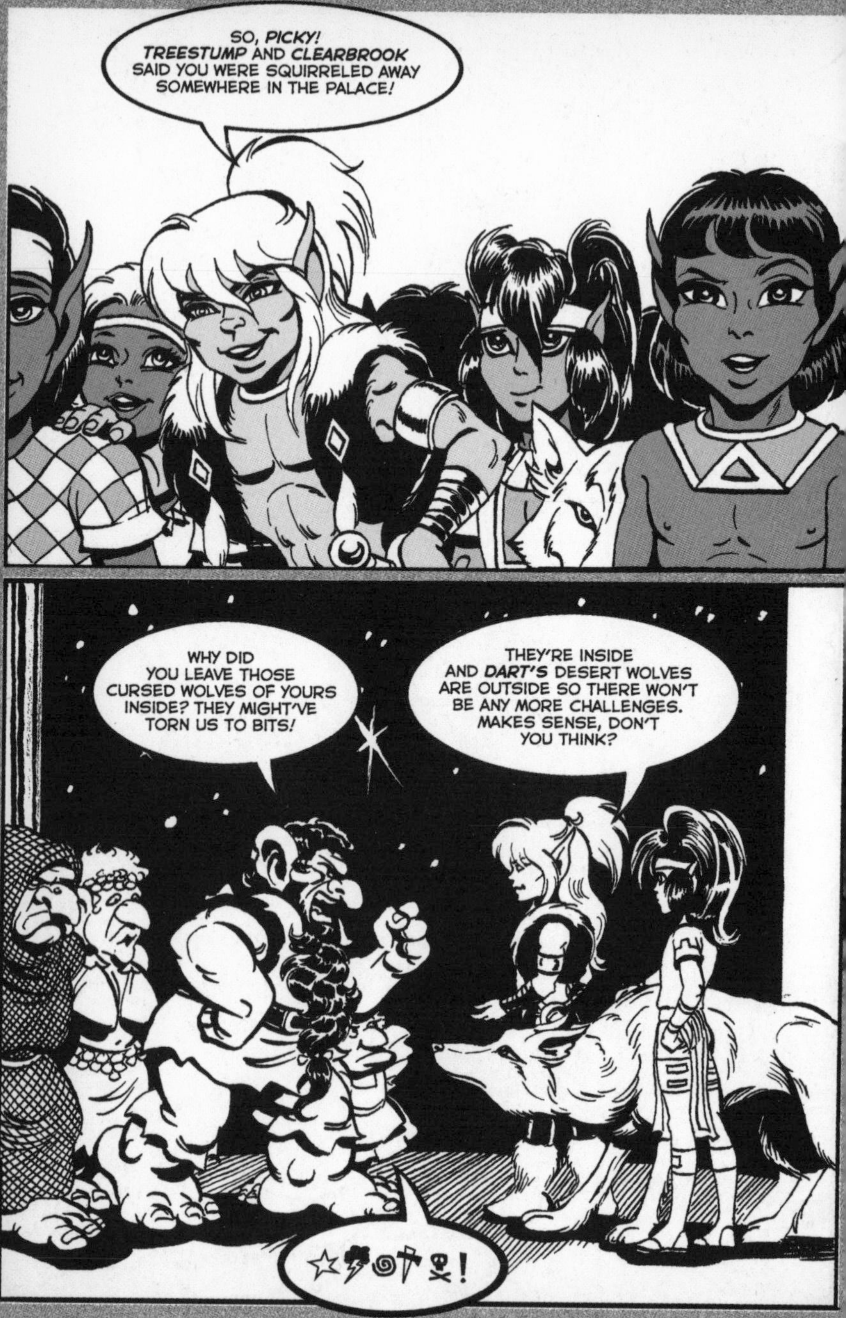
SO, PICKY! TREESTUMP AND CLEARBROOK SAID YOU WERE SQUIRRELED AWAY SOMEWHERE IN THE PALACE!
WHY DID YOU LEAVE THOSE CURSED WOLVES OF YOURS INSIDE? THEY MIGHT'VE TORN US TO BITS!
THEY'RE INSIDE AND DART'S DESERT WOLVES ARE OUTSIDE SO THERE WON'T BE ANY MORE CHALLENGES. MAKES SENSE, DON'T YOU THINK?
!

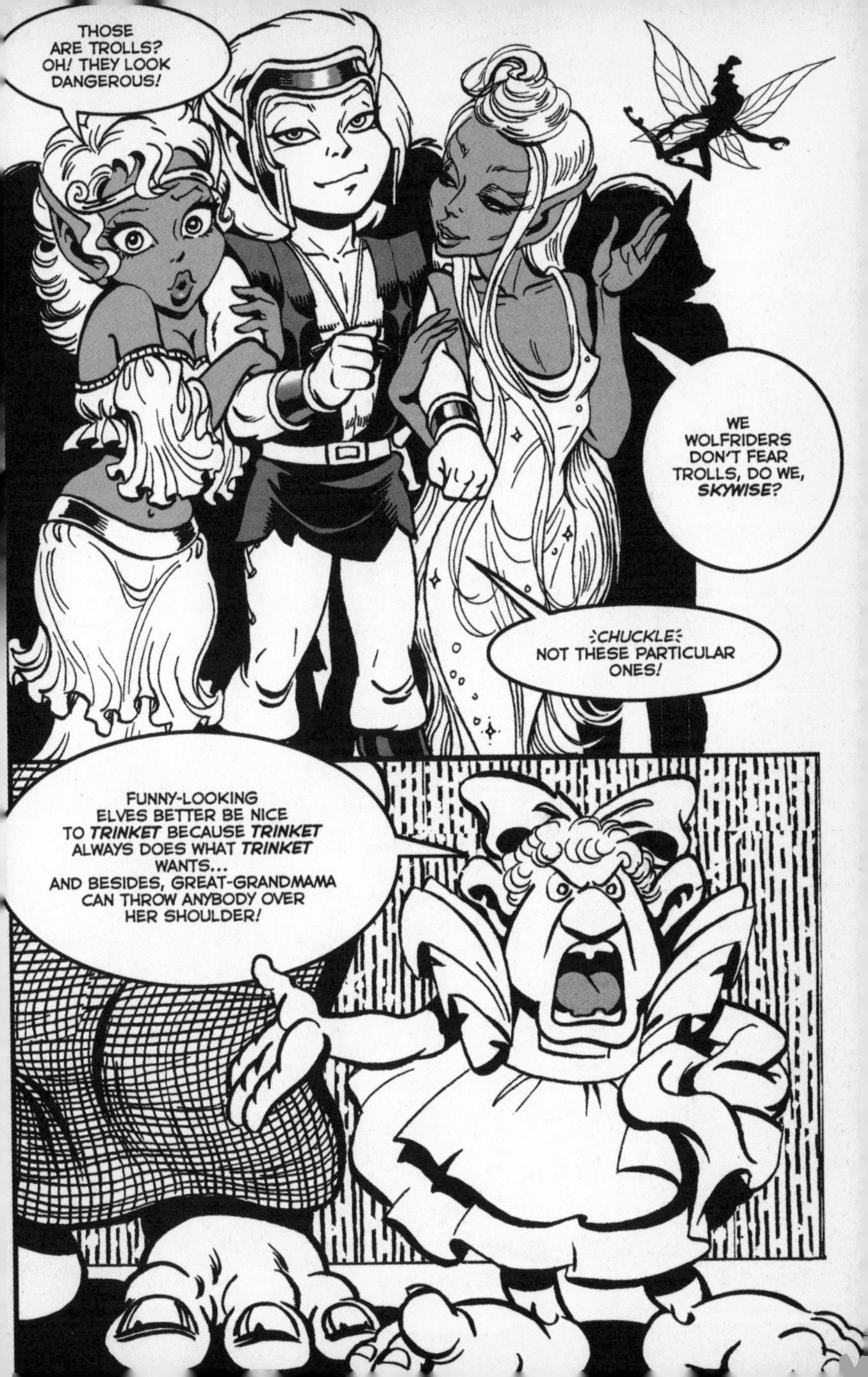
THOSE ARE TROLLS? OH! THEY LOOK DANGEROUS!
WE WOLFRIDERS DON'T FEAR TROLLS, DO WE, *SKYWISE*?
CHUCKLE NOT THESE PARTICULAR ONES!
FUNNY-LOOKING ELVES BETTER BE NICE TO *TRINKET* BECAUSE *TRINKET* ALWAYS DOES WHAT *TRINKET* WANTS... AND BESIDES, GREAT-GRANDMAMA CAN THROW ANYBODY OVER HER SHOULDER!

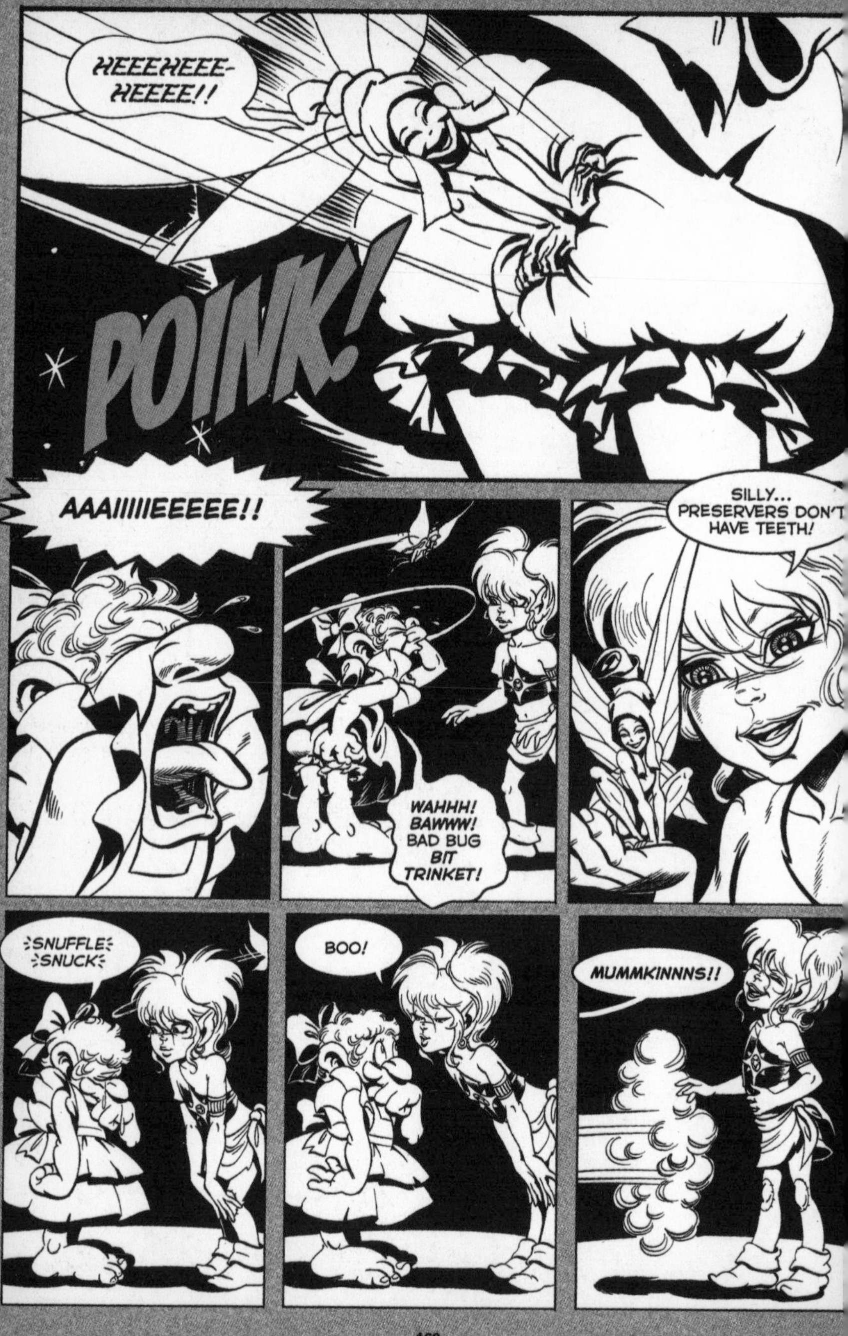
HEEEHEEE-
HEEEEE!!
POINK!
AAAIIIIIEEEEE!!
WAHHH!
BAWWW!
BAD BUG
BIT
TRINKET!
SILLY...
PRESERVERS DON'T
HAVE TEETH!
SNUFFLE
SNUCK
BOO!
MUMMKINNNS!!

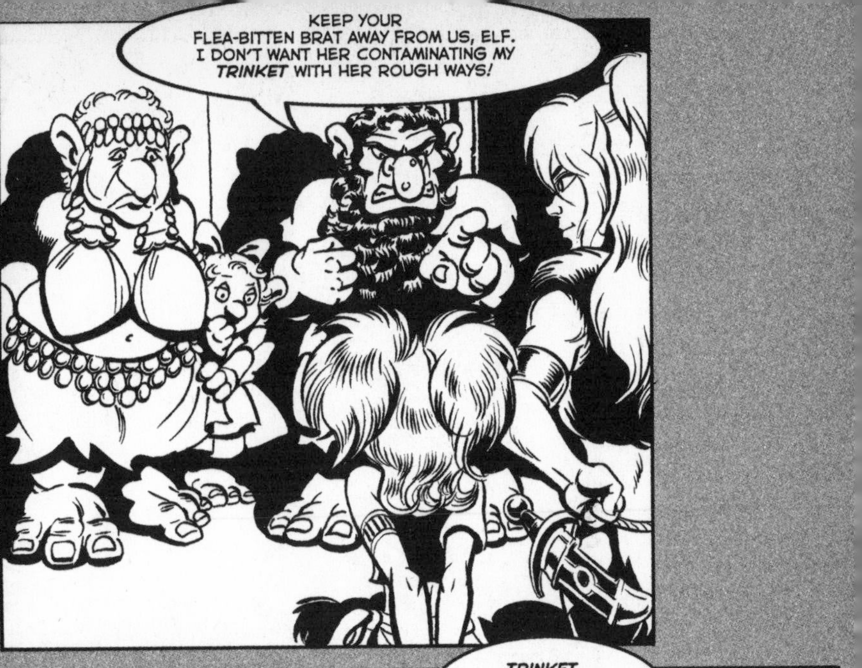
KEEP YOUR FLEA-BITTEN BRAT AWAY FROM US, ELF. I DON'T WANT HER CONTAMINATING MY *TRINKET* WITH HER ROUGH WAYS!

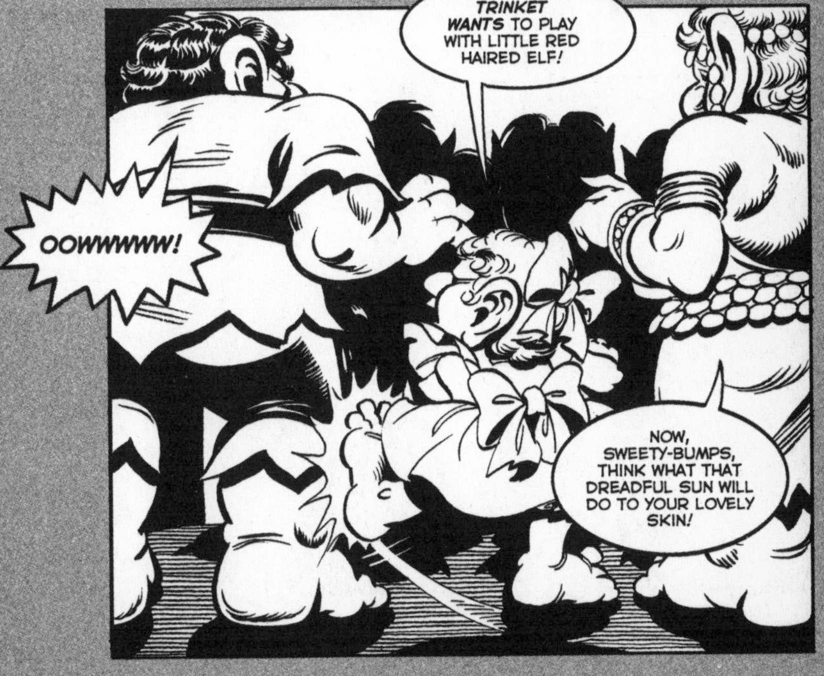
TRINKET WANTS TO PLAY WITH LITTLE RED HAIRED ELF!
OOWWWWW!
NOW, SWEETY-BUMPS, THINK WHAT THAT DREADFUL SUN WILL DO TO YOUR LOVELY SKIN!

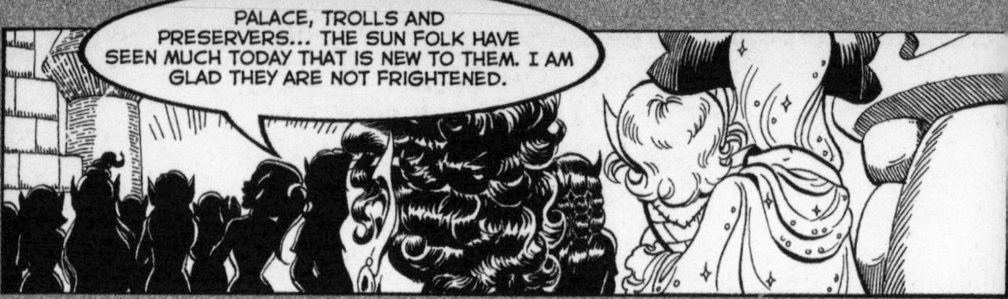
PALACE, TROLLS AND PRESERVERS... THE SUN FOLK HAVE SEEN MUCH TODAY THAT IS NEW TO THEM. I AM GLAD THEY ARE NOT FRIGHTENED.

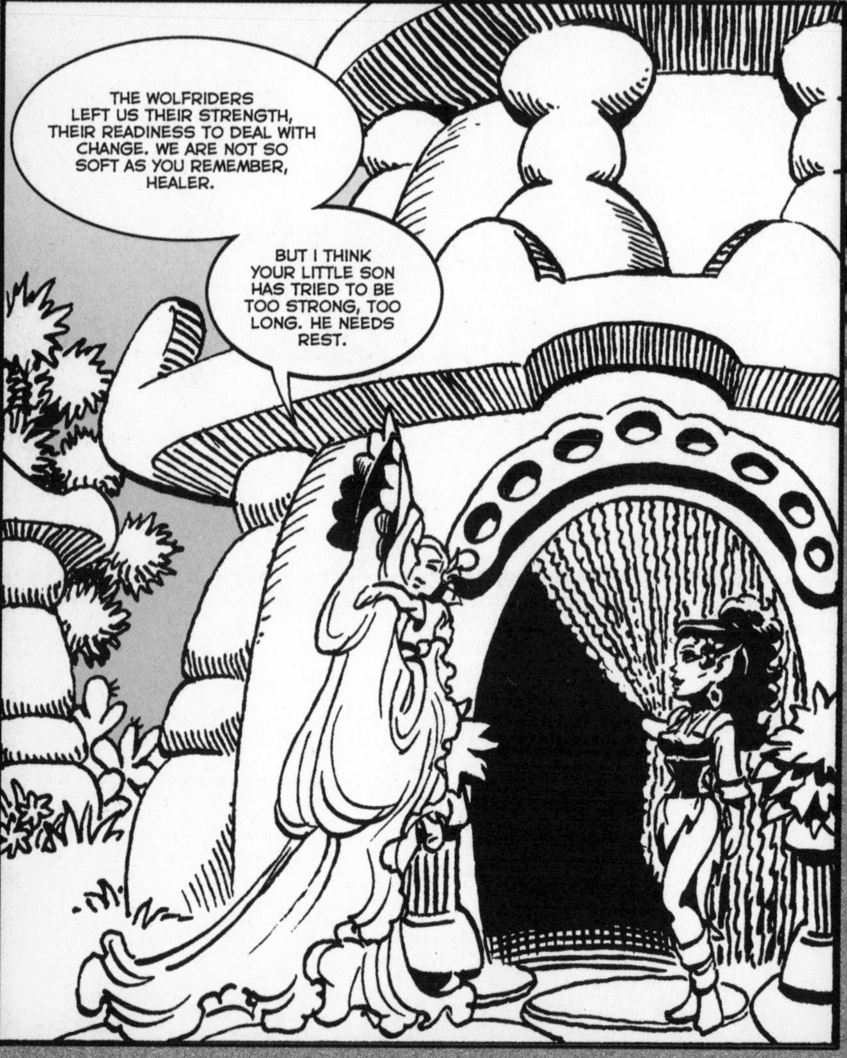
THE WOLFRIDERS LEFT US THEIR STRENGTH, THEIR READINESS TO DEAL WITH CHANGE. WE ARE NOT SO SOFT AS YOU REMEMBER, HEALER.
BUT I THINK YOUR LITTLE SON HAS TRIED TO BE TOO STRONG, TOO LONG. HE NEEDS REST.

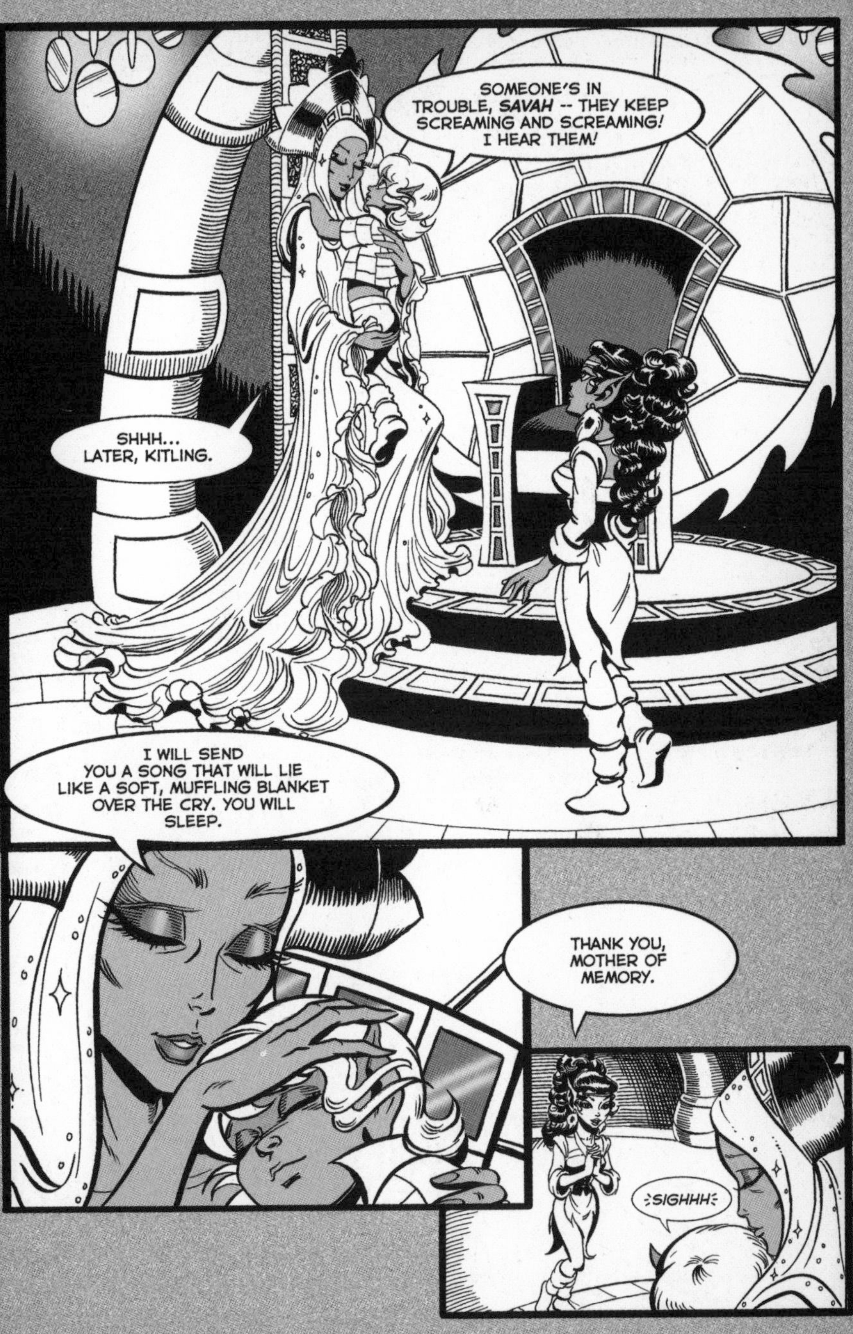
SOMEONE'S IN TROUBLE, SAVAH -- THEY KEEP SCREAMING AND SCREAMING! I HEAR THEM!
SHHH... LATER, KITLING.
I WILL SEND YOU A SONG THAT WILL LIE LIKE A SOFT, MUFFLING BLANKET OVER THE CRY. YOU WILL SLEEP.
THANK YOU, MOTHER OF MEMORY.
SIGHHH

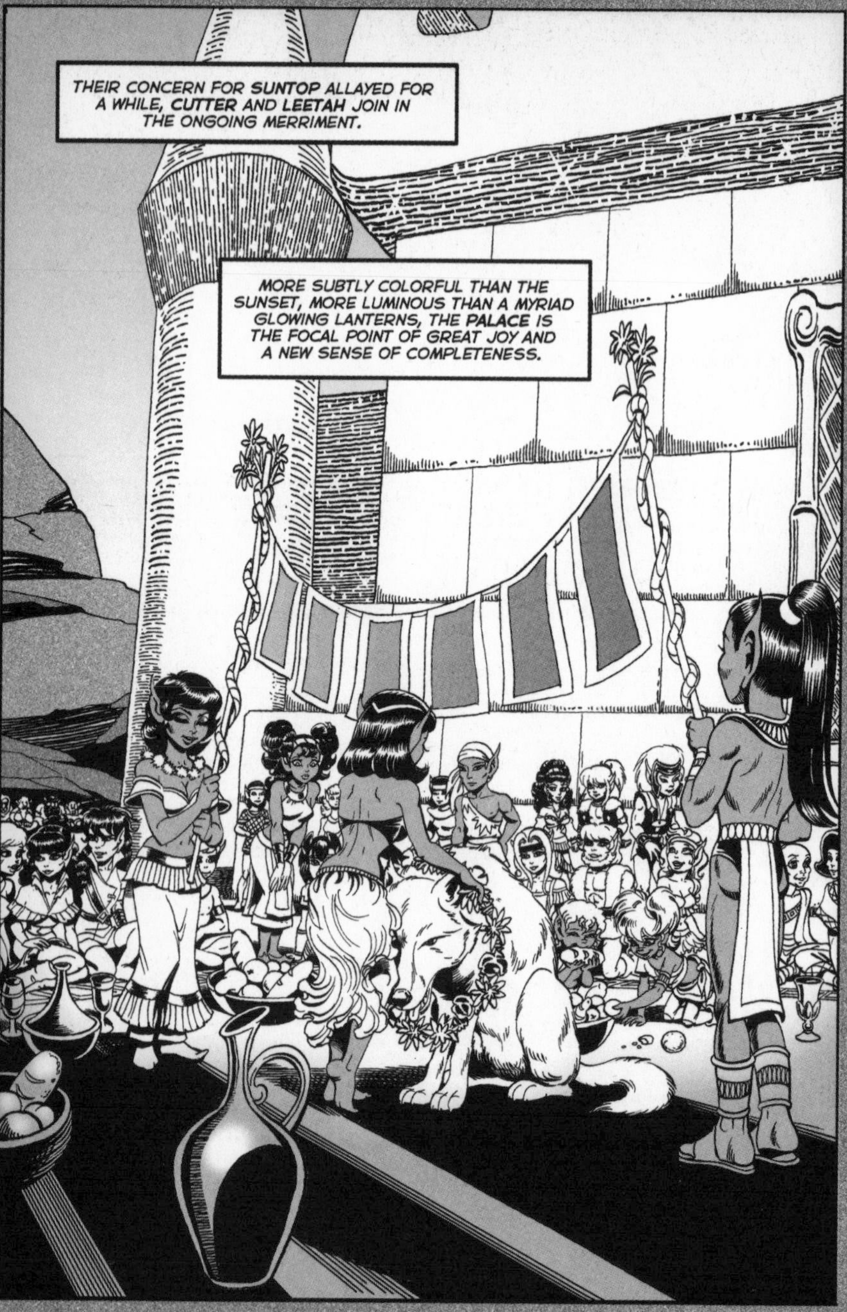
THEIR CONCERN FOR SUNTOP ALLAYED FOR A WHILE, CUTTER AND LEETAH JOIN IN THE ONGOING MERRIMENT.
MORE SUBTLY COLORFUL THAN THE SUNSET, MORE LUMINOUS THAN A MYRIAD GLOWING LANTERNS, THE PALACE IS THE FOCAL POINT OF GREAT JOY AND A NEW SENSE OF COMPLETENESS.

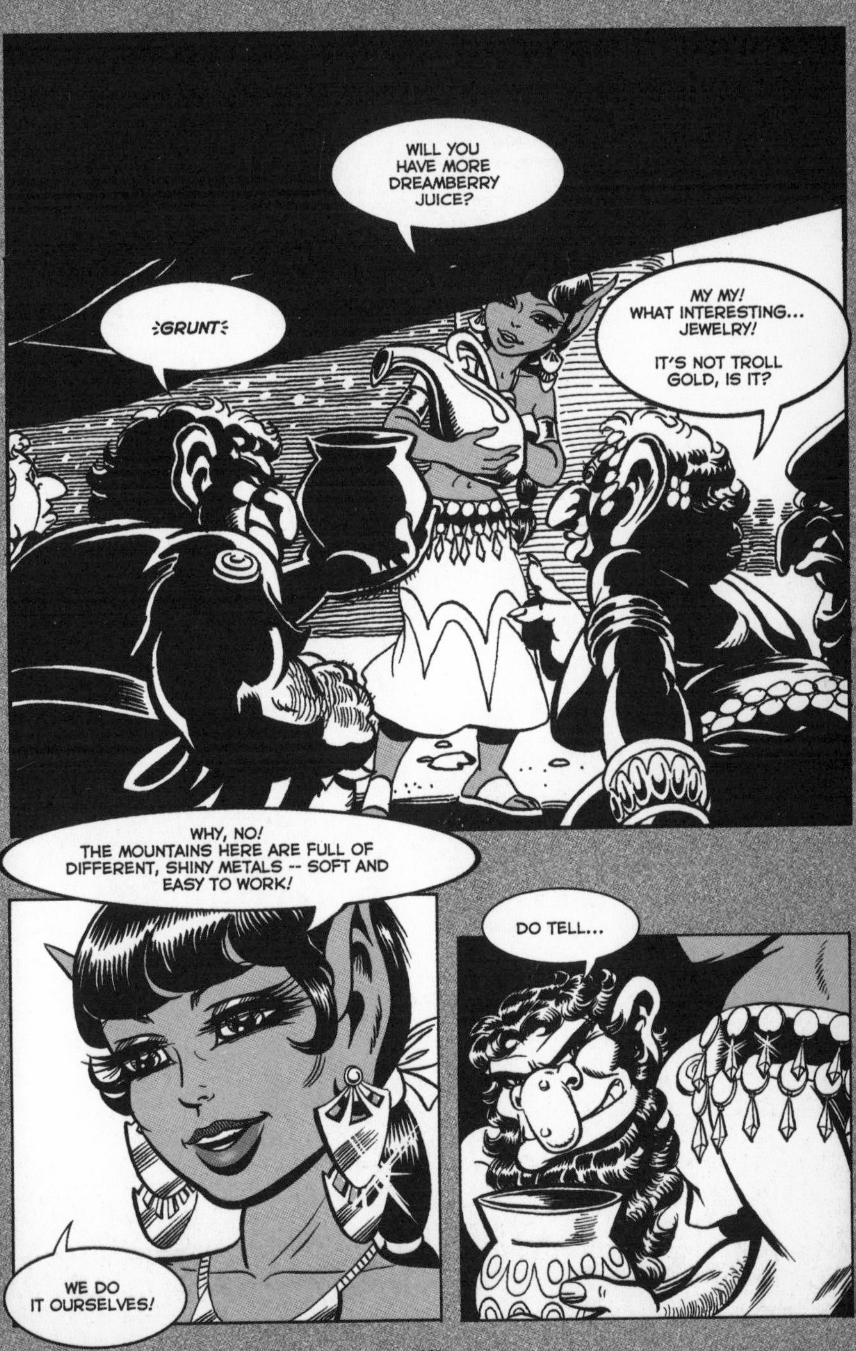
WILL YOU HAVE MORE DREAMBERRY JUICE?
GRUNT
MY MY! WHAT INTERESTING... JEWELRY!
IT'S NOT TROLL GOLD, IS IT?
WHY, NO! THE MOUNTAINS HERE ARE FULL OF DIFFERENT, SHINY METALS -- SOFT AND EASY TO WORK!
WE DO IT OURSELVES!
DO TELL...

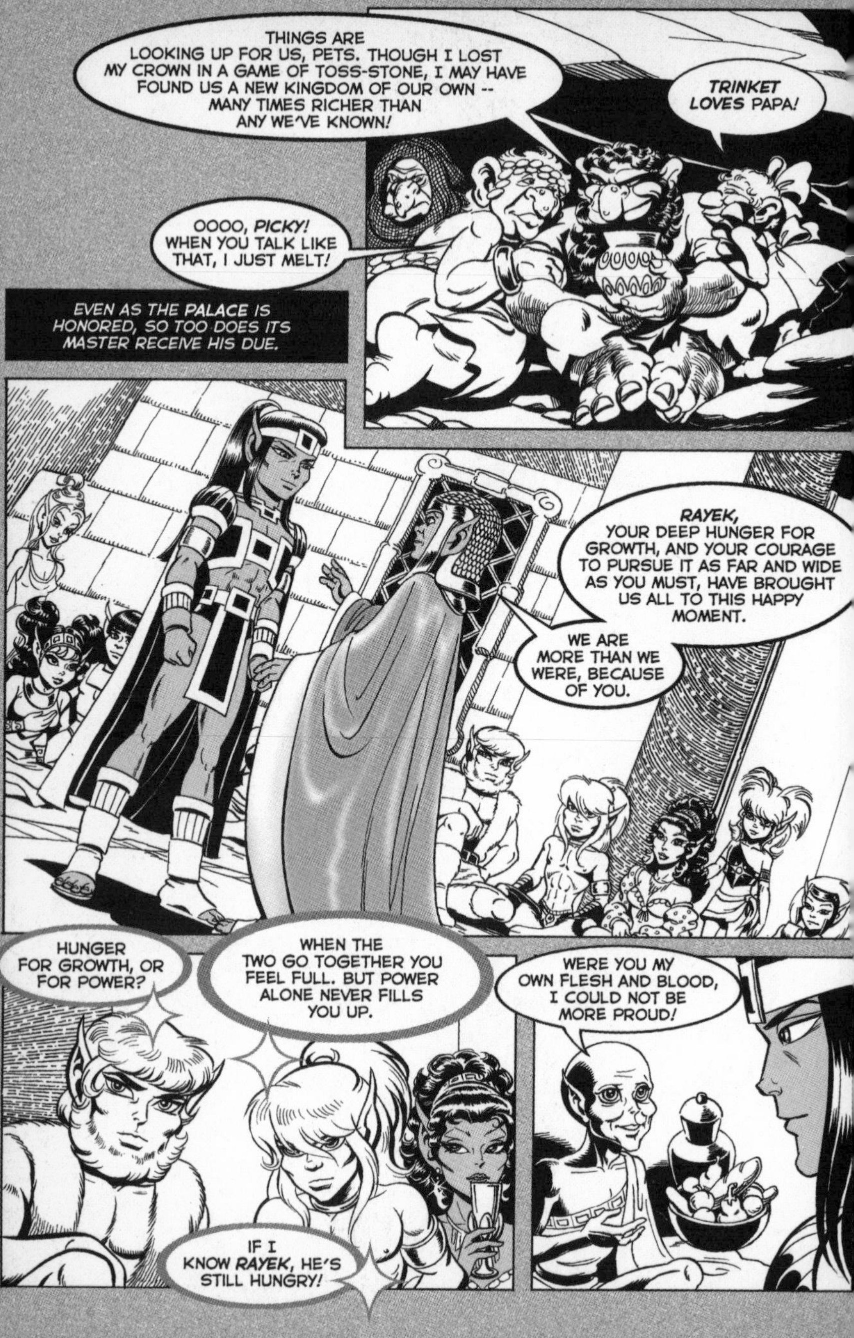
THINGS ARE LOOKING UP FOR US, PETS. THOUGH I LOST MY CROWN IN A GAME OF TOSS-STONE, I MAY HAVE FOUND US A NEW KINGDOM OF OUR OWN -- MANY TIMES RICHER THAN ANY WE'VE KNOWN!
TRINKET LOVES PAPA!
OOOO, PICKY! WHEN YOU TALK LIKE THAT, I JUST MELT!
EVEN AS THE PALACE IS HONORED, SO TOO DOES ITS MASTER RECEIVE HIS DUE.
RAYEK, YOUR DEEP HUNGER FOR GROWTH, AND YOUR COURAGE TO PURSUE IT AS FAR AND WIDE AS YOU MUST, HAVE BROUGHT US ALL TO THIS HAPPY MOMENT.
WE ARE MORE THAN WE WERE, BECAUSE OF YOU.
HUNGER FOR GROWTH, OR FOR POWER?
WHEN THE TWO GO TOGETHER YOU FEEL FULL. BUT POWER ALONE NEVER FILLS YOU UP.
IF I KNOW RAYEK, HE'S STILL HUNGRY!
WERE YOU MY OWN FLESH AND BLOOD, I COULD NOT BE MORE PROUD!

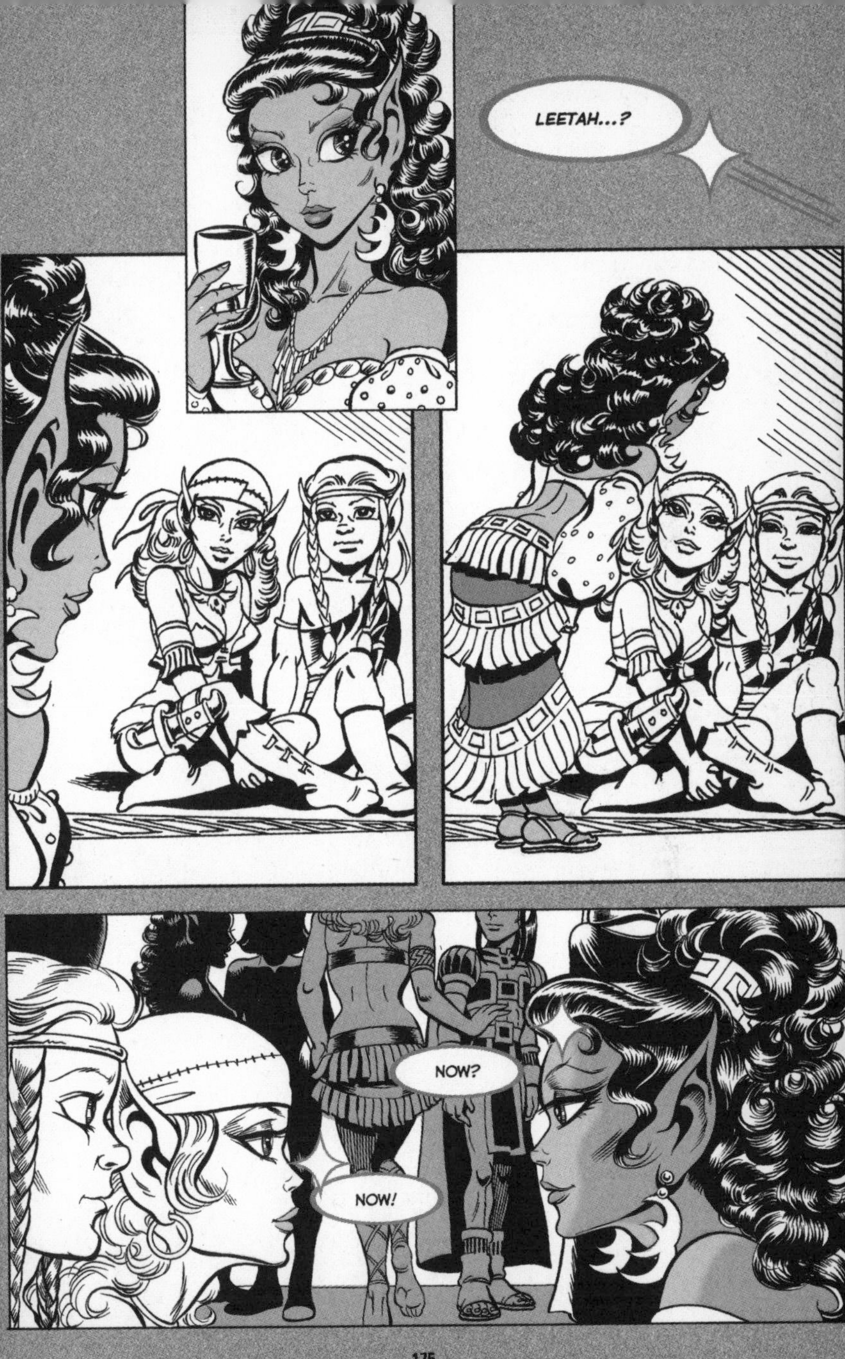
LEETAH...?
NOW?
NOW!

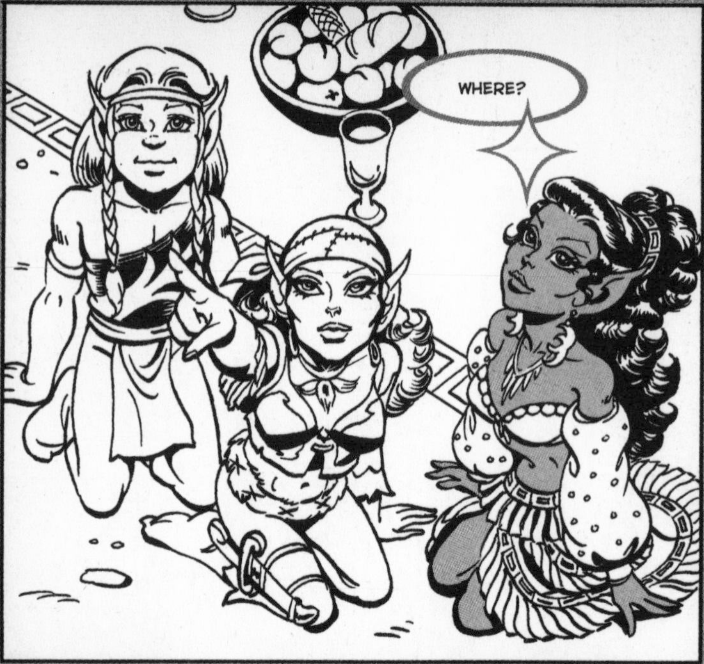
WHERE?

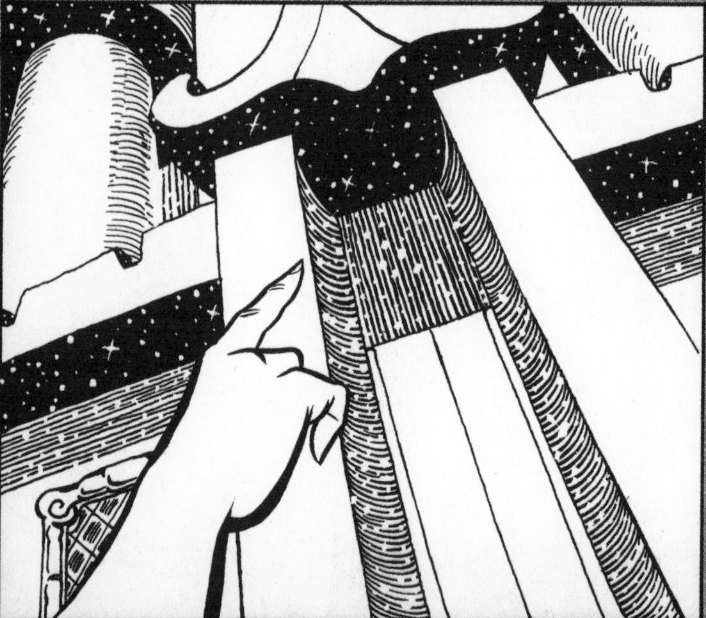

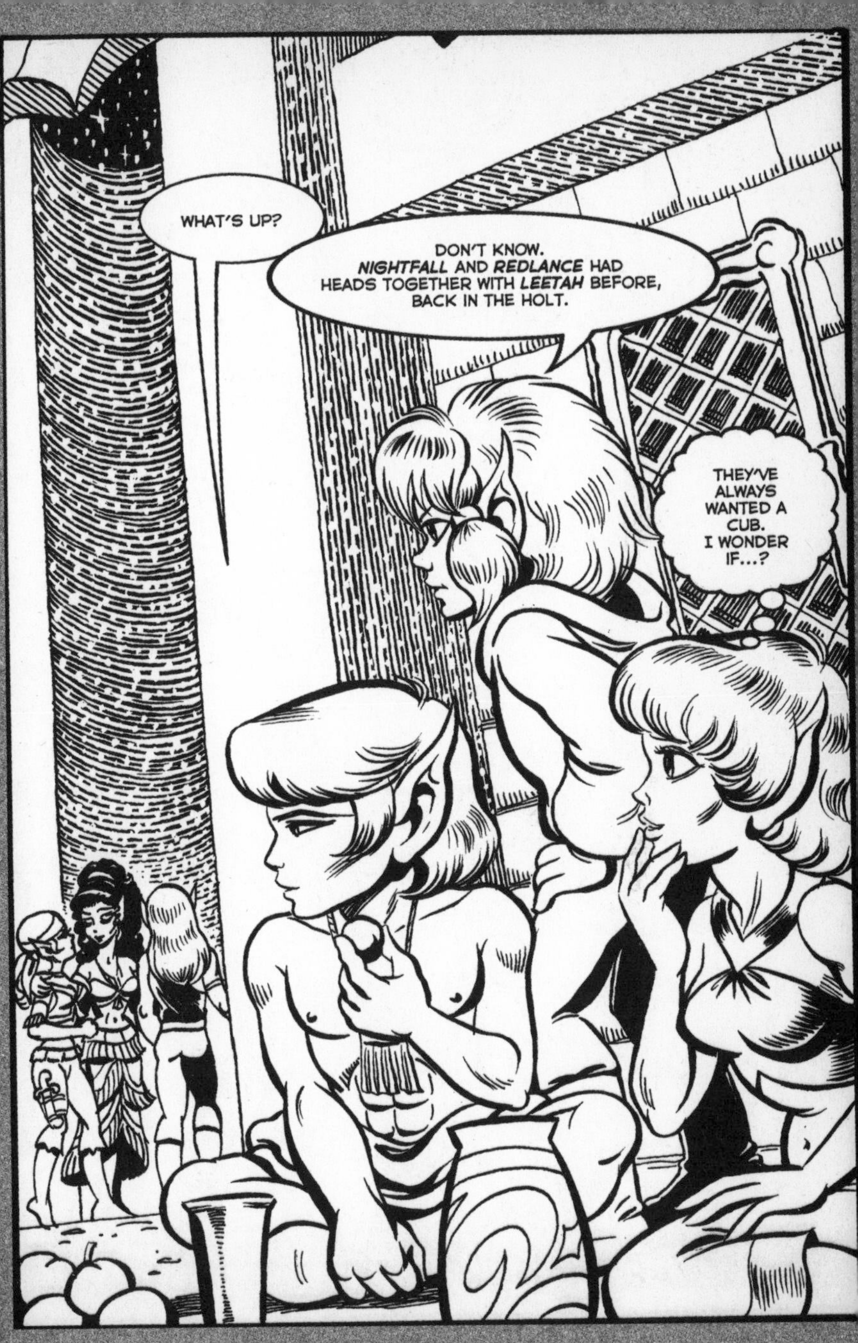
WHAT'S UP?
DON'T KNOW. NIGHTFALL AND REDLANCE HAD HEADS TOGETHER WITH LEETAH BEFORE, BACK IN THE HOLT.
THEY'VE ALWAYS WANTED A CUB. I WONDER IF...?

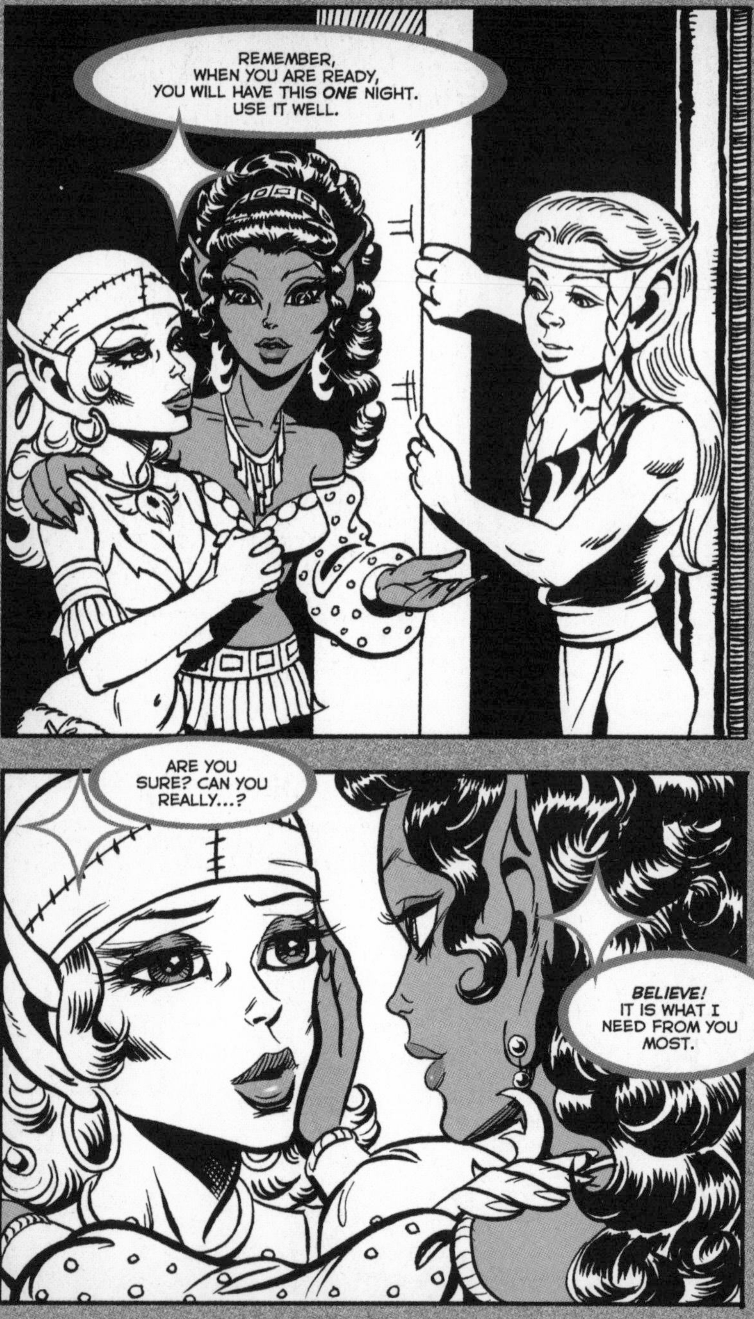
REMEMBER, WHEN YOU ARE READY, YOU WILL HAVE THIS *ONE* NIGHT. USE IT WELL.
ARE YOU SURE? CAN YOU REALLY...?
BELIEVE! IT IS WHAT I NEED FROM YOU MOST.

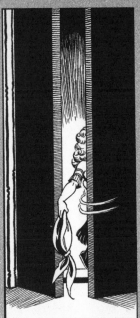
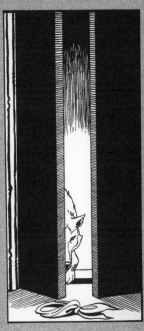

WHAT? *WHAAAT??* WHAT ARE THEY DOING?!

HAHAHA! SOMETHING *RAINSONG* AND I NEVER NEEDED A HEALER'S HELP TO DO!

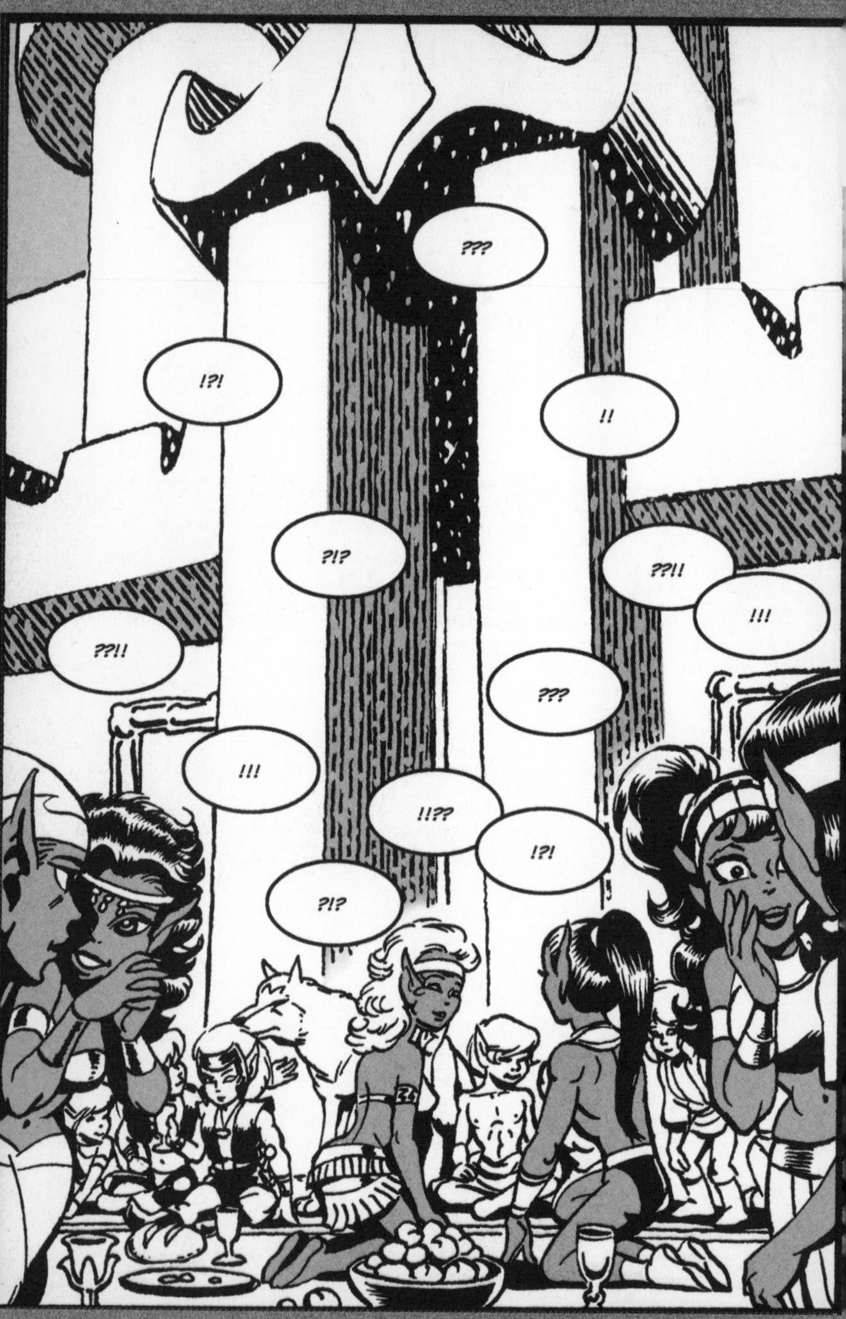
???
!?!
!!
?!?
??!!
!!!
??!!
???
!!!
!!??
!?!
?!?

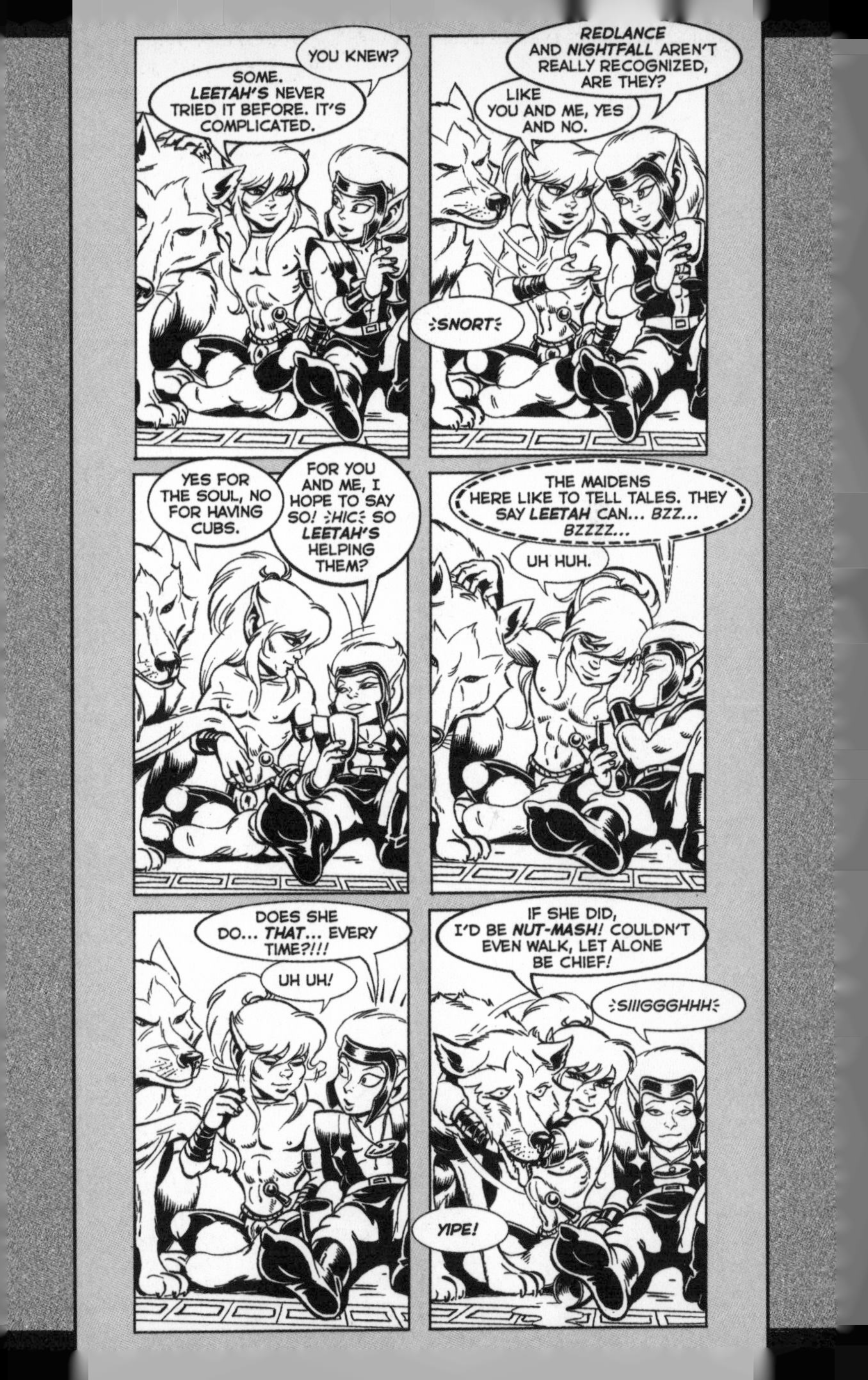
YOU KNEW?
SOME. LEETAH'S NEVER TRIED IT BEFORE. IT'S COMPLICATED.
REDLANCE AND NIGHTFALL AREN'T REALLY RECOGNIZED, ARE THEY?
LIKE YOU AND ME, YES AND NO.
SNORT
YES FOR THE SOUL, NO FOR HAVING CUBS.
FOR YOU AND ME, I HOPE TO SAY SO! HIC SO LEETAH'S HELPING THEM?
THE MAIDENS HERE LIKE TO TELL TALES. THEY SAY LEETAH CAN... BZZ... BZZZZ...
UH HUH.
DOES SHE DO... THAT... EVERY TIME?!!!
UH UH!
IF SHE DID, I'D BE NUT-MASH! COULDN'T EVEN WALK, LET ALONE BE CHIEF!
SIIIGGGHHH
YIPE!

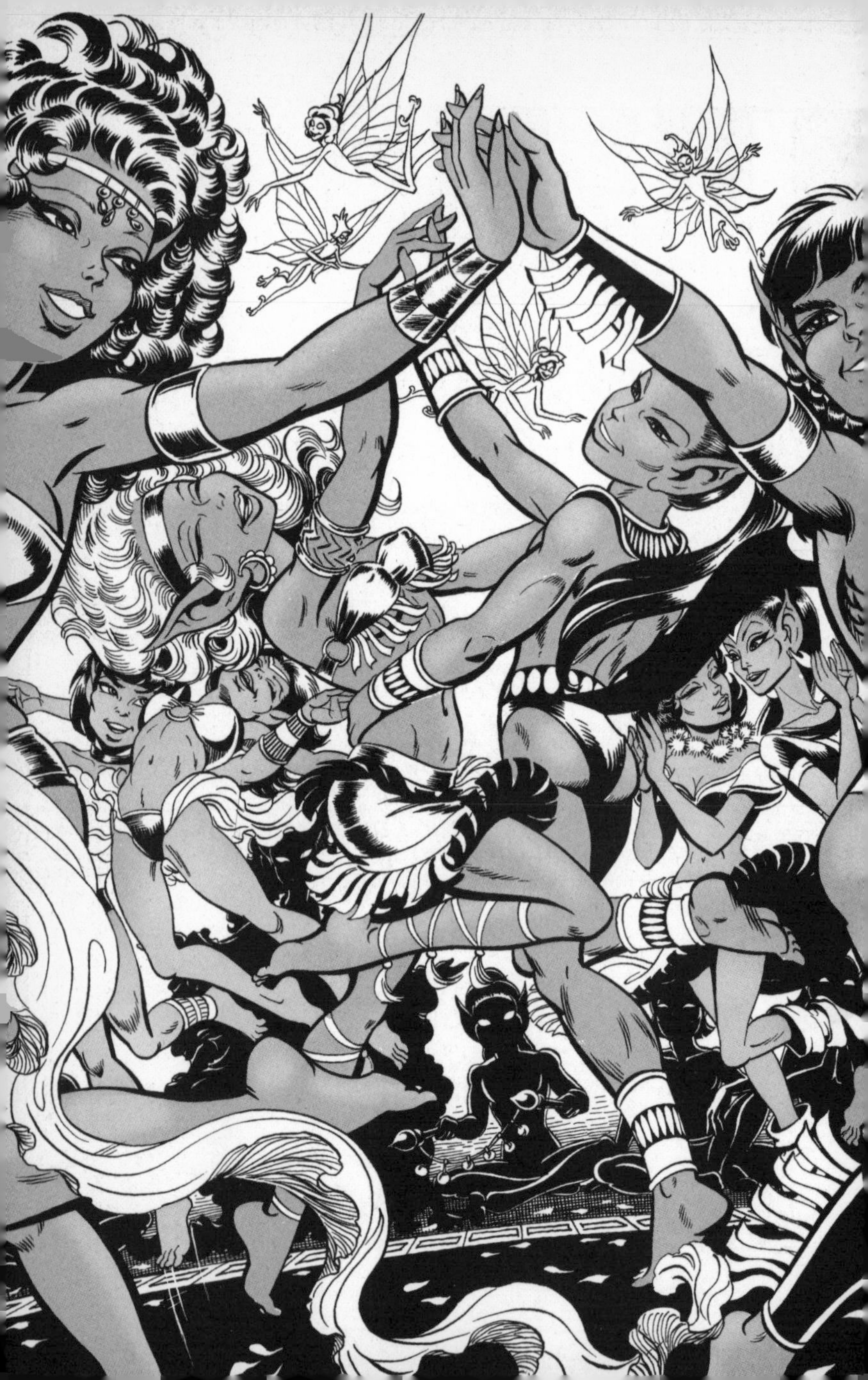

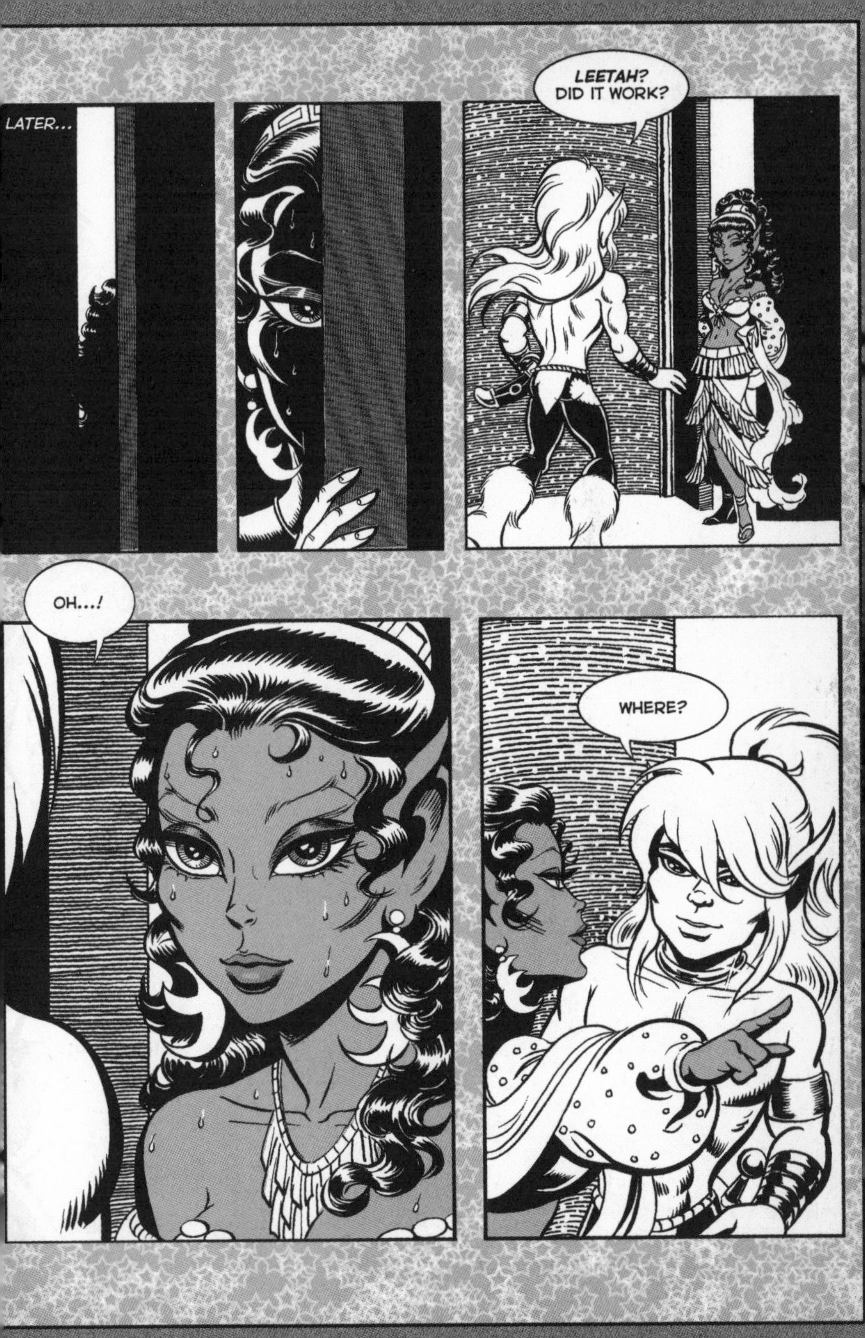
LATER...
LEETAH? DID IT WORK?
OH...!
WHERE?

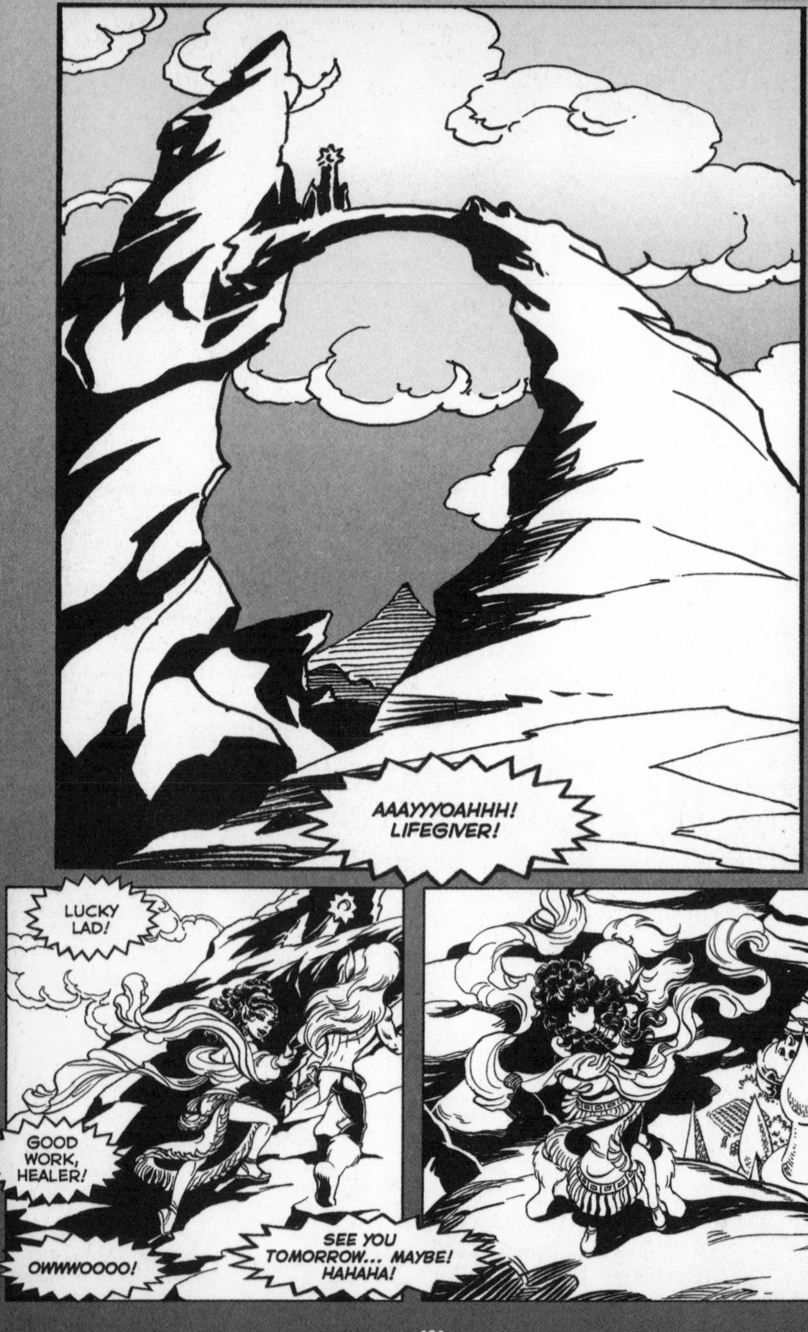
AAAYYYOAHHH! LIFEGIVER!
LUCKY LAD!
GOOD WORK, HEALER!
OWWWOOOO!
SEE YOU TOMORROW... MAYBE! HAHAHA!

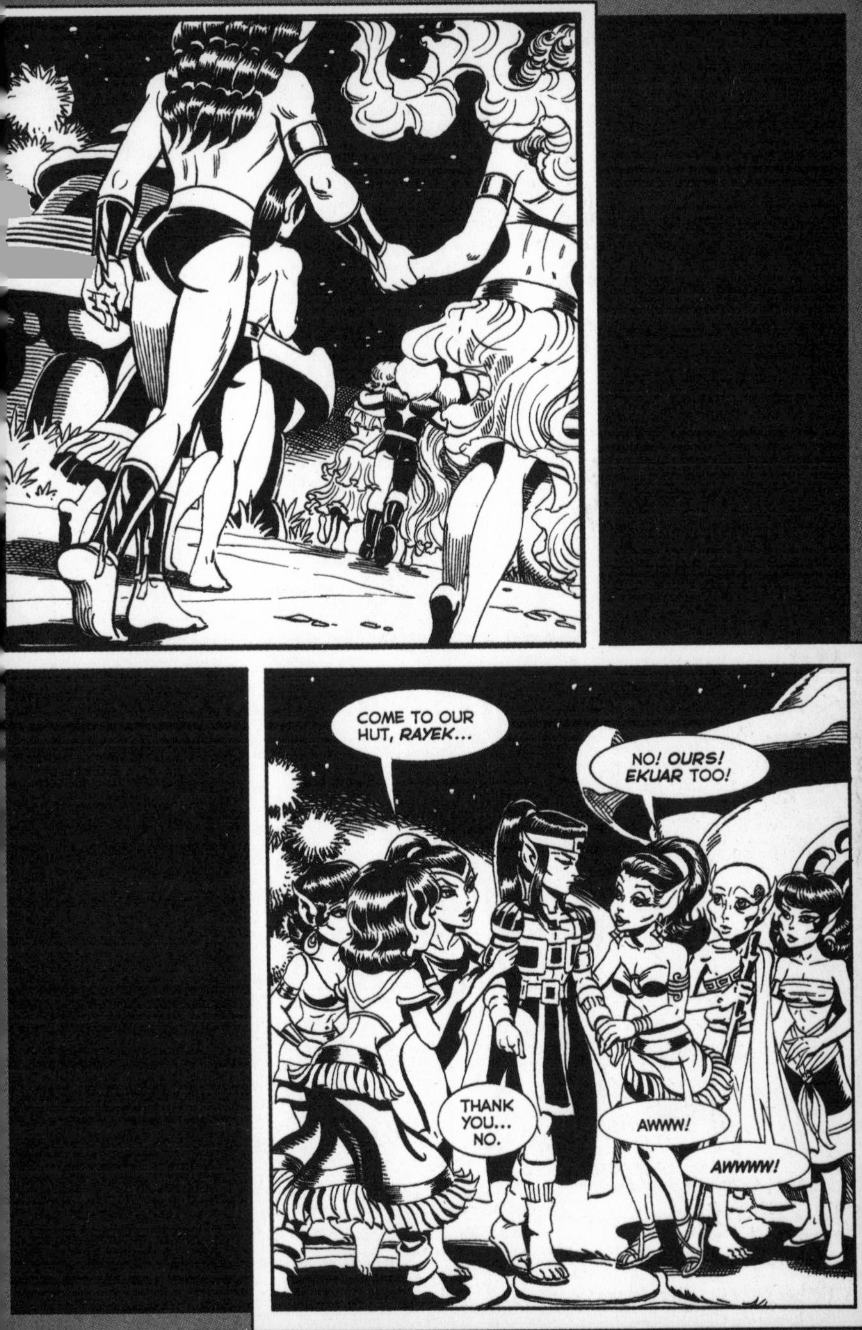
COME TO OUR HUT, RAYEK...
NO! OURS! EKUAR TOO!
THANK YOU... NO.
AWWW!
AWWWW!

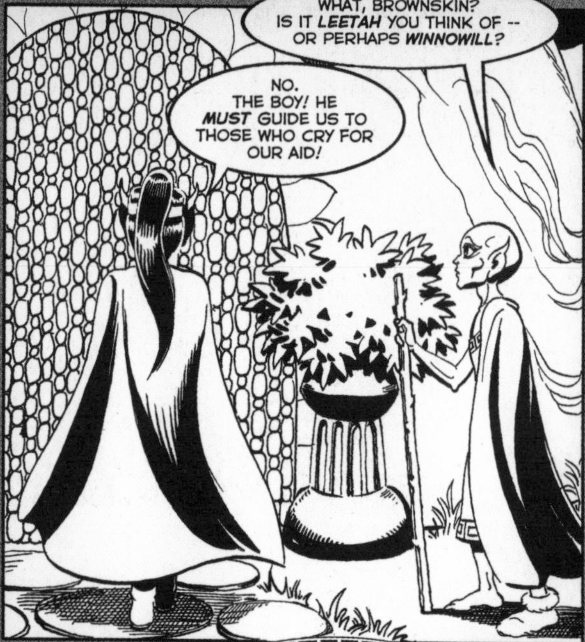
WHAT, BROWNSKIN? IS IT LEETAH YOU THINK OF -- OR PERHAPS WINNOWILL?
NO. THE BOY! HE MUST GUIDE US TO THOSE WHO CRY FOR OUR AID!
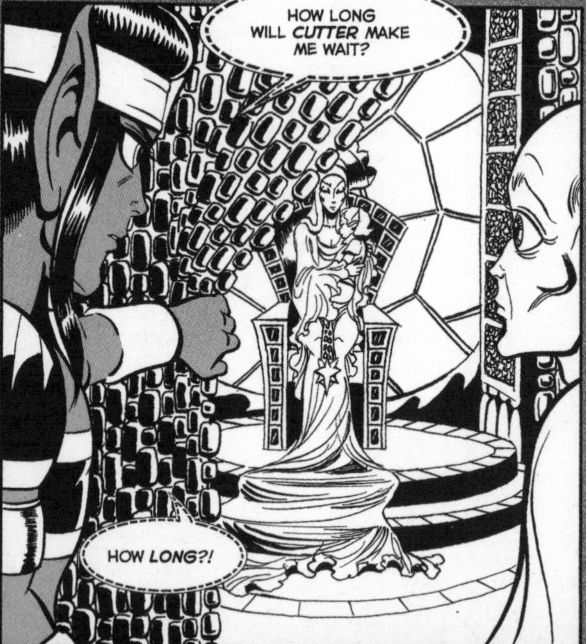
HOW LONG WILL CUTTER MAKE ME WAIT?
HOW LONG?!

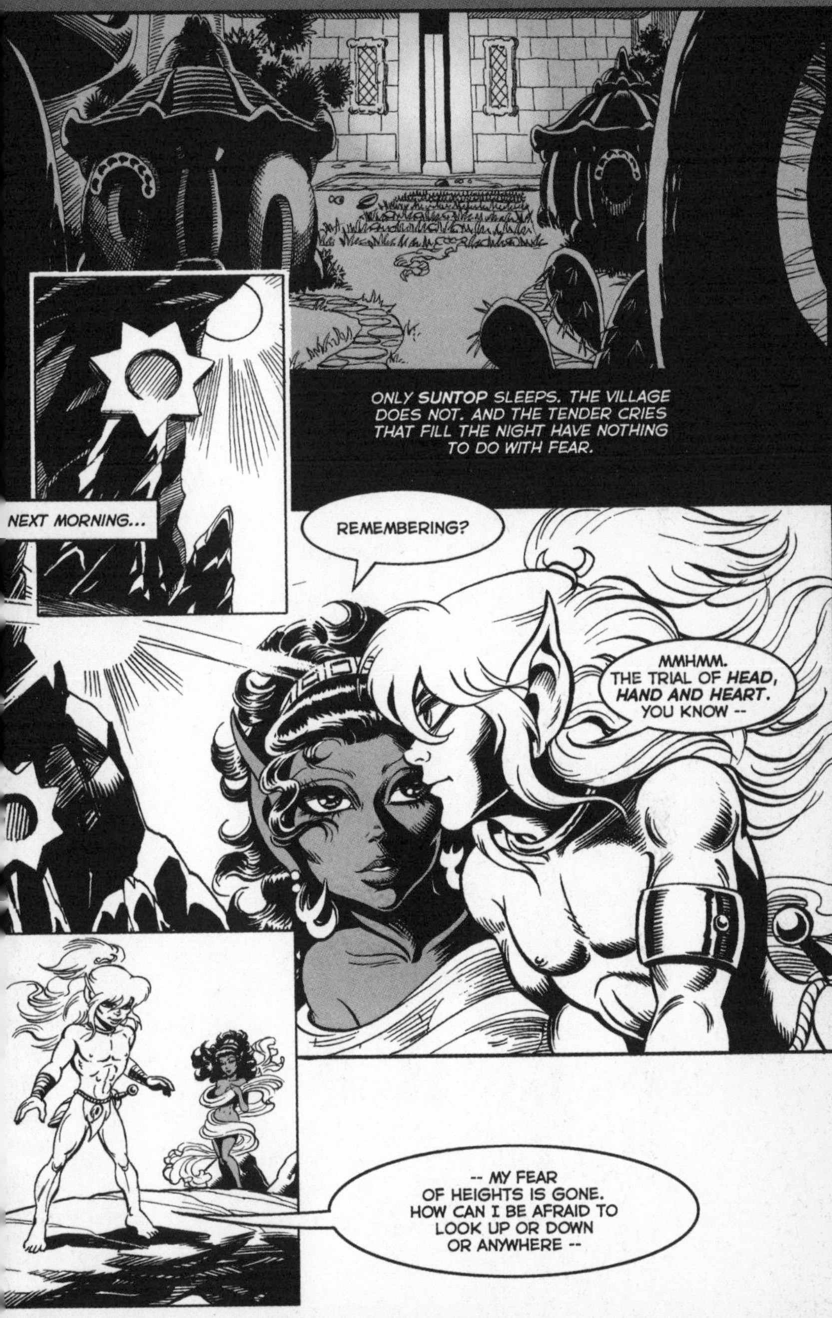
ONLY SUNTOP SLEEPS. THE VILLAGE DOES NOT. AND THE TENDER CRIES THAT FILL THE NIGHT HAVE NOTHING TO DO WITH FEAR.
NEXT MORNING...
REMEMBERING?
MMHMM. THE TRIAL OF HEAD, HAND AND HEART. YOU KNOW --
-- MY FEAR OF HEIGHTS IS GONE. HOW CAN I BE AFRAID TO LOOK UP OR DOWN OR ANYWHERE --

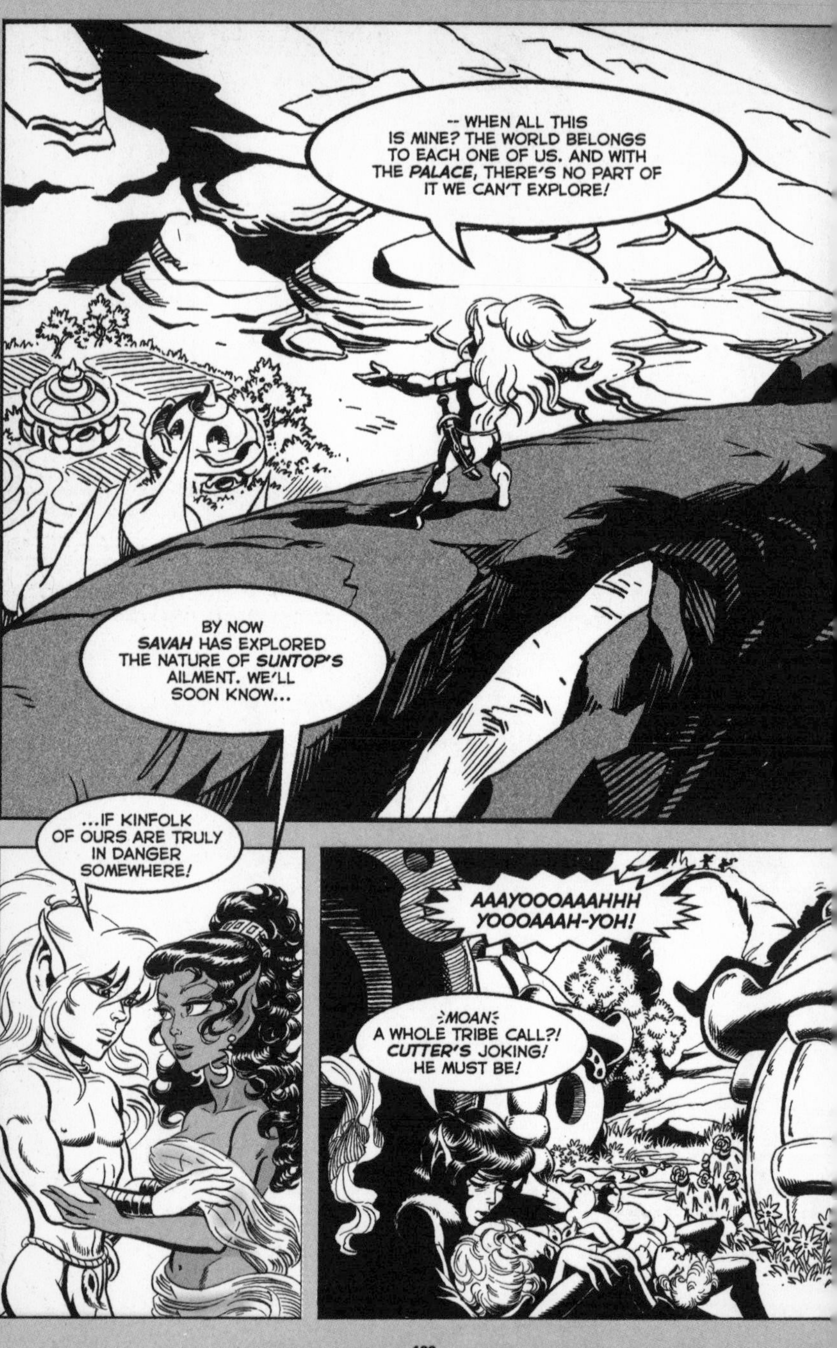
-- WHEN ALL THIS IS MINE? THE WORLD BELONGS TO EACH ONE OF US. AND WITH THE *PALACE*, THERE'S NO PART OF IT WE CAN'T EXPLORE!
BY NOW *SAVAH* HAS EXPLORED THE NATURE OF *SUNTOP'S* AILMENT. WE'LL SOON KNOW...
...IF KINFOLK OF OURS ARE TRULY IN DANGER SOMEWHERE!
AAAYOOOAAAHHH YOOOAAAH-YOH!
MOAN
A WHOLE TRIBE CALL?! *CUTTER'S* JOKING! HE MUST BE!

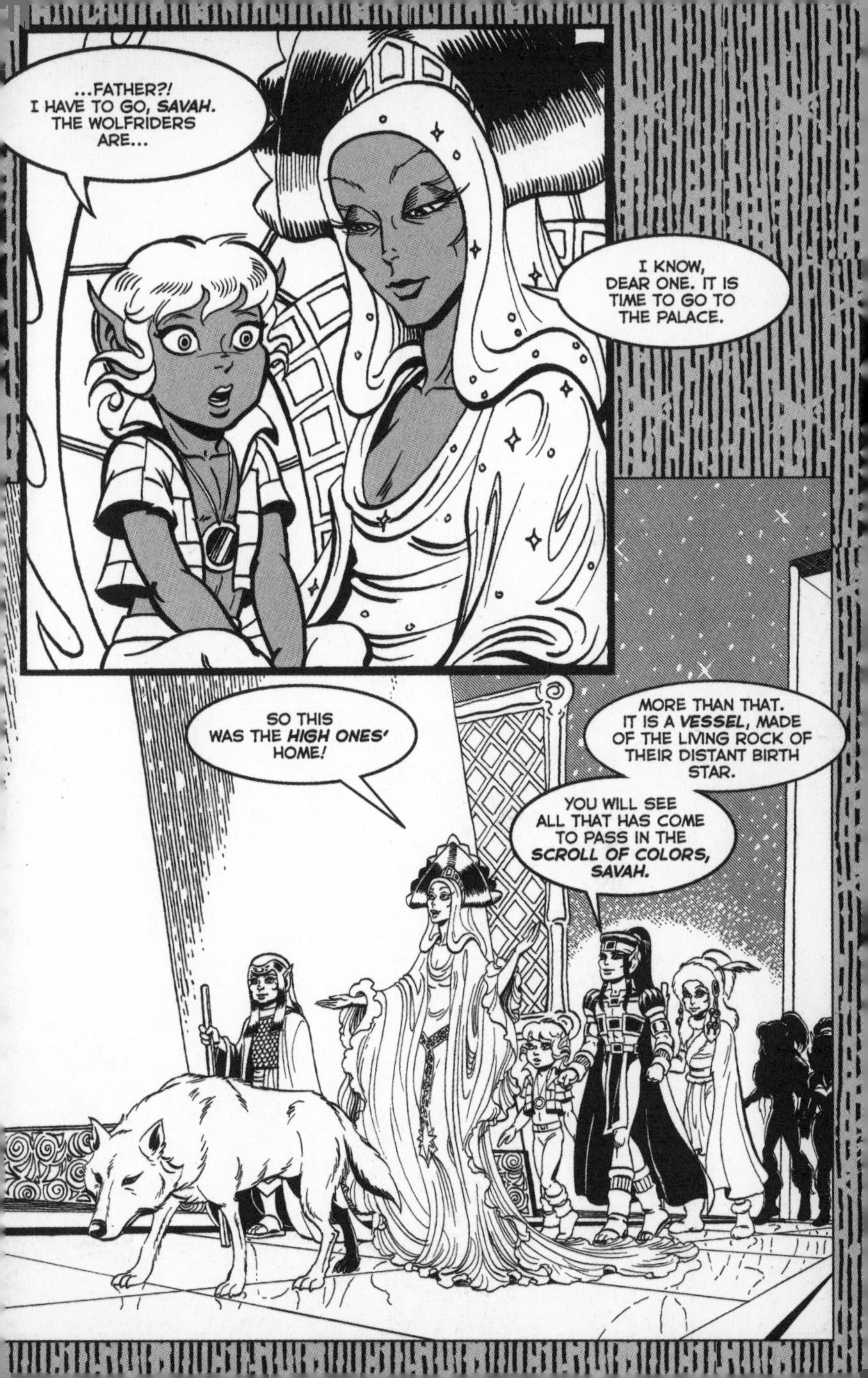
...FATHER?! I HAVE TO GO, SAVAH. THE WOLFRIDERS ARE...
I KNOW, DEAR ONE. IT IS TIME TO GO TO THE PALACE.
SO THIS WAS THE HIGH ONES' HOME!
MORE THAN THAT. IT IS A VESSEL, MADE OF THE LIVING ROCK OF THEIR DISTANT BIRTH STAR.
YOU WILL SEE ALL THAT HAS COME TO PASS IN THE SCROLL OF COLORS, SAVAH.

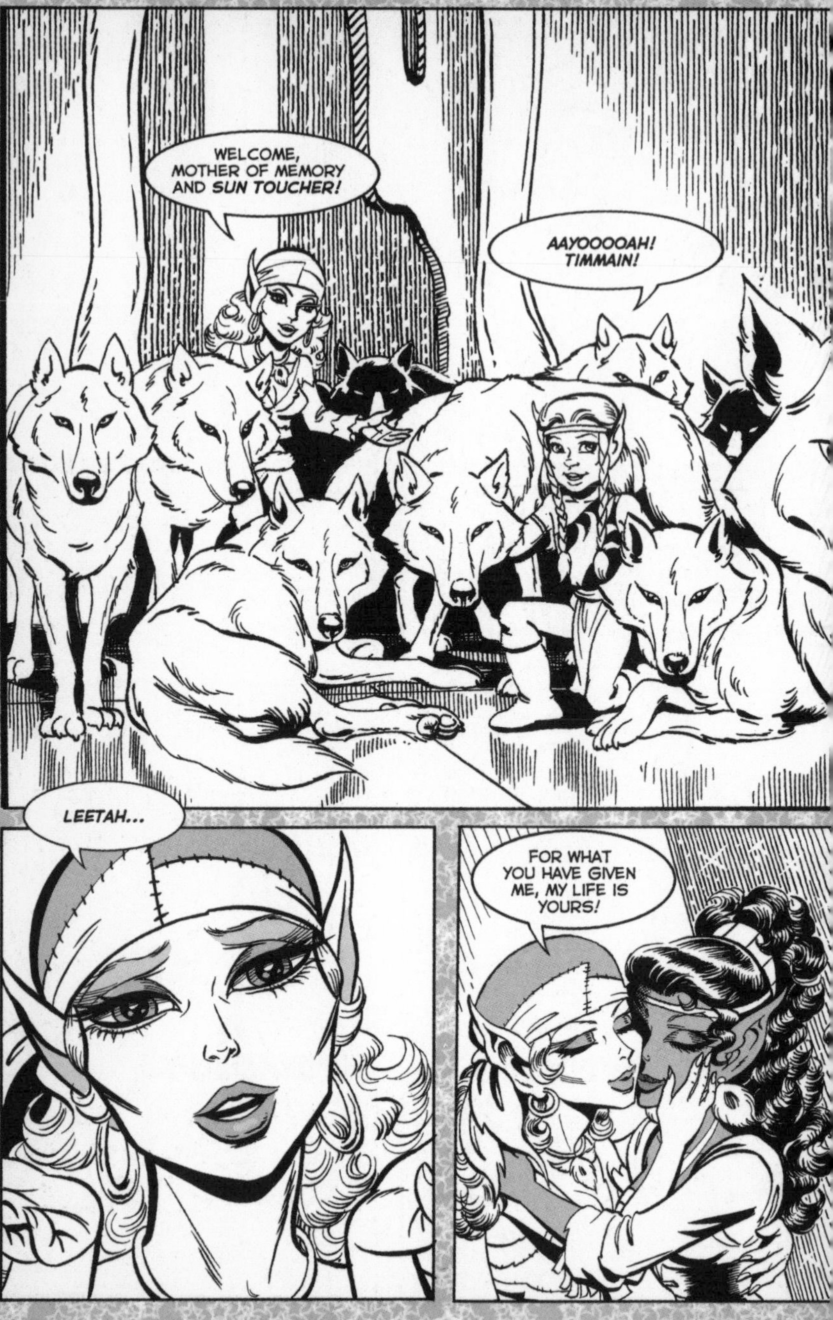
WELCOME, MOTHER OF MEMORY AND SUN TOUCHER!
AAYOOOOAH! TIMMAIN!
LEETAH...
FOR WHAT YOU HAVE GIVEN ME, MY LIFE IS YOURS!

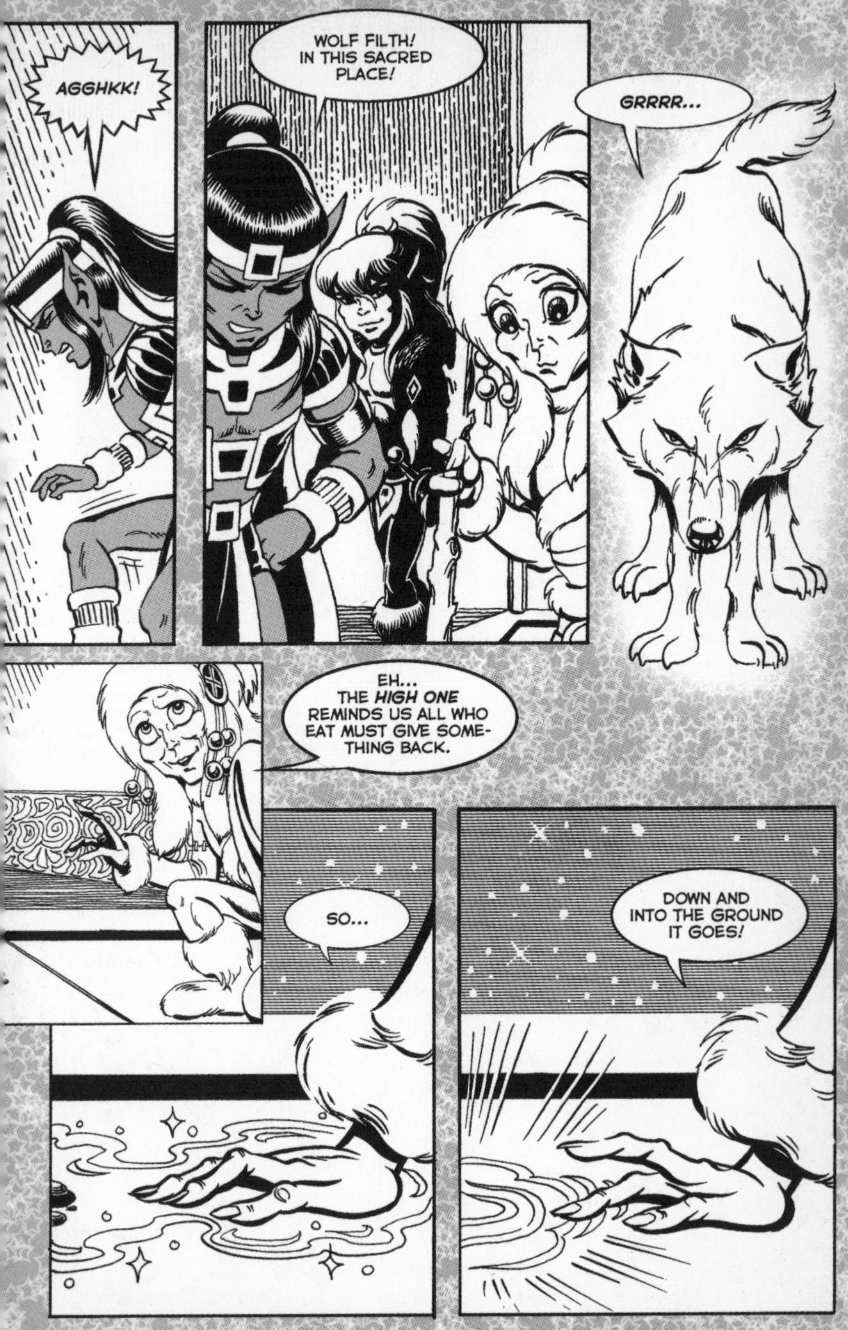
AGGHKK!
WOLF FILTH! IN THIS SACRED PLACE!
GRRRR...
EH... THE *HIGH ONE* REMINDS US ALL WHO EAT MUST GIVE SOME-THING BACK.
SO...
DOWN AND INTO THE GROUND IT GOES!

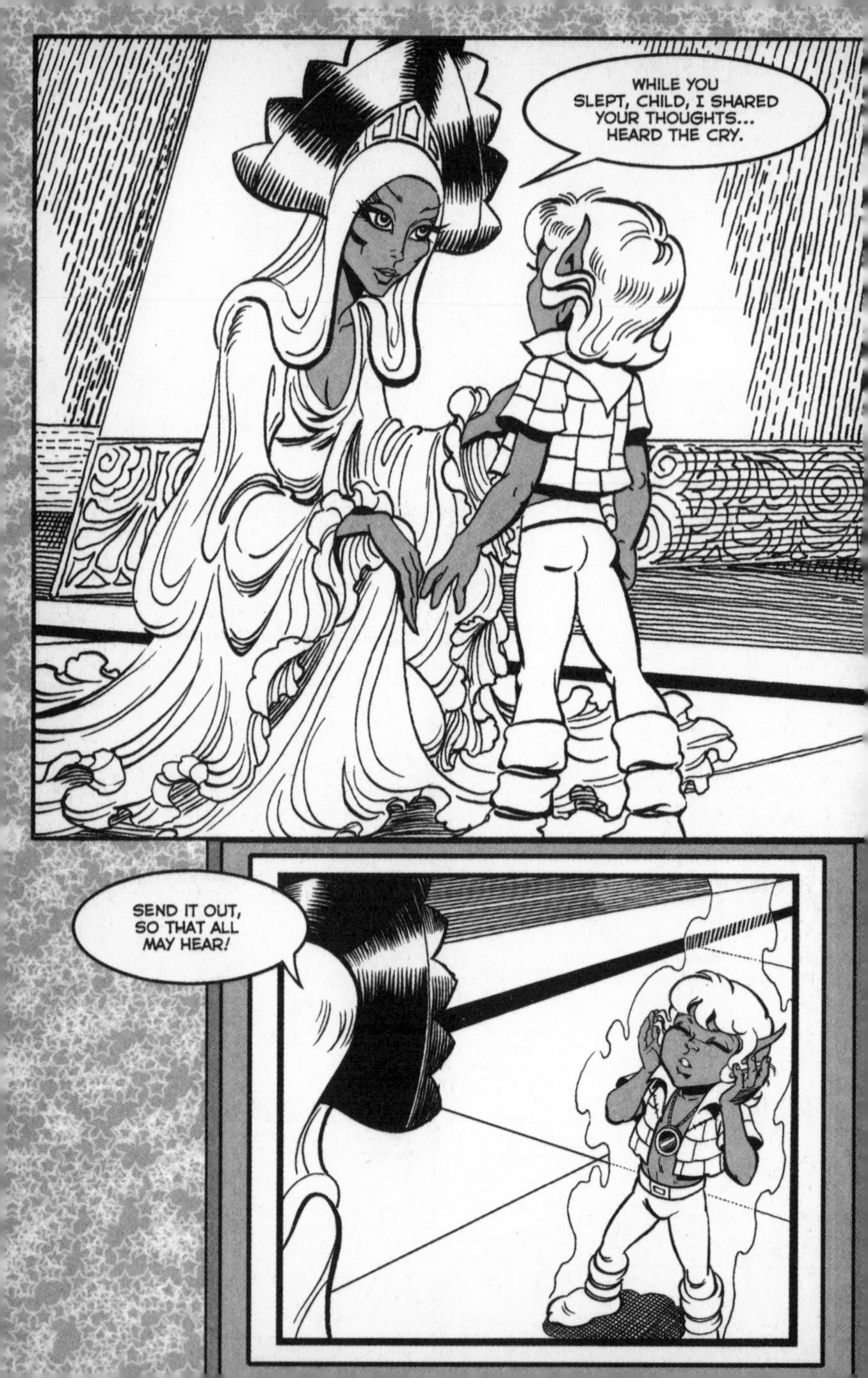
WHILE YOU SLEPT, CHILD, I SHARED YOUR THOUGHTS... HEARD THE CRY.
SEND IT OUT, SO THAT ALL MAY HEAR!

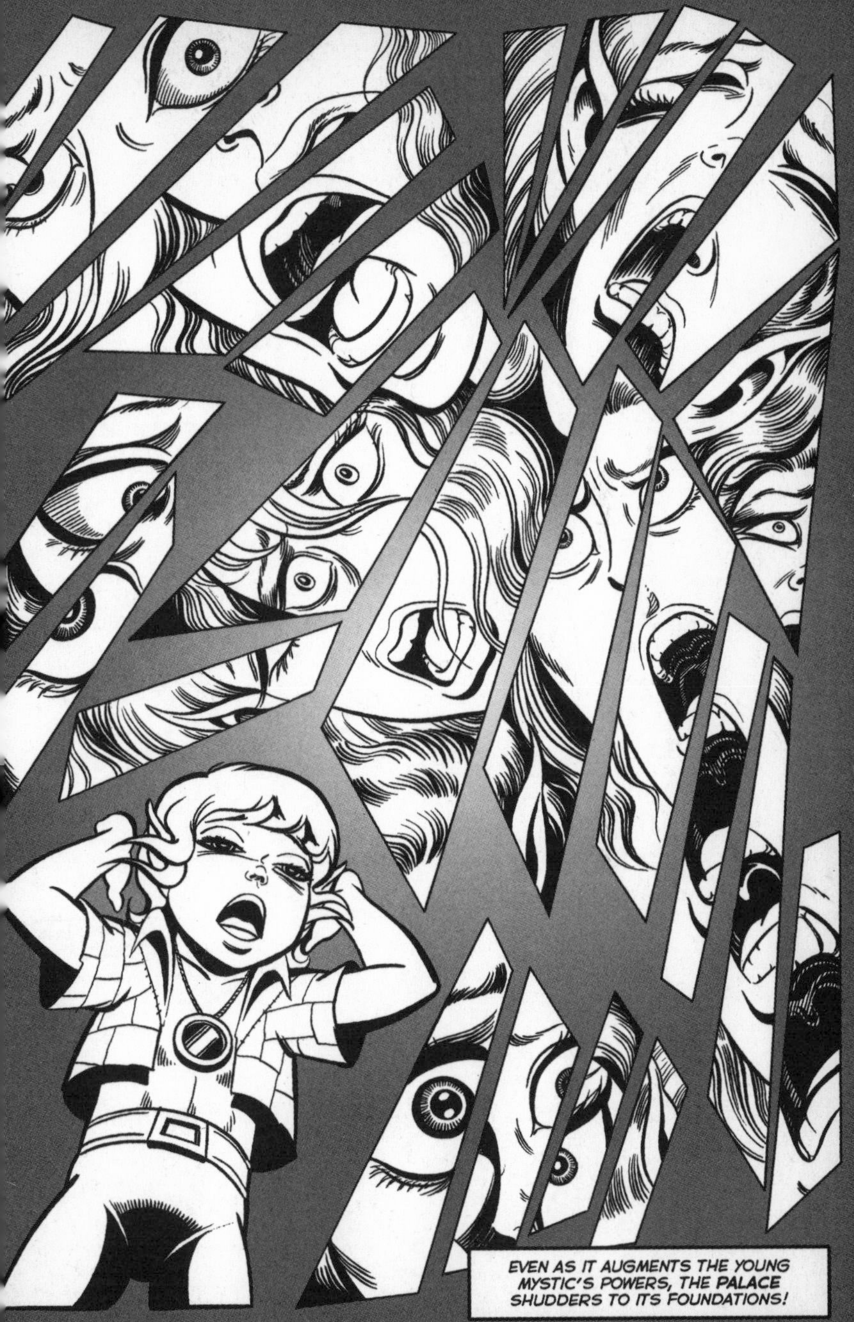
EVEN AS IT AUGMENTS THE YOUNG MYSTIC'S POWERS, THE PALACE SHUDDERS TO ITS FOUNDATIONS!

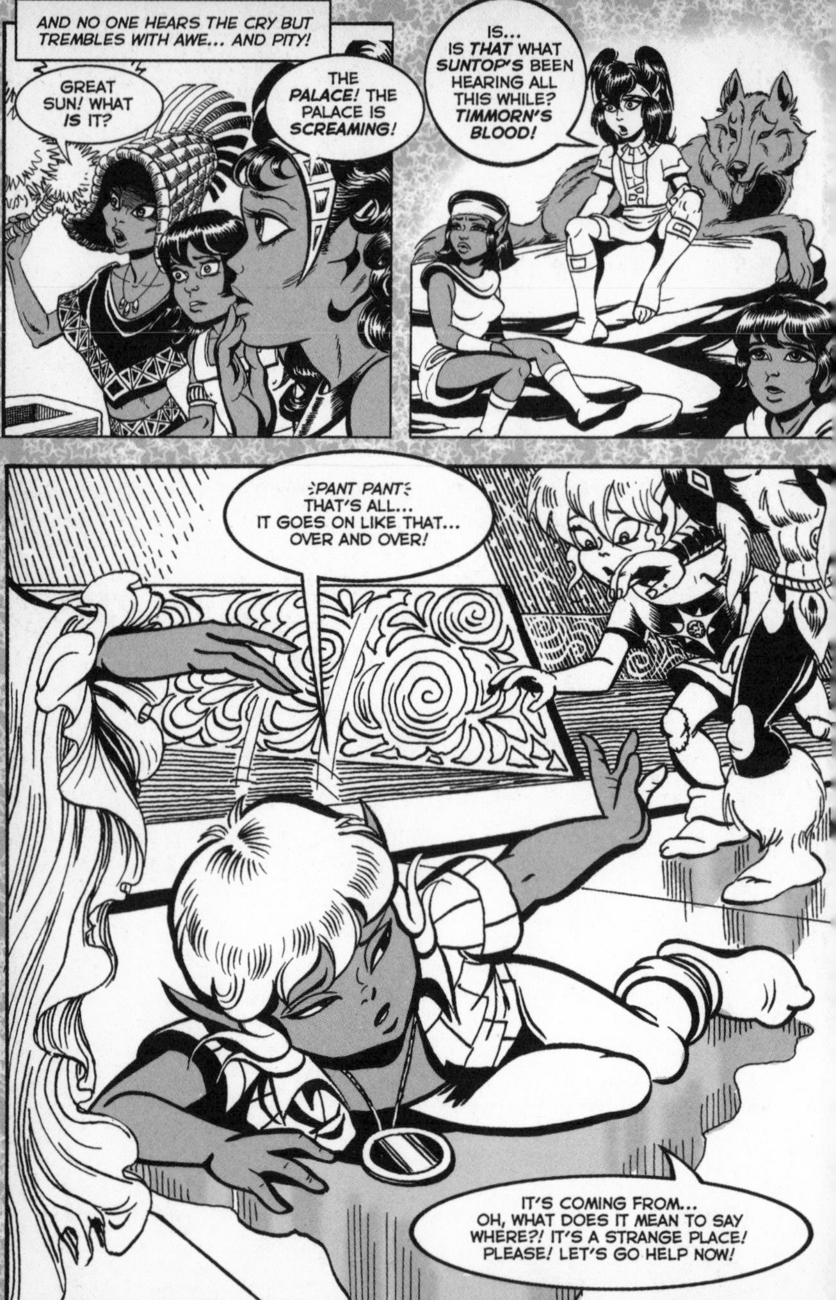
AND NO ONE HEARS THE CRY BUT TREMBLES WITH AWE... AND PITY!
GREAT SUN! WHAT IS IT?
THE PALACE! THE PALACE IS SCREAMING!
IS... IS THAT WHAT SUNTOP'S BEEN HEARING ALL THIS WHILE? TIMMORN'S BLOOD!
PANT PANT THAT'S ALL... IT GOES ON LIKE THAT... OVER AND OVER!
IT'S COMING FROM... OH, WHAT DOES IT MEAN TO SAY WHERE?! IT'S A STRANGE PLACE! PLEASE! LET'S GO HELP NOW!

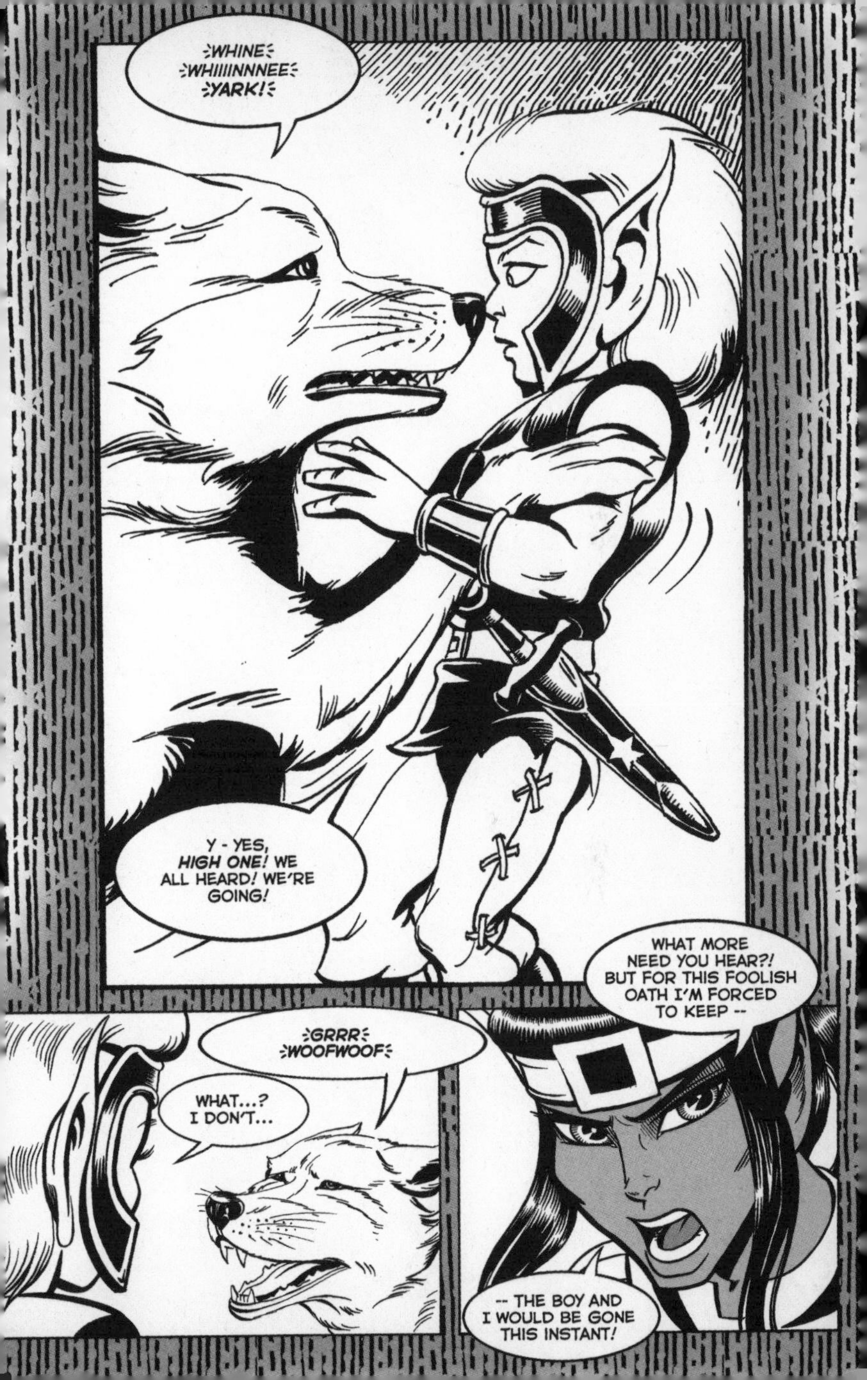

WHINE
WHIIIINNNEE
YARK!
Y - YES, HIGH ONE! WE ALL HEARD! WE'RE GOING!
GRRR
WOOFWOOF
WHAT...? I DON'T...
WHAT MORE NEED YOU HEAR?! BUT FOR THIS FOOLISH OATH I'M FORCED TO KEEP --
-- THE BOY AND I WOULD BE GONE THIS INSTANT!

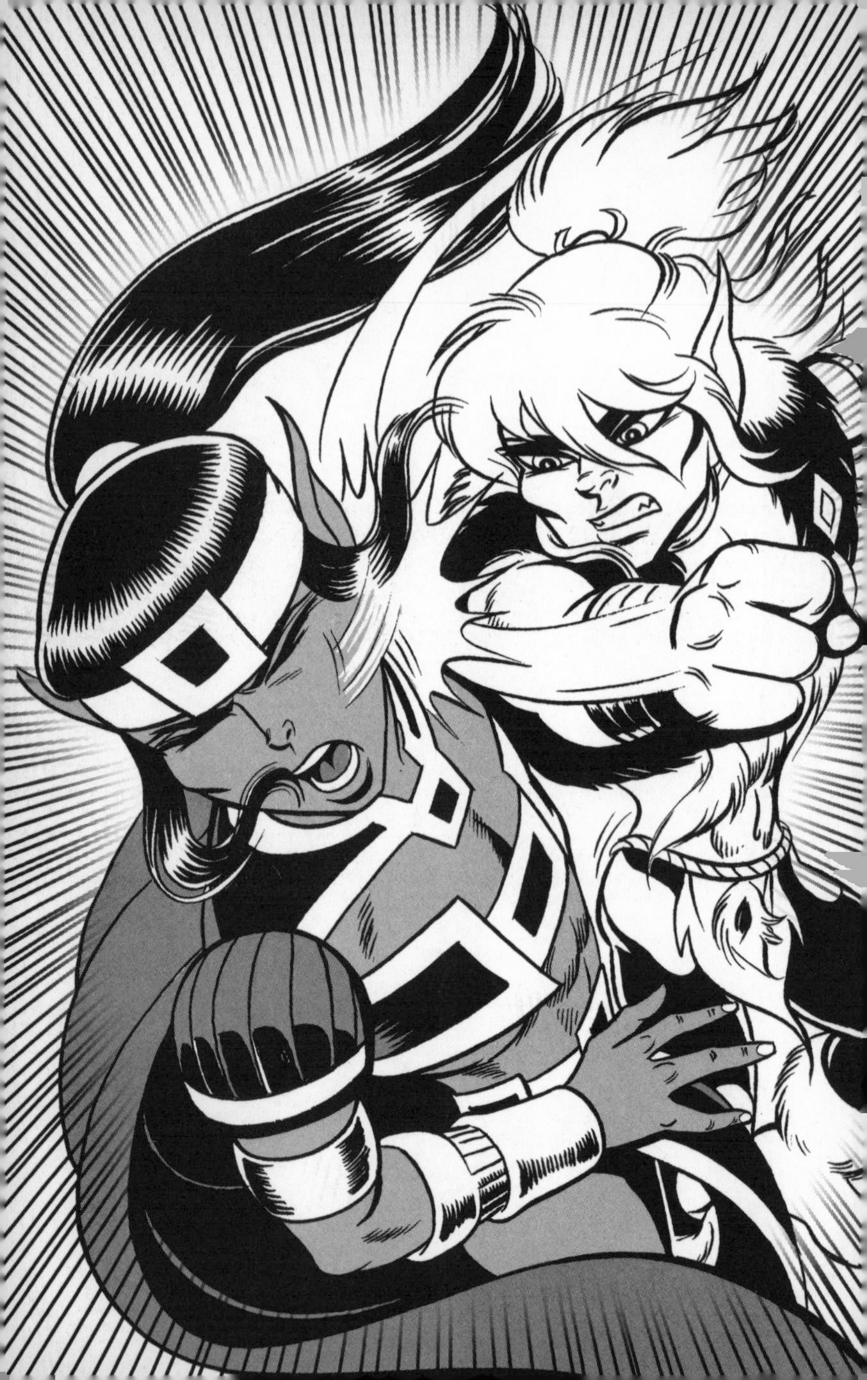

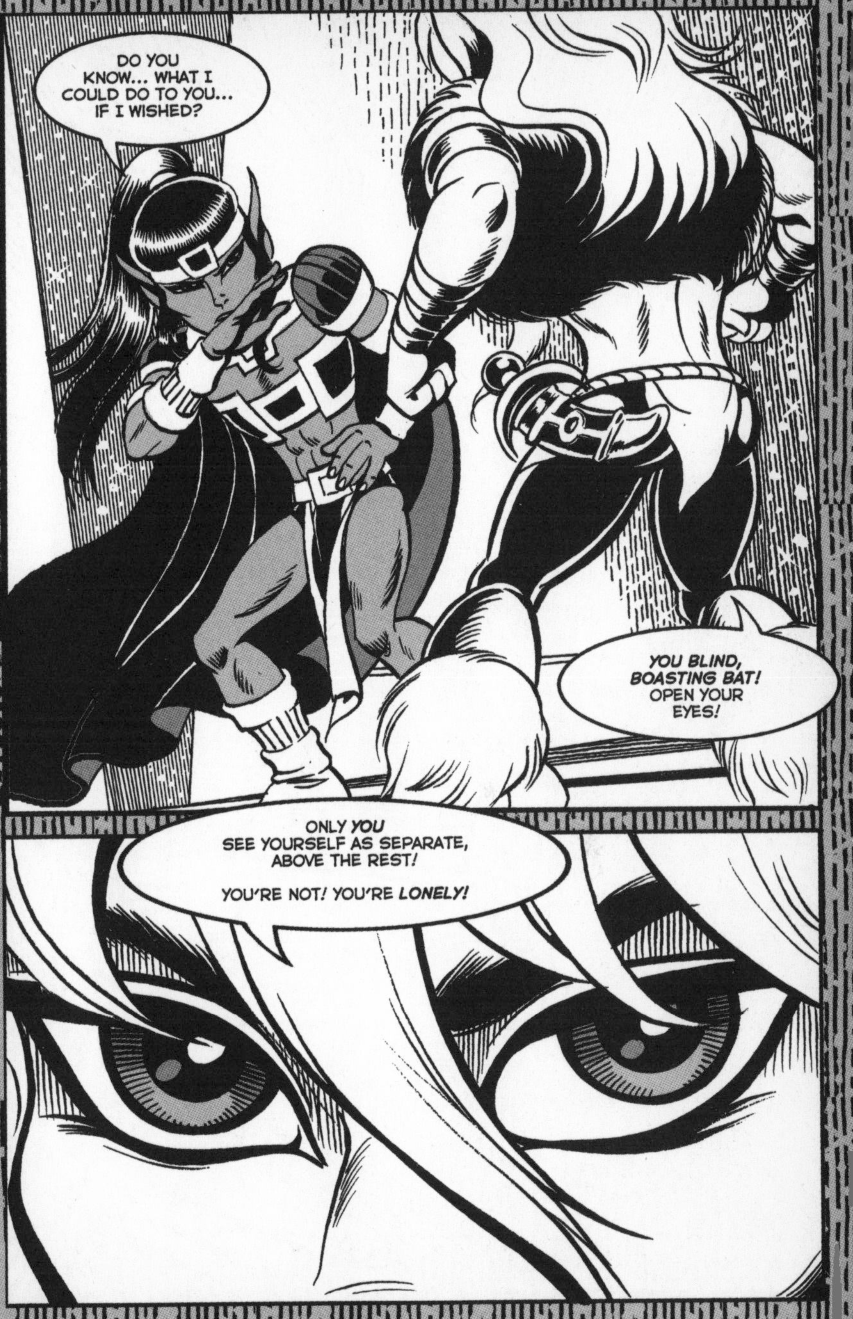
DO YOU KNOW... WHAT I COULD DO TO YOU... IF I WISHED?
YOU BLIND, BOASTING BAT! OPEN YOUR EYES!
ONLY YOU SEE YOURSELF AS SEPARATE, ABOVE THE REST!
YOU'RE NOT! YOU'RE LONELY!

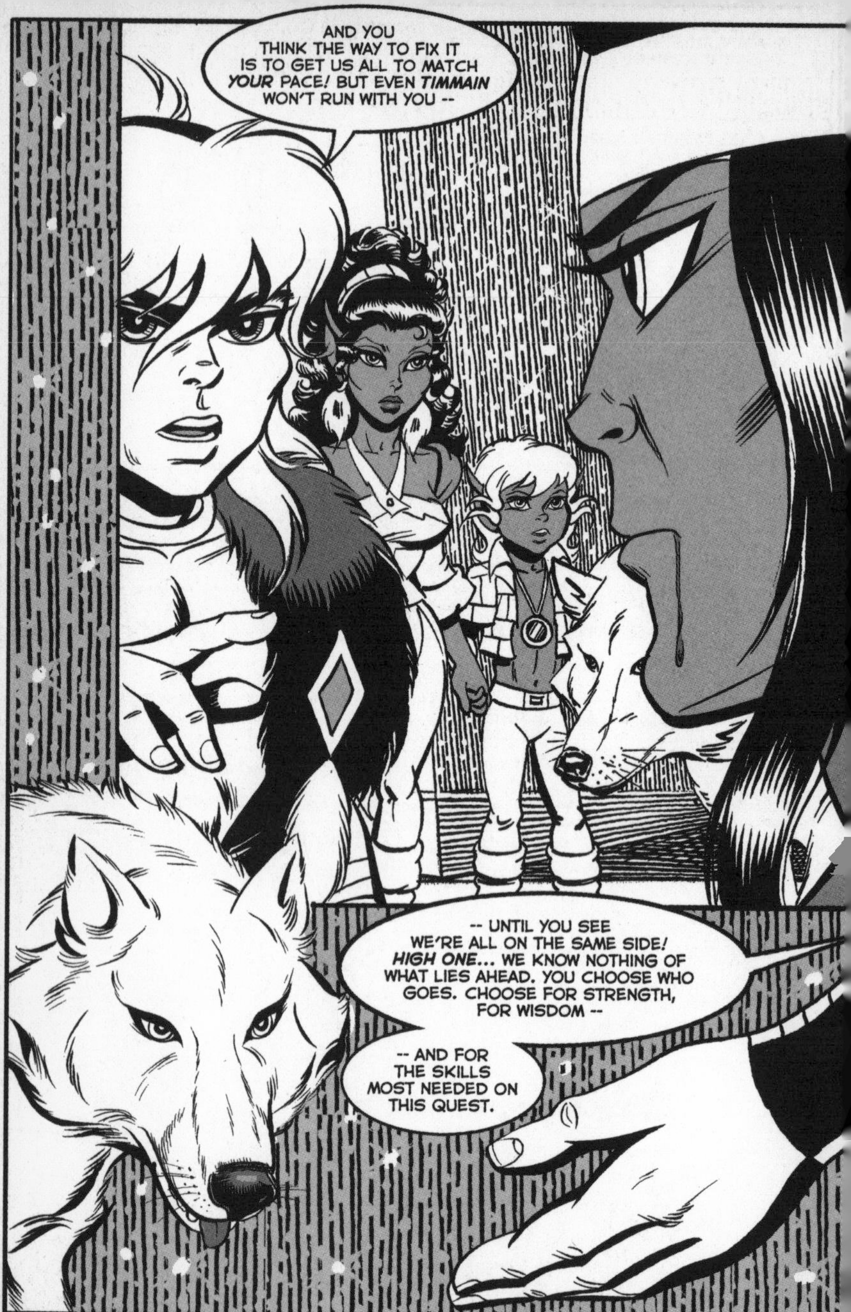
AND YOU THINK THE WAY TO FIX IT IS TO GET US ALL TO MATCH *YOUR* PACE! BUT EVEN *TIMMAIN* WON'T RUN WITH YOU --
-- UNTIL YOU SEE WE'RE ALL ON THE SAME SIDE! *HIGH ONE*... WE KNOW NOTHING OF WHAT LIES AHEAD. YOU CHOOSE WHO GOES. CHOOSE FOR STRENGTH, FOR WISDOM --
-- AND FOR THE SKILLS MOST NEEDED ON THIS QUEST.

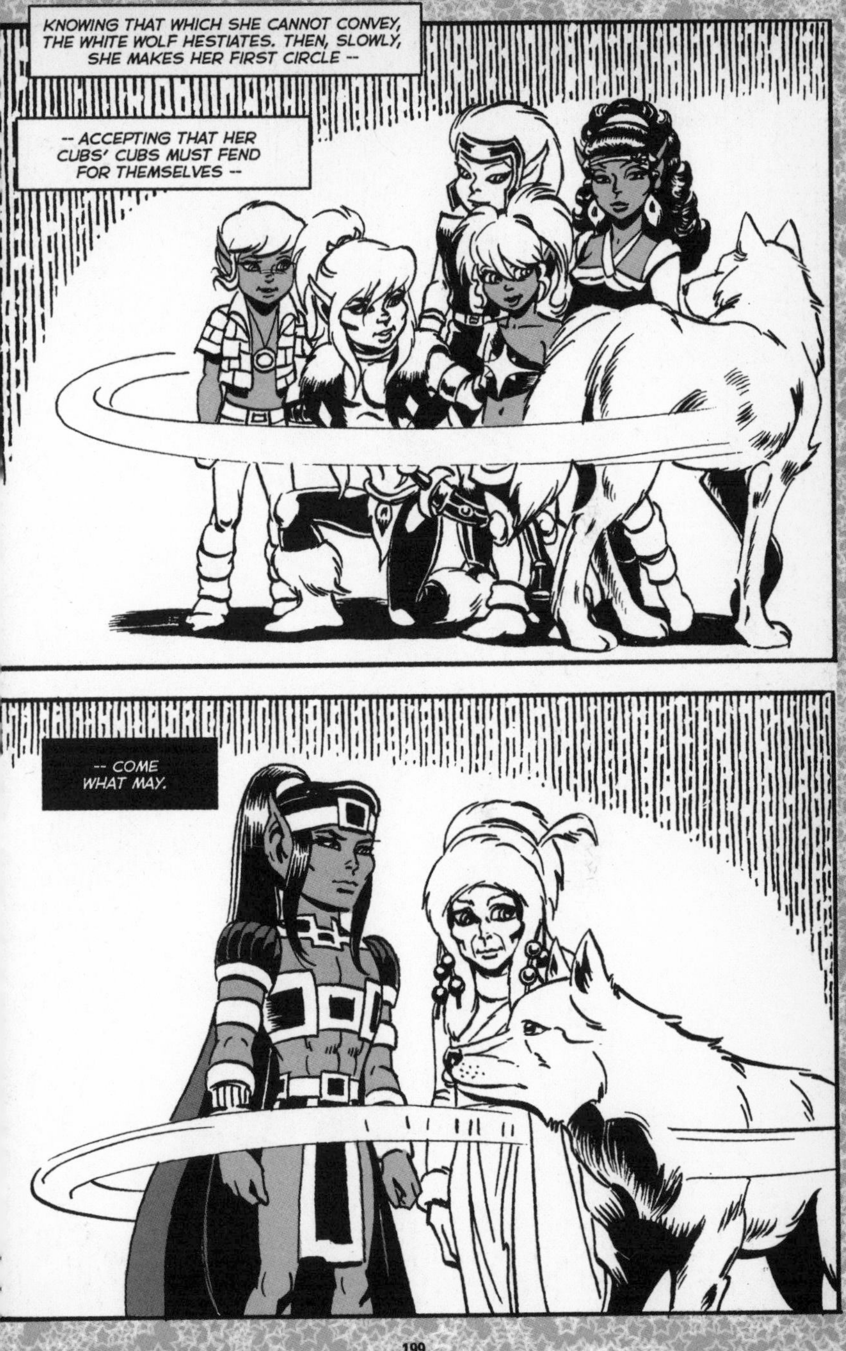
KNOWING THAT WHICH SHE CANNOT CONVEY, THE WHITE WOLF HESTIATES. THEN, SLOWLY, SHE MAKES HER FIRST CIRCLE --
-- ACCEPTING THAT HER CUBS' CUBS MUST FEND FOR THEMSELVES --
-- COME WHAT MAY.

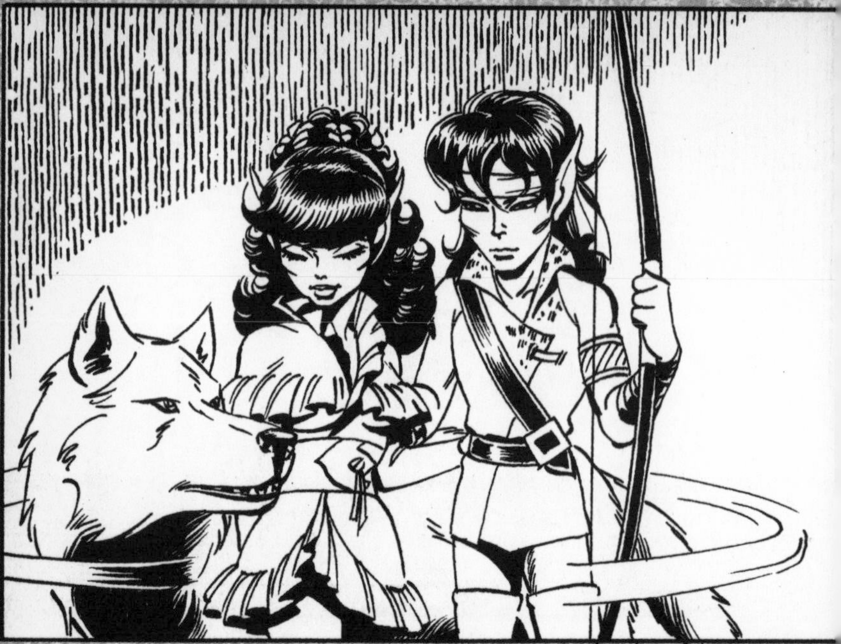

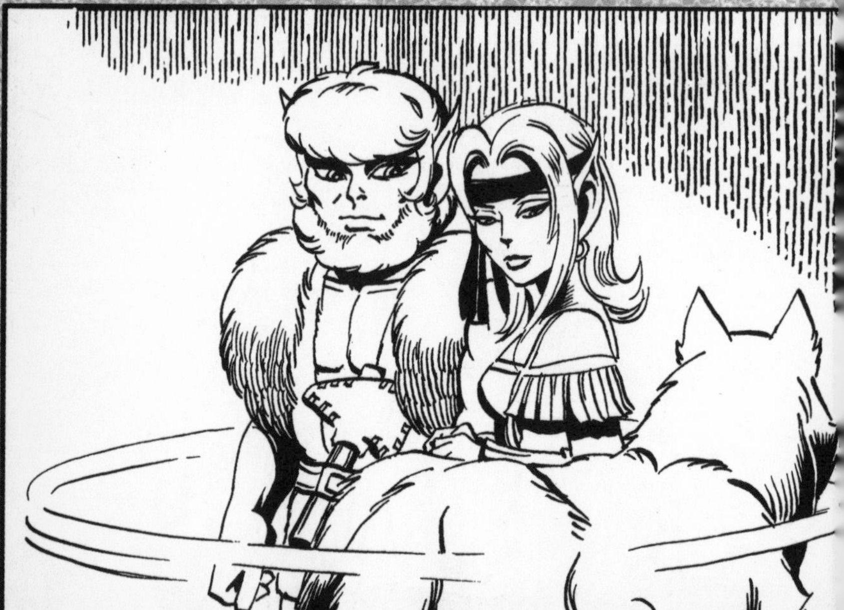

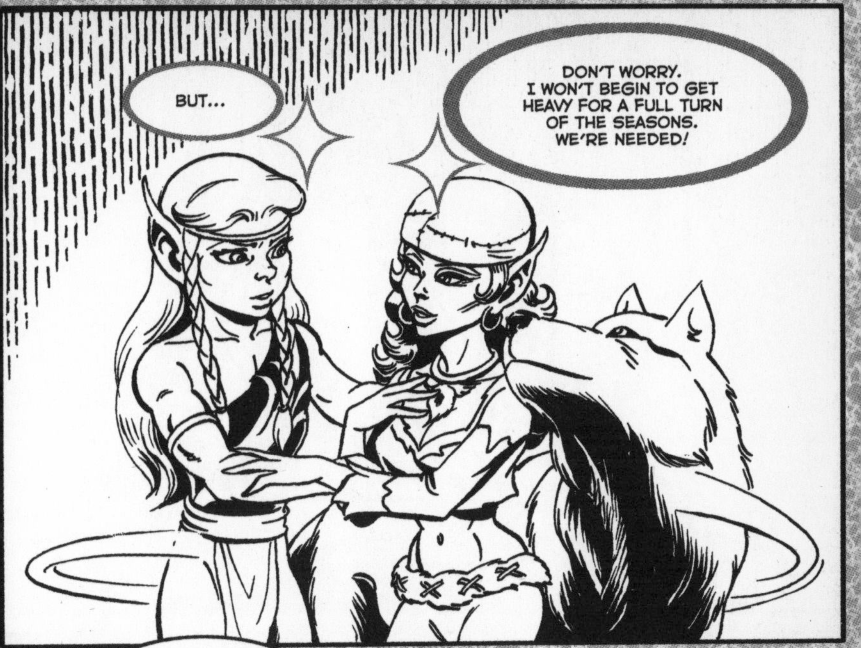
BUT...
DON'T WORRY. I WON'T BEGIN TO GET HEAVY FOR A FULL TURN OF THE SEASONS. WE'RE NEEDED!

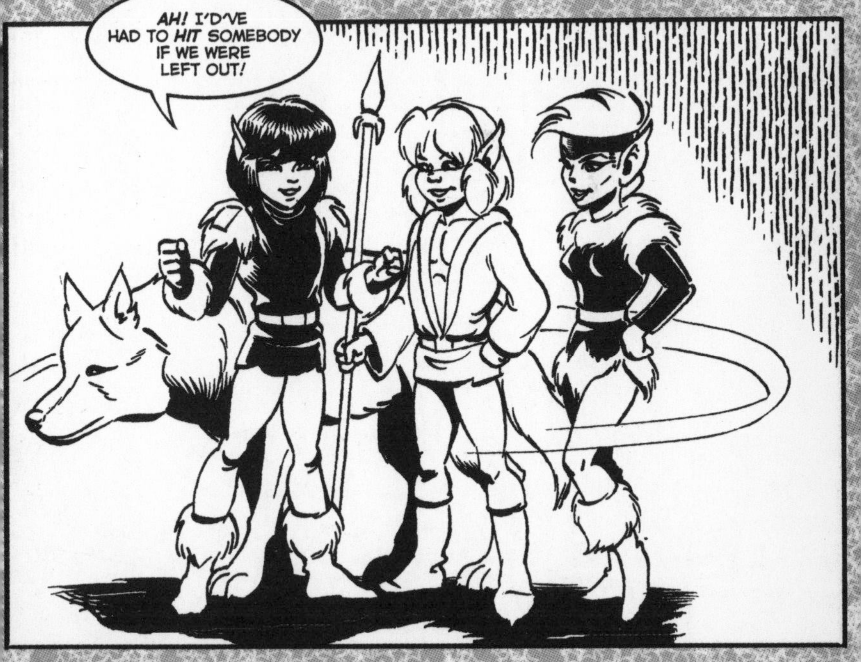
AH! I'D'VE HAD TO HIT SOMEBODY IF WE WERE LEFT OUT!

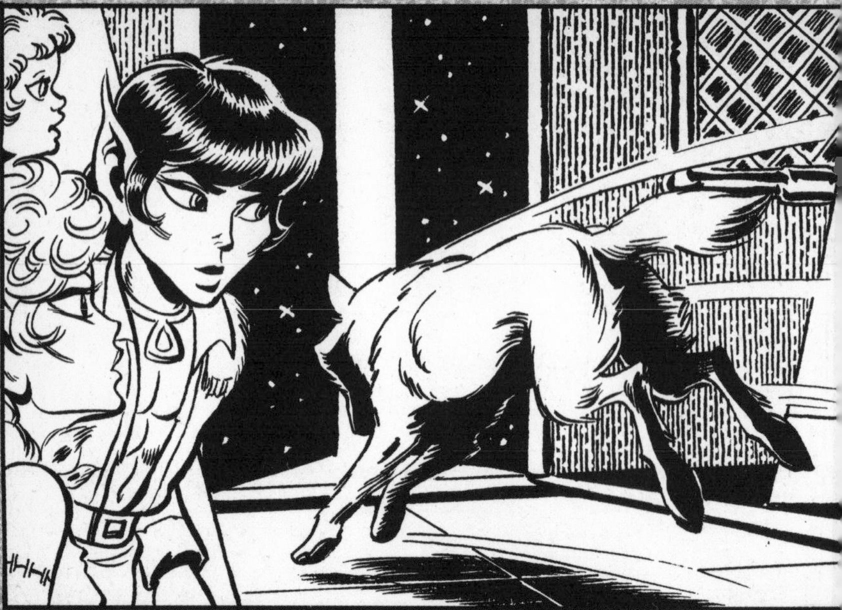

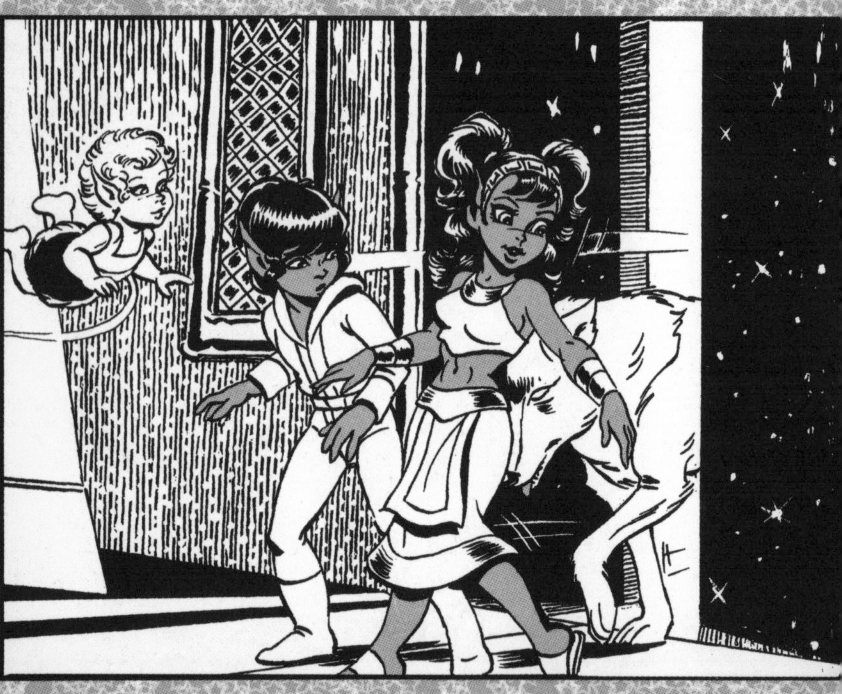

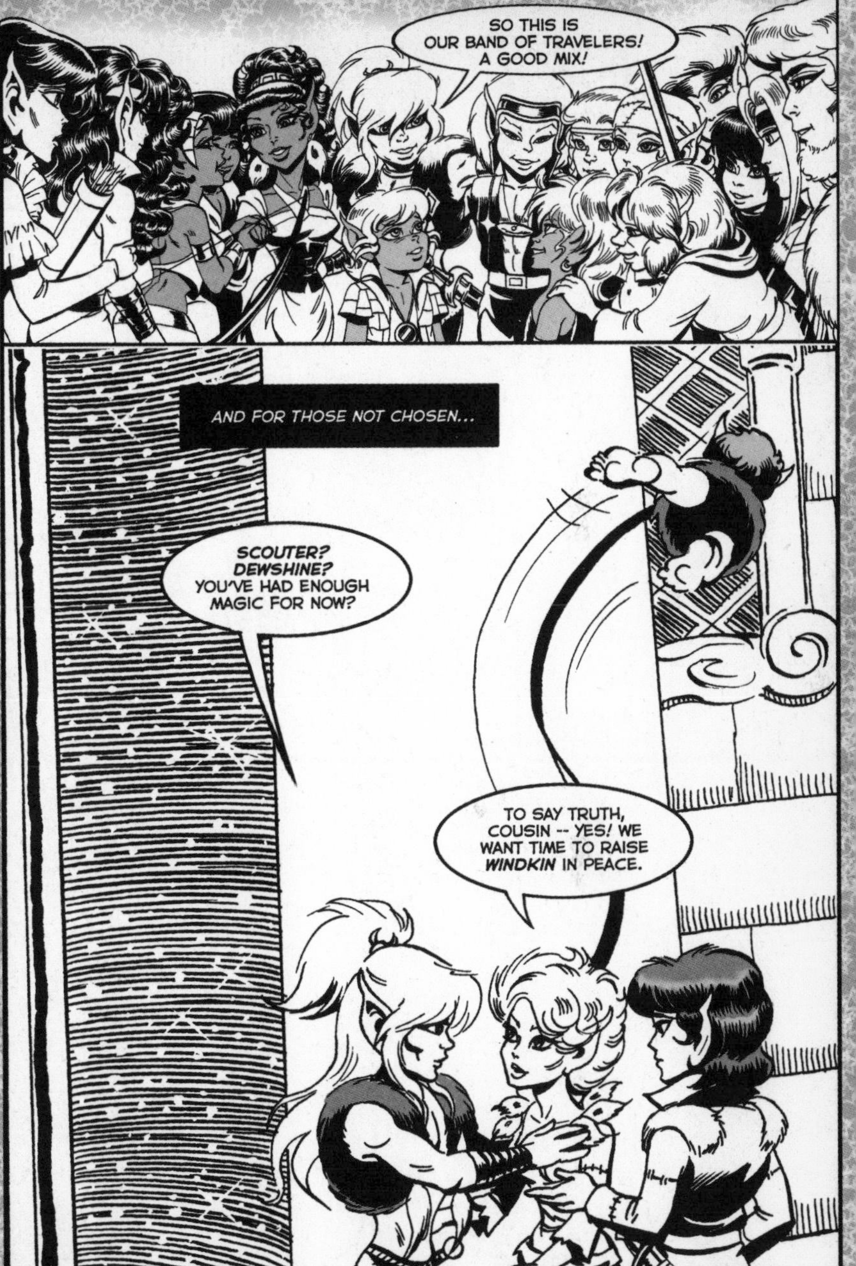
SO THIS IS OUR BAND OF TRAVELERS! A GOOD MIX!
AND FOR THOSE NOT CHOSEN...
SCOUTER? DEWSHINE? YOU'VE HAD ENOUGH MAGIC FOR NOW?
TO SAY TRUTH, COUSIN -- YES! WE WANT TIME TO RAISE WINDKIN IN PEACE.

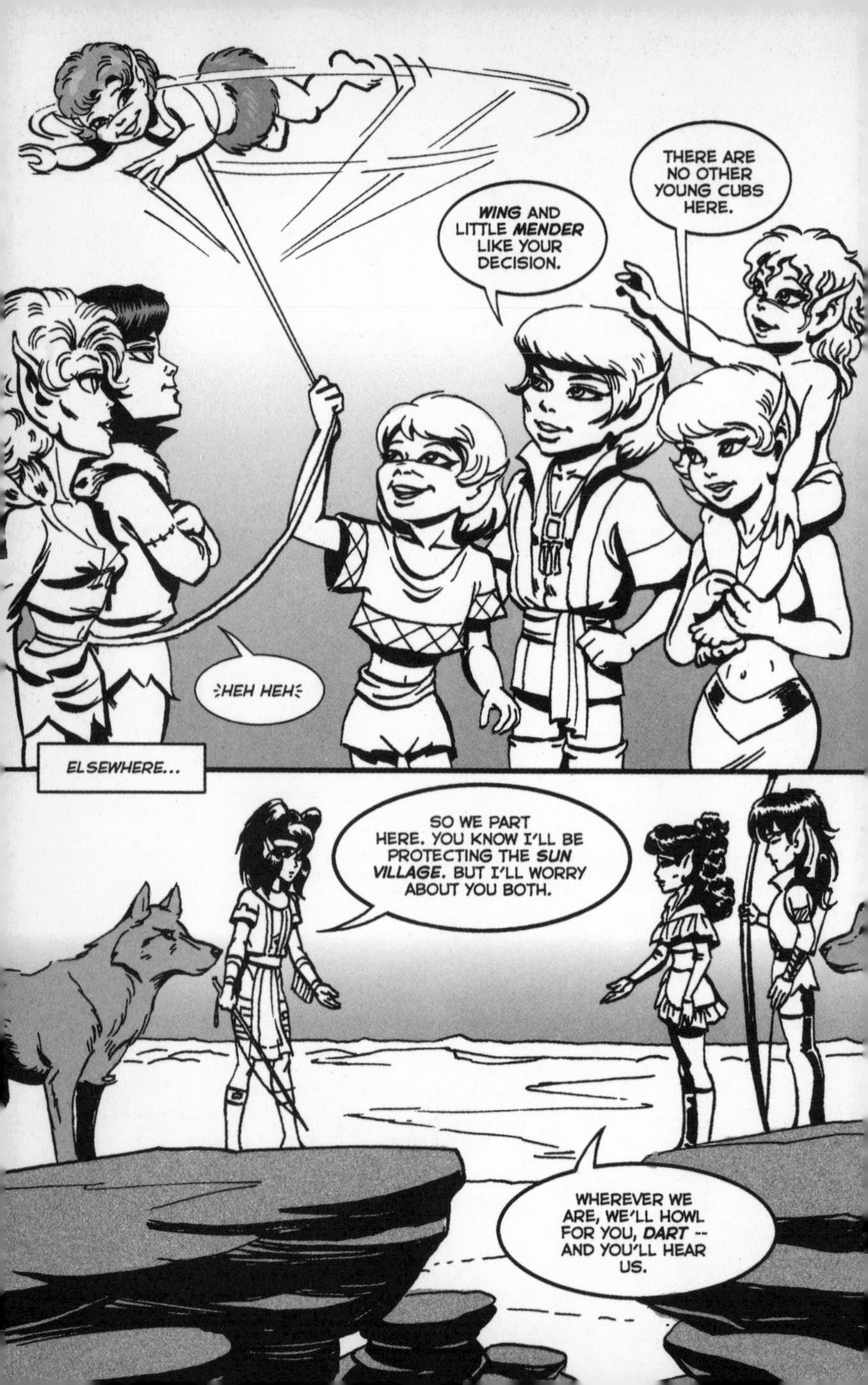
WING AND LITTLE MENDER LIKE YOUR DECISION.
THERE ARE NO OTHER YOUNG CUBS HERE.
HEH HEH
ELSEWHERE...
SO WE PART HERE. YOU KNOW I'LL BE PROTECTING THE SUN VILLAGE. BUT I'LL WORRY ABOUT YOU BOTH.
WHEREVER WE ARE, WE'LL HOWL FOR YOU, DART -- AND YOU'LL HEAR US.

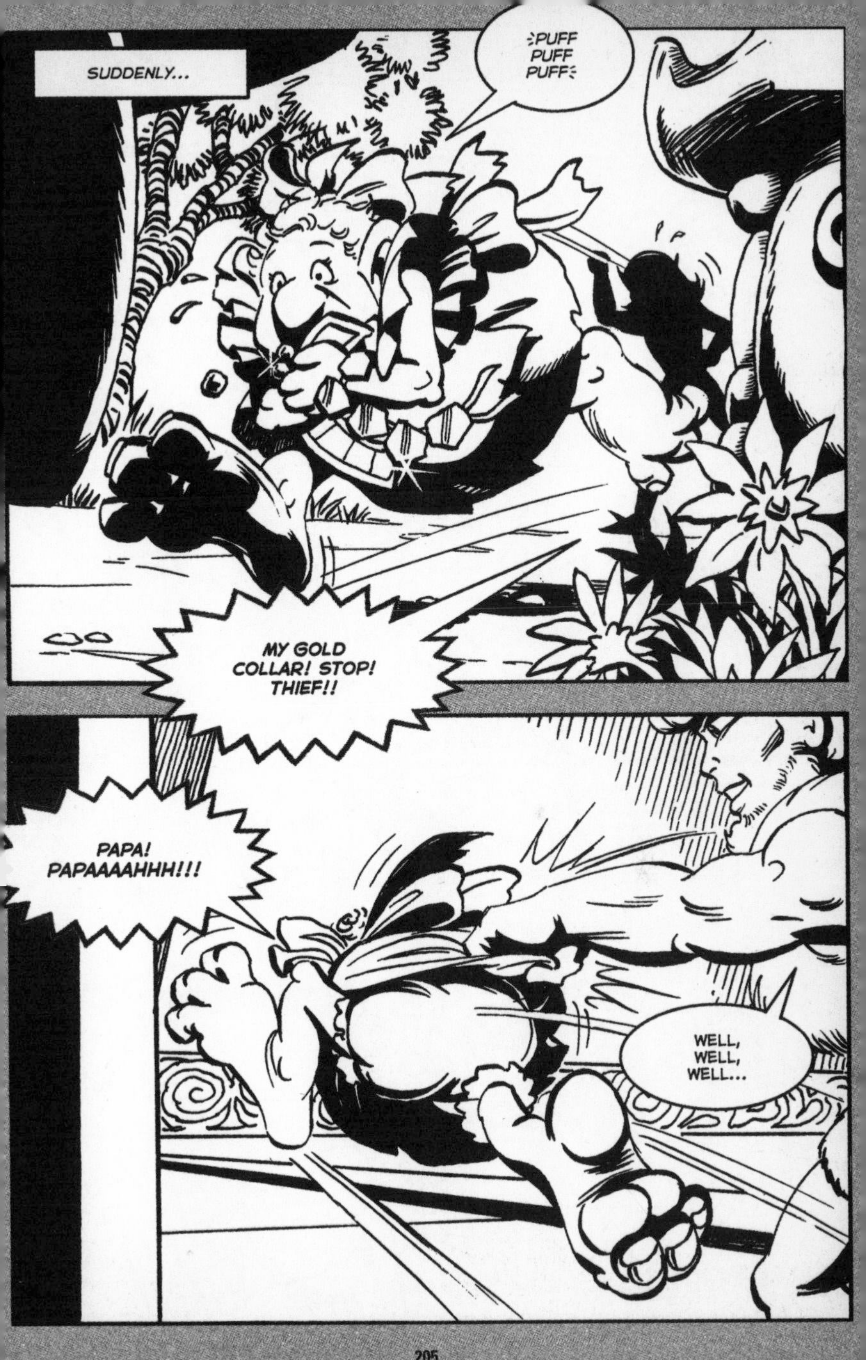
SUDDENLY...
PUFF PUFF PUFF
MY GOLD COLLAR! STOP! THIEF!!
PAPA! PAPAAAAHHH!!!
WELL, WELL, WELL...

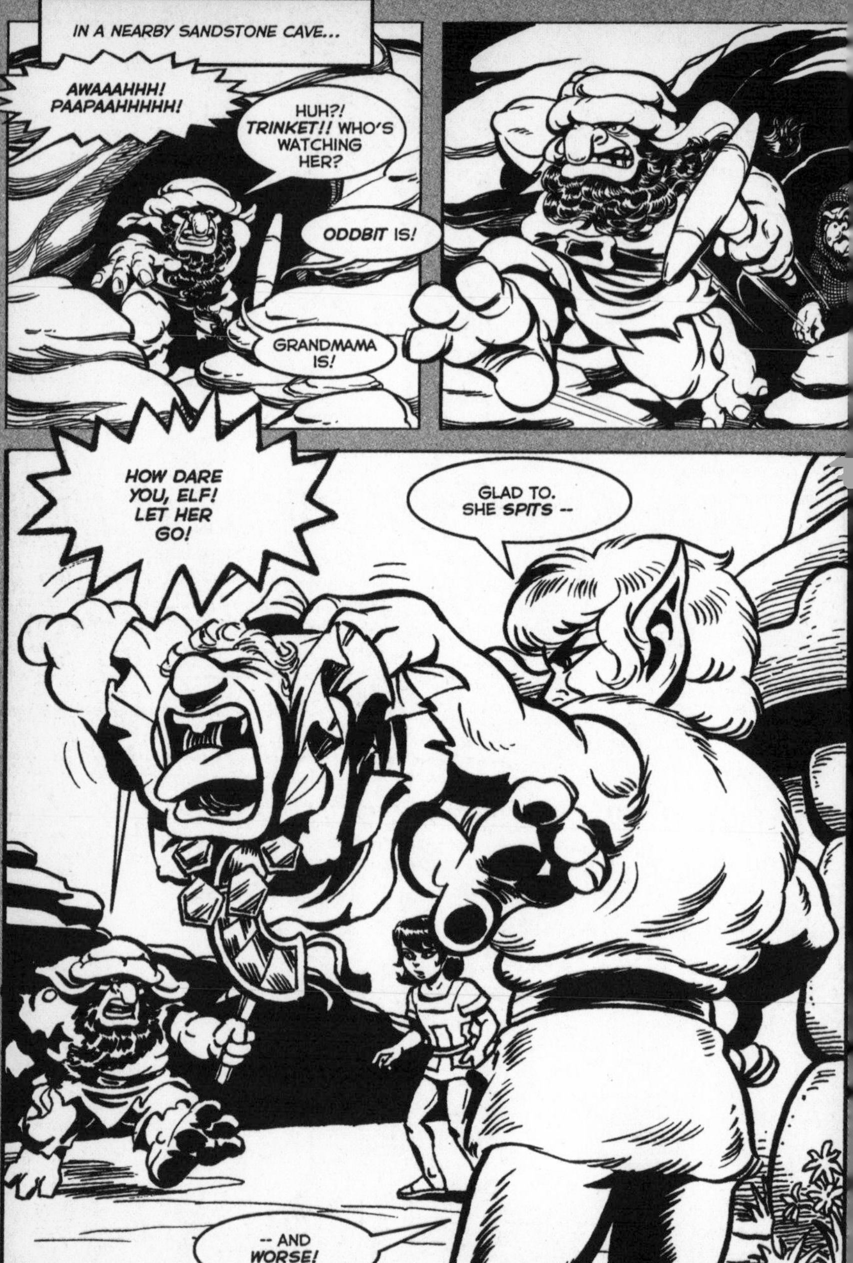
IN A NEARBY SANDSTONE CAVE...
AWAAAHHH! PAAPAAHHHHH!
HUH?! TRINKET!! WHO'S WATCHING HER?
ODDBIT IS!
GRANDMAMA IS!
HOW DARE YOU, ELF! LET HER GO!
GLAD TO. SHE SPITS --
-- AND WORSE!

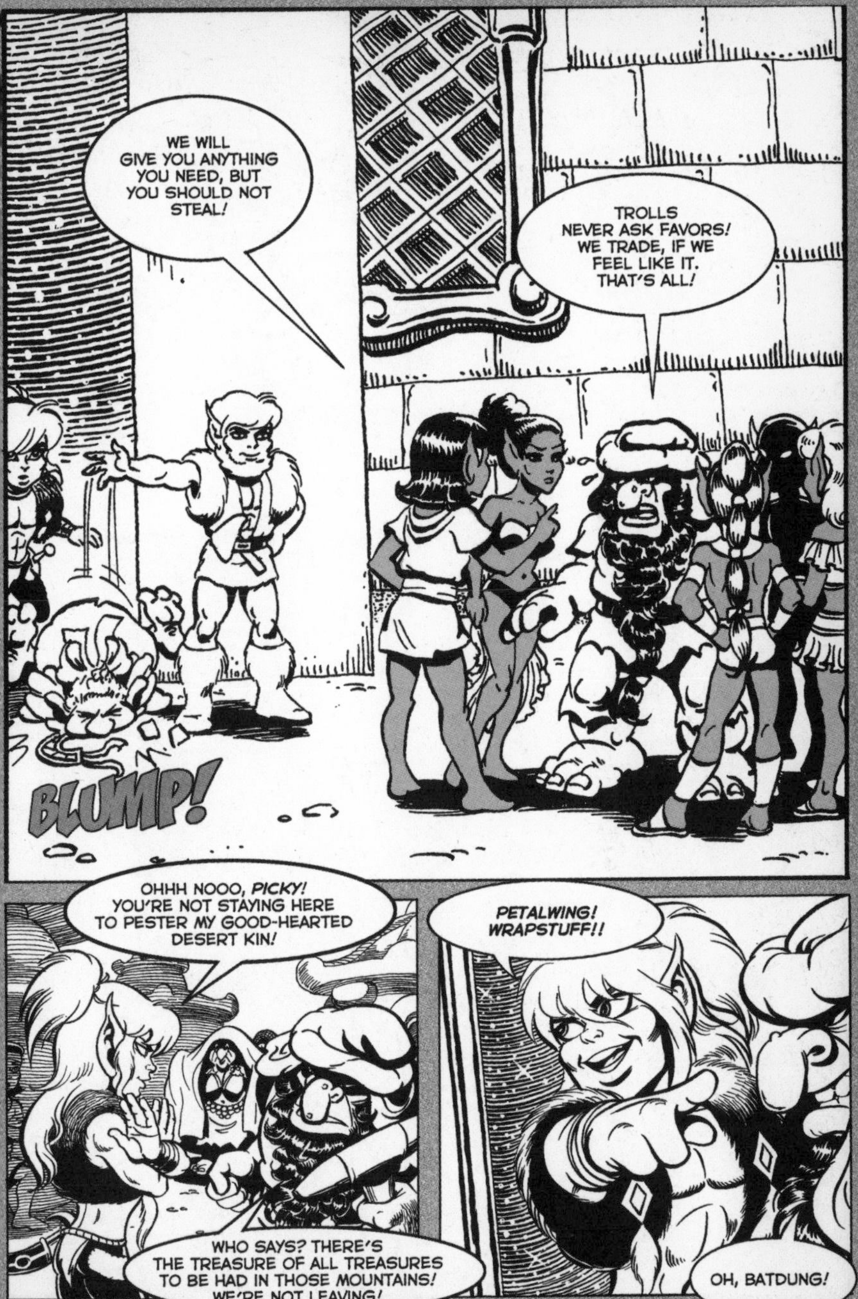
WE WILL GIVE YOU ANYTHING YOU NEED, BUT YOU SHOULD NOT STEAL!
TROLLS NEVER ASK FAVORS! WE TRADE, IF WE FEEL LIKE IT. THAT'S ALL!
BLUMP!
OHHH NOOO, PICKY! YOU'RE NOT STAYING HERE TO PESTER MY GOOD-HEARTED DESERT KIN!
WHO SAYS? THERE'S THE TREASURE OF ALL TREASURES TO BE HAD IN THOSE MOUNTAINS! WE'RE NOT LEAVING!
PETALWING! WRAPSTUFF!!
OH, BATDUNG!

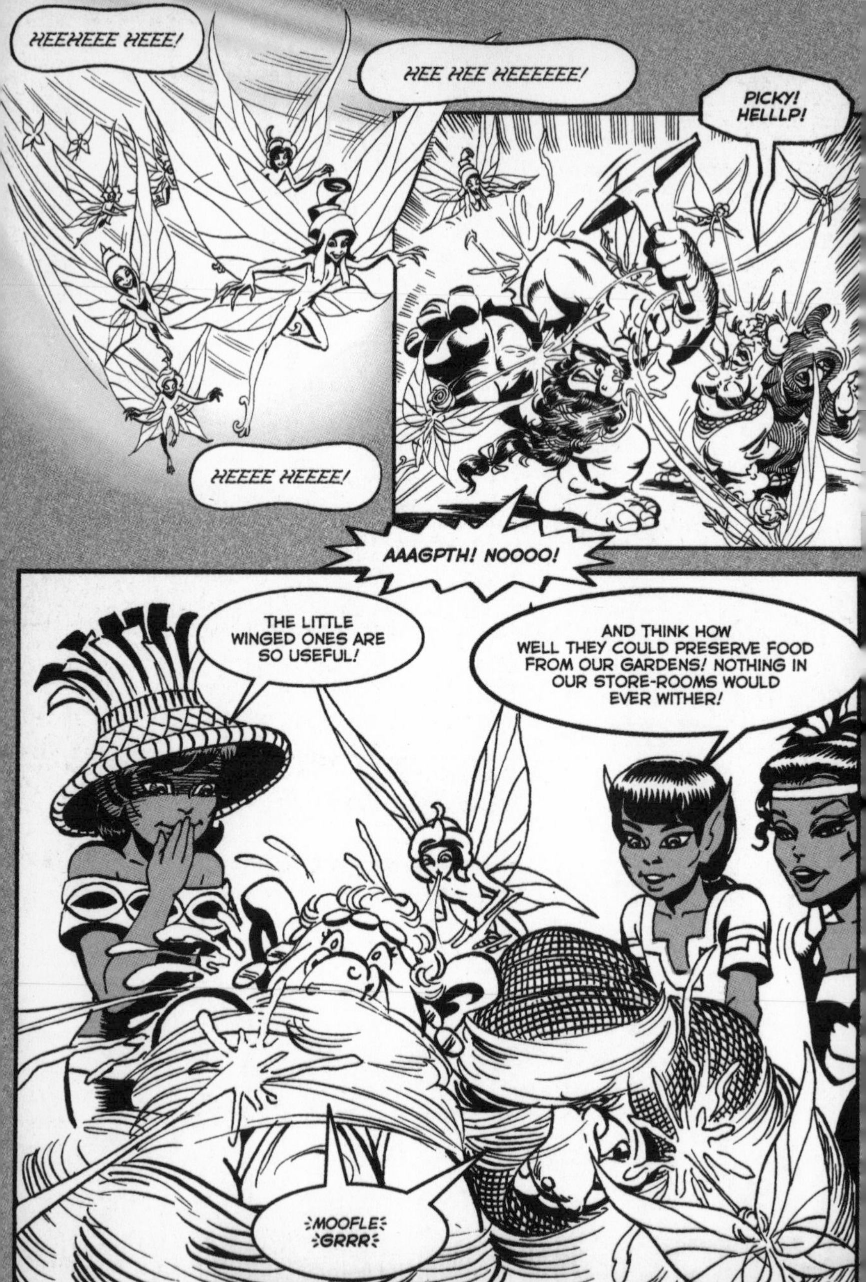
HEEHEEE HEEE!
HEE HEE HEEEEEE!
PICKY! HELLLP!
HEEEE HEEEE!
AAAGPTH! NOOOO!
THE LITTLE WINGED ONES ARE SO USEFUL!
AND THINK HOW WELL THEY COULD PRESERVE FOOD FROM OUR GARDENS! NOTHING IN OUR STORE-ROOMS WOULD EVER WITHER!
MOOFLE GRRR

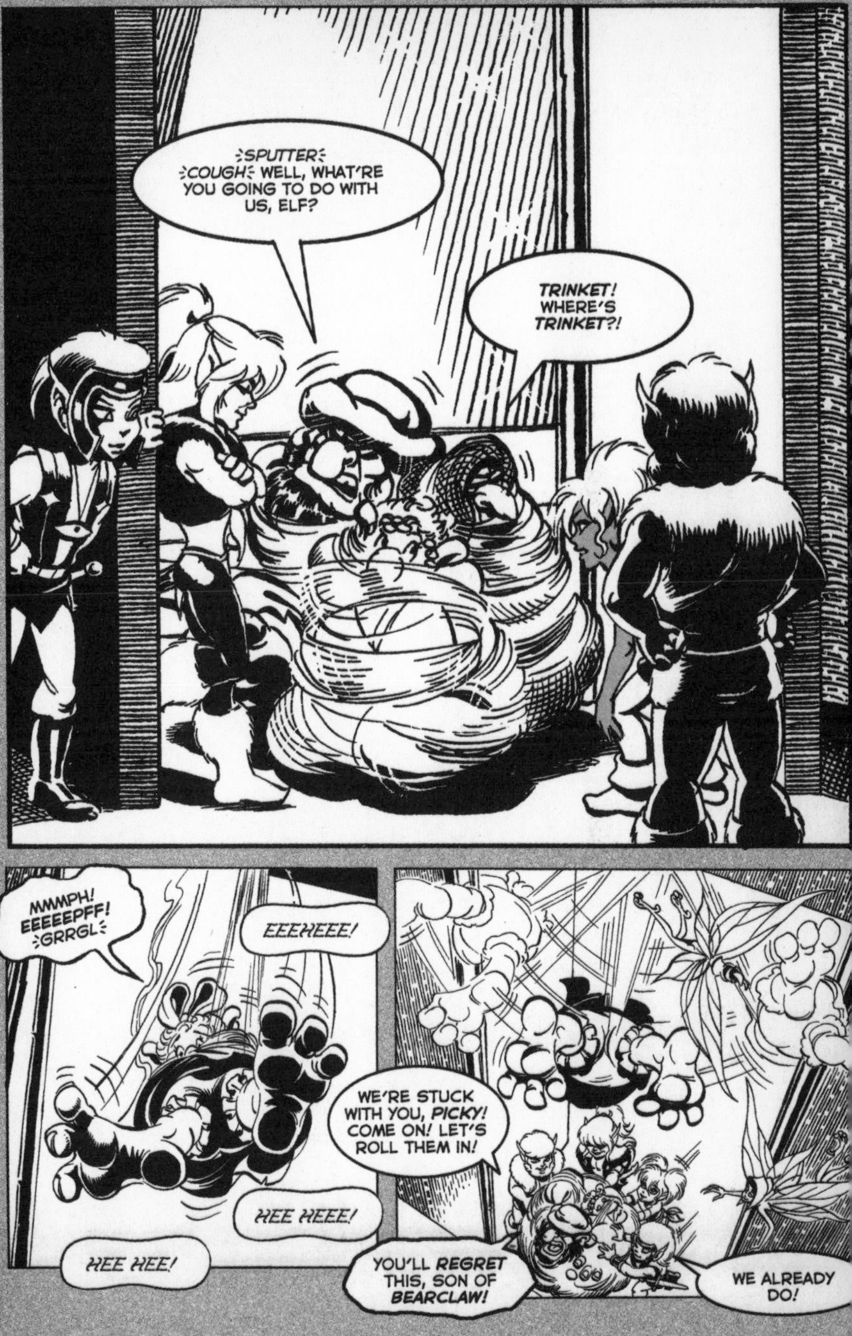

SPUTTER
COUGH WELL, WHAT'RE YOU GOING TO DO WITH US, ELF?
TRINKET! WHERE'S TRINKET?!
MMMPH! EEEEEPFF! GRRGL
EEEHEEE!
HEE HEEE!
HEE HEE!
WE'RE STUCK WITH YOU, PICKY! COME ON! LET'S ROLL THEM IN!
YOU'LL REGRET THIS, SON OF BEARCLAW!
WE ALREADY DO!

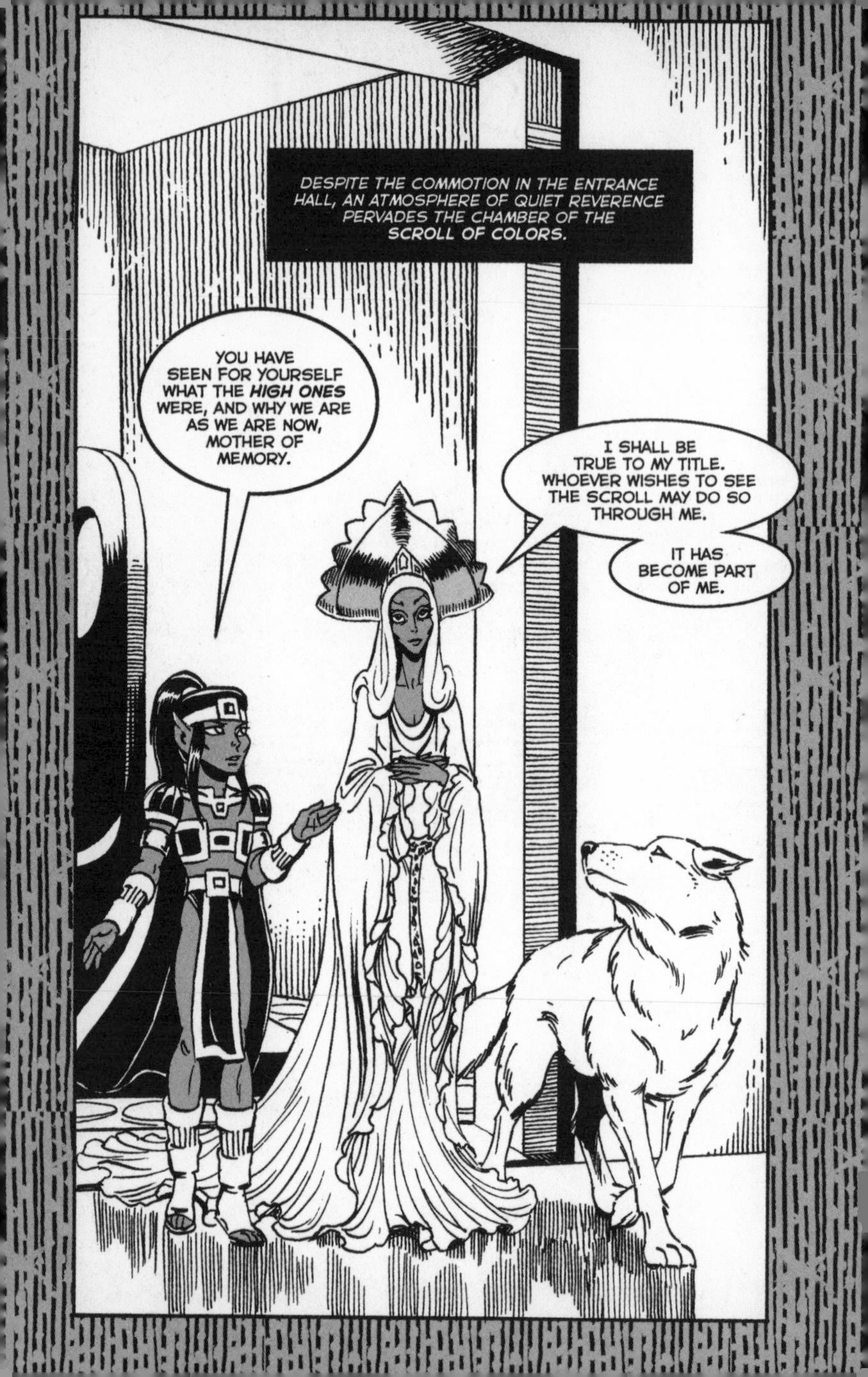
DESPITE THE COMMOTION IN THE ENTRANCE HALL, AN ATMOSPHERE OF QUIET REVERENCE PERVADES THE CHAMBER OF THE SCROLL OF COLORS.
YOU HAVE SEEN FOR YOURSELF WHAT THE *HIGH ONES* WERE, AND WHY WE ARE AS WE ARE NOW, MOTHER OF MEMORY.
I SHALL BE TRUE TO MY TITLE. WHOEVER WISHES TO SEE THE SCROLL MAY DO SO THROUGH ME.
IT HAS BECOME PART OF ME.

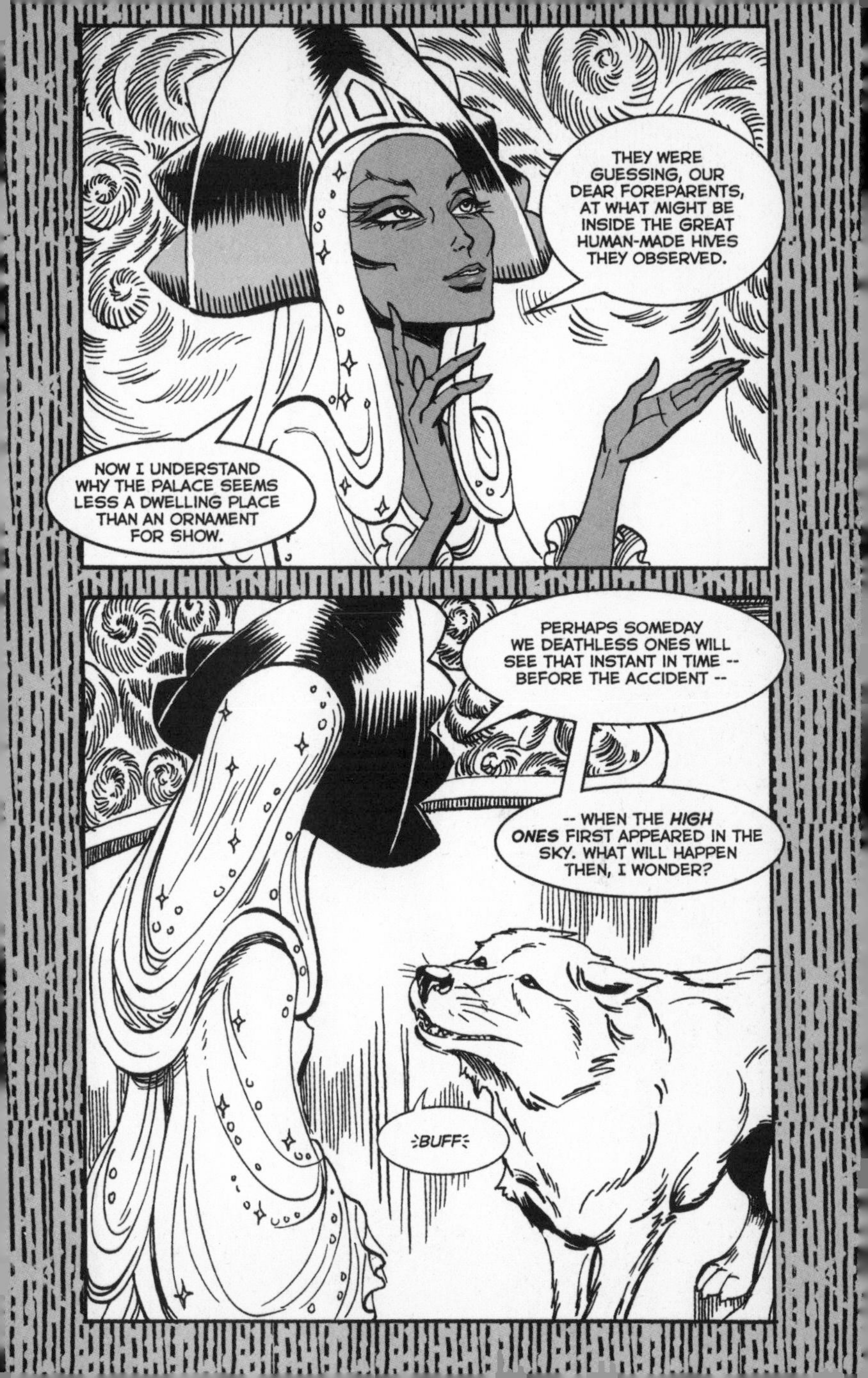
THEY WERE GUESSING, OUR DEAR FOREPARENTS, AT WHAT MIGHT BE INSIDE THE GREAT HUMAN-MADE HIVES THEY OBSERVED.
NOW I UNDERSTAND WHY THE PALACE SEEMS LESS A DWELLING PLACE THAN AN ORNAMENT FOR SHOW.
PERHAPS SOMEDAY WE DEATHLESS ONES WILL SEE THAT INSTANT IN TIME -- BEFORE THE ACCIDENT --
-- WHEN THE *HIGH ONES* FIRST APPEARED IN THE SKY. WHAT WILL HAPPEN THEN, I WONDER?
BUFF

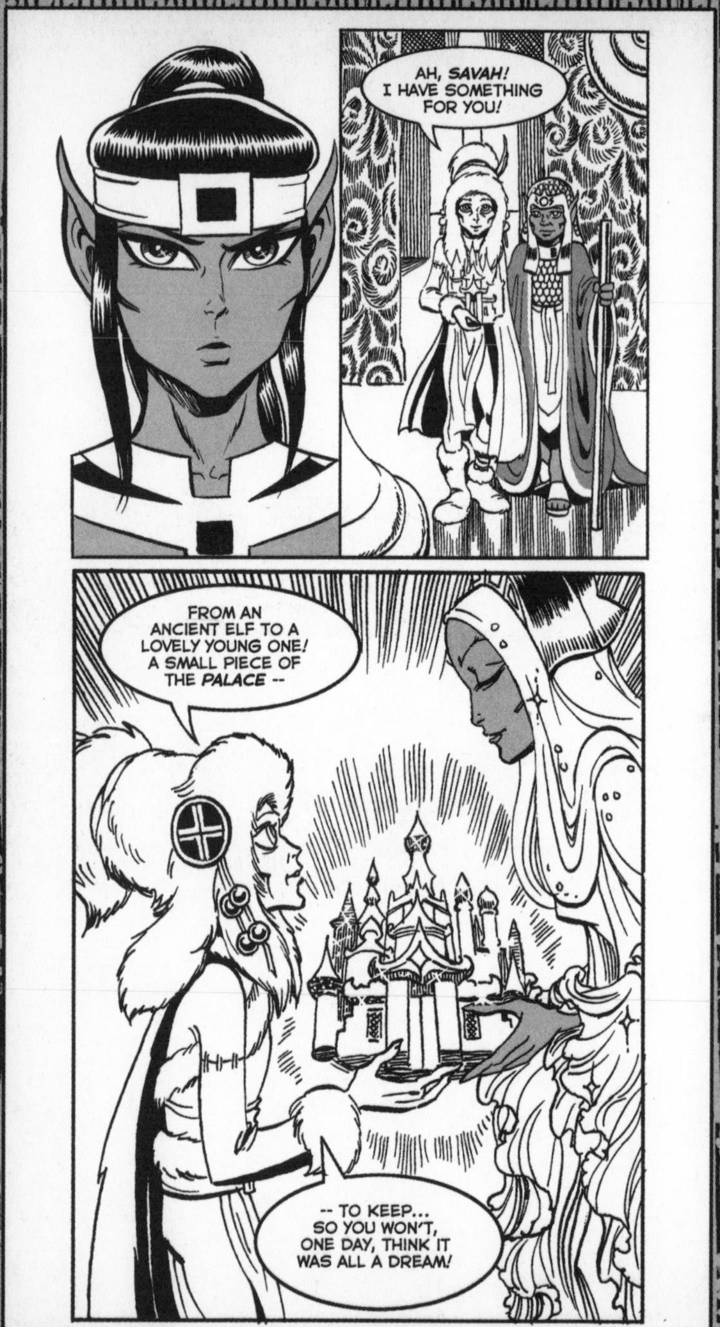
AH, *SAVAH!* I HAVE SOMETHING FOR YOU!
FROM AN ANCIENT ELF TO A LOVELY YOUNG ONE! A SMALL PIECE OF THE *PALACE* --
-- TO KEEP... SO YOU WON'T, ONE DAY, THINK IT WAS ALL A DREAM!

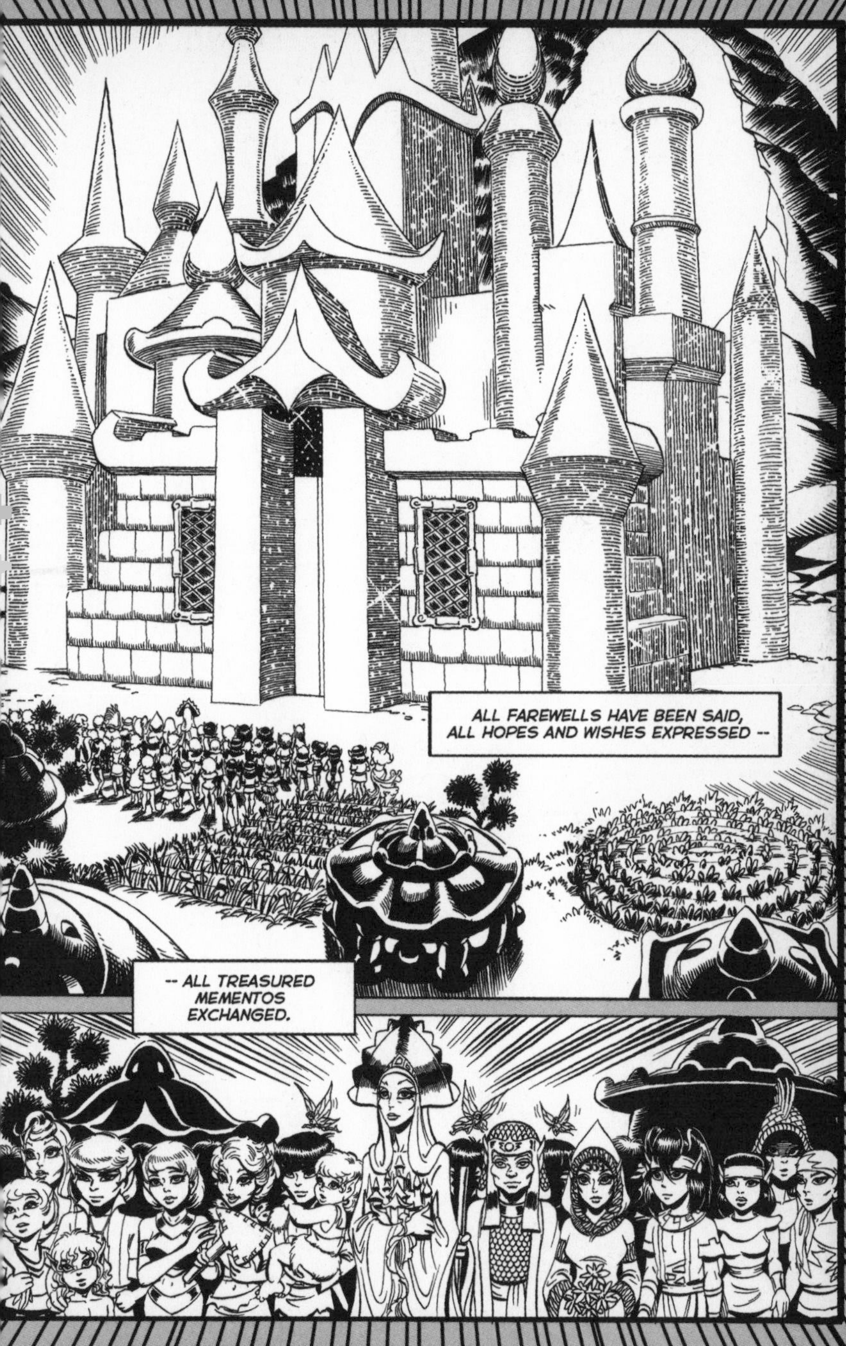
ALL FAREWELLS HAVE BEEN SAID, ALL HOPES AND WISHES EXPRESSED --
-- ALL TREASURED MEMENTOS EXCHANGED.

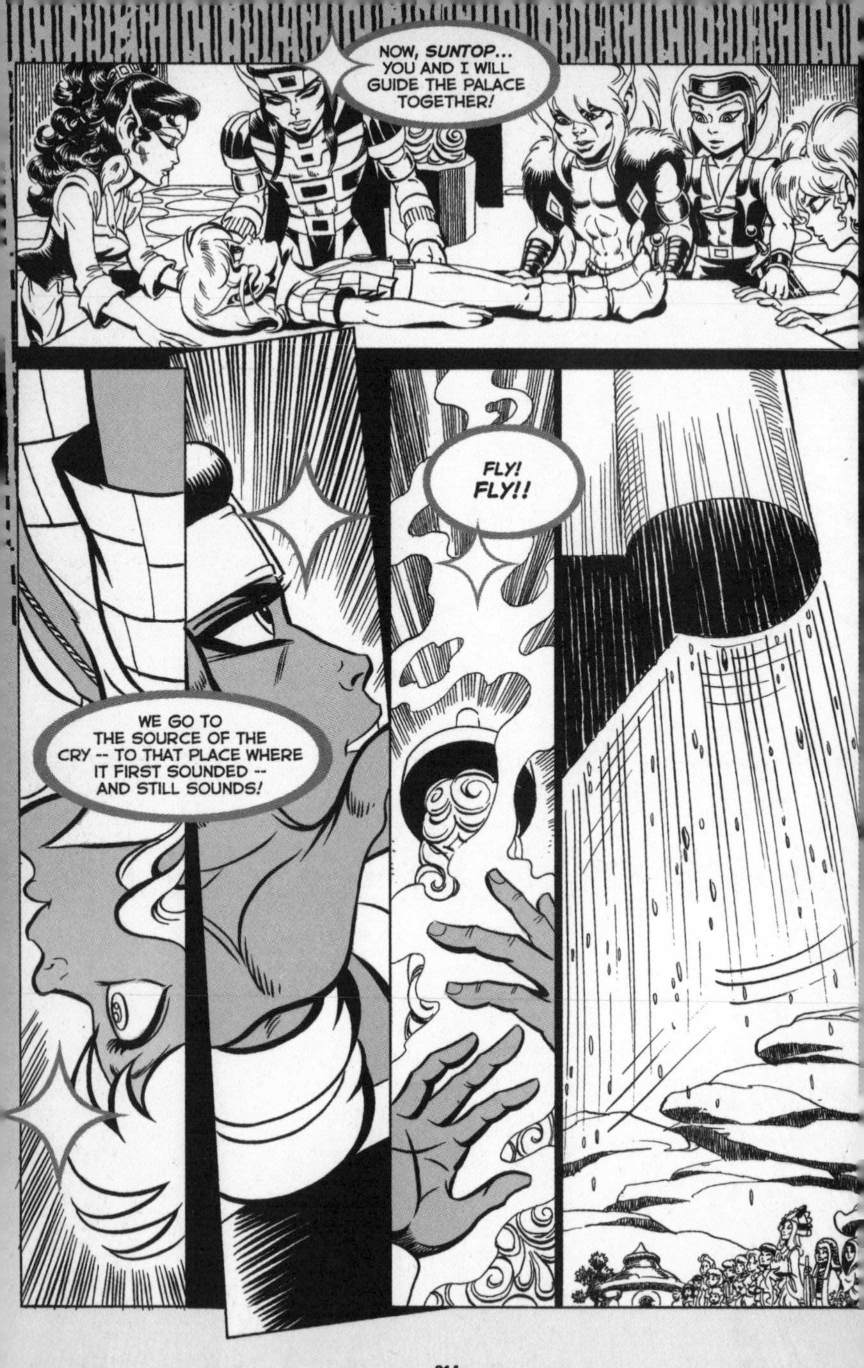
NOW, *SUNTOP*... YOU AND I WILL GUIDE THE PALACE TOGETHER!
WE GO TO THE SOURCE OF THE CRY -- TO THAT PLACE WHERE IT FIRST SOUNDED -- AND STILL SOUNDS!
FLY! FLY!!

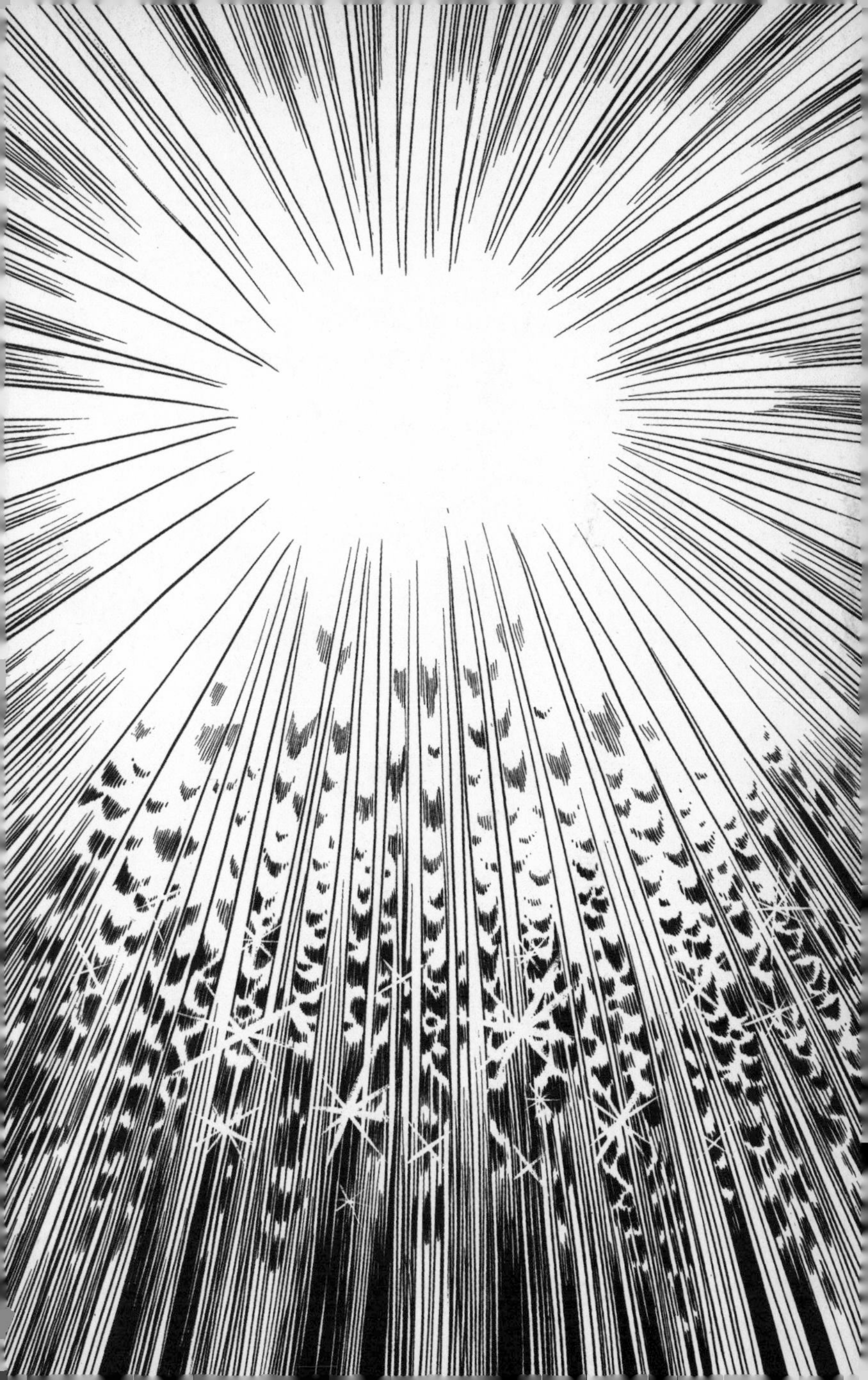

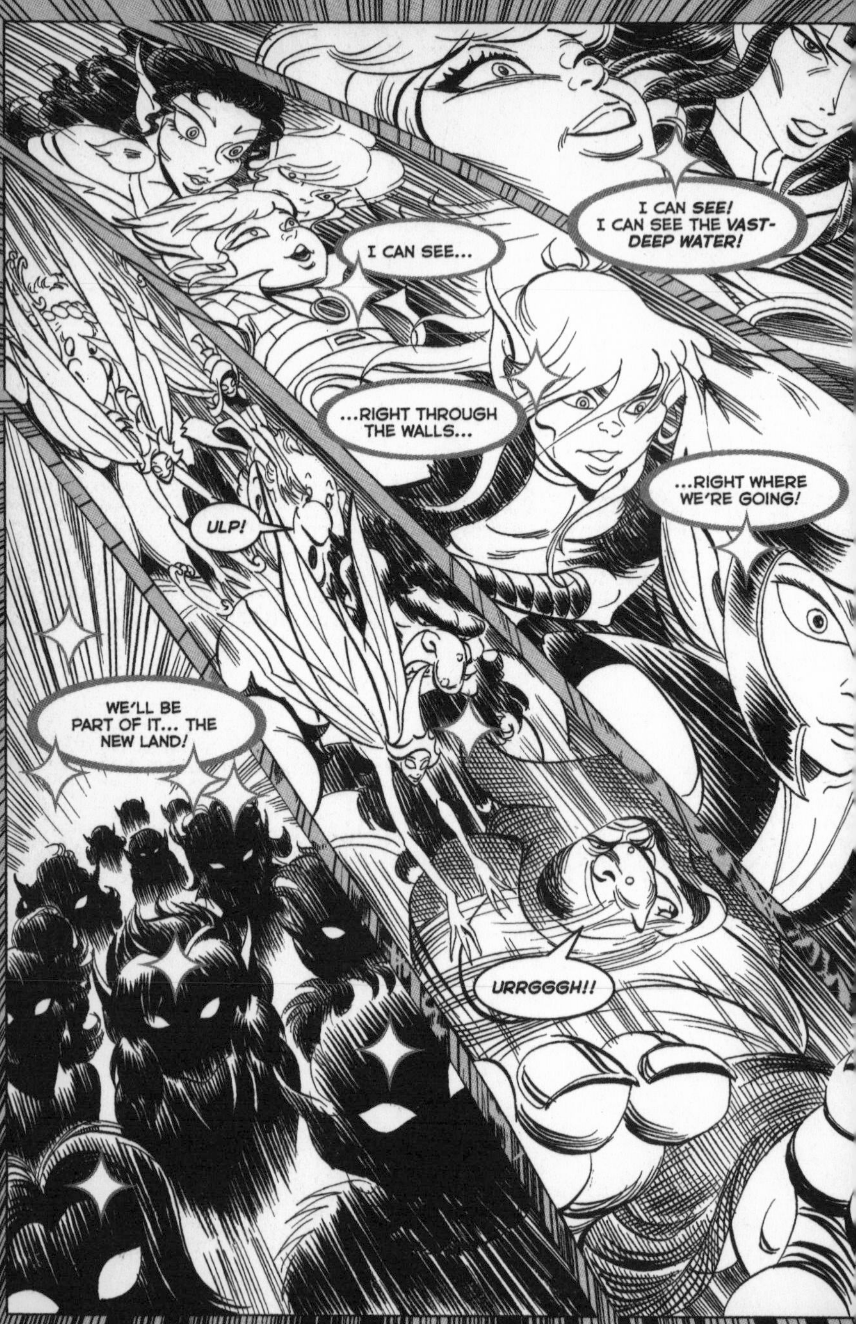
I CAN SEE...
I CAN SEE! I CAN SEE THE VAST-DEEP WATER!
...RIGHT THROUGH THE WALLS...
...RIGHT WHERE WE'RE GOING!
ULP!
WE'LL BE PART OF IT... THE NEW LAND!
URRGGGH!!

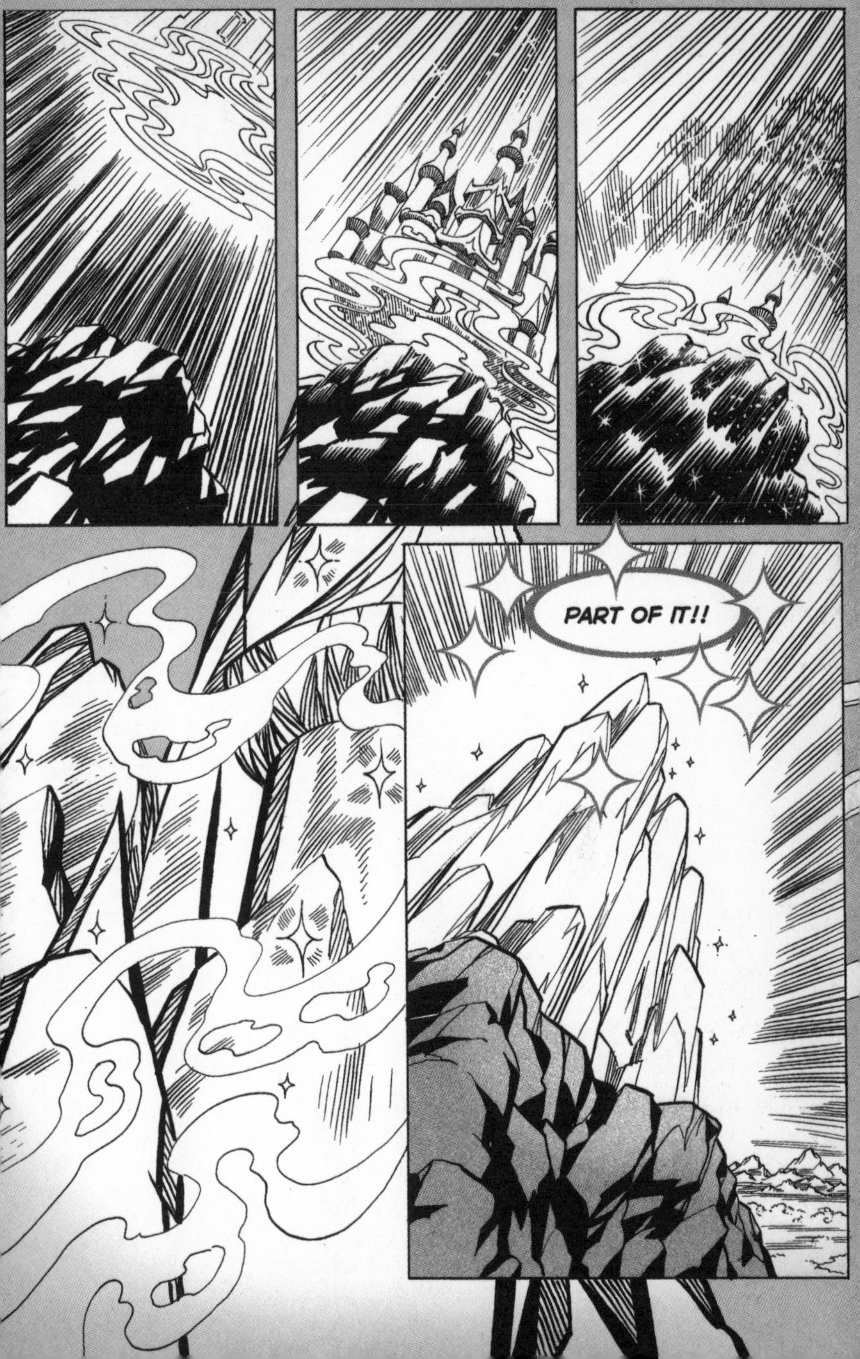
PART OF IT!!

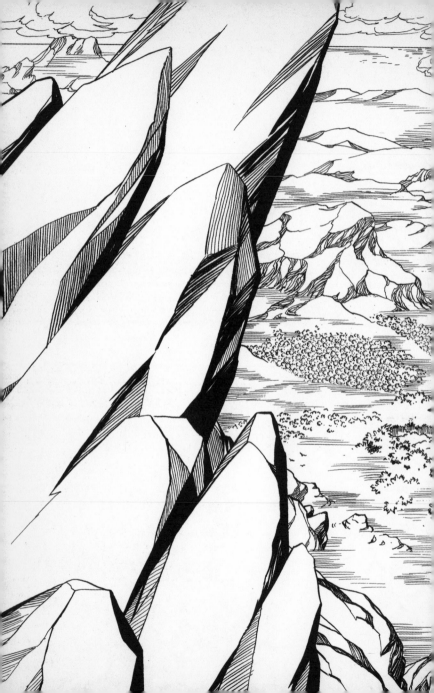

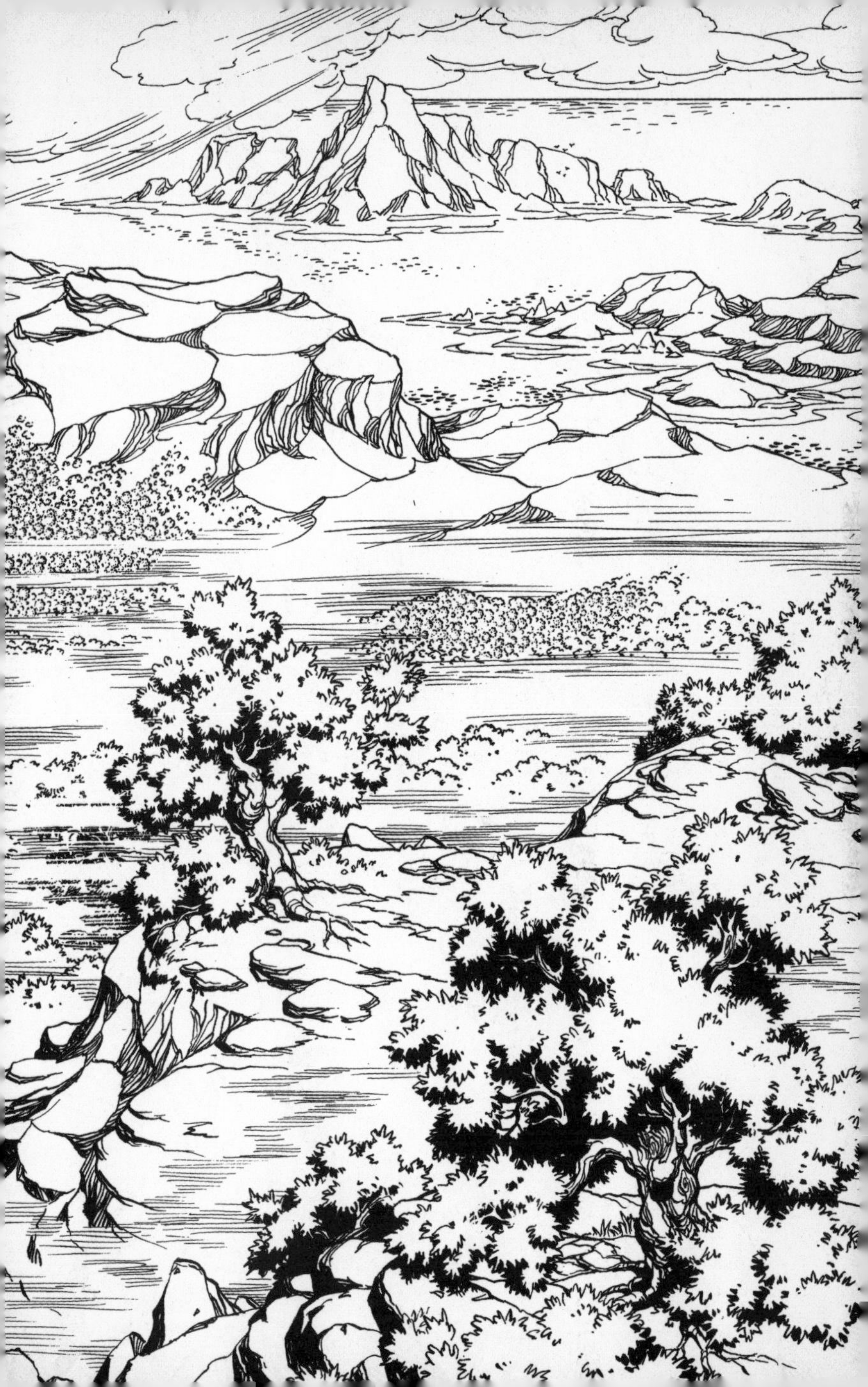

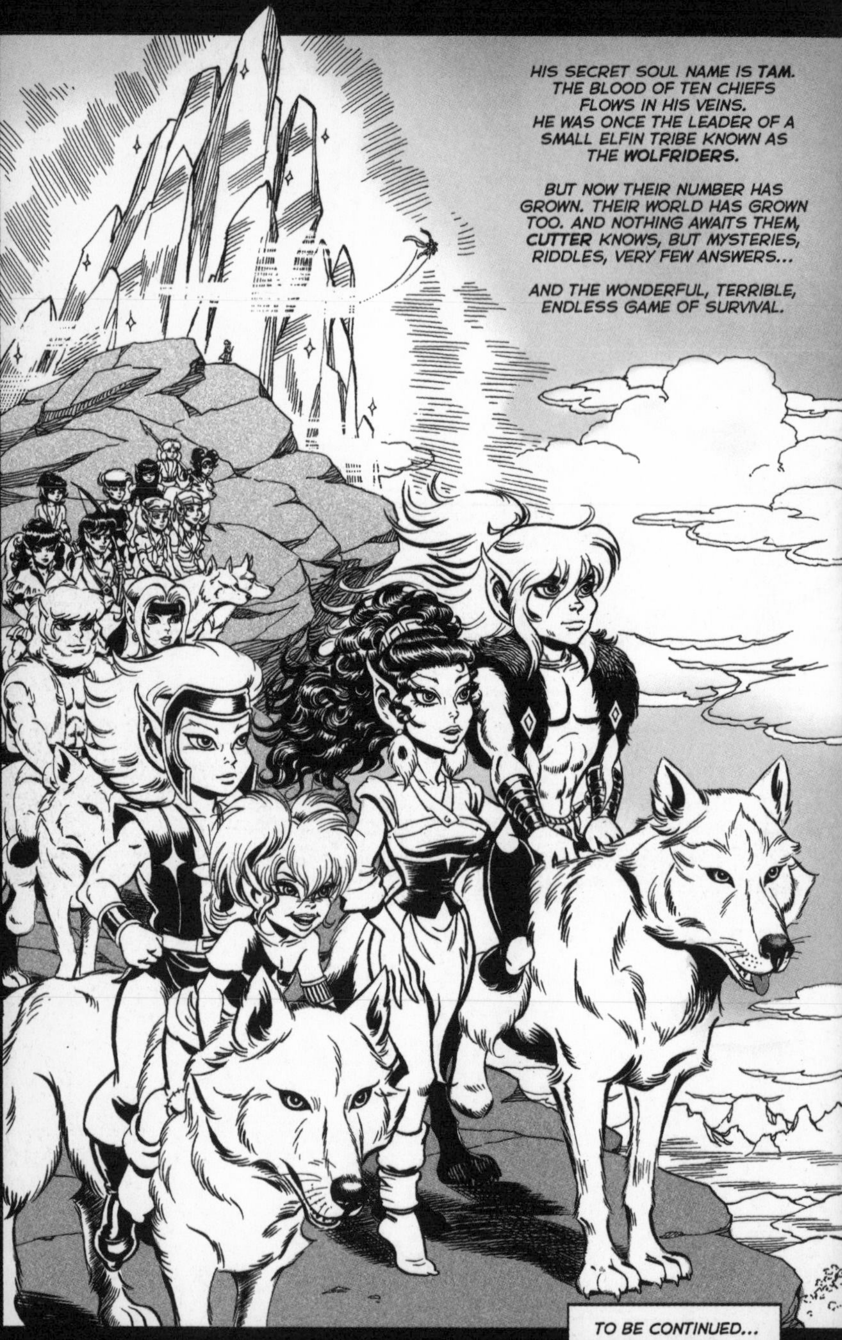
HIS SECRET SOUL NAME IS TAM.
THE BLOOD OF TEN CHIEFS
FLOWS IN HIS VEINS.
HE WAS ONCE THE LEADER OF A
SMALL ELFIN TRIBE KNOWN AS
THE WOLFRIDERS.
BUT NOW THEIR NUMBER HAS
GROWN. THEIR WORLD HAS GROWN
TOO. AND NOTHING AWAITS THEM,
CUTTER KNOWS, BUT MYSTERIES,
RIDDLES, VERY FEW ANSWERS...
AND THE WONDERFUL, TERRIBLE,
ENDLESS GAME OF SURVIVAL.
TO BE CONTINUED...

IN THE
NEXT VOLUME

Rayek, chasing his mad dream to silence the cry from beyond, has stolen Leetah, Suntop and Ember – Cutter's very heart and soul – and taken them to the Palace of the High Ones. Cutter desperately seeks them, not knowing Rayek has taken them to the one place he can never find!

Look for this latest addition in DC Comics' new library of ElfQuest stories in

OCTOBER
2005

VOLUME FIVE

1 ELFQUEST: WOLFRIDER

WENDY & RICHARD PINI

VOLUME TWO

2 ELFQUEST: WOLFRIDER

WENDY & RICHARD PINI

VOLUME FIVE

1 ELFQUEST: THE GRAND QUEST

WENDY & RICHARD PINI

VOLUME TWO

2 ELFQUEST: THE GRAND QUEST

WENDY & RICHARD PINI

VOLUME THREE

3 ELFQUEST: THE GRAND QUEST

WENDY & RICHARD PINI

VOLUME FOUR

4 ELFQUEST: THE GRAND QUEST

WENDY & RICHARD PINI

COMPACT EDITIONS

WOLFRIDER: Volume One & Two

THE GRAND QUEST: Volume One

THE GRAND QUEST: Volume Two

THE GRAND QUEST: Volume Three

THE GRAND QUEST: Volume Four

THE GRAND QUEST: Volume Five

THE GRAND QUEST: Volume Six

THE GRAND QUEST: Volume Seven

THE GRAND QUEST: Volume Eight

THE GRAND QUEST: Volume Nine

THE ELFQUEST LIBRARY

FROM